Cosmopolitanism and the Geographies of Freedom

Previously Published Wellek Library Lectures

The Breaking of the Vessels
Harold Bloom (1983)

In the Tracks of Historical Materialism
Perry Anderson (1984)

Forms of Attention
Frank Kermode (1985)

Memoires for Paul de Man
Jacques Derrida (1986)

The Ethics of Reading
J. Hillis Miller (1987)

Peregrinations: Law, Form, Event
Jean-François Lyotard (1988)

A Reopening of Closure: Organicism Against Itself
Murray Krieger (1989)

Musical Elaborations
Edward W. Said (1991)

Three Steps on the Ladder of Writing
Hélène Cixous (1993)

The Seeds of Time
Fredric Jameson (1994)

Refiguring Life: Metaphors of Twentieth-Century Biology
Evelyn Fox Keller (1995)

The Fateful Question of Culture
Geoffrey Hartman (1997)

The Range of Interpretation
Wolfgang Iser (2000)

History's Disquiet: Modernity and Everyday Life
Harry Harootunian (2000)

Antigone's Claim: Kinship Between Life and Death
Judith Butler (2000)

The Vital Illusion
Jean Baudrillard (2000)

Death of a Discipline
Gayatri Chakravorty Spivak (2003)

Postcolonial Melancholia
Paul Gilroy (2005)

On Suicide Bombing
Talal Asad (2007)

Cosmopolitanism and the Geographies of Freedom

David Harvey

COLUMBIA
UNIVERSITY
PRESS
NEW YORK

Columbia University Press
Publishers Since 1893
New York Chichester, West Sussex

Library of Congress Cataloging-in-Publication Data
Harvey, David, 1935–
Cosmopolitanism and the geographies of freedom / David Harvey.
p. cm. — (Wellek Library lectures in critical theory)
Includes bibliographical references and index.
ISBN 978-0-231-14846-7 (cloth : alk. paper) — ISBN 978-0-231-51991-5 (ebook)
1. Geography—Philosophy. 2. Cosmopolitanism. 3. Liberty. 4. Liberalism.
I. Title. II. Series.

G70.H33 2009
910.01—dc22 2009009053

Columbia University Press books are printed on permanent and durable acid-free paper.
This book is printed on paper with recycled content.
Printed in the United States of America

c 10 9 8 7 6

EDITORIAL NOTE

The Wellek Library Lectures in Critical Theory are given annually at the University of California, Irvine, under the auspices of the Critical Theory Institute. The following lectures were given in May 2005.

The Critical Theory Institute
Gabriele Schwab, Director

Contents

Preface

This book began as the Wellek Library Lectures in Critical Theory delivered in the University of California at Irvine in May 2005. It was both a privilege and a pleasure to spend time with the critical theorists at Irvine, and I thank the organizers and the participants for their generosity, their warm reception, and their intellectual engagement.

I had originally intended to publish the three lectures more or less as given, but as I began to revise them, I found myself increasingly convinced that I needed to fill them out and expand them into something like the current form. I had been surprised and honored to be asked to deliver these lectures, given the intellectually illustrious and formidable list of previous participants. The surprise derived in part from my status as a geographer, since I have long been used to the somewhat lowly status of that discipline in the academic pecking order of prestige. To say one is a geographer in academic circles (or anywhere else for that matter) is either to meet up with bemused looks or to provoke witty comments about Indiana Jones exploring the Amazon or having snow on one's boots. But these sorts of typical responses then placed an added obligation on me to state as clearly and comprehensively as I could what a critical theory of geography might look like and to explain the role such a critical theoretical perspective might play in the social sciences and the humanities more generally. To do this required serious engagement with some difficult subject matter and a lengthier exposition than had been possible in the original three lectures. Our intellectual task, as Einstein once put it, is "to be simple but no simpler," and I hope I have here managed to live up

to that command. I have, over the years, had the great privilege to work with and around a host of sympathetic colleagues who have had much to say about what a critical geography is about. The occasional meetings of the International Critical Geographers group have always been stimulating, and as more and more disciplines, such as anthropology and cultural studies, increasingly take up ideas about space, place, and environment as crucial to their mission, so there has been a welcome expansion of the terrain upon which a critical geographical theory can operate.

I have benefited immensely from the innumerable critical discussions I have been privileged to engage in across a wide range of disciplines in lectures, seminars, presentations, and panel discussions over the years. This makes it difficult to single out particular individuals for thanks, but I do want to acknowledge the importance of this ongoing dialogue and to state incontrovertibly that this book is as much a product of that collective engagement as it is a product of my own imagination. I would be seriously amiss, however, were I not to specifically acknowledge the tremendous stimulus that comes from teaching at the Graduate Center of the City University of New York, where close colleagues and students from anthropology, geography, sociology, and beyond come together in ways that are as seriously dedicated to critical inquiry as they are to creating a mutually supportive atmosphere for learning.

Cosmopolitanism and the Geographies of Freedom

Prologue

The concepts of freedom and liberty have played a huge role in the history of what might be called The American Ideology, with all manner of material consequences. On the anniversary of the terrorist attacks of September 11, 2001, for example, an op-ed piece under President George W. Bush's name appeared in the *New York Times*. He there avowed that we "are determined to stand for the values that gave our nation its birth" because a "peaceful world of growing freedom serves America's long term interests, reflects enduring American ideals and unites America's allies." He then concluded that humanity now "holds in its hands the opportunity to further freedom's triumph over its age-old foes," adding, for good measure, that "the United States welcomes its responsibility to lead in this great mission."[1] These sentiments were in broad accord with the tendency in the United States to interpret the September 11 events as an attack upon distinctively American values of freedom and liberty, rather than upon the main symbols of U.S. military and financial power. In the weeks that followed, the Bush administration frequently signaled its intention to lead a distinctively American campaign "to further freedom's triumph over its age-old foes." Two years later, after the formal reasons given for the invasion of Iraq, orchestrated as a response to the September 11 attacks, were proven wanting, Bush increasingly resorted to the theme that the "freedom" of Iraq was a sufficient moral justification for the war. Bringing freedom, liberty, and democracy to a recalcitrant world in general and to the Middle East in particular became a persistent theme in Bush's speeches.

British prime minister Tony Blair took a far more cosmopolitan position. When he addressed the U.S. Congress in July 2003, shortly after the Iraq mission was supposedly accomplished, he proposed a friendly amendment to Bush's emphasis upon American values. "There is a myth," he said, "that though we love freedom, others don't; that our attachment to freedom is a product of our culture; that freedom, democracy, human rights, the rule of law are American values, or Western values. Members of Congress, ours are not Western values, they are the universal values of the human spirit."[2] Bush thereafter modified his rhetorical claims. In a speech before a select gathering of British notables in Whitehall in November 2003, he said: "The advance of freedom is the calling of our time. It is the calling of our country. From the fourteen points [Woodrow Wilson] to the four freedoms [Roosevelt] to the speech at Westminster [Ronald Reagan], America has put its power at the service of principle. We believe that liberty is the design of nature. We believe that liberty is the direction of history. We believe that human fulfillment and excellence come in the responsible exercise of liberty. And we believe the freedom we prize, is not for us alone. It is the right and capacity of all mankind."[3]

In his acceptance speech before the Republican National Convention in September 2004, Bush took the argument one step further. "I believe America is called to lead the cause of freedom in a new century, I believe that millions in the Middle East plead in silence for their liberty. I believe that given the chance they will embrace the most honorable form of government ever devised by man. I believe all these things because freedom is not America's gift to the world, it is the Almighty's gift to every man and woman in this world." And in his inaugural speech of January 2005, Bush further consolidated this theme. "We go forward with complete confidence in the eventual triumph of freedom. Not because history runs on the wheels of inevitability. It is human choices that move events. Not because we consider ourselves a chosen nation. God moves and chooses as he wills." While "history has an ebb and flow of justice," he observed, it "also has a visible direction, set by liberty and the author of liberty."[4]

The transition from distinctive American values through universal human values to values given by nature to, finally, the Almighty's intelligent design is of rhetorical as well as substantive interest. Bush, on this final reading, evidently saw himself leading the United States in its great mission to realize God's intelligent design on earth. Major decisions could then be cast within a stark and unyielding moral frame in which the absolutes of good and evil are frequently invoked and righteousness trumps nuanced realities. The excessive resort to militarism partially derives from this, because, as Vice-President Cheney put it, "you don't negotiate with evil, you defeat it."

But what is also compelling about these speeches—and Bush made many of them even before the events of September 11—is the stark contrast between the nobility and high moral tone of their universal pronouncements and the ugly facts upon the ground: the documented murder through torture of prisoners under U.S. care in Bagram in Afghanistan; the degrading photographs from Abu Ghraib; the denial of Geneva Convention rights to anyone deemed by the Bush administration to be unlawful or enemy combatants; the painful pictures of shuffling prisoners held without trial for years in Guantanamo Bay; the U.S. Army refusal to keep records of "collateral deaths" thought to number more than 100,000 in Iraq in the first year of occupation; the "rendition" for interrogation to countries that practice torture of suspects arbitrarily (and, it turns out, often mistakenly) picked up anywhere in the world. The evidence mounts that these transgressions against human rights and decency are systemic rather than the result of the actions of a few "rotten apples" in the military barrel (as the administration often averred). In 2005, Amnesty International for one condemned the Bush administration for "atrocious violations" of human rights in Afghanistan, Iraq, and Guantanamo Bay. Within the United States, the Patriot Act restricted civil liberties, while abroad, the administration, despite noble pronouncements to the contrary, in no way ceased support for repressive, authoritarian, and sometimes ruthlessly dictatorial governments (Uzbekistan, Pakistan, Algeria, to name a few) when this served U.S. interests.

It is tempting, of course, to dismiss Bush's speeches as rhetorical shams and peculiar to him. That would be a profound mistake. David Brooks, a conservative columnist for the *New York Times*, argues, correctly in my view, that they must be taken seriously. We should not assume, he says, that the real America "is the money-grubbing, resource-wasting, TV-drenched, unreflective bimbo of the earth" and that all this high-toned language "is just a cover for the quest for oil, or the desire for riches, dominion, or war."[5] While it almost certainly is a partial cover for these more venal aims, Brooks is quite right to insist that it is far from being "just" a cover. The ideals that Bush propounded have, it turns out, a longstanding political resonance in the United States at both elite and popular levels.

Consider, for example, the record of those with whom Bush most closely identified—Woodrow Wilson of the Fourteen Points, Franklin Delano

Roosevelt of the Four Freedoms, and Ronald Reagan. In his Whitehall speech Bush made much of the fact that the last person to stay at Buckingham Palace was Woodrow Wilson, "an idealist, without question." Bush recounted how at a dinner hosted by King George V in 1918, "Woodrow Wilson made a pledge. With typical American understatement, he vowed that right and justice would become the predominant and controlling force in the world." Yet this was the same Woodrow Wilson whose attorney general launched the infamous "Palmer raids" against immigrants and "anarchists" that culminated in the executions of Sacco and Vanzetti (now pardoned as innocent). The Wilson administration ruthlessly crushed the Seattle general strike in 1918 and exiled the leaders, dubbed "Reds," to the newly minted Soviet Union. It imprisoned Eugene Debs for speaking out against the war and escalated its interventionism in Central America to put U.S. Marines into Nicaragua for more than a decade. The power politics that lay behind Wilson's idealism were anything but pleasant. What Wilson actually meant when he again and again pledged to bring freedom and liberty to the whole world was this: "Since trade ignores national boundaries and the manufacturer insists on having the world as a market, the flag of his nation must follow him, and the doors of the nations which are closed against him must be battered down. Concessions obtained by financiers must be safeguarded by ministers of state, even if the sovereignty of unwilling nations be outraged in the process. Colonies must be obtained or planted, in order that no useful corner of the world may be overlooked or left unused."[6]

Bush's willingness to violate "the sovereignty of unwilling nations" and the enunciation of a "preemptive strike" military strategy (in violation of U.N. doctrine) whenever U.S. interests (commercial as well as military) are threatened, sits firmly in this Wilsonian tradition, as did his frequent association of personal freedom and democracy with free markets and free trade. Wilson's invocation of the seventeenth-century principle known as *res nullius* in his commentary on implanting colonies is also telling. Most famously advanced by John Locke to justify the colonization of North America, this principle states that unoccupied or "unused" land could rightfully be appropriated by those who would render it more fruitful and more productive of value. That the land should become more productive of value is the key point. This was how the English justified their dispossession of the Irish in the seventeenth century (just as eminent domain can now be used in the United States to dispossess homeowners to make way for higher value uses such as box stores). "We're sometimes faulted for a naïve faith that liberty can change the world," Bush said in his Whitehall speech, adding, "if that's an error it came from reading too much John Locke and Adam Smith." While the idea of Bush reading either seems far-fetched, his concern to situate himself in this seventeenth- and eighteenth-century liberal tradition is clear.

In "saving capitalism from the capitalists," as he himself put it, FDR likewise launched all manner of domestic and international preemptive strikes against democratic governments and union power. He threw aside all constitutional protections in the name of security by illegally interning 120,000 Japanese Americans. Roosevelt's enunciation of the "Four Freedoms" as the basis for a new world order appealed solidly to liberal conceptions of individualism and private property rights. These last principles were subsequently enshrined in the U.N. Declaration on Human Rights and were incorporated into the charters of a set of international institutions (the United Nations and what are known as the Bretton Woods institutions, such as the World Bank and the International Monetary Fund) that were designed at the outset to consolidate freedoms of the market and to function largely as instruments of U.S. imperial power. That power was backed by a coalition (later based formally in NATO, in particular) of what is now known as "the willing" seeking to preserve the economic and political stability of a crisis-prone capitalism at all costs in the midst of a Cold War against the spread of communism. The Universal Declaration was clearly meant to embarrass the Soviet Union. The policies then set in motion culminated, after Roosevelt's death, in the peculiar combination of a generous though self-interested Marshall Plan abroad and a very undemocratic McCarthyism at home. The United States insisted upon decolonization on the part of European powers, only to replace the European imperial regimes with distinctive forms of U.S. neocolonialism. The U.S.–backed overthrow of democratically elected governments in Iran in 1953 and Guatemala in 1954 (the list goes on and on) and support for any dictator who cared to take an anticommunist line confirmed U.S. contempt for the sovereignty of unwilling nations, as well as for any sense of the international rule of law. For his part, Reagan's dedication to the cause of freedom was mired in, among many other things, attacks upon union power and the dismantling of many forms of social protection, coupled with tax cuts for the rich, deregulatory and environmental scandals at home, and the Iran-contra scandal (centered on illegal support for the war against the Sandinistas in Nicaragua), along with active support for military dictatorships and chronic abuse of human rights throughout much of Latin America.

Neil Smith, in his trenchant analysis of the "three moments" of U.S. globalization in the twentieth century, neatly connects the dots between these different articulations of the U.S. version of freedom's march.[7] He highlights the continuities between Woodrow Wilson's Fourteen Points through FDR's Four Freedoms to the present phase of what he calls "the endgame" of globalization. The persistent pattern, over a century or more, of noble rhetoric coupled with grubby practices on the ground is as startlingly obvious as it is highly disturbing. The invocation of the Enlightenment and its special version known as "American exceptionalism" (the idea that the United States is different, outside of, inherently good and therefore beyond any external constraints) takes us onto tricky terrain, for it is customary in these postmodern times to attribute many of our contemporary ills to the hubris, errors, and omissions of Enlightenment thinking. But, as Foucault for one argues, we cannot just wish the Enlightenment away. "We must free ourselves," he writes, "from the intellectual blackmail of being for or against the Enlightenment."[8] We have no choice except to come to terms with the fact that we are all, in some sense or another, heirs to its consequences. And this is far from being a peculiarly Western view because Mao, Nehru, Nasser, Nyerere, and Nkrumah (just to name a few significant political leaders from the developing and postcolonial world) were as much directly implicated in this tradition as those who, such as Ghandi, Franz Fanon, and Edmund Burke, defined themselves against it.

In the United States, as Neil Smith observes, the Enlightenment liberalism that inheres in "the political economy of Adam Smith, Kant's cosmopolitanism, the willed reason of Rousseau, Hume's practical empiricism and of course John Locke's juridical politics of property and rights" is not "the political antithesis of contemporary conservatism but its political backbone." "With Kant's more enigmatic aspirations for cosmopolitan citizenship in the background, Locke and Smith together provided twin intellectual inspirations for a series of interlocked beliefs" about liberty, equality, and freedom that "anchored the political flowering of capitalism and the self-understanding of bourgeois society and its individualism." These are the beliefs and the political-economic laws and practices that Woodrow Wilson represented and that President Bush promised to impose, by hook or by crook, by violence or by peaceful means, upon the rest of the world.[9]

Of course, this persistent strain of thinking within the U.S. political tradition has met with opposition. It has by no means been hegemonic.

A populist nationalism has often dominated and operated as a powerful check upon liberal international engagements. The isolationism of the 1920s, centered at the time within the Republican party, stymied Wilsonian internationalism at home (the Senate rejected joining the League of Nations), while the imperialist policies of the European powers checked it abroad. George W. Bush's republicanism, initially cast in populist nationalist terms, was geared to avoiding international engagements, such as the "nation building" that the Clinton administration had pursued in Kosovo and (disastrously) in Somalia. Bush was openly scornful of nation building abroad and a form of liberalism that by the late 1960s favored managing the market (both at home and abroad) through strong government domestic interventions and costly adventures abroad (including full-scale wars in Korea and Vietnam). Bush's subsequent advocacy of Wilsonian liberal international idealism, including attempts at democratization and nation building in Afghanistan and Iraq, suffused with the rhetoric of individual liberty and freedom, signaled a major political break in how this strain in U.S. foreign policy was to be articulated. The September 11 attacks and the subsequent declaration of a global war on terror allowed populist nationalism to be mobilized *behind* rather than *against* Wilsonian internationalism. This is the real significance of the widespread claim (accepted within the United States but not elsewhere) that the world fundamentally changed with September 11. That this is where the neoconservatives wanted to be all along is also deeply relevant. Their longstanding minority views could now become dominant at least for a time within the administration, if not hegemonic within the country. By contrast, large segments of the Democratic party, along with the traditional Republican right wing, have become comfortable with ideas of protectionism and isolationism (eventually looking to abandon the Iraq venture to its ugly fate). True-blue conservatives, such as William Buckley, mindful of the strong tradition of noninterventionism in the affairs of others that stretches back at least to Edmund Burke, became ferocious critics of the Iraq venture.

Bush and the neoconservatives are not alone in their global vision for a new world order founded in liberty and freedom. Both neoliberals and neoconservatives can agree that free markets and free trade and strong private property rights should form the political-economic grounding of the global order. The neoliberal utopianism that has swept around the world since the mid-1970s and engulfed state after state, to the point where even political parties of the left as well as many key international institutions (such as the World Bank and the International Monetary Fund) embrace its fundamental tenets, presumes that personal and individual freedom is best assured by strong private property rights and the institutions of a free market and free trade. On this point Bush the younger and Clinton, as well as Thatcher and Blair, could easily agree. It is against this background that Bush's justification of a preemptive war against Iraq and a program to democratize the Middle East can partially be understood. We must, he said, "use our position of unparalleled strength and influence to build an atmosphere of international order and openness in which progress and liberty can flourish in many nations." The United States has no imperial designs, he claimed. We merely "seek a just peace where repression, resentment and poverty are replaced with the hope of democracy, development, free markets and free trade." The U.S. aim is to "promote moderation, tolerance and the nonnegotiable demands of human dignity—the rule of law, limits on the power of the state, and respect for women, private property, free speech and equal justice."[10]

Again, it is tempting to dismiss this rhetoric as the friendly mask for the less benign face of authoritarian neofascism at home and militaristic imperialism abroad. While undoubtedly such dark undercurrents flowed freely in U.S. politics as well as among certain elements within the Bush administration, I think this would be a profound misreading if taken too one-sidedly. To begin with, this is certainly not the self-perception of the majority of U.S. citizens whose libertarian traditions are easily aroused through such rhetoric. Nor can it account for those other aspects of U.S. policy in which there is a marked generosity, both public and private, toward the rest of the world. The widespread support for "doing good in the world" and for engaging in charitable and philanthropic works (whether it be on the part of the Gates and Soros Foundations or U.S. emergency assistance and governmental aid) may be misguided or misplaced (and often passes with strings attached), but it cannot easily be construed as merely a mask for some nefarious purpose.

To dismiss what Bush was about misses what seems to me an essential and much broader point: all universalizing projects, be they liberal, neoliberal, conservative, religious, socialist, cosmopolitan, rights-based, or communist, run into serious problems as they encounter the specific circumstances of their application. Noble phrases and ideals crumble into shoddy excuses, special pleadings, misunderstandings, and, more often than not, violent confrontations and recriminations. If the U.S. effort to democratize Iraq has run into problems, then NATO has its problems to stabilize Afghanistan and the U.N. to bring the rule of law and democratic governance to a newly independent East Timor, much as Britain once had its problems in Cyprus, India, and Kenya; the French long ago in their invasion of Egypt; the Catholic Church in Latin America; the Soviet Union in Central Europe and Afghanistan; the Chinese in Tibet; and the Sandinistas with the Mesquite Indians on the Atlantic Coast. The list goes on and on. Such dismal histories leave a bitter taste. From them derives an understandable reticence to embrace universal solutions and utopian ideals of any sort. This gives us pause before we rush in to define any alternative universalizing project, such as that proposed through a revival of cosmopolitan governance or some international regime based on universal human rights. Such skepticism is pervasive, not only among postmodernists and the followers of thinkers like Foucault who explicitly reject all metatheoretical attempts at universal solutions as negative utopias. The reticence is widespread within the social movements that converge on the World Social Forum. While on the one hand these movements insist that "another world is possible" and that there is an alternative to neoliberal capitalism and imperialism, many of them, on the other hand, avidly resist articulating any global conception as to what such an alternative might look like and actively refuse to contemplate any global form of organized power. To take that path, they believe, is to embark upon a project that is bound to fail, to inflict more misery than it assuages, if not to produce an authoritarianism even worse than that which currently prevails. The new global order will emerge, it is said, from the million and one microprojects to be found all around the world as people grapple with the circumstances of their daily lives and seek tangible and practical ways to improve their lot.

While I shall ultimately dispute this view, it is plainly important to have a solid grasp of why seemingly noble universal projects and utopian plans so often fail. The blatant and evident failures of the Bush administration to live up to its noble rhetoric allow us to reflect upon this more general problem. The first and most obvious step in such an inquiry is to see to what degree failure results from the lack of understanding of the particular circumstances of the democratizing project's application. There are innumerable instances when this in itself seems to constitute a major part of the problem. Most commentators now retrospectively agree that the kind of knowledge of Iraq's history, geography, anthropology, religious traditions, and the like that would be necessary to have even a smidgen of a chance of managing the transition to something resembling U.S. democracy in an occupied Iraq was sadly lacking. Hardly surprisingly, "stuff happened" (in Donald Rumsfeld's memorable words), and the situation in Iraq quickly ran out of control. But it is precisely at this point that this sort of explanation of failure itself runs out of control. The supposition is that there is some secure foreknowledge of the circumstances that could have guaranteed success. But what kind of knowledge would that be, where could it be found, and how secure could it possibly be?

The vital importance of adequate knowledge of circumstantial and local conditions is frequently evoked. The development economist Jeffrey Sachs, for example, learned from bitter experience that the systemic theories of development economics (derived, of course, from the universalistic economic principles set out by Locke and Adam Smith) cannot be applied without "a commitment to be thoroughly steeped in the history, ethnography, politics and economics of any place where the professional advisor is working."[11] Without an adequate knowledge of geography (by which he mainly means physical environment and relative location), history, anthropology, sociology, and politics, we are bound to end up with egregiously erroneous solutions to pervasive problems of global poverty and environmental degradation. But with Sachs, the universal principles remain untouched. The circumstances affect only the applications. Seyla Benhabib, in contrast, sees a tension—a whole series of internal contradictions—between the universality of human rights theories and their application in different cultural situations. Our fate, she says, "is to live caught in the permanent tug of war between the vision of the universal" and attachments to "particularistic cultural and national identities." She also notes that universal theories have particularistic origins and invariably bear the traces of their origins. It was Parisian men, after all, who proclaimed "the rights of man." When the U.S. constitution, frequently taken as a global model, was framed with the famous opening line of "We the people," it articulated the views of "a particular human community, circumscribed in space and time, sharing a particular culture, history and legacy; yet this people established itself as a democratic body by acting in the name of the 'universal.'"[12] For Benhabib, there is a tense, dynamic, and often contradictory relation between the universals and the particulars. The concepts of freedom and liberty that Bush now projects onto the rest of the world inevitably bear the traces of the circumstances of their particular origin in U.S. history. There is, therefore, always an imperializing moment in any attempt to make that particular formulation, drawn from the one place and time, the foundation for universal policy. To note this is not necessarily to dismiss any such universal principle as illegitimate, but to recognize that the translation of a local finding into a universally accepted norm is itself a complicated process that requires building consent and understanding rather than brutal imposition of the sort now advocated in that theory of "military humanism" that was used to justify NATO military intervention in Kosovo and the bombing of Serbia.[13]

Similar caveats can be advanced when considering the current revival of interest in Kant's cosmopolitanism as a unifying vision for global democracy and governance. Martha Nussbaum, a leading advocate of the return to a cosmopolitan morality as a new way of being in the world, parallels her advocacy with an argument for an entirely different educational structure (and pedagogy) appropriate to the task of rational political deliberation in a globalizing world. "Our nation," she complains, "is appallingly ignorant of most of the rest of the world." That ignorance is fundamental to understanding why "the United States is unable to look at itself through the lens of the other and, as a consequence, [is] equally ignorant of itself." In particular, Nussbaum goes on to argue: "To conduct this sort of global dialogue, we need knowledge not only of the geography and ecology of other nations—*something that would already entail much revision in our curricula*—but also a great deal about their people, so that in talking with them we may be capable of respecting their traditions and commitments. Cosmopolitan education would supply the background necessary for this type of deliberation" (emphasis added).[14]

Nussbaum's appeal to adequate and appropriate geographical, ecological, and anthropological understandings interestingly echoes Kant's opinion. Young men, he argued, needed an understanding of anthropology and geography in order to better understand the world. "The revival of the science of geography," he wrote, "would create that unity of knowledge without which all learning remains only piece-work."[15] And, in Kant's view, this knowledge must be popular (that is, accessible to all) and pragmatic (useful), as well as scientific. He regularly taught both geography and anthropology alongside his logic, metaphysics, and ethics. He evidently tried—unsuccessfully, as we shall see—to practice what he preached. But in the extensive debate that occurred around Nussbaum's appeals for the revival of a cosmopolitan morality, the critical role that education in anthropology, geography, and the environmental sciences might perform passed by unexamined. Nussbaum makes no attempt to define what a "cosmopolitan education" in these subjects might be about. Nor does she consider the possibility, so important to Benhabib, that the cosmopolitan principles themselves may have to be modified or even radically reformulated (as in the case of human rights theory) under the impact of the geographical, ecological, and anthropological particularities encountered.

If Nussbaum had paid more attention to these forms of knowledge, she might have noted the troubling fact of the difficult histories of both anthropology and geography as disciplines that had their origins in and have been seriously scarred by an intimate connection with colonialism, imperialism, militarism, and racism. While efforts have been made to eradicate the worst legacies of such tainted origins, traces still remain. But now we have also to face the equally troubling fact that these knowledges continue to be incorporated into, for example, the military apparatus to monitor, remotely sense, target and guide missiles, or to shape strategies of counter-insurgency. Geographical and anthropological knowledges are very much shaped by the institutional frameworks within which they are embedded; the World Bank, the CIA, the Vatican, and corporations, as well as the media, all promote specific ways of knowing, and these are often radically different from each other (the geographical knowledge purveyed by the tourist industry is very different from that found within the World Health Organization). Popular geographical knowledges (or lack thereof) have very often been put to crude political uses, even become embedded in government propaganda machines. When, for example, Bush characterized the world in terms of an "Axis of Evil" that includes Iraq, Iran, and North Korea, when particular states are arbitrarily designated as "rogue states" or "failed states," then a distinctive map of the world is constructed that tacitly defines a legitimate terrain of potentially preemptive military action, which no one is in a position to gainsay without adequate counter-knowledge. Those cartoons of Reagan's or Bush's map of the world are amusingly instructive, but they also sometimes have deadly consequences. And it has precisely been the trope of U.S. foreign policy in particular, as Neil Smith points out, to conceal the actual geography of what Henry Luce back in 1942 dubbed "the American Century," because U.S. geopolitical ambition has been global and universal, rather than specifically territorially focused, all along. Preferring not to state U.S. aims in terms of some "vastly different geography," Luce advocated the use of big and "majestic" words like "Democracy, Freedom and Justice," and in the process deliberately trivialized all forms of geographical knowledge. Smith concludes: "possessing the new global power, he sensed, meant not having to care about the world's geography. Precisely because geography was everything—the American century was global—it was simultaneously nothing."[16] Cultivating the geographical ignorance of which Nussbaum complains has, for many years in the United States, been a cardinal if covert aim of national educational policy.

But when whole territories, cultures, and peoples are demonized or infantilized as backward and immature, when whole swaths of the populated globe (such as Africa) are dismissed as irrelevant because they are unproductive of sufficient value, and when the studied and deliberate cultivation of geographical, ecological, and anthropological ignorance on the part of the mass of a population permits small elites to orchestrate global politics according to their own narrow interests, then the seeming banality and innocence of geographical knowledges appears more insidious. It is not simply that the devil lies in the geographical details (though it all too frequently does). It is the very political nature of the details that needs to be understood. Scientific understandings of global warming and greenhouse gasses, to cite a most recent and blatant example, get perverted by interventions of scientists with dubious credentials supported by lucrative contracts from the major energy companies. But this is then how oppositional politics always gets framed. When environmental groups challenge the World Bank's financial support for mega-dam projects, they invariably situate the proposed dam against the background of specific geographical, ecological, and anthropological conditions that allow losses and destructions to be highlighted—in contrast to the typical World Bank report that depicts the dam as some grand symbol of modernity generating rural electricity for a grateful populace en route to achieving a much superior standard of living. The core of the conflict often resides in which geographical, ecological, and anthropological description is deemed correct.

How then, to return to Nussbaum's seemingly innocent suggestion, are we to incorporate always conflictual and controversial as well as often perverse and self-serving forms of geographical knowledge into cosmopolitan projects? The danger of the unwitting deployment of political propaganda by way of geographical descriptions looms large. The revisions in our geographical, ecological, and anthropological curricula that might serve the purposes of Nussbaum's cosmopolitan education desperately call for critical examination. But few, particularly those in power, care to focus on the question as a matter of public urgency. In this book I seek to address this lacuna explicitly. I will concentrate mainly on the case of geography, since that is the terrain with which I am most familiar. But there are innumerable overlaps with anthropology, as well as with ecology and the environmental sciences, and I see no reason to police any fictitious borders that some may wish to impose upon overlapping and highly interactive fields of study. My aim is to probe both the possibilities and the difficulties of achieving a cosmopolitan education in geography (alongside ecology and anthropology) that might meaningfully contribute to, perhaps even radically reformulate, the drive to construct a new cosmopolitan intellectual order appropriate for an emancipatory and liberatory form of global governance.

John Locke, incidentally, also recognized the foundational importance of adequate geographical knowledge to his universal project. "Without a knowledge of geography," he wrote, "gentlemen could not even understand a newspaper."[17] Unfortunately, President George W. Bush, according to his own account, did not even care to read the newspapers.

Part One
Universal Values

Chapter One
Kant's Anthropology and Geography

I begin with Kant because his inspiration for the contemporary approach to cosmopolitanism is impossible to ignore. I cite perhaps the most famous passage from his essay on "Perpetual Peace": "The peoples of the earth have entered in varying degrees into a universal community, and it is developed to the point where a violation of laws in *one* part of the world is felt *everywhere*. The idea of a cosmopolitan law is therefore not fantastic and overstrained; it is a necessary complement to the unwritten code of political and international law, transforming it into a universal law of humanity."[1]

Kant's conception of cosmopolitan law arises in the context of a certain kind of geographical structure. The finite quality of the globe defines limits within which human beings, by virtue of their common possession of the surface of the earth, are forced to accommodate (sometimes violently) with each other. Human beings have the inherent right, if they so desire, to range across the surface of the earth and to associate with each other (through trade and commerce, for example). Means of transport (Kant mentions the ship and the camel) facilitate increasing contacts over space. But in Kant's schema, the earth's surface is presumed to be territorially divided into sovereign states. These will tend in the long run to become both democratic and republican. Inhabitants will then possess distinctive rights of citizenship within their states. Relations between states will be regulated by a growing requirement to establish perpetual peace because of increasing interdependence through trade and commerce. War between states becomes less likely for two reasons. First, in a democratic state it will be necessary to gain the consent of a public that would have to bear the brunt of the costs. The habit of sovereigns, emperors, and the nobility of waging war for reasons of personal prestige or aggrandizement will be constrained. Second, trade disruptions from war would inflict greater and greater losses as the levels of economic interdependence between states increased. The cosmopolitan ethic requires that individuals (presumed citizens of one state) would have the right to hospitality when they cross clearly defined borders (particularly for purposes of trade): "Hospitality means the right of a stranger not to be treated as an enemy when he arrives in the land of another. One may refuse to receive him when this can be done without causing his destruction; but so long as he peacefully occupies his place, one may not treat him with hostility. It is not the right to be a permanent visitor that one may demand. A special contract of beneficence would be needed in order to give an outsider a right to become a fellow inhabitant for a certain length of time. It is only the right of temporary sojourn, a right to associate, which all men have. They have it by virtue of their common possession of the surface of the earth, where, as a globe, they cannot infinitely disperse and hence must finally tolerate the presence of each other."[2]

Cosmopolitan right is, therefore, circumscribed. "The right of hospitality," Benhabib notes, "occupies that space between human rights and civil rights, between the right of humanity in our person and the rights that accrue to us insofar as we are members of specific republics."[3] The presumption of a sovereign (preferably democratic and republican) state authority defined by its distinctive territoriality lies at the basis of this formulation. For purposes of citizenship the territoriality of the state is regarded as an absolute space (that is, it is fixed and immovable and has a clear boundary). But it is the universal (that is, deracinated) right to hospitality that opens the absolute spaces of all states to others under very specific conditions.

Kant's formulation of the cosmopolitan ethic has been the subject of considerable analysis and debate. But no one has cared to explore the implications of Kant's assumptions about geographical structure for the cosmopolitanism he derives. The only substantive discussion I can find concerns the role that the common possession of a finite globe plays in Kant's justification of cosmopolitan right. The consensus seems to be that "the spherical surface of the earth constitutes a circumstance of justice but does not function as a moral justificatory premise to ground cosmopolitan right."[4] This conclusion is understandable. To conclude otherwise would be to commit the naturalistic fallacy or, worse still, to fall into a crude environmental determinism (the idea that spatial structure—the sphericity of the globe—has direct causative powers). But relegation of the geographical circumstances to the status of a mere "circumstance of justice" is not the end of the issue. It is as if the nature of the geographical space has no bearing in relation to principles applied to it. Though the material (historical and geographical) circumstances may be contingent, this does not mean that the characterization of those circumstances in the form of anthropological and geographical knowledges is irrelevant to the formulation of a cosmopolitan ethic. Nussbaum and, as we shall see, Kant himself clearly think the circumstances matter. And so, it turns out, does Foucault. So how and why does it matter?

Kant's philosophical teaching concentrated on logic, metaphysics, and ethics. But he also taught geography and anthropology on a regular basis. Is there any relation between these teachings? His writings on anthropology and particularly geography have, until very recently, been generally ignored or relegated to a zone of insignificance in relation to his three major critiques. The Anthropology has, however, been translated into several languages and subjected to some commentary. Foucault, for example, translated the Anthropology into French in 1964, promising a deeper analysis of it in a subsequent publication. He never made good on this promise (though he did leave behind an extended commentary that is now finally available to us). Kant's Geography is known hardly at all (Foucault, interestingly, barely mentions it). Whenever I have in the past questioned Kantian scholars about it, their response has almost always been the same. It is "irrelevant," "not to be taken seriously," or "there is nothing of interest in it." There is as yet no published English edition (though there is a translation of Part I as a master's thesis by Bolin). A French version finally appeared in 1999, and an English translation is scheduled.[5] There is as yet no serious study of Kant's Geography in the English language other than May's, coupled with occasional forays by geographers into understanding Kant's role in the history of geographical thought (without any attempt to link this to his metaphysics or ethics). The introduction to the French edition of the Geography does attempt an evaluation, and a recent English-language conference bringing together philosophers and geographers finally promises serious examination of the problems the Geography poses.[6]

This historical neglect of the Geography does not accord with Kant's own assessment. He went out of his way to gain an exemption from university regulations in order to teach geography in place of cosmology.

He taught geography forty-nine times, compared to the fifty-four occasions when he taught logic and metaphysics, and the forty-six and twenty-eight times he taught ethics and anthropology, respectively. He explicitly argued that geography and anthropology defined the "conditions of possibility" of all knowledge. He considered these knowledges a necessary preparation—a "propaedeutic" as he termed it—for everything else.[7] While, therefore, both anthropology and geography were in a "precritical" or "prescientific" state, their foundational role required that they be paid close attention. How else can we interpret the fact that he taught geography and anthropology so persistently alongside his metaphysics and ethics? Though he signally failed in his mission, he plainly thought it important to bring anthropology and geography into a more critical and scientific condition. The question is: why did he think so?

F. Van de Pitte, in his introduction to the Anthropology, provides one answer to this question. As Kant increasingly recognized that "metaphysics could not follow the method of pure mathematics," then, as Kant himself put it, "the true method of metaphysics is basically the same as that introduced by Newton into natural science." Metaphysics must rest, therefore, upon a scientific understanding of human experience. But if metaphysics now was to begin in experience, where would it find the fixed principles in terms of which it could build with assurance? As Kant himself expressed it, the variations in taste and different aspects of man give to the flow of experience an uncertain and delusive character. "Where shall I find fixed points of nature which man can never shift and which can give him indications of the shore on which he must bring himself to rest?"

Kant, according to Van de Pitte, turned to Rousseau's writings to find an answer. There he discovered that "because man can consider an array of possibilities, and which among them is more desirable, he can strive to make himself and his world in a realization of his ideals." This could be so because human beings possessed powers of rational thought (though mere possession of these powers did not guarantee their appropriate use). But this meant in turn that metaphysics need no longer be purely speculative. It must proceed "in terms of clearly defined absolute principles derived from man's potential."[8] By what means, then, could man's potential be established, if God and traditional cosmology could not provide the answer?

At several points in his articulation of the cosmopolitan ethic, Kant expresses the view that the ethic arises out of nature or out of human nature (he sometimes seems to conflate the two). The cosmopolitan ethic is therefore based on something other than pure speculation or idealism. Kant (unlike President Bush) refuses to invoke any notion of God's design. The attention Kant pays to both geography and anthropology then makes more sense. If theology and cosmology could no longer provide adequate answers to the question "what is man?" (hence Kant's determination to eliminate cosmology from the curriculum and replace it with geography), then something more scientific was needed. Where was that "science of man" to come from, if not from anthropology and geography? The distinction between geography and anthropology rested, in Kant's view, on a difference between the "outer knowledge" given by observation of "man's" place in nature and the "inner knowledge" of subjectivities (which sometimes comes close to psychology in practice). This dualism bears a heavy burden, for it underpins the supposedly clear distinctions between object and subject, fact and value and, ultimately, science and poetry that have bedeviled Western thought ever since. He began teaching geography first (in 1756), and much of what he there examines concerns the physical processes that affect the earth's surface and human life upon it. This suggests a certain initial attraction to an underlying theory of environmental determinism as providing a potentially secure scientific basis for metaphysical reflection (and, as we shall see, many of the examples he evokes in his geography reflect that tendency). His later turn to anthropology (which he began teaching in 1772), and the fact that he paid far greater attention to elaborating upon it (even preparing it for publication) in his later years, suggests that he increasingly found the inner knowledge of subjectivities more relevant to his philosophical project. "As a result," Foucault provocatively suggests, "the notion of a cosmological perspective that would organize geography and anthropology in advance and by rights, serving as a single reference for both the knowledge of nature and the knowledge of man, would have to be put to one side to make room for a cosmopolitical perspective with a programmatic value, in which the world is envisaged more as a republic to be built than a cosmos given in advance."[9] It is significant that the final passages of the Anthropology address the whole question of cosmopolitan law directly, while there is no mention of this topic in the Geography.

Consider first, then, the implications of his Anthropology. The work amounts to a detailed inquiry into our species being (it foreshadows, therefore, Marx's examination of the concept in *The Economic and Philosophic Manuscripts of 1844*). The purpose is plain enough. Not only must we understand what we have been about and how we now are as a human species: we must also understand what we can become by virtue of our particular capacities and powers. Human nature is not fixed but evolving, and by studying that evolution we can say something about the destiny of the human race. Foucault, in his commentary, is as profoundly admiring of Kant's capacity to ask these questions as he is critical of Kant's actual answers. "Man is not simply 'what he is,' but 'what he makes of himself.' And is this not precisely the field that Anthropology defines for its investigation?" Foucault asks. The Anthropology is, therefore, in Foucault's view, a central rather than marginal text in relation to the three major philosophical critiques that Kant contributed. Amy Allen summarizes Foucault's argument this way:

> Thus, Foucault suggests, the Anthropology (perhaps unwittingly) breaks open the framework of the critical philosophy, revealing the historical specificity of our a priori categories, their rootedness in historically variable social and linguistic practices and institutions. Foucault's reading of Kant's Anthropology thus suggests that Kant's system contains the seeds of its own radical transformation, a transformation that Foucault will take up in his own work: namely the transformation from the conception of the a priori as universal and necessary to the historical a priori; and the related transformation from the transcendental subject that serves as the condition of possibility of all experience to the subject that is conditioned by its rootedness in specific historical, social and cultural circumstances.[10]

This transition in thinking from a disembodied to a rooted human subject is critical, and the vehicle is in the first instance supplied by the Anthropology. Kant's views on our species being are not confined to his text on Anthropology, so on this point some contextualization is needed. Kant generally rejects any notion of the inherent goodness of humanity. He does not appeal to any figure of the noble savage or of Godly innocence. "Everything," he says, "is made up of folly and childish vanity, and often of childish malice and destructiveness."[11] Enlightenment, he says in his celebrated essay on that subject, depends upon "man's emergence from his self-incurred immaturity," defined as the inability to use understanding "without the guidance of another." Only a few, Kant suggests, "have succeeded in freeing themselves from immaturity and in continuing boldly on their way," while all manner of prejudices (even the new ones created in the course of revolution) "will serve as a leash to control the great unthinking mass." For enlightenment to progress depends on "the most innocuous form" of freedom—"the freedom to make public use of one's reason in all matters." While we live in an age of enlightenment, we do not live in an enlightened age. This way of thinking enters into the final passages of the Anthropology. Human beings, he says:

> cannot be without peaceful coexistence, and yet they cannot avoid continuous disagreement with one another. Consequently, they feel destined by nature to develop, through mutual compulsion and laws written by them, into a cosmopolitan society which is constantly threatened by dissension but generally progressing toward a coalition. The cosmopolitan society is in itself an unreachable idea, but it is not a constitutive principle. . . . It is only a regulative principle demanding that we yield generously to the cosmopolitan society as the destiny of the human race; and this not without reasonable grounds for supposition that there is a natural inclination in this direction. . . . [W]e tend to present the human species not as evil, but as a species of rational beings, striving among obstacles to advance constantly from the evil to the good. In this respect our intention in general is good, but achievement is difficult because we cannot expect to reach our goal by the free consent of individuals, but only through progressive organization of the citizens of the earth within and toward the species as a system which is united by cosmopolitical bonds.[12]

The mission of Kant's anthropology—written, as he insists, from "a pragmatic point of view"—is, therefore, to define "the conditions of possibility" for that "regulative principle" that can lead us from a condition of folly and childish vanity, from violence and crude brutality, to "our destiny" of a peaceful cosmopolitan society. This entails an analysis of our cognitive faculties, of our feelings (of pleasure and displeasure), and of desire (the influence on Foucault's work is obvious). It also entails reflection on how and why natural endowments ("temperaments") are transformed by human practices into "character." Kant writes: "what nature makes of man belongs to temperament (wherein the subject is for the most part passive) and only what man makes of himself reveals whether he has character."[13] While this introduces an unfortunate dichotomy between our "animal" and our "civilized" being, it does open up the possibility for the ongoing work of perpetual transformations of character. Pheng Cheah summarizes Kant's argument as follows:

> As natural creatures with passions and sensuous inclinations, we are, like things and animals, creatures of a world merely given to us and are bound by the same arational mechanical laws of causality governing all natural objects. However, as moral subjects we are self-legislating rational agents. We belong to a transcendent realm of freedom we create for ourselves, a world that encompasses all rational beings governed by universal laws we prescribe through our reason. The moral world is supersensible and infinite because it is not subject to the blind chance of meaningless contingency that characterizes finite human existence . . . culture provides a bridge to the transcendent world of freedom because it minimizes our natural bondage by enhancing the human aptitude for purposive self-determination . . . [it] liberates the human will from the despotism of natural desires and redirects human skill toward rational purposes by forming the will in accordance with a rational image.[14]

The general proposition that "man makes himself" carries over very strongly, of course, into the Marxist tradition. Echoes of Kant's transcendent definition of freedom can also be heard in Marx's pronouncement that "the realm of freedom actually begins only where labour which is determined by necessity and of mundane considerations ceases" and that this "lies beyond the realm of material production."[15] Kant reflects on how far we have progressed in reshaping temperaments into character through the making of culture by examining differentials in national character and cultures. The text is lighthearted, anecdotal, and on occasion deliberately amusing in the national stereotypes it evokes. But this should not detract from the seriousness of Kant's purpose. Human beings have made themselves differently in different places and produced different cultures. Our task—and on this point Kant's arguments are surely powerfully to the point—is to exercise both judgment and intelligence with respect to this process: "Just as the faculty of discovering the particular for the universal [the rule] is called judgment, so the faculty of discovering the universal for the particular is called intelligence. Judgment concentrates on detecting the differences within the manifold as to partial identities; intelligence concentrates on marking the identity within the manifold as to partial differences. The superior talent of both lies in noticing either the smallest similarity or dissimilarity. The faculty to do this is acuteness, and observations of this sort are called subtleties, which, if they do not advance knowledge, are either called empty sophistries or conceited prattlings."[16]

Judged against this high-sounding standard, Kant's own formulations often appear unduly crude (if not as empty sophistries and conceited prattlings). Throughout the Anthropology we are assaulted by all manner of seemingly prejudicial statements about race, class, gender, and nation. His statements on the nature of woman and the feminine character will likely outrage even the mildest feminist (though they will probably delight some ardent evangelicals). In seeking to understand the differentiations that plainly occurred within our species being, Kant initiated the idea (which later had a very unfortunate history) that the question of race should be put upon a purely scientific footing. And his consideration of the roots of national identity is problematic: "By the word people (populus) we mean the number of inhabitants living together in a certain district, so far as these inhabitants constitute a unit. Those inhabitants, or even a part of them, which recognize themselves as being united into a civil society through common descent, are called a nation (gens); the part which segregates itself from these laws (the unruly group among these people) is called rabble (vulgus), and their illegal union is called a mob (agere per turbas), a behavior which excludes them from the privileges of citizen."[17]

Not all residents, by this account, qualify as citizens. It all depends, according to Kant, upon the "maturity" of the individual, a normative concept of rational behavior that Foucault challenges head on in his essay "What Is Enlightenment?"[18] Is a character like Baudelaire to be excluded from citizenship, Foucault asks, by virtue of what Kant would almost certainly consider his irrational immaturity? And what happens when—as Kant, along with most other Enlightenment thinkers, holds—women are by definition considered immature and therefore incapable of participating in public life?

The definition and significance to humanity of nationhood by common descent, however, leads Kant to one of his most important conclusions. A singular world government could only exist as monarchical despotism because it would have to erase and suppress national differences based upon common descent within territorial configurations. A world government of that sort would, in short, go against nature and human nature. The only form of cosmopolitan government that will work is one based on a federation of independent (preferably democratic and republican) nation-states. This may or may not be a good idea, but it is important to recognize that Kant's derivation of it arises out of his highly questionable anthropological conception of the nation-state as a civil society based on common descent (to say nothing of the exclusion of "troublesome elements"—however defined—from rights of citizenship). This presumption also helps explain why the cosmopolitan right to cross borders is so circumscribed and why the right to hospitality must be temporary. Permanent residence for foreigners is inconsistent with the requirement of common descent. Those, like Benhabib, who want to extend the rights of migrants in meaningful ways have therefore to struggle mightily with the restrictions of the Kantian cosmopolitan frame. The real problem lies, however, in the questionable anthropological foundations for Kant's arguments. But if Kant's specific anthropological foundation is rejected, as I think it must be, then the question arises as to what is or what might be an adequate anthropological foundation for understanding the territorial structures of human association. Indeed, questions might reasonably be asked as to whether the cosmopolitan ethic requires any kind of anthropological foundation whatsoever. Plainly, both Nussbaum and Foucault, as well as Kant, believe it does.

An examination of Kant's Geography raises even deeper problems. The lack of interest in it on the part of Kant scholars is understandable since its content is nothing short of an intellectual and political embarrassment. As R.-P. Droit remarks, reading it "comes as a real shock" because it appears as "an unbelievable hodge-podge of heterogeneous remarks, of knowledges without system, of disconnected curiosities."[19] The thought that this might provide a secure foundation for metaphysical reflection is just absurd. To be sure, Kant seeks to sift the sillier and obviously false tales from those that have some factual credibility, but we are still left with a mix of materials more likely to generate hilarity than scientific credibility. But there is a more sinister side to it. While most of the text is given over to often bizarre facts of physical geography (indeed, that was the title of his lectures), his remarks on "man" within the system of nature are deeply troubling. Kant repeats without critical examination all manner of prejudicial remarks concerning the customs and habits of different populations. Thus we find:

> In hot countries men mature more quickly in every respect but they do not attain the perfection of the temperate zones. Humanity achieves its greatest perfection with the White race. The yellow Indians have somewhat less talent. The Negroes are much inferior and some of the peoples of the Americas are well below them.

> All inhabitants of hot lands are exceptionally lazy; they are also timid and the same two traits characterize also folk living in the far north. Timidity engenders superstition and in lands ruled by Kings leads to slavery. Ostoyaks, Samoyeds, Lapps, Greenlanders, etc. resemble people of hot lands in their timidity, laziness, superstition and desire for strong drink, but lack the jealousy characteristic of the latter since their climate does not stimulate their passion greatly
>
> Too little and also too much perspiration makes the blood thick and viscous. . . . In mountain lands men are persevering, merry, brave, lovers of freedom and of their country. Animals and men which migrate to another country are gradually changed by their environment. . . . The northern folk who moved southward to Spain have left progeny neither so big nor so strong as they, and which is also dissimilar to Norwegians and Danes in temperament.[20]

Burmese women wear indecent clothing and take pride in getting pregnant by Europeans, the Hottentots are dirty and you can smell them from far away, the Javanese are thieving, conniving and servile, sometimes full of rage and at other times craven with fear. It is difficult to attribute any notion of rationality or maturity to such populations.

This, surely, cannot be the kind of geography that Nussbaum has in mind. When projected into a world of sovereign democratic and republic states, it conjures up a threatening image of unwashed Hottentots, drunken Samoyeds, conniving and thieving Javanese, and hordes of Burmese women lusting to become pregnant by Europeans, all clamoring for the right to cross borders and not be treated with hostility. It is precisely in such geographical "circumstances" that we can better understand why Kant included in his cosmopolitan ethic and in his notion of justice the right to refuse entry (provided it does not result in the destruction of the other), the temporary nature of the right to hospitality (provided the entrant does not create any trouble), and the condition that permanent residency depends entirely on an act of beneficence on the part of a sovereign state that in any case always has the right to deny rights of citizenship to those who create trouble. Only those who exhibit maturity, presumably, will be granted the right to stay permanently. Again, those like Benhabib who struggle mightily to loosen the constraints of Kantian cosmopolitan law as it relates to the rights of migrants in effect have to undo the hidden trace of these geographical preconceptions upon Kant's formulation of cosmopolitan law.

None of this has gone away. Acrimonious debates about the rights of minorities and of migrants to be received "without hostility" even on a temporary basis abound in our contemporary world. All manner of prejudicial and stereotypical conceptions about "others" and "strangers" exist, even among highly educated political elites. Denial of rights of citizenship to strangers on the grounds that they are immature and not like us is all too familiar. And while Kant's excursus into the idea of national character may be barely acceptable, the long tradition of writing on the "peculiarities" of the English, the particularities of the French, the Spanish, or the Italians, and the like by eminent and much respected writers (such as P. Anderson, T. Zeldin, and L. Barzini, with tacit support from epic works such as that of E. P. Thompson on *The Making of the English Working Class*)[21] suggests that Kant was onto something. Furthermore, when political philosophers of the stature of John Rawls (most particularly in *The Law of Peoples*) and Michael Walzer (particularly in *Spheres of Justice*) ground their arguments in something akin to Kant's original idea with respect to national character and culture, then we have to take the whole question of the anthropological and geographical rootedness of political philosophy, if not of politics itself, far more seriously than is our wont[22]

Kant's geographical depictions can, of course, be excused as mere quotations from or echoes of Montesquieu and other scholars with environmental determinist and racist leanings, such as Hume and Buffon (to say nothing of the lore that Kant picked up from merchants, missionaries, and sailors passing through Königsburg). Many of the fervent defenders of universal reason and of universal rights at that time, Droit notes, cheerfully peddled all manner of similarly prejudicial materials, making it seem as if racial superiorities and ethnic cleansings might easily be reconciled with universal rights and ethics (though Kant, to his credit, did go out of his way to condemn colonialism on the grounds that this was occupation without permission and therefore a violation of cosmopolitan law).[23] And all manner of other extenuating circumstances can be evoked: Kant's geographical information was limited; his course in geography was introductory, meant to inform and raise issues rather than solve them; and Kant never revised the materials for publication (the text that comes down to us was compiled from Kant's early notes—around 1759—supplemented by those of students, and there is controversy over how corrupted the text is relative to other, later versions given during the 1790s).[24] And his later shift in emphasis toward the

Anthropology in any case suggests a gradual progress away from some of the grosser forms of environmental determinism that are featured in his Geography.

But that Kant's Geography is of such uncertain genealogy and an embarrassment to boot is no justification for ignoring it. Indeed, this is precisely what makes it so interesting, particularly when set against his much-vaunted universal ethics and cosmopolitanism. Dismissal of his Geography does not accord with Kant's own positioning of it as a "condition of possibility" and as a "propaedeutic" for all other forms of reasoning (including his metaphysics and his ethics). The problem is that Kant failed entirely to bring geographical knowledge out of its "precritical state" and place it on a rational, scientific basis. He later hinted as to why. He simply could not make his ideas about final causes work on the terrain of geographical knowledge. "Strictly speaking," he wrote (in a passage that Clarence Glacken regards as key), "the organization of nature has nothing analogous to any causality known to us,"[25] and this problem blocked his ambition to construct geographical understandings in a style akin to Newtonian natural science. If this is so, then his metaphysics and his ethics lack the solid scientific foundations he considered essential to their formulation. They revert to the sphere of mere speculation as to "man's species being."

The problem that Nussbaum poses of how anthropological and geographical knowledges might be better constructed and positioned in relation to the "proper" formulation of a cosmopolitan ethic is left open by Kant, and hardly anyone has cared to investigate it since. Most contemporary commentators either ignore this question or, as does Seyla Benhabib or Tim Brennan, attempt to deal with some of the issues that Kant left dangling through ad hoc adjustments to his concept of cosmopolitan law.[26] Laudable though such adjustments may be, these writers deal with symptoms rather than underlying structural problems, not only with Kant's original formulations but with almost all subsequent work on the subject. So what would it take, then, to reconstruct anthropological and geographical knowledges in a way that could better inform struggles over the proper conception of cosmopolitan law? How, in short, should we attempt to answer Nussbaum's foundational demand for a proper set of geographical and anthropological understandings? And what, under contemporary conditions, could "proper" possibly mean? While such questions may appear daunting, if not unanswerable in any simple sense, this should not deter us from investigating them.

Foucault's position on this is interesting. He seems to have been profoundly affected by his reading of Kant's Anthropology and clearly saw this as a propaedeutic to Kant's ethics. And his own writings bear the trace of that influence throughout. But Foucault apparently never read Kant's texts on geography. He did, however, make frequent use of spatial concepts. This was particularly evident in the relatively early and long-unpublished essay on heterotopia—about which more anon—and in his careful delineation of spatial forms (such as his celebrated use of the panopticon) in his inquiries into prisons and hospitals in texts like *Madness and Civilization* and *Discipline and Punish*. He accepted that spatiality was a key concept and initially at least seems to have accepted Kant's views on how space should be understood. But later in life, he also openly worried, perhaps with a critique of Kant as well as his own formulations of heterotopia in mind, at the way "space was treated as the dead, the fixed, the undialectical, the immobile," while "time, on the contrary, was richness, fecundity, life, dialectic."[27] If "space is fundamental in any form of communal life," then space must also be "fundamental in any exercise of power," he argued. More surprisingly, when asked in 1976 by the editors of the newly founded radical geography journal *Hérodote* to clarify his arguments on space and geography, Foucault gave evasive and seemingly incomprehending answers to what, on the whole, were quite reasonable probing questions. By refusing again and again to elaborate or even speculate on the material grounding for his vast arsenal of spatial metaphors, he evaded the issue of a geographical knowledge proper to his or anyone else's understandings (even in the face of his use of actual spatial forms such as the panopticon to establish his themes). He failed, furthermore, to give tangible material meaning to the way space is "fundamental to the exercise of power." Yet this is what he eventually did say by way of conclusion: "I have enjoyed this discussion with you because I've changed my mind since we started. Now I can see that the problems you put to me about geography are crucial ones for me. Geography acted as the support, the condition of possibility for the passage between a series of factors I tried to relate. Where geography itself was concerned, I either left the question hanging or established a series of arbitrary connections. . . . Geography must indeed necessarily lie at the heart of my concerns."[28]

Foucault here accords, albeit somewhat reluctantly, a parallel status of "condition of possibility" for geography to that earlier assigned to Kant's anthropology. It is, therefore, the geographical rootedness in specific historical, social, and cultural circumstances—the historical and geographical a priori if you will—that now must be taken into account. So how then are we to understand this relation between the geographical as opposed to the historical a priori, and what role does this play in relation to Foucauldian ethics (to say nothing of politics)? In an attempt to find some answers to this question, Foucault subsequently submitted a series of questions to the editors of Hérodote as to how he should properly understand what geography was about.[29] But his questions indicated that he equated geographical knowledge with the study of spatiality and spatial order. Why did he take such a limited and undialectical view of what geography might be about?

Critical engagement with Kant here provides some useful pointers, for, as May argues, it is possible to reconstruct some of Kant's putative principles of geographical knowledge from the general corpus of his writings. Geography was not only a precursor, as we have seen, but also, together with anthropology, a synthetic end-point of all of our knowledge of the world (understood as the surface of the earth as "man's" habitation). And Kant saw this end-point as more than simply a posteriori knowledge of the world. It is in some sense constructive of our "destiny" for actually living in the world. In other words, we need not only to examine what our geography and anthropology have been and are, but consider what they might become.

Geography, however, looks at "man" as a "natural object within the system of nature." In the eighteenth century this meant that geographical knowledge was prone to those forms of environmental determinism that could all too easily lurch over (as we have already seen in Kant's case) into blatant racism. But the general question Kant poses, of how to understand the metabolic relation between human evolution and environmental transformations, is as vital now as ever. Just because Kant plainly got it wrong is no excuse for ignoring the question. And environmentalism has by no means disappeared. In the contemporary work of Jared Diamond and Jeffrey Sachs, as we will later see, it even acquires a seeming scientific respectability. How to conceptualize "man" as a "natural object within the system of nature" remains a core question, and how we answer it will affect not only the technicalities of application of cosmopolitan law but the whole destiny of humanity.

But Kant excluded environmental history from the definition of geography per se. Geographical knowledge concerns the study of spatial order alone, he argued. History is considered distinctive because it provides a narration in time. These two synthetic forms of knowledge—in turn quite distinct from analytic sciences such as physics and biology—should not be confused with each other. Geography (along with other spatial sciences such as archaeology and astronomy) synthesizes analytical findings in terms of space, and history does so with respect to time. This separability of space and time, particularly with respect to the organization of knowledge, positions Kant in the Newtonian tradition with regard to the nature of space and time. But Kant also recognized a problem with the Newtonian adaptation of the Cartesian theory of space and time. If space and time are considered infinite, absolute, and empty of all matter, then they are unavailable to our understandings through direct perceptual experience. Kant's answer was that space and time are accessible to our intuitions; our knowledge of them is synthetic a priori. This opens up all sorts of possibilities in principle for non-absolute definitions of space and time, but there is no sign in Kant's work that human intuition would uncover any other scientific truth save that of the Newtonian absolute system with respect to the world of experience. Kant in effect uses Leibniz to seal in an absolute Newtonian view of a separable space and time.[30] This, as we shall see later, seriously inhibits the Kantian perspective. Kant's geography is then defined as an empirical form of knowledge about spatial ordering and spatial structures alone, and this definition dominates Foucault's perspective in his questions to the editors of Hérodote. Kant's definition of the Geography as a "synoptic discipline synthesizing findings of other sciences through the concept of *Raum* [area or space]" has been influential in the history of German and US Geography with unfortunate results.[31] R. Hartshorne, in *The Nature of Geography*, published in 1939 under the auspices of the Association of American Geographers, used Kant's ideas to dismiss entirely the possibility of a field called historical geography (except as comparative statics) much to the umbrage of Carl Sauer, the main practitioner of historical and cultural geography in the United States from the 1920s onward.[32] The particularity of spatial positioning, furthermore, is marked, Hartshorne argued, by contingency, and under this restrictive definition geography can only be concerned with the unique and the particular. This contrasts radically with the universality that attaches to the concept of a unidirectional time that might point us teleologically toward our destiny of cosmopolitan governance. F. Schaeffer was later to dispute Hartshorne's interpretation of Kant, provoking a series of vitriolic exchanges, by arguing that it was perfectly feasible to determine universal laws of spatial order (applying geometric models to settlement patterns, as in the central-place theories of Christaller and Lösch, for example). Under another interpretation of Kant's scheme of things, favored by May, spatial ordering produces regional and local truths and laws, as opposed to universals. These local laws are derived territorially by way of the specific rules of citizenship within the history of nation-states defined in terms of common descent. This "absolute" Newtonian conception of space (and of time) then frames Kant's territorial anthropological approach to cosmopolitan law, much as it also frames Rawls's and Walzer's approach to questions of local justice. Kant's map of the world is equivalent to a Mercator projection with absolute borders of nation-states clearly defined. This perspective of absolute entities in space underpins Foucault's concept of heterotopia, and this in turn may have influenced Foucault's view that metatheory is inadmissible and that the politics of the contingent and the local (including local knowledges) is all that matters.[33]

May does not tell us how Kant proposed to relate local truths and laws (such as national character) to the universals of reason (humanity in the abstract). But if May's account is right, then Kant's geographical and anthropological knowledges appear potentially in conflict with his universal ethics. What happens, for example, when universal ethical ideals are applied to issues of global governance in a world in which nation-states set up their own distinctive rules consistent with their national character? Worse still, how do we apply a universal ethic to a world in which some people are considered immature or inferior and others are thought indolent, smelly, or just plain untrustworthy? Either the smelly Hottentots, the lazy Samoyeds, the thieving Javanese, and the indecent Burmese women have to reform themselves for consideration under the universal ethical code (thereby flattening out all kinds of geographical and cultural differences in favor of some normative definition of maturity), or the universal principles operate across different geographical conditions as an intensely discriminatory code masquerading as the universal good. There are reasonable grounds for inferring that Kant actually thought the former, since in his famous essay "What is Enlightenment?" he made much ado about human "maturity" as a necessary condition for proper engagement in a public realm where certain freedoms were institutionally established and politically guaranteed. His rules for the exclusion of troublesome elements from citizenship within a sovereign democratic republic support that view. But, as we have also already seen, the supposedly universal principles laid out in his specification of cosmopolitan law entail all manner of hidden concessions to a certain version of anthropological and geographical realities. One suspects that it is precisely the attraction of Kant's cosmopolitanism that it can somehow sustain a veneer of attachment to some theory of universal goodness while allowing, even justifying, innumerable concessions to prejudicial exclusions on the ground. From this perspective it may even legitimately be claimed that Bush is a true Kantian.

This is, as many have recognized, a fundamental and unresolved difficulty in Kant's whole approach to knowledge. Hannah Arendt puts the dilemma this way: "The chief difficulty in judgment is that it is 'the faculty of thinking the particular'; but to think means to generalize, hence it is the faculty of mysteriously combining the particular and the general. This is reasonably easy if the general is given—as a rule, a principle, a law—so that the judgment merely subsumes the particular under it. The difficulty becomes great if only the particular be given for which the general has to be found. For the standard cannot be borrowed from experience and cannot be derived from outside. I cannot judge one particular by another particular; in order to determine its worth."[34]

Kant's answer, as we have seen, is to invoke that acute intelligence that acknowledges subtleties. But then the danger is the production of "empty sophistries and conceited prattlings." The version of Kant's geography that has come down to us amounts to an incoherent bunch of anecdotic particulars for which the general has yet to be found. To this day, geographical knowledge continues to lie very much in this state, in spite of some of the best efforts of geographers and others to reform its ways. Kant's anthropology, though more systematic, is also deeply flawed. And contemporary anthropology, in spite of the efforts of its best practitioners, has hardly eliminated "empty sophistries and conceited prattlings" (particularly in its so-called "postmodern" guise). All of this would not be a problem were it not for the fact that the political consequences (as in Iraq, Rwanda, Palestine, and Darfur) can on occasion be nothing short of catastrophic.

What appears so dramatically with Kant has widespread ramifications for politics. Popular geographical and anthropological knowledges in the public domain (in the United States in particular) are either entirely lacking or of a similar prejudicial quality to that which Kant portrayed. Stereotypes about geographical "others" abound, and prejudicial commentary can be heard daily in casual conversations even in elite circles (listen in to any conversation about Mexicans, sub-Saharan Africans or Arabs in university common rooms, let alone upon the street, and see how quickly stereotypes are invoked and pass unchallenged).

It then becomes all too easy for the U.S. government (or any other government for that matter) to portray itself as the bearer of universal principles of justice, democracy, liberty, freedom, and goodness, while in practice operating in an intensely discriminatory way against others judged different, unfamiliar, or in some sense lacking in proper qualifications or human qualities. Bush, for example, propounds his version of the Kantian cosmopolitan ethic while shock and awe over Baghdad and the horrors of thousands of Iraqi deaths, plus the sordid sights of Abu Ghraib, bring us back to what in the technical language of remote sensing is referred to as the "ground-truthing" of abstract concepts in relation to anthropological and geographical realities.

This contrast between the universality of Kant's cosmopolitanism and his ethics, and the awkward and intractable particularities of his anthropology and geography is therefore of critical importance. If knowledge of the latter defines (as Kant himself held) the "conditions of possibility" of all other forms of practical knowledge of the world, then on what grounds can we trust Kant's cosmopolitanism if his anthropological and geographical groundings are so suspect? Yet there is a way to see this as a fruitful starting point for discussion. For while it is possible to complain endlessly about "the damage done by faction and intense local loyalties to our political lives,"[35] it is also important to recognize how "human passions" (which Kant believed to be inherently aggressive and capable of evil) so often acquire a local and disruptive expression. In the face of this, it will take a tremendous effort to even approach that cosmopolitan state of which we are, at least in Kant's judgment, potentially capable. Is there, then, some way in which we can facilitate that effort by answering Nussbaum's call for a radical overhaul in our curricula for the teaching of geography, ecology, and anthropology? Kant identifies the questions but fails to provide adequate answers. He may have lived in an age of Enlightenment but it was most certainly not, as he himself understood, an enlightened age. We are then faced with an interesting choice. We can either reject the whole Enlightenment project, along with all of Bush's rhetoric about freedom and liberty, as a sordid and hypocritical justification for imperial rule and global domination or accept the basic thrust of what the Enlightenment (and its U.S. off-shoot) was about, with the clear understanding that that particular stab at enlightenment was not enlightened enough. And one of the prime areas of knowledge that remains to be reconstructed is that of "appropriate" anthropological and geographical understandings that can illuminate the way to a genuinely cosmopolitan future. But behind this there lies a certain imperative that pushed the whole question of cosmopolitanism and a federated republicanism into the forefront of Kant's concerns. Why, for example, do we need borders, and why do we need to cross them, anyway? On this point it is clear that the needs of trade and private property are paramount, and that implies that the legal requirements of merchant and landed capital in particular and perhaps even of capital in general play a highly significant closet role in Kant's formulations.

Chapter Two
The Postcolonial Critique of Liberal Cosmopolitanism

It is one thing to go after the abstractions of Kant's ethical cosmopolitanism but quite another to take on the philosophy and practices of liberalism. But this is precisely what a group of postcolonial writers, inspired by Eric Stokes and culminating in the works of Dipesh Chakrabarty and, above all, Uday Singh Mehta, have done so brilliantly with respect to the ideas and practices of nineteenth-century British liberalism in India. Mehta puts it this way: "Liberal theoretical claims typically tend to be transhistorical, transcultural, and more certainly transracial. The declared and ostensible referent of liberal principles is quite literally a constituency with no delimiting boundary: that of all humankind. The political rights that it articulates and defends, the institutions such as laws, representation, contract all have their justification in a characterization of human beings that eschews names, social status, ethnic background, gender and race."[1]

The individualism it contemplates is deracinated, universal, given over, in true Kantian fashion, to a cosmopolitanism of reason and rational action. This remains as true today as it did in the eighteenth century. It was exactly in this spirit, for example, that President Clinton could greet China's admission to the World Trade Organization with the comment that it opened up China to the rule of law (as if China had no preexisting body of law). And it was, as we have seen, the liberal tradition of John Locke and Adam Smith that Bush invoked in his Whitehall speech defending his politics of spreading liberty and market freedoms everywhere. Liberalism is vigorously expressive of a universal ethic: it refuses to privilege (at least in principle) any particular spatial or temporal context: "By rendering nature and the encounter with it sentimentally inert, Locke denies locational attachments as having any individual significance in relation to political identity. The sentiments in a person 'coming from' or 'belonging to' a *place*, and of those sentiments being constitutive of his of her identity, are all deemed politically irrelevant. . . . By not acknowledging natural or geographical distinctions along with their corresponding emotional attachments as having any political value, Locke and much of the subsequent British liberal tradition cannot give credence to the claims of territoriality that undergird most political identities and nationalisms." [2]

The facts of geography and anthropology are occluded, if not actively repressed, within liberal theory (and its derivative discourses such as economics) because they are judged irrelevant to the universality of its basic conceptions. The geographical and anthropological conditions only become relevant at the moment of application. But reflection on actual outcomes reveals a problem: how could eminent liberals, such as J. S. Mill, hold onto their pristine liberal ideals while denying the right of self-determination and basic liberties such as representative governance to India? How could they insist that it was perfectly right that India remain under the tutelage of British imperial rule, and why did it take such a long struggle for Indians to gain their independence from a supposedly liberal empire? As in Kant's case, we find that the devil resides in the otherwise occluded anthropological and geographical details. "The details structure the outcome," notes Mehta, "without of necessity violating the presumed inclusionary vision." For Mill in particular, Mehta argues, local conditions "placed limits on the scientific aspirations of legislation and theory in general." So what was it about these "local conditions" that justified such limitations?[3]

Exclusion from the benefits of self-governance could be justified in two ways. Under the first, a particular space and people were demonized or declared "savage" or "barbarian" and in extreme cases, as with the indigenous populations of North America, considered so close to nature as to be beyond incorporation into any concept of a civilized world. In the extreme case (such as that which Clayton describes for Vancouver Island) this means the erasure of all mention of indigenous populations as having an existence, let alone political organization or rights.[4] A territory is depicted as empty and open for settlement by those colonists who could justify their rights to property by mixing their labor with the land in a true Lockean fashion. Descriptions of native practices, insofar as they were bothered with at all, provided discursive and ultimately legal support within the liberal framework for a politics of dispossession of those considered to be "unworthy savages." Since native populations were deemed to be part of nature, and since the subordination of nature to the god-given imperative to be fruitful and multiply was central to "our" holy mission on earth, then the domination of native populations was both legitimate and noble.

The second modality, which became more general in India, was to treat the indigenous population as not yet educated or mature (the Kantian phrase is apt) enough to justify inclusion in the liberal regime of power and rights: "India is a child for which the empire offers the prospect of a legitimate and progressive parentage and toward which Britain, as a parent, is similarly obligated and competent. For both the Mills and Macaulay this point is the justification of denying democratic rights and representative institutions to Indians, along with various other imperial interdictions. The idea has a distinguished pedigree and in the liberal tradition originates in Locke's characterization of tutelage as a necessary stage through which children must be trained before they acquire the reason requisite for expressing contractual consent."[5]

This "infantilizing" of whole peoples is a common enough trope. The French took up the idea with a vengeance in the wake of the French Revolution by arguing, as did Boissy d'Anglas in 1796, that the immaturity and laziness of the colonized peoples mandated that they forever "remain content with being subject to wise and peaceful government by just and humane men who are enemies of tyranny."[6] Rockefeller appealed to it as the basis for neocolonial interventions in Latin America (in particular, Venezuela, which just happened to have oil) in the early years of the twentieth century. It was registered within the liberal tradition at the turn of the twentieth century as "the white man's burden." It continues to be expressed, though less openly, in contemporary languages of development aid or Peace Corps missions, and the whole discourse of "backwardness" and "underdevelopment." It has been a serious problem in Marxist internationalism and radical developmentalism as well: consider the seriously flawed Sandinista approach to incorporation of the Atlantic Coast Mesquite Indians into Nicaraguan development in the 1980s and the disastrous consequences that followed as the CIA cynically exploited Mesquite Indian discontent to parlay it into the Nicaraguan "Contra" movement. The politics of such infantilization are implicit in Kant's depiction of Enlightenment as a condition of human "maturity" of judgment (or "maturity of their faculties," as J. S. Mill put it). Either way, the effect has been, Mehta concludes, to embed a politics of exclusion into the heart of nineteenth-century European liberal theories and practices with respect to empire. The trace of such exclusionary practices exists throughout the whole history of liberal capitalism, and it taints the contemporary neoliberal project as well.

This poses a deeper analytical and epistemological problem concerning the role and positionality of historical, anthropological, and geographical knowledges ("the details") in giving rise to such exclusionary political outcomes. For Chakrabarty, J. S. Mill's refusal to grant self-governance depended purely upon the historicist argument that "Indians or Africans were not yet civilized enough to rule themselves. Some historical time of development and civilization (colonial rule and education, to be precise) had to elapse before they could be considered prepared for such a task. Mill's historicist argument thus consigned Indians, Africans and other 'rude' nations to an imaginary waiting room of history. In doing so, it converted history into a version of this waiting room." [7]

Since Europe (or "the West" more generally) was always progressing faster, it was then easy to justify prolonging everyone else's stay in the waiting room indefinitely. Mehta partially concurs with this argument: the conception of history and progress lies at the root of the problem. "Cosmopolitanism," he writes, "without the problematic of universal history generates and aspires to an ethics, but it does not issue in a program of paternalism and interventionist collective action."[8] It was only when Kant inserted the idea of universal history into his argument—the idea that "man makes himself" and that temperament can give way to character—that cosmopolitanism came to depart fundamentally from the purely ethical cosmopolitanism of the Stoics. J. S. Mill distinguished himself from Locke's liberalism in exactly the same way. The idea of historical progress and of leaders and followers produces exclusions that can last in perpetuity.

Chakrabarty's answer to this dilemma is to "provincialize Europe." There are, he argues, separate spaces apart from Europe (such as India or Bengal) within which separate and equally valid temporalities/histories hold. Progress may proceed differentially and unevenly, but there is no waiting room to which any one people is confined. Chakrabarty makes no attempt, however, to justify the existence of the distinctive spaces to which he appeals, treating geographical entities such as India or Bengal as self-evident, and conveniently ignoring the substantial evidence that the very idea of "India" was itself a British imperial construction (albeit subsequently nurtured and nuanced by the rise of Indian nationalism). Mehta agrees that there are "multiple and extant temporalities and life forms" in different places. But he goes further than Chakrabarty by seeing anthropological and more particularly geographical conditions and knowledges as integral to understanding how imperial rule came to be justified within liberal theory. In somewhat tortuous prose (always an interesting indicator of a certain conceptual difficulty) he argues for "a hermeneutics of spatially contemporaneous life forms whose differences, at least a priori, exist on the same ontological plane and must therefore be understood in terms of a relationality of heterogeneous spatial simultaneity and not homogeneous temporal linearity."[9] I think he means by this that space is discontinuous, social, and relational, and that it is just as important as time in the shaping of political identities. The smooth Euclidean/Newtonian (to which I would add Kantian) space and time that frames both liberal theory and universal history was an erroneous fiction that permitted Mill "to imagine the world as a connected and smooth surface, uniformly available to a fixed grid of knowledge." The occlusion of anthropology and geography within liberal theory and practice then becomes the problem. According to Mehta, the question of space and geography "rarely gets raised to the level of theoretical attention." Political theory is confronted with the problem, as Kant would put it, of "particulars for which the general has yet to be found."

Oddly, Mehta ignores entirely the substantive work, some of it by geographers, that has paid a great deal of theoretical attention to questions of space and geography. The failure to register any of these findings in his analysis can, of course, be dismissed as yet another lamentable example of disciplinary myopia, but it unfortunately has some very substantive effects, for it is exactly at this point, and perhaps for this reason, that Mehta's argument begins to go seriously awry. He repeatedly points to the deficiencies of a liberal theory that is unable to appreciate the significance of place, locality, and geography to political identity formation: "Liberals have failed to appreciate that territory is both a symbolic expression and a concrete condition for the possibility of (or aspirations to) a distinct way of life, and that in the modern epoch it gathers together many of the associations through which individuals come to see themselves as members of a political society. To invoke a metaphor prevalent in early liberal theorizing, territory is the *body* of the polity, which, not unlike the human body, marks the perimeter within and through which its identity is constituted and the specific expression of its autonomy is molded."[10]

Liberals, as a consequence, "were unable to recognize and appreciate the political integrity of various nonconsensual societies." The empire they built was therefore almost predestined to encounter some form of parochialism and nationalism as a political response. Even when oppositional "nationalists invoked the language of liberal universalism, they alloyed it with the textured realities of locally imagined and physical landscape. And geography was often their more powerful tool."[11] The language here is interesting. We find, once more, the Kantian (and even Foucauldian) "condition of possibility" argument opened up, but its potentiality as a point of critical engagement is immediately interred within a deeply problematic biological metaphor with dangerous associations to social Darwinism. This metaphor of the body politic is not without its possibilities, but used uncritically it can all too easily lead us into the nether world of fascism. In Mehta's case, the turn is toward a consideration (and a rehabilitation in many ways) of Edmund Burke (that great opponent of the French revolution and of the British empire). Burke, we are told, did not eschew universals, for he held that "territory or place is a fundamental condition of collective and individual political identity. Moreover, it constitutes the ground through which notions such as duty, obligation, order and freedom come to have the political meaning that they do." Burke, according to Mehta, "takes seriously the sentiments, feelings and attachments through which peoples are, and aspire to be, 'at home.' This posture of thought acknowledges that the integrity of experience is tied to its locality and its finitude. . . . By doing so, it is congruent with the psychological aspects of experience, which always derive their meaning, their passionate and pained intensity, from within the bounded, even if porous, spheres of familial, national, or other narratives."[12]

Again and again in his impassioned attacks upon the British imperial presence in India, Burke invoked the facts of geography as he saw them as a primary rhetorical strategy to deny the legitimacy of British occupancy. Writes Mehta: "territory or location is both a metaphor and an important physical fact that captures the psychological and emotional conditions of individuals viewing themselves as members of a distinct society. . . . Both history and geography, notwithstanding the contestations that attend them, facilitate the creation of that sense of bounded togetherness, through which itself the notion of sharing in something comes to be effective and available to normative and institutional modification."[13]

In a brilliant series of reversals, Burke sees the British imperialists as the wild and unruly children, incapable of mature engagement with the merely different, let alone the radically unfamiliar: "Burke's cosmopolitanism does not rely on the strategy of aligning societies that are in fact contemporaneous in their affective attachments, along a temporal grid that moves them 'backward' on account of their difference, so as to give a linear coherence to the idea of the progress. Once one recognizes, as Burke does, that human experience gains its density from the passionate commitment that a life form produces, then the challenge of cosmopolitanism is to understand these forms as contemporaneous ways of being in the world."[14]

From this perspective Burke constructs what Mehta calls a "cosmopolitanism of sentiments." There is much that is seemingly positive in this argument. It would not be hard, for example, to assimilate the idea of such sentiments into Nussbaum's quest for cosmopolitanism as an ethos and as a moral standpoint; as we shall see later, this is how Anthony Appiah arrives at his conception of a "rooted cosmopolitanism." But much depends on the nature of the sentiments expressed. And on this point there is much that is deeply problematic in Mehta's argument: the appeal to permanence and the supposed "integrity" and "finitude" of place-based experience; the absolute spaces within which such sense of belonging has its provenance; and, above all, the "singularities" of place and geography that Burke believes can be negotiated only by "mature" adults engaging in free conversations. Mehta, to his credit, recognizes that Burke nowhere explains "the psychological and cognitive operations through which place comes to acquire its crucial relation to identity."[15] In earlier setting up some relational propositions regarding the nature of space, and in recognizing that boundaries can be imposed that have nothing to do with affections or any sense of dwelling, Mehta also indicates that territories may have porous borders and therefore a fluid rather than permanent meaning. And in appealing to Frantz Fanon's view of place as "the zone of occult instability where people dwell," Mehta temporarily concedes the inherent instability of all geographical and anthropological attachments. But these nuances get lost in the overall argument. Mehta, understandably appreciative of Burke's attack upon imperial rule in India, fails to see that Burke's favoring of entailed inheritance (the "rights of true-born Englishmen") over universal rights provided—as Arendt, for one, points out—"the ideological basis from which English nationalism derived its curious touch of race feeling" as well as its "later obsession with inheritance theories and eugenics."[16] Mehta ignores all such potential pitfalls and drives remorselessly to a conclusion: "Human beings are not born blank slates; instead they inherit a mass of predispositions from an unfathomable past bounded by the variations of time and place. It is the emplacement within these points of reference that gives to individuals, and to communities, a sense of their integrity and self-understanding from which alone life can be, and is, richly experienced—indeed, from which alone moral action is possible."[17]

Read as an absolute conclusion this is nothing short of appalling, given the emphasis upon integrity and unfathomability, and, above all, that it is from this exclusive positionality of community in place *alone* that moral action is possible. This is, to put it mildly, disempowering of all other forms of critique based in any universals (such as justice or human rights) whatsoever. Chakrabarty, for his part, recognizes the danger and neatly sidesteps it. While he holds, on the one hand, that "the universal and the analytical produce forms of thought that ultimately evacuate the place of the local," he recognizes, on the other hand, that "we need universals to produce critical readings of social injustices."[18] Without this last perspective it becomes impossible to condemn exclusionary communitarianism and even fascist violence. That Mehta should take such a position appears odd, since he also coauthored a perceptive article critical of the activities of Shiv Sena, a local nativist-turned-religious-nationalist movement in Mumbai, generally blamed for the extraordinary violence in 1992–93 in which more than a thousand people (mostly Muslims) were killed and perhaps hundreds of thousands more were forced to flee the city during months of violence and rage.[19] This is not, I imagine, the kind of "moral action" that Mehta would either support or condone. But how can we criticize Shiv Sena's own sense of integrity and self-understanding except by appeal to moral precepts that arise outside of its enclosure within that place and its members' claims to being the only authentic inhabitants of Maharastra? Mehta has unwittingly substituted Burke's racially charged concept of localized entailed inheritance (Kant's sense of the *gens*) for Mill's paternalism.

The sentiments Mehta expresses here are very Heideggerian. He actually reads Heidegger as "deeply Burkean" in his sensibility.[20] This embrace of Heidegger is not unique to Mehta. In recent times it has acquired considerable purchase among postcolonial thinkers more generally. Chakrabarty, for example, also seeks to understand the experience of liberal empire by triangulating between the polarities of Heidegger and Marx, using the former to evoke all the facts of geography and the fragmented temporalities that the liberal imperialists as well as, in Chakrabarty's view, the Marxists so fatally ignore. There is, these authors seem to propose, no other way to compensate for liberal or socialist universalism and by extension

Kantian failings other than by leaping straight from the Kantian frying pan into the Heideggerian fire. Why Heidegger's thought is privileged as the way by which the obviously pertinent facts of geography can be incorporated into political theory remains somewhat of a mystery.

Mehta suggests that the pertinent facts of geography can be subsumed under the political and psychological significance of "place and history as constitutive of human identity." Concerns of this sort, whether inspired by Burke or not, are common currency even among conservatives. Desirous of conserving hierarchies and genealogies of power and privilege, many conservatives are concerned to preserve the social, cultural, and ecological milieus that nourish such social relations. Any threat to these milieus must therefore be taken seriously and, if possible, resisted. From this perspective, the geographer Carl Sauer, writing in 1938, constructed a blistering denunciation not only of Spanish colonialism but of the subsequent ravages and depredations of capitalist neocolonialism throughout Latin America. Complaining that "in our impatience to get at universals" we grossly neglected "the complexities of our own natural history," Sauer characterized the "expansion of European commerce, peoples and governments" as initiating a "tragic age" in which over a mere century and a half "more damage has been done to the productive capacity of the world than in all of human history preceding."[21] In the wake of World War II he quieted his critique, almost certainly for political reasons, only to return to it in *The Early Spanish Main*, a book that Anthony Pagden characterized (in his introduction to a later edition) as a major contribution to understanding the dark side of the Columbian exchange. Sauer was no romantic. He understood that societies change and evolve. The tragedy, in Sauer's view, was that the rich possibilities in the region were so "ruthlessly and idiotically thrown away," in large part because of Columbus's "lack of understanding not merely of where he was but of the possible consequences of his being there." Far from being a great geographer, Columbus was an ignoramus who initiated "a pattern of conquest and settlement that was repeated all over Spanish America" with disastrous and tragic consequences—consequences "that we, for all our scientific rationalism, have done very little to rectify." Sauer opened up themes that later became more common currency in the works of Pagden, Walter Mignolo, and other Latin American scholars, the lesson being that the Latin American experience, while quite different, has been just as authentically and destructively postcolonial as that of South Asia.[22] The South Asian scholars who defined the postcolonial field have, Mignolo argues, no privileged experience of how Enlightenment reason and liberalism worked to their own detriment and certainly should have no lock on postcolonial theorizing (an interesting case of how the geographical circumstances of knowledge production have a distinctive role to play in theory construction). But it is also worth noting that the critical and anti-imperialist perspectives of a traditional geographer like Carl Sauer, writing in the 1930s, have been totally ignored in the postcolonial literature.

There is, interestingly, a left-wing version of this same argument, most clearly represented in the antiglobalization movement and its theorists. In the "postdevelopmental theory" of Arturo Escobar, for example, we find the obvious objection that the universals of Western developmentalism and neoliberal globalization are far too insensitive to local difference and that much of what passes for fair trade is neocolonial in structure and therefore exploitative in the extreme (particularly with respect to the extraction of natural resources). We also find a total rejection of all universal developmental models in favor of local, place-based initiatives out of which real alternatives to a globalizing capitalism can supposedly be constructed. Escobar proposes "a reassertion of place, noncapitalism, and local culture against the dominance of space, capital and modernity that are central to globalization discourse," in the belief that this will "result in a theory of postdevelopment that makes visible the possibility for reconceiving and reconstructing the world from the perspective of place-based cultural and economic practices." Escobar appeals to the "novel debates" that have been generated around the theme of economy and place, in which "place is asserted against the dominance of space and noncapitalism against the dominance of capitalism." Place is here conceptualized as "the other" to the space of globalization. A discussion of place is presumed to "afford an important perspective towards rethinking . . . the question of alternatives to capitalism and modernity."[23] But this immediately raises the questions of how we can reasonably construe space and place as in some way oppositional concepts, and why space might be linked to liberal theory, globalization, and modernity, while place is the terrain of its oppositional other. And while Escobar guardedly cautions against "reifying places, local cultures and forms of noncapitalism as 'untouched' or 'outside of history,'" there is nevertheless an overwhelming tendency to regard "local models of nature and the economy, and the social movements linked to them," as the unique source of postdevelopmentalism. In this Escobar comes close to embracing Mehta's appalling vision of place-bound sentiments as the sole acceptable form of moral judgment. These are, clearly, issues that need to be debated. But it is also clear that the geographical conceptual apparatus deployed—in this instance, the proper relation between space and place—has a key role to play in formulating political understandings as well as transformative possibilities.

Burke's appeal to the facts of geography "as he saw them" as the fundamental argument against British imperialism and Mehta's endorsement of Burke's position likewise raise the question as to what, exactly, those facts might be and how they may best be represented and theorized. If, after all, Columbus was so disastrously wrong, why should we assume that Burke was any more right about India than Bush was about Iraq? On this point there is another story to be told from the postcolonial world that simultaneously supports and subverts Mehta's contentions, while seriously challenging the opposition between space and place set up in Escobar's account. India, as a coherent geographical entity, was, according to Matthew Edney, very much a British imperial rather than indigenous conception. The fundamental moment in this definition was the mapping of the subcontinent by British surveyors. Mapmaking

> was integral to British imperialism in India, not just as a highly effective informational weapon wielded strategically and tactically by directors, governors, military commanders, and field officials, but also as a significant component of the "structures of feeling" which legitimated, justified and defined that imperialism. The surveys and maps together transformed the subcontinent from an exotic and largely unknown region into a well-defined and knowable geographical entity. The imperial space of India was a space of rhetoric and symbolism, rationality and science, dominance and separation, inclusion and exclusion. Its horizontal spatial boundaries, which enclosed, divided, and so gave political meaning to an otherwise homogeneous space, merged imperceptibly with the vertical boundaries of the empire's social hierarchies. The empire might have defined the map's extent, but mapping defined the empire's nature.[24]

The triangulation of India was about constructing and imposing spatial order. In accepting the Kantian separation of space from time, it eviscerated all signs of history and collective memory. It created a new knowledge of India that was crucial to the colonial disciplinary apparatus. "The British engineer-surveyor looked at the Indian landscape as a surgeon looks at his patient, as an item to be thoroughly investigated, measured and prodded so that maladies and imperfections might be identified, understood, adjusted, controlled, and so cured." The subtext was that British culture was "rational, liberal, precise and proper," as opposed to Hindu conceptions—for example, of spatiality—that were considered by the British to be mystical and cosmological even when mathematically and geometrically elegant. Part of the British project was to "free the mind" of the Hindus "of the fetters of unreasoning belief," and to that end the Hindus were invited to submit to the logic of the maps the British had made of them, to abandon all sense of their own history, and to take on that "structure of feeling" that every trueborn Englishman was supposed to possess. The British aim, in what most concede in the annals of cartography to be a magnificent achievement, was to produce a single, uniform cartographic archive that could be used for rational and effective rule (including, of course, the extraction of wealth through taxation). However, the information the British produced "did not represent a perfect, empirically known truth, as they thought it did, but instead constituted contested knowledge of a socially constructed reality." It was not that the British falsified, but that their spatial conception of the world—Newtonian and Cartesian—produced a particular kind of homogeneous, universal, and ahistorical knowledge ("managed and controlled in London"!) that was partial in what it could represent:

> The rational uniform space of the British maps of India was not a neutral, value-free space, it was a space imbued with power relations, with the fact that the British controlled (or had the power to control) the land depicted and that they could impose India-wide legislation and reforms in a manner impossible for earlier rulers. Imperial space was a space of boundaries . . . rationalized and fixed by the force of imperial adjudication. In this respect imperial space used boundaries as a mechanism for equating abstract space with the concrete reality of territory. In a major conceptual reversal, boundaries were no longer vague axes of dispute (frontiers) between core areas of Indian polities, but were configured as the means whereby these core areas were now defined. Political territories were no longer defined with respect to the physical features that characterized them or which bounded them; they were not defined by the complex "feudal" interrelationships of their rulers. The British suborned the character of those territories to a mathematical space even as they reduced political structures to the "rule of law."[25]

To administer a place called India through the perspective of the map was to administer a population that supposedly had no history, memory, or any other mark of identity save location within the grid of a uniform Euclidean space imposed cartographically upon a far more complicated space. How Indian nationalists took all of this apparatus to construct their own sense of national identity is a major story of Indian colonial and postcolonial history. They could not and indeed would not abandon the map. Their task was to find some way to fill the map they were inheriting and refill it with a meaning that was distinctly their own, even as it replicated part of that "structure of feeling" that the British legacy imparted. Herein lay the origins of a powerful constructed myth of Indian statehood, a myth that to this day has enormous power in the Indian political consciousness. Broken into fragments, as Partha Chatterjee points out, the myth of nationhood within the cartography that the British left behind conjoins the Indian sense of space, place, and geography with a peculiarly abstract and modernist understanding of time and history.[26]

While Kant was anticolonial in principle, his rationalist vision of a spatial ordering quite separate from temporalities and from histories proved eminently adaptable to British imperial and colonial rule. It was, therefore, by no means as value-free and neutral as it seemed. The deracinated theory of liberalism proved even more pernicious when brought to earth with the aid of a cartographic reason that treated of space as abstract, universal, and absolute. In that context, and that context alone, the idea of geography and place as a potential source of an oppositional politics makes sense. But it is curious that so many postcolonial thinkers concerned with the Indian case would resort to Heidegger for sustenance. Clearly, the kinds of "geographical facts" that Burke had in mind, and that Mehta also invokes, to say nothing of the space-time world of myths and origins that Heidegger presents, are very different from the spatial rationalities of Descartes and Newton. But this is not the only kind of oppositional thought as to the salience of place and geography. Indeed, the danger lurks that postcolonial theory will rest secretly imprisoned within a cartographic image of India bequeathed by British imperial rule, all the while trying to stuff it full, as it were, with hefty doses of Heideggerian mythology.

That this is not the only path to take is best illustrated in the "cartographic" essays of Chandra Mohanty. She points out that there is plenty of work still to be done to decolonize postcolonial theory itself. While hers begins as a distinctively feminist and to some degree universal quest to recognize and undo the ways "in which we colonize and objectify our different histories and culture, thus colluding with hegemonic processes of domination and rule," she refuses the idea of a universal feminism in favor of negotiating a path between a "debilitating ossification of difference," on the one hand, and the fluid relationalities of power and struggle that result in both real and conceptual "cartographies of struggle," on the other.[27] Her cartography is neither fixed nor held hostage, as it is in Mehta's case, to some "unfathomable past bounded by the variations of time and space." And this cartography is radically different from that which was imposed by imperial rule. Place (and "home" in particular) is vital to how we both construct and understand the world, but the cartographies of struggle that we construct are not imprisoned in any fixed space (if only because, as we move house from, for example, country to city, we often encounter radically different experiences and understandings of the world as we change locations). Furthermore, solidarities and alliances (key political terms in Mohanty's formulations) can be and are built across space, turning fixed boundaries into porous borders in such a way as to realize feminist, anticolonial, and anticapitalist struggles through the uneven geographical development of political dynamics. In her case, the pursuit of freedom is not located inside a fixed geography. It entails, rather, the construction of an entirely new and different geography (practically as well as conceptually) around relational principles of belonging that entail a completely different definition of space and place to that contained either in the Kantian or the Heideggerian schemas. While the oppressions of the British form of cartographic reason are palpable, there is no point articulating a false resistance to these by resort to Burkean and Heideggerian formulations that, in their own way, are just as oppressive. Whichever way we look, therefore, we find a deep significance to how we build our conceptual cartographies and make our actual geographies. And at the center of this effort lies the theoretical and practical conundrum of how we can and should understand the evidently problematic relation between space and place.

Chapter Three
The Flat World of Neoliberal Utopianism

Thomas Friedman begins his best-seller, *The World Is Flat*, with an account of an epiphany experienced on a golf course in downtown Bangalore in southern India. His playing partner, pointing "to two shiny glass-and-steel buildings off in the distance, just behind the first green," suggested he aim either at IBM or at Microsoft. After he had gotten to the eighteenth green (having encountered Hewlett Packard and Texas Instruments on the back nine), Friedman called his wife to say, "Honey, the world is flat." Free-market globalization and rapid technological changes have, he says, produced a world of

> digitalization, virtualization, and automation of almost everything. The gains in productivity will be staggering for those countries, companies and individuals who can absorb the new technological tools. And we are entering a phase where more people than ever before in the history of the world are going to have access to these tools. . . . I think this new era of globalization will prove to be such a difference in degree that it will be seen, in time, as a difference in kind. That is why I introduced the idea that the world has gone from being round to flat. Everywhere you turn, hierarchies are being challenged from below or transforming themselves from top-down structures into more horizontal and collaborative ones. . . . Henceforth, more and more economies [will] be governed from the ground up, by the interests, demands and aspirations of the people, rather than from the top down by the interests of some narrow ruling clique.[1]

As he travels from country to country, meeting with CEOs, techno-geeks, and pundits, Friedman finds them everywhere integrating themselves into global networks, actively cultivating the deployment of the new technologies, creating unheard-of efficiencies, and, it goes without saying, making plenty of money. He describes unparalleled technological and organizational changes, particularly in the information technology (IT) sector (at one point he even happily pleads guilty to the charge of technological determinism, erroneously attributing such a theory to Marx, having liberally quoted from *The Communist Manifesto*). Behind this there exist important macroeconomic reforms. Initiated "by a small handful of leaders in countries like China, Russia, Mexico, Brazil and India" (and often relying upon authoritarian state powers to accomplish their goals), country after country has been pushed "into more export-oriented free-market strategies—based on privatization of state companies, deregulation of financial markets, currency adjustments, foreign direct investment, shrinking subsidies, lowering protectionist tariff barriers, and introduction of more flexible labor laws." These countries' leaders, he says, confronted "the irrefutable fact that more open and competitive markets are the only sustainable vehicle for growing a nation out of poverty, because they are the only guarantee that new ideas, technologies, and best practices are easily flowing into your country and that private enterprises, and even government, have the competitive incentive and flexibility to adopt those new ideas and turn them into jobs and products." But two other conditions are necessary for a country to succeed. First, the state has to stimulate innovation and structure a regulatory environment favorable to entrepreneurialism and to personal accountability and responsibility. Constructing such a good business climate is the top-down part of the magical formula for economic success. Second, there has to be a parallel shift in bottom-up, grass-roots cultural understandings. The people of a country have to internalize "the values of hard work, thrift, honesty, patience, and tenacity," and be "open to change, new technology, and equality for women." In other words, everyone has to embrace contemporary bourgeois virtues and a neoliberal work ethic if they and the countries they inhabit are to succeed in today's competitive environment.[2] As with Kant's cosmopolitanism, we all have to become the same everywhere in order to qualify for admission to the regime of universal (in this case neoliberal) rights and benefits.

Friedman's is a brilliant but hyped-up caricature of the neoliberal world view that currently reigns supreme. The erasure of geographical and anthropological differences is striking, although at times it seems as if these do pose barriers to be overcome. A universal system of private property rights, free markets, and free trade together form the privileged, if not the sole, institutional framework within which the universal virtues of liberty and freedom can be realized. This is the supposed "irrefutable fact" upon which all of our hopes for a decent future must, according to Friedman, be founded. President Bush (not one of Friedman's favorite politicians) makes a similar argument: repression, resentment, and poverty will everywhere be countered "with the hope of democracy, development, free markets and free trade," because these have already proven "their ability to lift whole societies out of poverty."[3]

Theories of this sort have been around for a very long time, but they took on their distinctive contemporary coloration in 1947, when a group of luminaries led by Friedrich von Hayek, Milton Friedman, Ludwig von Mises, and several others formed the Mont Pelerin Society. They claimed that individual rights, including freedoms of thought and expression, were everywhere being "progressively undermined by extensions of arbitrary power" and "by a decline of belief in private property and the competitive market," adding that "without the diffused power and initiative associated with these institutions it is difficult to imagine a society in which freedom may be effectively preserved."[4] The role of the state with its monopoly of violence is, therefore, to create and support private property rights and free-market practices and to promote the integrity of money and a good business climate. But the state should go no further because, according to the theory, it cannot possibly possess enough information to second-guess market signals (prices), and because powerful interest groups (such as the infamous "K Street" lobbyists who currently so corrupt politics in Washington, D.C.) will inevitably distort and bias state interventions for their own benefit.

Neoliberal theorists have been particularly assiduous in cultivating the myth of private property as the guarantor of liberty and freedom. They convert the eighteenth-century view of the virtues of private property when embedded in a social system of moral obligations (of the sort that serious scholars of the time, such as Hugo Grotius and Adam Smith, went to great pains to specify) into an absolute fetish of property as an untrammeled and exclusive individual right to do exactly as one pleases with what one owns. In neoliberal theory, any restraints upon the exercise of private property rights are construed as an unconstitutional form of "takings." This fetish belief is illustrated in what Thomas Friedman considers the "brilliant and innovative work" of Hernando de Soto.[5] Usually depicted as an indigenous "third world theorist" from Peru, de Soto was in fact raised and educated in Geneva and early on gained the support of the Atlas Foundation for Economic Research, a right-wing North American neoliberal think tank. With its funding and advice, de Soto set up his Institute for Liberty and Democracy in Lima, Peru, and promptly became one of the leading voices in the neoliberal movement in the global South. Endorsed by Margaret Thatcher, Milton Friedman, and a host of other neoliberal luminaries as an indigenous thinker, he published books that became international best-sellers, exercising considerable influence over development theory (including that of the World Bank).

De Soto argued that poverty in the global South was self-inflicted rather than imperialistically, neocolonially, or capitalistically generated: the main barrier to development was the lack of clear title to ownership of assets, particularly land and housing. Ownership would open access to credit markets and integrate those in the informal economy into the global market, thereby ending poverty. The implementation of de Soto's ideas, at first under his direction but later taken over by the Peruvian government and then by the World Bank, did not produce the expected results for the 1.2 million people who gained title in Peru. The one tangible effect seemed to be that adults worked more hours, while their children worked less. This was lauded in the World Bank and the mainstream press, as well as by Thomas Friedman, as a positive outcome. But, as Timothy Mitchell shows, the finding is probably more a product of how the data were collected than a reflection of people's daily lives, to which I would add that even if it were properly substantiated, the idea that it is beneficial to the people who work more hours, as opposed to the people they work for, is far from proven.[6]

The idea that individualized private property, as a universal value, is a necessary condition for economic development and poverty alleviation has, however, no historical substantiation. Britain stood at the origin and dominated the world of industrial capitalism for a century or more while the crown, the church, the Oxford and Cambridge colleges, and a few aristocratic families controlled around two-thirds of the land. In practice, granting property rights to impoverished populations opens them up to market exploitations. In Egypt, the effect of reconceptualizing what used to be called "the informal economy" as a private property–led "microenterprise" economy (along lines recommended by de Soto) and of integrating it into "microlending" credit structures is, as J. Elyachar reports, far from benign. It seeks to impose market valuations and discipline upon a traditional workshop culture and to extract value out of that culture at relatively high rates of return. While neoliberals applaud such projects, the real effect, as Elyachar depicts it, is to create a "market of dispossession." Such practices are now gathering strength around the world as microcredit is more and more touted as the solution to global poverty. Initiated in the first instance as a noncommercial scheme to provide very small amounts of capital to large numbers of very poor people (especially women), microcredit projects are now touted by commercial financial institutions as a way to bring large numbers of people into the disciplinary apparatus of the market while extracting high rates of return (in some instances as high as 20 percent). This conversion of philanthropic microcredit into a commercially viable system of microfinance is of considerable significance. It is an attempt to impose the cultural change (a self-disciplinary apparatus) that Friedman considers crucial to creating the flat world of neoliberalism. This now refracts back into philanthropic practices. A new school of philanthropists (trained in the ways of Wall Street) now believes, David Gross reports, that "fighting poverty effectively relies on the creation of low-wage factories, as well as the establishment of lending institutions that charge rates that many Americans would deem usurious."[7]

This astonishing view that the poor will benefit the more they are disciplined by the market—and, incidentally, exploited by the rich—is not at all uncommon. Earlier, it was John Turner's famous anarchist-inspired advocacy in the mid-1970s of self-help housing in the *favelas* and slums of the world that was so delightedly seized upon by McNamara's World Bank as the key to reducing the travails of poverty and underdevelopment. It was supposed to give rise to a populist capitalism that would work for all and thereby abolish poverty. The scheme failed to realize its aims (though some intermediaries became wealthy), and poverty is worse than ever, as excruciatingly documented in recent reports on the state of our "planet of slums."[8] Private property arrangements, we should remember, have any chance to work only when, as Grotius and Adam Smith long ago insisted, the "moral sentiments" that regulate social interactions are of the requisite quality. The noncommercial microcredit schemes for which Yunnus, the originator, received the Nobel Peace Prize, incorporated this moral element, while the now numerous commercially grounded microfinance schemes do not.

The failure of neoliberals to imagine the consequences of imposing private property rights and monetized market institutions on divergent geographical, ecological, and anthropological situations is one of the more astonishing conceits of our times. In 2003, for example, the United States mandated the privatization of all state-owned assets and enterprises in occupied Iraq, full ownership rights of Iraqi businesses by foreign firms, the opening of Iraqi banks to foreign control, no barriers to foreign direct investment or to the repatriation of profits out of Iraq, and the elimination of nearly all trade barriers. The attempt to impose this free-market fundamentalism on Iraq, without any regard for the country's complex social structures and history, has contributed to the disastrous collapse of the country's political economy. The turn toward more neoliberal policies had, however, gathered steam throughout the world from the 1970s onward, led most spectacularly by the market reforms initiated in the United States under Reagan and in Britain under Thatcher. Social democratic, developmental, interventionist, and *dirigiste* states that had dominated global capitalism in the period from 1945 until the mid-1970s were bit by bit reformed along more neoliberal lines. In some instances (as in Chile after the coup of 1973), the changes were violently imposed. In other instances, neoliberal reforms were mandated as part of the solution to serious financial crises. Many of the formerly successful "developmental states" in East and Southeast Asia, for example, were pushed into partial neoliberalization through the catastrophic debt crisis of 1997–98.[9] Elsewhere the reforms were pushed through by some mix of external pressures (typically orchestrated by the U.S. Treasury operating through its control over the International Monetary Fund [IMF] and the World Bank) and internal dynamics in which local elites sought political-economic advantage from neoliberal reforms.

I have analyzed the rise of neoliberalism as a purported answer to the economic crisis of the 1970s in detail elsewhere. Although neoliberalization promised in principle a world free of excessive state interference, in practice states have been heavily involved in producing a good business climate (often subsidizing capital and curbing the aspirations of labor), in bailing out financial institutions when they are threatened, and in integrating business into government through public-private partnerships (and other structures of governance) or through the legalized corruption of electoral processes (hence all those lobbyists in Washington). Neoliberalization also promised rapid economic growth and an expansion of the world market that would redound to the benefit of all. What actually occurred was something quite different. Neoliberalism broadly failed to stimulate worldwide growth.[10] But it did entail relentless attacks upon forms of social solidarity incompatible with a system based on personal responsibility and individual initiative. It also saw significant state withdrawals from social provision. The reduction in barriers to trade and the opening up of global markets helped generate rapid shifts in the location of economic activity, in part accounting for the vast wave of deindustrialization and social disruption in working-class communities and even whole city-regions. "Offshoring" became a household word. While there were gains to be had from increasing trade, these gains were unevenly distributed, both geographically and socially. The power of finance capital, for example, was much enhanced, while the powers of organized labor were much reduced as state after state sought and in some instances violently imposed greater flexibility upon its labor markets. Furthermore, the advocates for the neoliberal way came to occupy positions of considerable influence in education (the universities and many think tanks\ set up during the 1970s by rich donors and corporations), in the media, in corporate board rooms and financial institutions, in key state institutions (treasury departments, the central banks), and also in those international institutions such as the IMF, the World Bank, and the World Trade Organization (WTO) that regulate global finance and trade. Neoliberalism became, in short, hegemonic as a universalistic mode of discourse as well as a foundation for public policies worldwide. It increasingly defines the commonsense way many of us interpret, live in, and understand the world. We are, often without knowing it, all neoliberals now.

This hegemonic shift, if we can call it that, permeates almost all attempts to grapple with what the term *globalization* means. In jumping on the globalization bandwagon, all manner of academics, policy makers, as well as purveyors of information in the popular media construct a picture of the world that is in essence no different from that which Friedman depicts (thus accounting for the popularity of Friedman's text). This is unfortunately true even within anthropology, where an influential analyst like Arjun Appadurai has taken a leading role in describing what he sees as the new conditions of globality. Within that frame, he holds, we must now understand not only what he calls "the social life of things" (that is, the worldwide trend toward the commodification of everything) but also the production of distinctive landscapes, such as "ethnoscapes," "technoscapes," "mediascapes," and the like, which then provide a certain kind of heuristic geographical framework through which we can interpret the anthropological diversity that is both actively produced and sustainable in a neoliberalizing world. The problem with such formulations is not that they are wrong per se, but that by presuming a singular and highly abstract force called "globalization" as the agent behind these changes, they give up on the necessity to "unpack" what that force is about, where it comes from, who is promoting it, and for what reasons. The world gets flattened conceptually almost by default. To begin with, the shift of language from terms like *capitalism* and *imperialism* to *globalization* performs a masking function as to the power relations involved. But in themselves these concepts are equally abstract and potentially flat, because they in turn tend to mask the contested and contradictory processes of uneven geographical development of the class forces both promoting and resisting globalization.[11]

For example, the idea that more and more economies will be governed, as Thomas Friedman asserts, "from the ground up by the interests, demands and aspirations of the people, rather than from the top down by some narrow ruling clique" is totally at odds with the immense and ever increasing concentrations of personal and corporate (particularly financial) power that have emerged in many areas of the world over the last thirty years. Wherever neoliberalization has occurred (from the United States to Mexico, Russia, South Africa, India, and now even nominally "socialist" China), social inequality has burgeoned. Neoliberalization has created a flat world for the multinational corporations and for the billionaire entrepreneur and investor class, but a rough, jagged, and uneven world for everyone else. As one of Friedman's informants cogently observed, neoliberal reforms made it possible, perhaps for the first time, "to stay in India and become one of *Forbes*'s richest people in the world."[12]

What amounts to a restoration and reconstitution of class power worldwide is of such significance (and so frequently ignored in social-scientific analyses of globalization) that it calls for documentation. Class power is, in itself, evasive because it is a social relation that eludes direct measurement. But one visible, necessary, and universal condition for its exercise is the accumulation of income and wealth in a few hands. The existence of such accumulations and concentrations throughout the world was being widely noted in U.N. reports by the mid-1990s. The net worth of the 358 richest people in the world was then found to be equal to the combined income of the poorest 45 per cent of the world's population—2.3 billion people. The world's 200 richest people, during the halcyon years of the so-called Washington Consensus, when neoliberalism ruled supreme, more than doubled their net worth in the four years to 1998, to more than $1 trillion. These trends subsequently accelerated, though unevenly. The share of the national income taken by the top 1 percent of income earners in the

United States more than doubled between 1980 and 2000, while that of the top 0.1 per cent more than tripled. The income of the 99th percentile rose 87 percent" between 1972 and 2001, while that of "the 99.9th percentile rose 497 percent. In 1985 the combined wealth of the *Forbes* 400 richest people in the US was $238 billion with an average net worth of $600 million, adjusted for inflation. By 2005, their average net worth was $2.8 billion and their collective assets amounted to $1.13 trillion — more than the gross domestic product of Canada. By 2006, the top 1 percent of Americans gained their highest share of the national income ever (more than 21 percent). Wealth and income inequality reached levels not seen since the 1920s (which perhaps explains why the 2008 financial crash looks rather similar to that of 1929). Much of this shift derived from rapidly rising rates of executive compensation. In 1980, the average chief executive in the US made about $1.6 million a year in 2004 dollars. By 1990 the figure had risen to $2.7 million; by 2004 it was about $7.6 million, after peaking at almost twice that amount in 2000. In other words, executive pay rose an average of 6.8 percent a year compared to the 0.8 percent a year increase in average worker pay. And then there are the hedge fund managers who supposedly play such a productive and central role in spreading risks that the top twenty-five of them personally took home no less than $250 million each on average in 2005. By 2006 several of them took home more than a billion dollars, and the top earner was reported to have gained $1.7 billion (setting off an obscene competition between the major cultural institutions in New York City to place him on their boards of directors). In 2007 the four leading managers received over $3 billion each in compensation. The heads of private equity firms, which surged into prominence in the 1990s (they specialize in taking public companies private, reorganizing them, and putting them back in the public domain at a huge profit), were reported to be receiving parallel levels of compensation. And to prevent traders from starting out on their own hedge fund ventures, the leading banks had to raise their rate of remuneration for leading personnel from the $10 million or so that had been the norm in 2000 to around $50 million in 2006 (the head of Goldman Sachs received $52 million, and the average bonus to traders was $685,000). The tax policies of the Bush administration have scandalously multiplied these disparities in the United States. Most of the benefits have gone to the top 1 percent of income earners and to those living off dividends and capital gains rather than on salaries and wages. The tax reform of 2006 delivered tax relief of approximately $20 to those at the center of the income distribution, while the top tenth of 1 percent, whose average income is $5.3 million, would save an average of $82,415.[13]

Such trends have not been confined to the United States. Wherever and whenever neoliberal policies have taken hold—and the geographical spread has been very uneven—massive disparities in income and wealth have ensued. Following the wave of privatizations in Mexico after 1988, fourteen Mexican billionaires appeared on the 1994 *Forbes* list of the world's wealthiest people, with Carlos Slim ranked twenty-fourth. In 2005 Mexico, with its very high rate of poverty, claimed more billionaires than Saudi Arabia, and by 2007 Slim was thought to have overtaken Bill Gates as the richest person in the world. Following the neoliberal reform wave in India in the 1990s, a dozen or more Indians appeared on the *Forbes* wealthiest list. Within a few years of "shock therapy" market reforms in Russia, seven oligarchs controlled nearly half of the economy, and there are now some twenty-seven billionaires in Russia, according to *Forbes* (creating a power base that Putin is furiously struggling to contain by a regrettable but understandable return to state authoritarianism). OECD countries registered big increases in inequality after the 1980s, as did the countries of Eastern Europe and the CIS. While firm and conclusive data are very hard to come by, abundant signs exist in China of the accumulation of massive private fortunes since 1980 (particularly in real estate development). A public offering on the Hong Kong Stock Exchange of a real estate company in southern China started by a poor farmer in 1997 raised $15 billion, "making the family of Yang Guoqiang perhaps the richest in China." The family's twenty-five-year-old daughter, who controls 60 percent of the shares, is now personally worth about $9 billion, more than George Soros or Rupert Murdoch. Margaret Thatcher's neoliberal reforms in Britain contributed to the top 1 percent of income earners doubling their share of the national income by 2000. Even more scandalously, we see that the very top group of British income earners tripled their share of the national income from 1997 to 2007 under the Labour Government of Tony Blair and under the economic management of that good socialist George Brown. ("We are intensely relaxed about people getting filthy rich," a Labour cabinet minister, Peter Mandelson, famously remarked). The so-called "developmental states" of East and Southeast Asia, which initially managed to combine strong growth with a reasonable equity of distribution (South Korea, Taiwan, and Singapore, in particular), have experienced a 45 percent increase in inequality indices since 1990, most of the change occurring after the fierce financial attack upon and subsequent forced neoliberalization of their economies in 1997–98. The vast fortunes of a few trading moguls in Indonesia escaped unscathed from this trauma, which left some 15 million Indonesians unemployed, and an Indonesian-based (though ethnically Chinese) trading group like that of Salim is now one of the wealthiest conglomerates in the world. The only measure of inequality that has diminished is that between countries, and this decline is almost entirely due to the astonishing growth performance of China, followed by India. Average per capita incomes in those countries have risen even as internal inequalities have surged.[14]

At the other end of the wealth scale, neoliberalization has done little or nothing to improve the condition of much of the world's impoverished and marginalized populations. The global labor force available to capital has tripled in size—to around 3 billion workers—since 1980. One-quarter of that increase arose out of population growth (largely in the poorer countries of Africa, Asia, and Latin America), but three-quarters can be attributed to the proletarianization through integration of Russia and Central Europe, as well as China, and the better integration of India and Indonesia into the global economy. The sheer size of these increases has put strong downward pressure on the remuneration of labor worldwide, but the political weakness of this newly available global labor force has provided capitalists of all sorts (from petty commodity producers to large global corporations) with a golden opportunity to engage in very exploitative practices (justified, as we have seen, as necessary for poverty reduction!). Toward the end of his account, Thomas Friedman acknowledges that "there are hundreds of millions of people on this planet who have been left behind by the flattening process or feel overwhelmed by it." As of now only 2 percent of the Indian population of 1.2 billion (according to Friedman's estimate) participates in the new prosperity epitomized by the view from the golf course in Bangalore. The rest of the Indian population is living under conditions either "unflat" (full of pain and despair) or "half flat" (full of anxiety, hoping and struggling to find a place). It never occurs to Friedman that his proposed solution—further flattening through the extension of neoliberal reforms—actually is the root of the problem of spiraling inequalities and deepening insecurities.[15] But this is precisely what neoliberal theory is so effective at disguising.

In the same way that Edmund Burke appealed to the facts of geography to critique British imperial practices in India, so the facts of geography, ecology, and anthropology are frequently used as sticks to beat upon the inappropriateness of neoliberal policies. For some, the problem lies primarily at the point of application. Joseph Stiglitz (once head of Clinton's Council of Economic Advisors) has complained vociferously at the way policy makers, particularly in the extremely powerful financial institutions like the U.S. Treasury and the IMF, indiscriminately apply a universal, "one size fits all," orthodox neoliberal approach to economic development everywhere. Appalled at the social devastation this wrought in Indonesia in 1998, he voiced his criticism of the IMF openly and shortly thereafter was forced out of his position as chief economist at the World Bank. While Stiglitz notes that the result of the Indonesian disaster was to favor Wall Street and U.S. financial interests, and to exacerbate rather than assuage local social and geographical inequalities, he fails to recognize that this enhancement of class power has been fundamental to what neoliberalism has always been about. Advantaging the rich was, in his account, an unfortunate by-product of policies created for other purposes, such as economic stabilization. Jeffrey Sachs (who teamed up with Angelina Jolie to do good works in impoverished parts of Africa) now broadly agrees with Stiglitz's diagnosis. "Today's development economics is like eighteenth century medicine, when doctors used leeches to draw blood from their patients often killing them in the process." The world's "money doctor"—the IMF—typically prescribes "budgetary belt-tightening for patients much too poor to own belts." The result has been "riots, coups, and the collapse of public services." Neoliberalism has all along, he argues, been "based on a simplistic, even simple-minded, view of the challenge of poverty. The rich countries told the poor countries: 'Poverty is your own fault. Be like us [or what we imagine ourselves to be—free market oriented, entrepreneurial, fiscally responsible] and you, too, can enjoy the riches of private-sector led economic development,'"[16] This is, of course, exactly what Friedman presupposes.

Others object that neglect of the cultural conditions within which capitalism can flourish leads to consummate errors of interpretation and judgment. Until the crisis of 1997–98, the remarkable growth performances that had occurred in East and Southeast Asia were frequently attributed to "Asian" or "Confucian" values (much as Protestant values were supposedly central to the rise of capitalism in Britain in the seventeenth and eighteenth centuries) and to long-embedded systems of mutual trust and reciprocity among businessmen (and it was almost entirely men within the confines of patriarchal relations). Known as *guanxi* among the Chinese, this system was widely admired for the ways in which it used cultural traditions in distinctive territorial settings to gain competitive economic advantage.[17] Neoliberal institutions such as the World Bank took to describing it in their reports as an excellent example of how market economies could work. Only when crisis struck was this system of social relations scathingly criticized as "crony capitalism" (as if K Street in Washington is not crammed with cronies). The solution, the neoliberals in the U.S. Treasury and the IMF held, was "good governance," to go back to the fundamentals of private property arrangements, pure competition, and properly functioning markets. This was, of course, the solution that just happened to be so beneficial to Wall Street and the financiers.

More fundamental criticisms of the violence and inhumanity of neoliberalization are articulated through social movements. In this the lack of respect for local social and ecological conditions looms large. Trenchant analyses by Walden Bello, Susan George, Arundhati Roy, Samir Amin, de Souza Santos, and many others who make up the umbrella Alternative Globalization Movement, have exposed the dark side of neoliberalization, with great emphasis upon particular destructions in particular places that have affected particular social groups (such as the Zapatistas, the indigenous populations and Hindu farmers in the Narmada Valley of India, the landless peasant movement in Brazil, or the Green Belt women's movement in Kenya). Hierarchical power has indeed been challenged, but by the Bolivarian revolution of Chavez and Morales in Latin America rather than by the entrepreneurial processes that Thomas Friedman had in mind.[18] The organizational form of the "malcontents" in the World Social Forum is far more in line, it turns out, with the horizontal and collaborative structures that Friedman idealizes than anything that can be found on Wall Street or in the City of London, let alone in the IMF or the WTO. Movements against the IMF, the WTO, and the G8 meetings have all emphasized the class and neo-imperialist character of these institutions, while emphasizing the local insensitivities of neoliberal policies in relation to actually existing anthropological, geographical, and ecological conditions. Criticism of neoliberalism, however, is not confined to the left and to social movements. The conservative political scientist John Gray, for example, complains that while the "Utopia of the global free market has not incurred a human cost in the way that communism did," yet "over time it may come to rival it in the suffering it inflicts." "We stand," he says, "on the brink not of the era of plenty that free-marketeers project, but a tragic epoch, in which the anarchic market forces and shrinking natural resources drag sovereign states into ever more dangerous rivalries," leading to "a world of war and scarcity at least as much as the benevolent harmonies of competition."[19] The spirit of Edmund Burke lives on.

Oppositional movements to neoliberalism frequently invoke the facts of geography, ecology, and anthropology to support their criticisms and their alternative visions. Local foods and food sovereignty, self-sufficient geographies, bioregional configurations, local trading systems, and the development of new and more intimate systems of social relations in new territorial structures become part of the rhetoric in the search for alternatives. Some proposals advocated e-linking from the global economy. In others, such as the International Forum of Globalization, a new geography of a "planetary system of economies made up of locally owned enterprises accountable to all their stakeholders" is envisaged as a way to overcome the alienation from nature and from fellow human beings produced by neoliberalization and globalization. Communitarian and localist in tone, such proposals still incorporate strong elements of liberalism, in the form of private property rights, individual initiative, and democratic institutions, even as they corral them within a much more intimately designed territorial structure of social relations. Nevertheless, such proposals view the production of a different kind of geography as essential to the achievement of a more egalitarian and satisfying mode of relating both to nature and to other human beings.[20] This poses the question of how that different geography might be produced and by whom, and this, in turn, requires a closer examination of the inherent geographical character of the neoliberal project.

Why, for example, in the face of its very patchy record of actual achievement and the multiple criticisms that have been voiced, has neoliberalism remained so influential, if not dominant? Part of the answer lies in the power of the neoconservative and neoliberal think tanks and the corporate-dominated media, as well as many segments of academia, to dominate the discussion. The power and prestige of economics as a discipline and its ahistorical and aspatial manner of theorizing also play a major role. Liberal and neoliberal economic theories assume a world of deracinated men and women; producers and consumers; buyers and sellers; entrepreneurs, firms, and megacorporations; and supposedly neutral but placeless institutions of market and the law. While conventional economic theory has long been concerned to explain differences in the wealth of nations (a very geographical/anthropological problem), it has signally failed to provide coherent answers, even though the discipline has been endowed with far more resources, prestige, and influence over public policy than all the other social sciences combined. In spite of a raft of recent innovations, the explanation within economic theory of differences in the wealth of nations remains as elusive as ever from within the closed (and totally aspatial) terms of its foundational propositions.[21]

That neoliberalism produces uneven geographical development is clear, but less clear is the way it uses uneven geographical, anthropological, and ecological developments (including those it produces) as means to promote the universality of its own world project, which has nothing to do with the well-being of the whole of humanity but everything to do with the enhancement of its own dominant forms of class power. Uneven geographical development, in short, has been not only a result but also a driving force of neoliberalization on the world stage. We need to consider how this is so.

The ease and fluidity with which capital, particularly money capital, moves across space—between, say, Bavaria, Bangalore, Birmingham, and Botswana—is illustrative of a dynamical relation between spaces, places, and ecological systems within the global economy. In this movement, minor differences in the qualities (physical, social, and political) of particular places in relation to investment requirements can be parlayed into significant profits for those doing the moving. At the same time, the increasing weight of fixed capital and social investments in place creates a new geographical landscape (a built environment and local cultures, for example) that requires a serious commitment to sustaining that humanly produced landscape into an indefinite future. This means active engagement on the part of certain capitalist class interests (sometimes in alliance with popular local forces), with a politics of protection of privileged places—even the golf course in Bangalore—from the fierce winds of open competition.

Competition between territories (states, regions, or cities) as to who has the best model for economic development or the best business climate has intensified in the more fluid and open systems of trading relations established after 1970. Successful states or regions put pressure on everyone else to follow their lead. Leapfrogging innovations put this or that state (Japan, Germany, Taiwan, the United States, or China), region (Silicon Valley, Bavaria, the Third Italy, Bangalore, the Pearl River Delta, or Botswana) or even city (Boston, San Francisco, Shanghai, Singapore, Barcelona, New York, or Munich) in the vanguard of capital accumulation. But the competitive advantages all too often prove ephemeral, introducing an extraordinary spatial volatility into global capitalism. Periodic episodes of localized growth have been interspersed with intense phases of localized creative destruction, usually registered as severe (and often socially devastating) financial crises in particular places at particular times. Argentina, for example, opened itself up to foreign capital and privatization in the 1990s and for a few years was the darling of Wall Street, only to collapse as international capital withdrew at the end of the decade. Financial collapse and social devastation were followed by a serious political crisis. Financial crises of this sort have proliferated all over the developing world, briefly devastating some economic giants, like South Korea, before leading to a recovery associated, as usual, with a radical transformation of class power. In other instances, such as Brazil and Mexico, repeated waves of structural adjustment and austerity have led to economic paralysis for the masses, while conferring considerable advantages on political-economic elites. That "success" was to be had somewhere and for someone obscures how neoliberalism has generally failed to stimulate strong and sustained global growth. The illusion is created that if only we all performed like the successful countries of the moment then we, too, could be successful.

As the role of the state shifts, from caring for the well-being of its citizens (under a paternalistic social democracy) to providing for a good business climate, so heightened interterritorial and interstate competition deepens neoliberal commitments. The decentralization of political powers here becomes a highly significant adjunct to the neoliberal project. If municipalities, cities, regions, and nation-states function as more or less autonomous, self-contained entrepreneurial units, then the intensification of competition between them forces all of them to offer more and more in the way of a good business climate to capital in order to sustain or attract investments and, hopefully, jobs. Increasing geographical decentralization of political power has been a very important feature of the historical geography of capitalism over the past thirty years. In China, for example, it was the controlled decentralization of economic decision making to regions, provinces, municipalities, and even villages that formed the basis for the remarkable economic development of the country after 1978.

What has to be offered in the way of a good business climate is not, however, entirely obvious. An adequate labor force is one necessary component, but the capitalist demand can vary all the way from low-waged and compliant to highly skilled and innovative labor supplies. Subsidizing companies to come to or stay in town is another familiar strategy, and during the 1980s in particular local governments throughout the capitalist world gave up vast subsidies from their public coffers to corporate capital (often going seriously into debt in the process). Intensifying interurban competition actually produces some curious geographical results. For example, the search for monopoly rents leads to a strong emphasis upon the commodification of unique features of an urban environment (such as cultural heritage). If such unique features (such as the Acropolis) do not already exist, then they have to be created (for example, by building signature architecture such as the Gehry Museum in Bilbao, staging unique cultural events such as film or art festivals, or bringing the Olympic Games to town). Urban administrations seek to build up symbolic capital through the development of so-called cultural, knowledge-based, or simply spectacle-driven industries. The marketing and selling of a city's reputation in itself becomes a big business.[22]

Intensifying interterritorial competition thus locks in the need to orient government (and structures of governance) more and more toward the provision of a good business climate, without any regard for the well-being of a local population and in some instances without any regard for the fiscal consequences. And the coercive laws of interterritorial competition ensure that there appears to be no alternative. If the world were anywhere near as flat as Friedman portrays it, then neoliberalism would not work.

Neoliberalism has proven a huge and unqualified success, both materially and ideologically, from the standpoint of the upper classes almost everywhere.[23] Countries that have suffered extensively, such as Mexico, have seen the massive reordering of internal class structures. With the media dominated by upper-class interests, the myth could be propagated that territories failed because they were not competitive enough—thereby setting the stage for even more neoliberal reforms, as well as increasing levels of subsidy to corporate interests. Increased social inequality (even super-exploitation of labor) within a territory is considered necessary to encourage the entrepreneurial risk and innovation that confers competitive power and stimulates growth. If conditions among the lower classes deteriorate, this is because they fail, usually for personal and cultural reasons, to enhance their own human capital (through dedication to education, the adoption of a Protestant work ethic, submission to work discipline, acceptance of flexibility, and all the other cultural adjustments that Friedman recommends). The idea is put about that problems arise only because of lack of competitive strength or because of personal, cultural, and political failings. In a Darwinian world, the argument goes, only the fittest should and do survive.

This brings us to a central conundrum. If the rich are to get much richer, and if neoliberalization is not generating much growth, then wealth and income must be redistributed either from the mass of the population toward the upper classes or from vulnerable to richer regions. Both movements entail what I call "accumulation by dispossession."[24] By this I mean a turn toward predatory accumulation practices of the sort that accompanied the rise of capitalism. These include the commodification and privatization of land and labor power, and the forceful expulsion of peasant populations from the land (as in Mexico and India in recent times); conversion of various forms of property rights (common, collective, state) into exclusive private property rights; suppression of rights to the commons; suppression of alternative (indigenous) forms of production and consumption; appropriation of assets (including natural resources); the slave trade (which continues today, particularly in the sex industry); usury; and, most devastating of all, the use of the credit system and debt entrapment to acquire the assets of others, most dramatically represented by the mortgage foreclosures that swept through the United States housing market beginning in 2006.

The primary aim of the vast global wave of privatization—a central tenet of neoliberal reform programs—has been to open up new fields for capital accumulation in domains hitherto regarded as off-limits to the calculus of profitability. Public utilities (water, telecommunications, transportation), social welfare provision (social housing, education, health care, pensions), public institutions (universities, research laboratories, prisons), and even warfare (as illustrated by the "army" of private contractors operating alongside the armed forces in Iraq) and the environment (trading in pollution rights) have all been privatized. The privatization of the *ejidos* in Mexico during the 1990s forced peasants off the land into the cities or to the United States (illegally) in search of employment. The Chinese state likewise dispossessed many peasants of their tacit land rights and transferred control over these assets (even in the absence of private property rights) to party elites. Eminent domain has been used by the state in the United States to release land for more profitable uses, at the cost of destroying viable communities. The intellectual property rights established through the so-called TRIPS agreement within the WTO defines genetic materials, seed plasmas, and all manner of other products as private property. Rents for use can be extracted from populations whose practices had played a crucial role in the development of these genetic materials. Some corporate executives now believe that patents and intellectual property will actually become components of greater value to a company than real estate, plant, and equipment. The global environmental commons (land, air, water) are being depleted and habitats degraded through the wholesale commodification of nature (as exemplified in capital-intensive agribusiness). The commodification of cultural forms, of people's histories and traditions, through tourism entails dispossessions. The music industry is notorious for its exploitation of grass-roots cultures and personal creativity. The reversion of common property rights won through years of class struggle (the right to a state pension, to welfare, to national health care) into the private domain has been one of the most egregious of all policies of dispossession pursued in the name of neoliberal orthodoxy. Assets are transferred from the public to the private domains where elites can more easily capture them. State power is frequently used to force such processes through, even against popular will.

Deregulation since the 1970s has allowed the financial system to become one of the main centers of redistributive activity through speculation, predation, fraud, and thievery. Stock promotions, asset stripping through mergers and acquisitions, the promotion of levels of debt incumbency that reduce whole populations, even in the advanced capitalist countries, to debt peonage (in the United States, household debt has tripled over the last thirty years even as wages have stagnated), to say nothing of corporate fraud and the raiding of pension funds: all these became central features of the capitalist financial system. The emphasis on stock values, which resulted from bringing together the interests of owners and managers of capital through the remuneration of the latter in stock options, led to market manipulations that brought immense wealth to a few at the expense of the many. The spectacular collapse of Enron was emblematic of a general process that dispossessed many people of their livelihoods and their pension rights. Beyond this, we also have to look at the speculative raiding—of the sort that sparked the Asian crisis of 1997–98—carried out by hedge funds and other major institutions of finance capital. These formed the cutting edge of accumulation by dispossession on the global stage, even as they supposedly conferred the positive benefit for the capitalist class of "spreading risks." For performing such functions, as we have seen, the leading hedge fund managers gained $250 million on average in remuneration in 2005 alone, a figure that paled into insignificance compared to the earnings of several managers in 2007 that exceeded $3 billion.

Beyond the speculative and often fraudulent froth that characterizes much of neoliberal financial manipulation, there lies a deeper process that entails the springing of "the debt trap" as a primary means of accumulation by dispossession. Crisis creation, management, and manipulation on the world stage have evolved into the fine art of deliberative redistribution of wealth from poor countries to the rich. Debt crises in individual countries, uncommon during the 1960s, became very frequent during the 1980s and 1990s, culminating in the financial crash of 2008, which caught much of Wall Street by surprise even as it spread losses (when it was supposed to spread risk) for almost everyone, everywhere. The more frequent the debt crises, the more the solution was touted that the rationalization of debt by assuming more but carefully structured debt was the solution (this is what the IMF became so expert at and which now guides the policies of the world's central bankers). Hardly any developing country remained untouched as crises were orchestrated, managed, and controlled both to rationalize the system and to redistribute assets largely from the poorer and more vulnerable economies back into the financial metropoles. R. Wade and F. Veneroso described the effects of the Asian crisis of 1997–98 this way: "Financial crises have always caused transfers of ownership and power to those who keep their own assets intact and who are in a position to create credit, and the Asian crisis is no exception . . . there is no doubt that Western and Japanese corporations are the big winners. . . . The combination of massive devaluations, IMF-pushed financial liberalization, and IMF facilitated recovery may even precipitate the biggest peacetime transfer of assets from domestic to foreign owners in the past fifty years anywhere in the world, dwarfing the transfers from domestic to US owners in Latin America in the 1980s or in Mexico after 1994. One recalls the statement attributed to Andrew Mellon: 'In a depression assets return to their rightful owners.'"[25]

While the 2008 financial crisis looks different, it actually fits all too well into this longer history. The only significant difference is that it is larger and more all-encompassing. Localized crises and devaluations have been orchestrated in the past to facilitate accumulation by dispossession without sparking a general collapse or too violent a popular revolt. The structural adjustment program administered by the Wall Street/Treasury/IMF complex of imperialist financial power takes care of the first, while it is the job of the *comprador* neoliberal state apparatus (backed by military assistance from the imperial powers) in the country or the sector that has been raided to ensure that unrest does not get out of hand. In 2008, however, the crisis that began in the United States quickly spread to engulf the whole world. The response followed the typical path taken by the IMF, but this time governments and central banks (rather than the IMF) bailed out the financial institutions while leaving it to the general public to pay, through some mix of unemployment, recession, loss of asset values (particularly housing), and an astonishing increase in the national debt. Some Wall Street institutions failed or were forcibly merged, but those that remain are more powerful than ever. The neoliberal rule of rescuing the financial institutions at the expense of the people was meticulously enforced at an unimaginable cost. Far from spelling the end of neoliberalism, the 2008 financial crisis was, from the standpoint of the consolidation of despotic class power, its culmination, even as it stripped away the veil of rhetoric concerning neoliberalism's supposed dedication to individual liberties and freedoms. Assets were, once more, returning to "their rightful owners"! It remains to be seen whether there will be popular revolt.

When epochal shifts of the sort that brought neoliberal globalization into its current position of overwhelming dominance occur, then all manner of other conceptual, ideological, political, and cultural transformations will likely accompany it (though not exactly of the sort that Friedman had in mind). De Sousa Santos notes, for example, that the term *governance,* rarely used before 1975, has in recent times become a dominant way to think about and practice politics. The ideology of governance is grounded in ideals of efficiency and rationality of administration, bringing together significant "stakeholders" (the favored term) to come up with "optimal" but "politically neutral" public policies. But this is a beguiling mask—so much so that it is presented by Aihwa Ong, for one, as the essence of neoliberalization. Grounded in the idea of "private-public partnerships" and elaborate mechanisms for bringing various stakeholders into a consensual coalition, governance effectively masks the class and social relations that are redistributing wealth and income to the affluent through a networked and decentered system of organized political-economic power.[26] But Ong never even considers, let alone interrogates, this possibility. The Michael Bloomberg administration of New York City is a classic example. A billionaire himself, he could effectively purchase the mayoralty unbeholden to anyone and announce an administrative system "above politics." He has indeed rationalized city government to a high level of efficiency and delivered much in the way of improvements in the city. But his aim is to make the city competitive in the global economy. Innumerable high-value development projects are reshaping the city. He prefers, as we have seen, not to subsidize businesses to come to the city but to attract high-quality businesses that can bear the costs of a high-value location. While he does not dare say so, the same principle applies to people. Manhattan has increasingly become a haven for the affluent classes, an astonishingly rich and often transnational capitalist class, active beneficiaries of what the "neutral" and "efficient" Bloomberg administration is able to deliver. To conceptualize this lopsided class project as if it is just about efficient governance is plainly misleading.[27]

D. Chandler highlights a parallel growth of interest in human rights under neoliberalization (particularly those rights grounded in individualism and private property). Before 1980, he notes, very little attention was paid to the matter. Advocacy groups (many of them transnational), nongovernmental organizations (NGOs), and grass-roots organizations (GROs) have likewise multiplied and proliferated since 1980. These organizations step into the vacuum left by the withdrawal of the state from social provision. In some instances this has helped accelerate state withdrawal from social provision, turning NGOs into "trojan horses for global neoliberalism."[28] Legal arrangements have necessarily had to adjust to these conditions, and the courts now take a more prominent role. The centrality of civil society (as opposed to the state) is increasingly emphasized in policy circles and governance practices. Effective actions and organizations within civil society are now often considered more important as a locus of social change than is the state apparatus. The drive to command state power in order to get things done is therefore considered less and less urgent. Voluntary associations become more prominent, while political parties decline. All these transformations are implicated in each other and register the depth and breadth of social and political changes associated with the neoliberal turn.

The underlying connections of these shifts with the rise of neoliberalism are reasonably easy to establish. The neoliberal ideological insistence upon the individual as foundational in political-economic life opens the door to extensive individual rights activism. By focusing on these individual rights, rather than on the creation of social solidarities and democratic structures, movements cast their opposition in neoliberal terms, which means within the legal apparatus or through civil-society organizational forms (the NGOs in particular). It is costly and time-consuming to go down legal paths, and the courts typically favor rights of private property and the profit rate over rights of equality and social justice. Yet corporations are considered legal individuals (except when they deem it important, as before the International Criminal Court, to deny such a status in order to avoid liability for anything they do). Even the state is considered a "virtual individual" (Kant's words) within the interstate system (though again, states have strategic ways to avoid, as in the case of the United States, liability for "crimes against humanity"). The frequent appeal to legal action reflects the neoliberal emphasis upon the rule of law and the preference to rely upon judicial and executive powers rather than those of representative democracy. Law replaces politics "as the vehicle for articulating needs in the public setting." Chandler concludes that the neoliberal elite's "disillusionment with ordinary people and the political process leads them to focus more on the empowered individual, taking their case to the judge who will listen and decide."[29] But there is a certain room for maneuver. The law can be challenged and revised, and some social movements, such as the landless peasant movement in Brazil, have achieved significant revisions in the legal code through their actions. Furthermore, the law is not monolithic across territories, even though it may be universal in its pronouncements. The need to coordinate legal arrangements across state boundaries creates innumerable areas of uncertainty. Over what space does the regulation of air safety or of labor processes extend, for example? In practice, the FAA rules set in the United States apply globally, since all airlines that fly into the lucrative U.S. market have to abide by them. Laws regulating environmental impacts or interstate commerce can, furthermore, be used for all manner of other purposes, such as arresting Mafia leaders or delaying the destructive operations of capitalist developers.

The NGOs sometimes do very good work and promote progressive politics. But they can often be elitist, unaccountable, and socially distant from those they seek to protect or help. They can conceal their agendas (which are often set by far-away donor organizations). More often than not, they seek integration within governance structures and then end up having to control their clientele rather than representing it. They presume to speak on behalf of those who cannot speak for themselves, and even to define the interests of those they speak for. When, for example, organizations agitate successfully to ban child labor in production as a matter of universal human rights, they may undermine economies where that labor is fundamental to survival. With their parents lacking any viable economic alternative, the children may be sold into prostitution instead (leaving yet another advocacy group to pursue the eradication of that). The universality presupposed in "rights talk" and the undoubted dedication of the NGOs and advocacy groups to universal principles sits uneasily with the local particularities and daily practices of political economic life.[30]

But there is another reason why a particular oppositional culture stressing rights and organizational mobilizations in civil society has gained so much traction in recent years. Accumulation by dispossession entails a very different set of practices from accumulation achieved through the expansion of wage labor in industry and agriculture. The latter, which dominated processes of capital accumulation in the 1950s and 1960s, gave rise to an oppositional culture (such as that embedded in trade unions and working-class political parties) that typically worked toward a social democratic compromise (if not outright socialist revolution). Dispossession, in contrast, is fragmented and particular—a privatization here, an environmental degradation there, a loss of identity or a financial crisis of indebtedness somewhere else. It is hard to oppose all this geographical specificity and particularity without appeal to universal principles. Dispossession entails the loss of rights. Hence the turn to a universalistic rhetoric of human rights, dignity, sustainable ecological practices, environmental rights, and the like, as the basis for a unified oppositional politics. This is what the transnational advocacy groups, NGOs, and GROs have become so expert and often effective in pursuing. And increasingly this is what radical oppositional politics is about.

The appeal to the universalism of rights is, however, a double-edged sword. It may and can be used with progressive aims in mind. The tradition that is most spectacularly represented by Amnesty International, Médécins sans Frontières, and others cannot be dismissed as a mere adjunct of neoliberal thinking. The whole history of humanism (both of the Western—classically liberal—and various non-Western versions) is too complicated for that. But the limited objectives of many rights discourses (in Amnesty's case, the exclusive focus, until recently, on civil and political as opposed to economic rights) makes it all too easy to absorb them within the neoliberal frame, even as an oppositional culture. Universalism seems to work particularly well with global environmental issues, such as climate change, loss of biodiversity through habitat destruction, and the like. But its results in the human rights field are more problematic, given the diversity of political-economic circumstances and cultural practices to be found in the world. As de Sousa Santos notes, it has generally proven more effective in defending the right to difference (hence its importance in fields such as women's and indigeneous rights and identity politics, where much has been accomplished) than in upholding the right to political-economic equality (fundamentally a class issue).[31] Furthermore, human rights issues have been coopted as "swords of empire" (to use Bartholomew and Breakspear's trenchant characterization).[32] More broadly, we can conclude with Chandler that "the roots of today's human rights–based humanitarianism lie in the growing consensus of support for Western involvement in the internal affairs of the developing world since the 1970s."[33] Domestically, public political debate is narrowed in debilitating ways. "Far from challenging the individual isolation and passivity of our atomised societies, human rights regulation can only institutionalize these divisions." Even worse, "the degraded vision of the social world, provided by the ethical discourse of human rights, serves, like any elite theory, to sustain the self-belief of the governing class."[34]

The temptation, in the light of this critique, is to eschew all appeal to universal rights and to the law as fatally flawed, as an untenable imposition of abstract ethics, and even as a mask for the restoration of class power. While these propositions deserve to be taken seriously, the terrain of rights cannot be abandoned to neoliberal hegemony. The critical connection forged between neoliberalization and the appeal to universals, ethical principles, and human rights should alert us. "Between two rights," Marx famously commented, "force decides."[35] There is a battle to be fought not only over which universals and which rights matter, but also over how universal principles and conceptions of rights shall be constructed and incorporated into law. If class restoration of the sort that has occurred under neoliberalism entails the imposition of a distinctive set of rights, then resistance to that imposition entails struggle for entirely different rights.[36] In particular, it suggests that it is collective rights and social solidarities around those rights rather than individual rights that really matter.

Behind all universal claims there lies, as always, the awkward problem of how to account for geographical, anthropological, and ecological differentiations. In the first instance this can be construed as a problem of sensitive application of universal neoliberal rights. The professional economist, argues Sachs, "requires a commitment to be thoroughly steeped in the history, ethnography, politics and economics of any place where the professional advisor is working." The IMF, for example, with its "one shoe fits all" vision, "has overlooked urgent problems involving poverty traps, agronomy, climate, disease, transport, gender, and a host of other pathologies that undermine economic development. Clinical economics should train the development practitioner to home in much more effectively on the key underlying causes of economic distress, and to prescribe appropriate remedies that are well tailored to each country's specific conditions." Geographical situation matters, because countries are "shaped profoundly by their location, neighborhood, topography, and resource base."[37] Many oppositional GROs, seeking to de-link from the global economy, likewise articulate their discontent with neoliberalism by appeal to the specificity of their own geographical situation in much the same way that postcolonial critics appeal to Burke and Heidegger to challenge the universal claims of liberal imperialism.

Kant recognized that geographical, anthropological, and ecological differentiations led to the construction of local truths, laws, customs, environmental exigencies, and even national characteristics. These are hard to reconcile with universal pronouncements about rights, justice, liberty, and freedom. Kant's answer was to proclaim the right for citizens of one state to be treated hospitably for a time in some foreign land, but not to stay indefinitely, particularly if they were not welcomed by indigenous inhabitants (hence Kant's principled objection to colonialism). Sovereignty and citizenship within the absolute confines of a territorially defined republican state anchored his arguments. The effect is to create innumerable spatial exclusions (on this point, at least, Ong's analysis of exceptions under neoliberalism is informative). The nature of the space within which the state held its sovereignty—its absolute qualities—permitted Kant to construe the state as a virtual individual in relationship to all other states constituting the state system. Competition as well as cooperation, war as well as trade, conflict as well as harmony among these virtual individuals became a central preoccupation of political theory as well as geopolitical practices. From Westphalia through the founding of the United Nations to the contemporary structures of global collaboration (such as the G8, the WTO, and various collaborative agreements like the European Union or the looser organizations of NAFTA or Mercosur,), attempts are constantly being made to construct adequate rules of the game to regulate international relations in peace and war, as well as with respect to economic, cultural, and social exchange, and the patterns of mobility of the people, capital, and commodities that these exchanges inevitably entail. That this does not always end in harmony should be evident, and John Gray's fear that it can all too easily descend into "a tragic epoch, in which the anarchic market forces and shrinking natural resources drag sovereign states into ever more dangerous rivalries" cannot be ignored.[38] One response to this threat has been to reinvent the cosmopolitan tradition as a way to transcend, or at least mitigate, the negative effects of the coercive laws of interterritorial and interstate competition. And it is to this possibility that we now turn.

Chapter Four
The New Cosmopolitans

By what set of institutional arrangements might all the inhabitants of planet earth hope to negotiate, preferably in a peaceful manner, their common occupancy of a finite globe? This was the question that animated Kant's cosmopolitan quest. If the question was prescient in 1800, when the global population was no more than 1 billion, then it is, surely, compelling today when the global population stands at 6.2 billion and rising. The benefits to be had and life-chances derived from open trade and commerce would be seriously curtailed, Kant held, unless merchants entering foreign lands were accorded the right to hospitality. The proliferation of trading relations should lead people to forego violent conflict and to seek out peaceable means to settle their differences. The vast increase in trade since Kant's time would seem to make some form of cosmopolitanism inevitable. What Kant missed, as P. Cheah points out, was "the potential of popular nationalism as an emancipatory force" in relation to the then prevailing systems of absolutist state and imperial rule. Kant did not "predict that the material interconnectedness brought about by capitalism would engender the bounded political community of the nation."[1] This was so even though Kant pioneered the theory of national character and the idea of national belonging through common bloodlines of descent. Kant also accepted without question the boundedness of a sovereign territorial state in absolute space that could then be conceptualized as a "virtual individual" within the interstate system. Kant's student, Herder, sought a radically different anthropology that focused on the binding force of cultural and political solidarities constructed in place. He understood, in ways that

Kant did not, how place and place-bound loyalties (as articulated by Burke and later by Heidegger) could dominate over the universality of abstract absolute space (of the sort that was put to use in the mapping of India).[2] The rise of nationalism (based, as Kant should have realized, in the construction of national character) and its increasing connectivity to class and state power throughout the nineteenth and early twentieth centuries effectively blocked any embrace of cosmopolitanism, with all manner of destructive consequences. After Kant, cosmopolitanism largely lay dormant as a subterranean challenge either to the ethics of a powerfully present competitive liberalism with all its class connotations or to a pervasive nation-state politics grounded in nationalism and class power.

Cosmopolitanism has now reemerged from the shadows and shaken off many of its negative connotations (from times when Jews, communists, and cosmopolitans were cast as traitors to national solidarities and at best vilified and at worst sent to concentration camps). Challenges mounted to the sovereign powers of the state (by, for example, the formation of the European Union and neoliberalization) and to the coherence of the idea of the nation and the state (through massive cross-border capital flows, migratory movements, and cultural exchanges) have opened a space for an active revival of cosmopolitanism as a way of approaching global political-economic, cultural, environmental, and legal questions. Influential thinkers, such as Nussbaum, Habermas, Derrida, Held, Kristeva, Beck, Appiah, Brennan, Robbins, Clifford, and many others, have written persuasively on the topic in recent years.

Unfortunately, cosmopolitanism has been reconstructed from such a variety of standpoints as to often confuse rather than clarify political-economic and cultural-scientific agendas. It has acquired so many nuances and meanings as to make it impossible to identify any central current of thinking and theorizing, apart from a generalized opposition to the supposed parochialisms that derive from extreme allegiances to nation, race, ethnicity, and religious identity. Some broad-brush divisions of opinion do stand out. There are, as usual, the differences that arise from within the academic division of labor, such that philosophers (concerned mainly with moral imperatives and normative principles), literary and cultural theorists (concerned with cultural hybridities and critiques of multiculturalism), and social scientists (focusing on the international rule of law and systems of global governance) all take their particular cuts at what might be meant by the resurrected term. As so often happens within the academy, these different traditions rarely communicate.

Passing strange that so many committed cosmopolitans avoid conversing with each other!

Martha Nussbaum, for example, constructs a moral cosmopolitan vision in opposition to local loyalties in general and nationalism in particular. Inspired by the Stoics and Kant, she presents cosmopolitanism as an ethos, "a habit of mind," a set of loyalties to humanity as a whole, to be inculcated through a distinctive educational program (including unspecified revisions to geographical, anthropological, and ecological curricula) emphasizing the commonalities and responsibilities of global citizenship. Against this universal vision are ranged all manner of hyphenated versions of cosmopolitanism, variously described as "rooted," "situated," "actually existing," "discrepant," "vernacular," "Christian," "bourgeois," "liberal," "postcolonial," "feminist," "proletarian," "subaltern," "ecological," "socialist", and so forth. Cosmopolitanism here gets particularized and pluralized in the belief that detached loyalty to the abstract category of "the human" is incapable in theory, let alone in practice, of providing any kind of political purchase on the strong currents of globalization and international interventionism that swirl around us. Some of these "countercosmopolitanisms" were formulated in reaction to Nussbaum's claims.[3] She was accused, for example, of merely articulating an appropriate ideology for the "global village" of the neoliberal international managerial/capitalist class. The famous line in the *Communist Manifesto*—"the bourgeoisie has through its exploitation of the world market given a cosmopolitan character to production and consumption in every country"—could all too easily be used against her.[4] In this we hear echoes of Antonio Gramsci's critical consideration of cosmopolitanism as "a culturally conditioned, disastrous detachment, which is specifically linked to imperialism, the false universal ecumenicism of the Catholic Church, and the development of a rootless, intellectualized, managerial class." The optimistic cosmopolitanism that became so fashionable following the Cold War, Craig Calhoun points out, not only bore all the marks of its history as "a project of empires, of long-distance trade, and of cities," it also shaped up as an elite project reflecting "the class consciousness of frequent travelers." As such, it more and more appeared as "the latest effort to revive liberalism" in an era of neoliberal capitalism. It is all too easy, concurs Saskia Sassen, "to equate the globalism of the transnational professional and executive class with cosmopolitanism." Even worse, as R. Wilson points out, is the habit in these postmodern times of packing into the term "not only the voluntary adventures of liberal self-invention and global travel, but also those less benignly configured mixtures of migration, nomadism, diaspora, tourism, and refugee flight," as well as the "traumas of the 'immigrant as global cosmopolitan,' carrier of some liberal and liberated hybridity, which, of course, the United States represents to the world as capitalist vanguard."[5]

There is, in any case, something oppressive about the ethereal and abstracted universalism that typically lies at the heart of any purely moral discourse. How can cosmopolitanism account for, let alone be sympathetic to, a world characterized by class divisions, multicultural diversity, movements for national or ethnic liberation, multiple forms of identity politics, and all manner of other anthropological, ecological, and geographical differences? How can it be vigilantly attentive to otherness, cope with what Mehta calls "unfamiliarity," and be sensitive to deeply etched cultural differences and geographical particularities? And why, some influential theorists ask,should the idea of nation and of state be cast so resolutely in opposition to cosmopolitanism when it takes a collectivity of states (Kant's federation of independent republics) to actually produce and police any genuinely cosmopolitan global order? What Cheah and Robbins call "cosmopolitics" then emerges as a quest "to introduce intellectual order and accountability into this newly dynamic space" of cosmopolitan argument, within which "no adequately discriminating lexicon has had time to develop."[6]

One strong current of opinion now holds, however, that a material basis for cosmopolitanism has already been constructed and that all that is lacking is an adequate theory to match these realities. There is surprisingly widespread acceptance of this view among cultural theorists as well as among social scientists impressed by the global integration of financial, production, and consumption networks and the mass migrations that have produced so many diasporas and so much cultural and ethnic mixing. It is generally accepted that the nation-state is no longer a sufficiently robust concept upon which to base analyses and that a new theoretical architecture is needed to deal with the new situation. A serious question then arises: is the new theory supposed merely to reflect or to critically engage with (and hopefully transform) the actualities of current practices? Contemporary cosmopolitanism often fuses the two approaches. In some cases this intermingling is productive, since it enables us to see how, say, transformations in international law that have occurred under pressures of neoliberalization since the 1970s have opened up new avenues for internationalist political critique while simultaneously reinforcing dominant class interests. The danger, however, is that seemingly radical critiques (as in the field of human rights) covertly support further neoliberalization and enhanced class domination.

This dilemma pervades the work of the sociologist Ulrich Beck. He argues that cosmopolitanization already exists, intensifying markedly since the 1990s. It has been

> stimulated by the postmodern mix of boundaries between cultures and identities, accelerated by the dynamics of capital and consumption, empowered by capitalism undermining national borders, excited by the global audience of transnational social movements, and guided and encouraged by the evidence of world-wide communication (often just another word for misunderstanding) on central themes such as science, law, art, fashion, entertainment, and not least, politics. World-wide perception and debate of global ecological danger or global risks of a technological and economic nature ('Frankenstein food') have laid open the cosmopolitan significance of fear. And if we needed any proof that even genocide and the horrors of war now have a cosmopolitan aspect, this was provided by the Kosovo War in spring 1999 when NATO bombed Serbia in order to enforce the implementation of human rights.[7]

All of this "urgently demands a new standpoint, the cosmopolitan outlook, from which we can grasp the social and political realities in which we think and act." We need "to break out of the self-centered narcissism of the national outlook and the dull incomprehension with which it infects thought and action," and "enlighten human beings concerning the real internal cosmopolitanization of their lifeworlds and institutions." A "realistic cosmopolitanism" cannot, however, "be developed in opposition to universalism, relativism, nationalism and ethnicism"; it has to be constructed as "their summation and synthesis." Nationalism and cosmopolitanism can "mutually complement and correct each other." Cosmopolitanization has to be understood, Beck concludes, as "a non-linear dialectical process in which the universal and the particular, the similar and the dissimilar, the global and the local are to be conceived, not as cultural polarities but as interconnected and interpenetrating principles."[8]

This intricate dialectical formulation is hard to interpret, and there is more than a shadow of suspicion that Beck is trying to have his cosmopolitan cake and eat it here. In practice he abandons dialectics in favor of celebrating an epochal shift from a first to a second kind of modernity, from a society dedicated to the management of production to one concerned to manage risks (both social and environmental) and from one in which the principle "international law trumps human rights" gives way to "human rights trumps international law." The first modernity "rests on the principle of collectivity, territoriality and borders," while the second appeals to the bearers of human rights as individuals rather than as collective subjects such as "people" and "state." These rights "are unthinkable without the universalistic claim to validity that grants these rights to all individuals, without regard to social status, class, gender, nationality or religion." There are, Beck concedes, murky areas that allow human rights to be misused for more venal aims. We must therefore guard against a "fake cosmopolitanism" that "instrumentalises cosmopolitan rhetoric—the rhetoric of peace, of human rights, of global justice—for national-hegemonic purposes" (and he cites the Iraq War as a recent example of this "fake" agenda).[9] It is, nevertheless, the universalism of individual human rights that grounds his cosmopolitanism.

On inspection, these rights turn out to be indistinguishable from those given in neoliberal theory. Beck does not consider other kinds of collective rights and solidarities. Critique here turns into justification. The political-economic ideology of possessive individualism is instantiated into a supposedly transcendent cosmopolitanism. Since rights require enforcement, Beck goes on to embrace "military humanism" of the sort the "liberal hawks" advocate in the United States and that NATO unleashed in the bombing of Serbia in defense of Kosovo. Beck even endorses the right of democratic governments (presumably of states he had earlier depicted as irrelevant and powerless!) to make preemptive threats of war or to take police actions (preferably collectively rather than unilaterally as has the United States in recent times) against leaders who abuse the human rights of their own populations.[10] It is hard to distinguish all this from the actual practices of Blair or even Clinton/Bush. The distinction between fake and real cosmopolitanism in Beck's scheme of things is as arbitrary and as blurred as is the distinction between neoliberalization and cosmopolitanism.

Beck also makes much of the purported cosmopolitan character of the European Union. Plainly, national sentiments have not disappeared, and in some respects they have been heightened within the Union, yet the adoption of a common legal framework and a common currency (though not for all), and the partial surrender of state sovereignty to the authorities in Brussels and the parliamentarians in Strasbourg, suggests acceptance of an alternative ordering of social relations on a vast terrain that now cuts across many languages and historical geographies from Poland to Portugal. European integration has made armed conflict between traditionally warring European nation-states more or less unthinkable, and has therefore realized one of Kant's visions: "a *pacific federation* (*foedus pacificum*) . . . would differ from a peace treaty (*pactum pacis*) in that the latter terminates *one* war, whereas the former would seek the end to *all* wars for good. This federation does not aim to acquire any power like that of a state, but merely to preserve and secure the freedom of each state in itself, along with that of the other confederated states. . . . [The union of states will secure] the freedom of each state in accordance with the idea of institutional right, and the whole will gradually spread further and further."[11]

Beck, Habermas, and others tend, therefore, to look upon the European Union as some kind of Kantian cosmopolitan construction.[12] They then reflect upon the possibility of expanding this system worldwide. The meaning of *nation* in Europe has simultaneously been challenged by the migratory movements both within and from without the European Union. The evident multiculturalism in many European countries that were once relatively ethnically and linguistically homogeneous allows the idea of nation to embrace everything from a backward-looking authenticity, supposedly rooted deep in ancient myths (as Le Pen and the fascist movement holds so dear in France), to an instantaneous embrace of the forward-looking idea of national citizenship and newly constructed cultural belonging by recent immigrants who form the backbone of, for example, the French soccer team.

All this lends a cosmopolitan allure to recent European developments. But it also obscures the kind of union that has actually been created. While the European Union had the grander aim of making war between traditionally warring states more and more unlikely, its actual mechanics, beginning with the Monnet Plan and the Coal and Steel Agreement that took effect in 1952, have always been primarily economic. The Maastricht Accord, negotiated between the European States in 1992, was a neoliberal rather than a cosmopolitan construction. The resistance to the proposed European Constitution in 2005 was cast by many on the left (particularly in France, where it was defeated in a referendum) as a vote against its neoliberal character (those on the right objected to its dilution of national identity and the loss of nation-state sovereignty). To be sure, being neoliberal, the institutions of the Union make much reference to the legal and political principles of individual rights. The E.U. therefore does partially correspond to Beck's ideal of a "cosmopolitan human rights regime," which opens up certain avenues for progressive politics, particularly with respect to legal and civil, as opposed to economic, rights. But the specific rights regime it promotes inhibits any serious challenge to the rising tide of capitalist class and corporate power.

To this problem Beck replies that "true" cosmopolitanism arises out of, but is quite different from, both neoliberalism and globalization. This is so because cosmopolitanization "comprises the development of multiple loyalties as well as the increase in diverse transnational forms of life, the emergence of non-state political actors (from Amnesty International to the World Trade [Organization]), the development of global protest movements against [neoliberal] globalism and in support of a different kind of [cosmopolitan] globalization. People campaign for the right to work, for global protection of the environment, for the reduction of poverty, etc. To this extent these are the beginnings (however deformed) of an institutionalized cosmopolitanism, for example, in the paradoxical shape of the anti-globalization movement, the International Court of Justice and the United Nations."[13] What de Sousa Santos calls a "subaltern cosmopolitanism" arises out of the global opposition to neoliberal globalization and imperialism.[14] But to make sense of this—and I will shortly attempt to do so—requires critical engagement with how the hegemonic theories and practices of neoliberal globalization and imperialism intersect with supposedly cosmopolitan practices. This is lacking in Beck's account. The result, as Alain Badiou says of the Mitterrandistes in France (to which I would add the Blairites in Britain), is to make any kind of revolutionary political project unthinkable. Political horizons are reduced to "the humanitarian preaching of ethics" and the "liberal-democratic canonization of human rights as the only horizon within which politics might be possible"—which is pretty much where Beck leaves us and where Nussbaum seems to want to be.[15] If this is what contemporary cosmopolitanism is about, then it is nothing other than an ethical and humanitarian mask for hegemonic neoliberal practices of class domination and financial and militaristic imperialism. It is inconceivable to Beck that, as Badiou and Rancière commonly hold, "the mainspring for the effervescent promotion of human rights and humanitarian interventions is a political nihilism, that its real aim is to have done with the very idea of an emancipatory politics."[16]

While this may sound an unduly harsh judgment, I fear it is rather too close to the mark for comfort with respect to much of the new cosmopolitanism. Consider, for example, the voluminous and highly prominent work of David Held. Like Beck, Held argues that the facts of globalization necessarily require a turn toward cosmopolitan forms of governance. After reviewing these facts, he proposes some core principles for a system of global governance. These principles are: "(1) equal worth and dignity; (2) active agency; (3) personal responsibility and accountability; (4) consent; (5) collective decision-making about public matters through voting procedures; (6) inclusiveness and subsidiarity; (7) avoidance of serious harm; and (8) sustainability." The principles fall into three clusters. The first (1–3) concerns the rights and responsibilities of individuals and is thoroughly neoliberal in tone; the second (4–6) states how the actions of individuals might best be collectivized; and the third (7–8) points toward the ends to which public decisions should be oriented. Cosmopolitanism ultimately denotes, says Held, "the ethical and political space occupied by the eight principles." He goes on to acknowledge that "while cosmopolitanism affirms principles which are universal in their scope, it recognizes, in addition, that the precise meaning of these is always fleshed out in *situated discussions*; in other words that there is an *inescapable hermeneutic complexity* in moral and political affairs which will affect how the principles are interpreted and the weight granted to special ties and other practical-political issues" (my italics).[17] This caveat has immense implications. Not only does it hold out the prospect of a totally fragmented world, in which everything from personal responsibility and accountability to sustainability gets interpreted any which way, thereby rendering the whole schema meaningless, but it also opens up Kant's hidden dilemma of how to square local laws with universal requirements.

What for Held is a mere moment of situated hermeneutic complexity would be the whole story for anyone with Burkean or Heideggerian leanings. The only answer Held proposes is to postulate a "layered cosmopolitanism," reflective of local, national, and regional affiliations. But he makes no attempt to understand how this layering is actually produced and at what scales. Nor does he examine the implications of "situatedness" and the "hermeneutic complexities" with which it may be associated. This would entail confronting directly the geographical, anthropological, and ecological preconditions that Nussbaum and Kant both consider important to any formulation of a cosmopolitan politics. Having all too briefly opened the Pandora's box of geographical relativism through confessing local forms of hermeneutical complexity, Held immediately slams it shut with the unexplained observation that his cosmopolitan principles effectively "delimit and govern the range of diversity and difference that ought to be found in public life." This allows him to claim (spuriously) that the "irreducible plurality of forms of life" to be found in different geographical situations is adequately factored into his cosmopolitanism and that his principles remain inviolable because they are of a sort that "all could reasonably assent to."[18] The use of "reasonably" as well as the "assent" inserted into the argument here is telling. It produces a powerful echo of Kant's (and Burke's) appeal to "mature individuals" as the only acceptable participants in discussions. The elitism (and potential class content) of this form of cosmopolitanism becomes clear.

But Held needs something else for his system of cosmopolitan governance to work: "there can be no adequate institutionalization of equal rights and duties without a corresponding institutionalization of national and transnational forms of public debate, democratic participation, and accountability. The institutionalization of regulative cosmopolitan principles requires the entrenchment of democratic public realms." This last conditionality could be viewed as an intensely radicalizing proposition in its own right. Three decades of neoliberalization have greatly diminished the scope and effectiveness of participatory democracy in many parts of the world (with the notable exception of Latin America, South Africa, and dubious democratization in what was once the communist bloc). The democratic deficit has been growing by leaps and bounds, particularly in the United States where, through the complex mix of legal and illegal corruptions, the only democracy left is that of raw money power. What Bush actually has in mind when he speaks of democratizing the Middle East is, by this measure, unthinkably corrupt. There is, however, an odd tendency in much of the new cosmopolitanism to assume that more or less adequate models of democracy have already been constructed within the framework of the leading nation-states and that the only problem remaining is to find ways to extend these models across all jurisdictions. This is what Held's idea of a "layered cosmopolitanism" attempts. The severe curtailment of the democratic public realm and the shift toward unaccountable juridical and executive power (often masked by the term *governance*) even within the leading nation-states passes by unremarked.[19]

Behind all these presentations lies a problem of understanding the shifting spatial scale of capitalistic activity and organization. Much of what now goes on under the rubric of "globalization" escapes the confines of the nation-state and requires (and to some degree has already produced) a broader territorial reach of law, regulation, and governance. This is particularly the case with environmental issues, such as global warming, acid deposition, stratospheric ozone depletion, and the like. Cosmopolitanism seeks to rationalize these new systems both procedurally and substantively, which means, Beck argues, that "the analysis of cosmopolitanization can and must be developed in both the spatial and the temporal dimensions." But he claims, rather surprisingly (and in total opposition to Mehta), that the spatial question "has already been worked out" and that it is only the temporal dimension that remains a problem. But when we turn to how he thinks the spatial dimension has been worked out, we simply find the banal idea that cosmopolitanization "replaces national-national relations with national-global and global-global relational patterns."[20] Beck evidently accepts unthinkingly the Kantian separation of space from time and believes that the sorts of geographical issues that exercised Burke and Mehta (let alone geographers and other spatial analysts like Lefebvre) have no relevance for his universal theorizations.

Part of the difficulty here arises out of coming to grips with the changing role of the nation-state. The sociological imagination (from C. Wright Mills's classic enunciation onward), as well as much of political and international relations theory, has long taken the nation-state as the solid and unquestioned framing for empirical analysis and social theory. The belated recognition that this is not (and never really was) an adequate geographical framework for investigating social and ecological relations has prompted the search for alternatives. Beck's work, for example, is primarily addressed to sociologists, urging them to break with their traditional state-centered approach to knowledge and adopt a more universal language. S. Sassen, another sociologist, likewise argues that "existing theory is not enough to map today's multiplication of non-state actors and forms of cross-border cooperation and conflict, such as global business networks, NGOs, diasporas, global cities, transboundary public spheres, and the new cosmopolitanisms." The problem is, she says, that "models and theories remain focused on the logic of relations between states and the scale of the state at a time when we see a proliferation of non-state actors, cross-border processes, and associated changes in the scope, exclusivity and competence of state authority over its territory." In this dispersion, she argues, the new digital technologies have played a major role. The Internet has also "enabled a new type of cross-border politics that can bypass interstate politics," and "this produces a specific kind of activism, one centered on multiple localities yet connected digitally at scales larger than the local, often reaching a global scale."[21]

The various specialized networks and domains of regulation, law, governance, and political activism spill over state boundaries to produce, Sassen argues, new spatialities and temporalities that unsettle existing arrangements. Sassen does not abandon the nation-state framework but seeks to reinterpret the nation-state's role, while acknowledging the rise of other important layers (as Held might put it) in global exchanges and governance. All this has tremendous implications for how we understand citizenship. In the Stoic cosmopolitan tradition we consider ourselves purely citizens of the world, but Kant modified that substantially, maintaining a federal structure to the interstate system and thereby injecting into the mix the connections between nation, state, sovereignty, and citizenship. But citizenship that used to be exercised mainly in bounded communities now has multiple locations. Some people have dual nationality, others carry multiple passports, and when it comes to allegiances, loyalties, and participation, many more have complicated relations with more than one space in the global economy simultaneously. Residents of New York City, for example, have important official positions in Jamaican and Chinese townships. This is also the case for corporate executives and the legal/accounting experts who operate across many borders; the government officials charged with managing the apparatus of interstate relations (including those in international institutions, as well as those engaged in international police work and intelligence gathering); the vast number of both legal and illegal migrant workers (the latter often performing active citizenship roles without any legal or political status); and the social movement activists with their coordinating cross-border networks. Internally, as A. Ong usefully points out, a country like China, with its complicated structure of special economic development zones of various kinds and its urban-rural legal distinctions (recently abolished), constructs an internal mosaic of definitions of citizenship. Benhabib points (as does Held) to the layered structure of citizenship rights that seems to emerge external to the nation-state (for example, within the European Union). There are, she says, "multiple levels of organization, association, and networks of interdependence" within the world, and "multilayered governance" can "ameliorate stark oppositions between global aspirations and local self-determination." If we view the world in this multilayered way, then "the question becomes one of mediating among these varied levels so as to create more convergence upon some commonly agreed-upon standards . . . but through locally, nationally, or regionally interpreted, instituted and organized initiatives."[22]

While there are strong parallels with Held's arguments on "layering" in this passage, Benhabib goes on to do battle with a powerful group of communitarian thinkers, most notably Michael Walzer, who takes a broadly Burkean position when he writes that "men and women do indeed have rights beyond life and liberty, but these do not follow from our common humanity; they follow from shared conceptions of social goods; they are local and particular in character." Walzer emphasizes the "distinctiveness of cultures and groups" and suggests that if this distinctiveness is valued ("as most people seem to believe"), then "closure must be permitted somewhere" and "something like the sovereign state must take shape and claim the authority to make its own admissions policy, and to control and sometimes restrain the flow of immigrants." Benhabib objects to this "anthropological" idea that "shared cultural commonalities will always trump human rights claims." The effect is to create a far too restrictive (spatial?) domain within which citizenship claims can be made.[23]

It will evidently be difficult to reconcile universal ethics with the undoubtedly deep feelings and emotional attachments that people have to their homes, their local traditions, and to various kinds of "imagined communities" (such as the nation). That human rights, duties, and obligations necessarily extend beyond the borders of the nation-state (or territorial jurisdiction) is clear. Beck's focus on a cosmopolitan human rights regime is, therefore, fully justified in principle. The problem, however, is that he and Held both have a very narrow and individualistic definition of rights, far too close to the neoliberal ethic for comfort. There are many different proposals for a proper conception of rights in relation to a just social order. Iris Marion Young, for example, in her influential text *Justice and the Politics of Difference*, drawing upon the experience of urban social movements, defines rights in opposition to what she calls "the five faces of oppression":[24] exploitation of labor in both the workplace and the living space; marginalization of social groups by virtue of their identity; powerlessness (lack of resources to participate meaningfully in political life); cultural imperialism (symbolic denigration of particular elements in the population); and violence (within the family as well as within society at large). The right to alleviate these oppressions by various forms of collective action lies outside the norms of neoliberal thinking. Nussbaum, for her part, locates her thinking in the philosophical tradition that stretches from Aristotle through Grotius to the young Marx of *The Economic and Philosophic Manuscripts of 1844* (where Marx takes up the Kantian concept of species being). Nussbaum takes from Grotius the idea that the human being must be understood "as a creature characterized both by dignity and moral worth" (ideas, it should be noted, fundamental to the Zapatistas) and by an "impelling desire for fellowship, that is for common life, not of just any kind, but a peaceful life, and organized according to the measure of intelligence, with those who are of his kind." Nussbaum here gives specific content to the rights that derive from our species being. She spells out a list of "central human capabilities" to which everyone might then be expected to aspire. These capabilities are

1. Life (of a normal length)
2. Bodily health (including adequate nourishment and shelter)
3. Bodily integrity (freedom to move and explore without encountering violence)
4. Liberty of the senses, imagination and thought
5. Emotions (expressive attachments, love and caring)
6. Practical reason (the acquired ability through education to identify ends and means)
7. Affiliation (adequate social relations, dignity and self-respect)
8. Relations to other species (to the world of nature)
9. Free play
10. Control over one's environment (political and material)

This formulation, which contrasts markedly with Held's way of constituting the space of cosmopolitan thinking, is outcome-based rather than procedural.[25]

In Nussbaum's articulation of the capabilities approach, she makes a number of noteworthy claims. As might be expected, she gives considerable philosophical depth to her arguments. Her critique of Rawls's influential extension of his theory of justice to relations between states in *The Law of the Peoples* is trenchant. "By assuming the fixity of states as his starting point," Rawls effectively prevents "any serious consideration of economic inequalities and inequalities of power among states." The upshot is that he ratifies "philosophically what the powerful nations of the world, especially the United States, like to do anyway," refusing to "change internally, whether in matters of human rights or in environmental matters or in matters of economic policy, either in response to the situation of the rest of the world or in response to international treaties and agreements."[26] One should not, Nussbaum concludes, grant "philosophical respectability" to such "an arrogant mentality that is culpably unresponsive to grave problems." Benhabib voices similar objections to the exclusionary nationalism that arises out of Rawls's contention that peoples and not states "are the relevant moral and sociological actors in reasoning about justice on a global scale." People do not, as Rawls presumes, live in bounded communities characterized by a clearly identifiable moral nature marked by common sympathies.[27]

Nussbaum believes that her capabilities approach also advances our understanding of human rights, since it emphasizes "many of the entitlements that are also stressed in the human rights movement: political liberties, freedom of association, the free-choice of occupation, and a variety of social and economic rights." The capabilities she defines are very different, however, from the rights that neoliberalism typically prescribes (and she explicitly refutes neoliberal interpretations of the U.S. Constitution). They also constitute a very different cosmopolitan space to that proposed by either Held or Beck. Capabilities give "important precision and supplementation to the language of rights."[28] This is the precision that Beck so sorely lacks. Had he adopted something like Nussbaum's list, his descent into a covert defense of neoliberalization and overt advocacy of military humanism would almost certainly have been halted. Nussbaum even claims that pluralism and the right to difference are protected from within the terms of the list she provides. In this she is, however, on shaky ground, even though her justifications are far more sophisticated than the cavalier assertions of Held on this point. While it is true that freedoms of thought and association are necessary conditions for the sustenance of pluralism, they are far from sufficient, and there are other capabilities, such as control over the political environment, that can all too easily work in an opposite, exclusionary direction. Furthermore, she neglects to consider how class, ethnic, gender, and other differences become instantiated in socio-spatial structures (such as the ghettoes of both rich and poor) that perpetuate differences (some but not all of which are unjust if not downright objectionable) by way of the geographical structures of segregation in human socialization. The deracinated and aspatial mode of her thinking can be subjected to exactly the same critical scrutiny to which Mehta subjected liberal and Lockean theory. Nussbaum does, however, make one other principled point: some capabilities (such as life and bodily integrity) cannot be realized without equality, while others (such as play and liberty of the senses) are best specified in terms of some minimum threshold beyond which all manner of differences can flourish. The capabilities approach is, therefore, only partially egalitarian. Finally, her approach has the advantage that it promotes an affirmative politics oriented to the achievement of incremental goals, rather than a politics derived from a list of duties and obligations that many would recoil from as too onerous.

There remains the difficulty, however, of specifying concrete means to realize such desirable outcomes. "Philosophy is good at normative reasoning and laying out general structures of thought," Nusbaum concedes, but "any very concrete prescriptions for implementation need to be made in partnership with other disciplines."[29] Her agenda is to lay out such a compelling moral vision of the good life that all who read her will be persuaded to think about how to get there. In this she succeeds well enough. Our world would unquestionably be a superior place if her capabilities approach were to displace the individualistic and market-driven ethics derived from neoliberal theory.

The suggestions Nussbaum does make on "how to get there" are, however, deeply problematic. Not only do they appear utopian and naïve, as well as onerous in the way that her capabilities approach supposedly avoids, but also some of the means she suggests turn out to be antagonistic to the ends. She begins by pointing out, correctly in my view, that while we are all, ultimately, responsible for realizing the capabilities for everyone else, in practice we need institutions through which much of that work must be accomplished. Much rests, therefore, on the nature and behavior of the institutions we construct. This is where her difficulties begin. For example, she suddenly mounts a strong and very surprising defense of the nation-state as a basic institution through which her capabilities approach might be realized, on the grounds that "the ability to join with others to give one another laws is a fundamental aspect of human freedom. Being autonomous in this sense is no trivial matter: it is part of having a chance to live a fully human life. In our day as in Grotius' time, the fundamental unit through which people exercise this fundamental aspect of human freedom is the nation-state: it is the largest and most foundational unit that still has any chance of being decently accountable to the people who live there. . . . Thus the nation state and its basic structure are, as Grotius already argued, a key locus for persons' exercise of their freedom."[30]

We need, she seems to be saying, some territorial/geographical form of organization to realize human capabilities, and the only way her universal and deracinated abstractions can be brought to earth is through the very same nation-state whose powers she had earlier, in the name of a principled cosmopolitanism, decried. Beck, Held, and Nussbaum all seem to run into the same problem without any sense of how complicated the problem is. In Nussbaum's case, her sudden resurrection of the nation-state as a positive site of human association permits her to reaffirm Kant's "moral belief that one should respect the sovereignty of any nation that is organized in a sufficiently accountable way, whether or not its institutions are fully just." One will then "refrain from military intervention into the affairs of that nation, and one will negotiate with its duly elected government as a legitimate government." While it certainly puts a brake upon Beck's swashbuckling military humanism, this positioning of the nation-state as a crucial mediator raises as many issues as it solves, for all the reasons we have already considered. As anarchist theorists are wont to correctly point out, there are many other ways in which to construct "foundational units" that are accountable.

There is a deep tension between Nussbaum's fierce commitment to antinationalism and her positioning of the nation-state as the primary institution through which capabilities will be realized. The universalities of the latter are in danger of being trumped by exactly that right to collective self-determination within the sovereign state that Rawls finds fundamental and to which Nussbaum so vociferously objects. The primary duty within each nation-state is, Nussbaum insists in a desperate attempt to rescue her position, to promote the capabilities she lists to at least a threshold level. The secondary duty is formulated as a simple Rawlsian moral argument: "nations should give a substantial proportion of their GDP to poorer nations." Both of these moral obligations are onerous in the extreme, and it is not hard to see how people might recoil from supporting them. Nussbaum does not even invoke (as someone like Pogge, in extending Rawls's views, does) the moral principle that something is owed to, say, Africa because of the history of colonial and neocolonial plundering of that continent by imperial powers and the continued extraction of surpluses through mechanisms of trade and resource exploitation. This is an astonishingly naïve view of what the contemporary state and the capitalistic organization of space are actually about. She also says that "multinational corporations have responsibilities for promoting human capabilities in the regions in which they operate" and that "the main structures of the global economic order must be designed to be fair to poor and developing countries."[31] But the neoliberal forms in which these institutional arrangements are currently cast are precisely designed to frustrate the capabilities she desires because they are largely designed and expertly utilized to sustain and enhance class power. Corporations through their globalization strategies have increasingly escaped regulation over the last thirty years. They have effectively stymied all attempts to regulate them internationally by setting up their own organization for corporate social responsibility (to which most of the world's leading corporations belong). When not merely engaging in public relations exercises, they use their power of social engagement and promotion to advance their neoliberalizing agenda (by setting up market advocacy NGOs, colloquially known as MANGOs, for example). Though they relish their standing as legal individuals in certain situations, they have made sure that this stops at the doors of the International Criminal Court, thus ensuring they cannot be sued for environmental damages or for abuse of human rights with respect to the labor they employ or the products they produce. They have ensured that corporate responsibility within the European Union is merely "voluntary," on the surprising grounds that they need to maintain sufficient flexibility to deal sensitively with geographical and cultural differences. Nussbaum's uncritical attachment to naïve liberal theories of the state, corporations, and markets lies in deep contradiction to the political and collectivist tradition derived from Aristotle, Grotius, and the young Marx that informs her capabilities approach.

These chronic failures on the part of the new cosmopolitans to ground their theories in spaces and places in effective ways or, when they naïvely attempt to do so, not to go much beyond conventional neoliberal wisdoms make it tempting to dismiss their whole line of argument as yet another moral or legalistic mask for the continuance of elite class and imperialist power. I think such dismissal is premature. We first need to ask: in what ways can a cosmopolitan project of opposition to cosmopolitan neoliberalism be formulated? There are, I first note, three ways in which cosmopolitanism can arise: out of philosophical reflection; out of an assessment of practical requirements and basic human needs; or out of the ferment of social movements that are engaged in transforming the world each in their own ways. Nussbaum draws heavily on the first, appeals to the second through the acknowledged influence of Sen's remarkable work on famines and food security, but ignores the third. I think it vital to integrate the diversity of thinking and practices of social movements into the analysis. This is the path that Iris Marion Young took in *Justice and the Politics of Difference*. In her final chapter, she attempts a derivation of what virtues are possible and reasonable, building upon an earlier analysis of the diverse faces of oppression as these are manifest in the tangible circumstances of contemporary city life. She specifies not only what the eradication of injustice demands, but also what a virtuous outcome would look like. In so doing she gives new meaning to universal concepts through the lenses of social movements, as well as from the geographical standpoint of contemporary urban life (albeit in the United States).[32]

De Sousa Santos follows a similar strategy with a more internationalist dimension (though without the urban emphasis). The excluded populations of the world need, he says, "a subaltern cosmopolitanism" expressive of their needs and reflective of their condition. "Whoever is a victim of local intolerance and discrimination needs cross-border tolerance and support; whoever lives in misery in a world of wealth needs cosmopolitan solidarity; whoever is a non- or second-class citizen of a country or the world needs an alternative conception of national and global friendship. In short, the large majority of the world's population, excluded from top-down cosmopolitan projects, needs a different kind of cosmopolitanism."[33] Our task as academics and intellectuals is not to speak for but to amplify the voice of "those who have been victimized by neoliberal globalization, be they indigenous peoples, landless peasants, impoverished women, squatter settlers, sweatshop workers or undocumented immigrants." Much of what is touted as "governance," he rightly argues, is suspect because it is merely "the political matrix of neoliberal globalization," even when it incorporates the poor or their representatives as relevant stakeholders. This is the primary way (as the case of microfinance so clearly demonstrates) in which "the hegemony of transnational capital and the main capitalist powers gets reproduced." The underlying tensions between the capitalistic and territorial logics of power that de Sousa Santos here identifies all too often lead directly, as I have shown elsewhere, into economic, political, and militaristic imperialism.[34] The political moves that occurred from the mid-1970s onward from "the central state to devolution/decentralization, from the political to the technical; from popular participation to the expert system; from the public to the private; from the state to the market" constructed the new neoliberal regime epitomized by the Washington Consensus. The silences within this governance matrix with respect to social justice, equality, and conceptions of rights that go beyond the liberal ideal of individual autonomy signal, in de Sousa Santos's view, "the defeat of critical theory."[35] Young and de Sousa Santos establish a critical perspective that is lacking in the formulations of Beck and Held, and which sadly disappears from Nussbaum's purview.

The more explicit formulation of what a subaltern cosmopolitanism might be about depends on how we characterize the counter-hegemonic social movements that are currently in motion. What is called "globalization from below" is generating considerable political energy for progressive changes in the global system. These struggles, Sassen argues, are geographically fragmented and specific. They are:

> global through the knowing multiplication of local practices. . . . These practices are also institution-building work with global scope that can come from localities and networks of localities with limited resources and from informal social actors. We see here the potential transformation of actors "confined" to domestic roles into actors in global networks without having to leave their work and roles in their communities. From being experienced as purely domestic and local, these "domestic" settings are transformed into microenvironments articulated with global circuits. They do not have to become cosmopolitan in this process: they may well remain domestic and particularistic in their orientation and remain engaged with their households and local community struggles, and yet they are engaging in emergent global politics. A community of practice can emerge that creates multiple lateral, horizontal communications, collaborations, solidarities, and supports.[36]

Sassen refuses to interpret all this in terms of "the cosmopolitan route to the global," and views it rather "as micro-instances of partial and incipient denationalization" or of "relational nationality."[37] De Sousa Santos, who would almost certainly concur with Sassen's description, would doubtless argue that this is precisely the form that a subaltern cosmopolitanism should and will take. I raise this point because it is impossible to characterize the cosmopolitanism incipient in social movements without confronting their geographical dispersal and frequently highly localized specificities, and also recognizing that their aim is not necessarily to change the world but to change the deleterious conditions in some particular part of it. If the only way that coal miners in Russia, sweatshop workers in Thailand, factory laborers in China, trafficked women in Europe, and lost children in Darfur can change the world is by revolutionizing the neoliberal global order, then so be it. There is nothing wrong with a subaltern cosmopolitan perspective remaining particularistic and local in orientation, provided the dialectical connectivity to global conditions is sustained. But at this point de Sousa Santos's view that the only task for critical intellectuals is to "amplify the voice of victimized" itself poses a barrier to deeper critical engagement. Vital though that role is, even a subaltern cosmopolitanism has to engage critically in the task of translation of particularist demands and local engagements into a common language of opposition to the neoliberal capitalism and imperialist strategies that lie at the root of current problems. But this in turn requires a far deeper understanding of how the geographical principles of space and place construction relate to the actual unfolding of any cosmopolitan project. In other words, we have to unpack what Held rushes over as "situated hermeneutic complexity" and answer the question that Nussbaum leaves dangling as to what kind of geographical, anthropological, and ecological knowledge is appropriate for a cosmopolitan education.

The glory of the dialectical method that Beck advocates but does not follow is that it can, when properly practiced, create a unity within and out of difference at the same time as it understands all too well the stresses and contradictions that arise through the uneven development of situated struggles around different conceptions of rights, capabilities, and governance. To operationalize all this entails, as Kant long ago noted, a particular combination of intelligence and judgment, the ability to generate acute and subtle understandings rather than "empty sophistries and conceited prattlings." None of us can claim to be immune from falling into errors of the latter sort. What does, therefore, require a prior moral and intellectual commitment is that we should offer each other mutual aid in developing the kinds of subaltern cosmopolitanisms (and the pluralization of the term is deliberate) that can generate emancipatory theory and politics across a politics of difference. This brings us back to the idea of a located and embodied, "actually existing" cosmopolitanism that, as Bruce Robbins puts it, acknowledges "the actual historical and geographical contexts from which it emerges" and does not regard the prospect of pluralizing and particularizing its propositions as somehow fatal to its global reach.[38] But for this to happen requires that we first answer the question that Nussbaum and Kant invoked and which everyone else at some point or other encounters (often with frustration, or in some instances with cavalier dismissal): what geographical, ecological, and anthropological knowledges would be required for any decent, and in this case subaltern, cosmopolitan project to succeed?

Chapter Five
The Banality of Geographical Evils

Liberalism, neoliberalism, and cosmopolitanism all leave Kant's suggested requirement for an adequate foundation in a science of geography to one side. Their universal claims are transhistorical, transcultural, and treated as valid, independent of any rootedness in the facts of geography, ecology, and anthropology. Theories derived from these claims dominate fields of study such as economics (monetarism, rational expectations, public choice, human capital theory), political science (rational choice), international relations (game theory), jurisprudence (law and economics), business administration (theories of the firm), and even psychology (autonomous individualism). These universal forms of thinking are so widely diffused and so commonly accepted as to set the terms of discussion in political rhetoric (particularly with respect to individualism, private property rights, and markets) in much of the popular media (with the business press in the vanguard), as well as in the law (including its international human rights variant). They even provide foundational norms in those fields of study—such as geography, anthropology, and sociology—that take differences as their object of inquiry.

There are two independent but overlapping lines of critical engagement with these universal theories. First is the political critique that their fundamental propositions and abstractions are biased in tems of class or ethnicity (Eurocentric and imperialist, in the case of cosmopolitanism). In appealing so often to the Robinson Crusoe story to illustrate the natural basis of their universal arguments, Marx wryly noted, the classical political economists failed to register that Robinson was "a true-born Briton" who, having conveniently rescued from the wreck watch, ledger, and pen and ink, was already capable of keeping a set of books.[1] The application of these universal theories therefore leads to the reinforcement of existing structures of class or geopolitical power, the production of increasing geographical and social inequality (with all of its attendant social stresses), and the plundering of the global commons. This was what Marx so brilliantly revealed in his deconstruction of liberal political economy (Crusoe myth and all) in *Capital*. The second line of critique focuses on the inherent faults of any theory formulated without reference to the realities of geography, ecology, and anthropology. If geographical knowledge really is a "condition of possibility" of all other forms of knowing, then how can it be so cheerfully ignored in universal theory? The two critiques become entangled when, for example, the tutelage administered by the British imperial regime in India in the name of John Stuart Mill's liberalism is excused because of the geographical and anthropological conditions (the Indians are not yet mature enough to govern themselves). The geographical and anthropological conception in this case provided a mask for the preservation of class structures within the British imperial state apparatus, in much the same way that Bush protected the incomes and assets of the superrich in the United States while purportedly promoting a purist quest for universal liberty and freedom in the messy geographical and anthropological worlds of Afghanistan, Iraq, and the Middle East. In all those cases, recalcitrant geographical details seemed to perpetually frustrate a noble mission (if only Sunnis and Shias would rationally collaborate in a neoliberal democracy in Iraq, and if only the Palestinians would not show the bad taste to vote for Hamas, then all would be well!). The devil as well as the difficulties, it seems, all too often get hidden in the geographical and anthropological details.

How this works politically should be a matter of great concern. In his State of the Union address in January 2003, for example, President Bush dramatically depicted the greatest threat to the security of the United States as an "axis of evil," constituted by certain states and their terrorist allies who were "arming to threaten the peace of the world."[2] The term *axis*, while it conveniently echoed the language of World War II, when the "free world" (albeit in alliance with the Soviet Union) confronted and defeated "the Axis Powers," also suggested a coherently organized geopolitical arc of evil-minded powers threatening world peace in general and U.S. interests in particular. In a country where Star Wars and fearful threats from evil empires had been a standard feature of popular culture during the Cold War years, the immediate political impact of such an image leaves little to the imagination. The problem was that two of the states named, Iraq (then governed by Sunnis) and Iran (governed by Shias), had waged a bitter war against each other during the 1980s, with the United States broadly supporting the former (Donald Rumsfeld's smiling handshake with Saddam Hussein in 1983 is symbolic) in spite of Saddam's war crimes (Iraq's use of biological warfare that the United States at the time downplayed). The third state, North Korea, for its part, was isolated from the other two both geographically and politically, but was nevertheless considered equally aberrant and therefore worthy of inclusion in the axis concept. Evil forces were, it seems, gathering in these territories. Designated as centers of evil, these countries had to be disciplined or, in extremis, subdued by main force.

Resort to this trick (for such it is) is not unique to Bush, nor is it confined to the United Statres. The government of Iran regularly reverses the compliment of being the incarnation of evil in the direction of the United States, and the influential Shi'a cleric in Iraq, Muqtada al-Sadr, greeted the U.S. invasion with the memorable words that "the little Satan has been deposed and the grand Satan has arrived." Ronald Reagan used to refer to the then Soviet Union as an "evil empire" that had to be fiercely resisted if not crushed. The demonizing of certain states, such as Cuba and Libya (followed now by Venezuela); the designation of this or that state as a "rogue state"; the dismissal of even erstwhile allies as representatives of some tired and stuffy "old Europe": all become part of a discursive world in which global geopolitical alignments get mapped and color-coded in terms of good and evil, mature or immature, barbaric or civilized, old or new, or "with us or against us." It has long been standard practice in the United States to take some territory, of which the public is woefully ignorant, and designate it as problematic or as harboring evil forces, in order to justify interventions, sanctions, or other prescriptive actions. The idea that international negotiations can be conducted or that economic and military wars can be waged on the basis of such flimsy geographical and anthropological conceptions is quite terrifying. The tension that arises between universal Enlightenment rationality (usually masking more venal commercial interests of the sort that Woodrow Wilson so explicitly revealed) and the geographical and anthropological details encompasses much of the world's troubled history from the seventeenth century onward.

In this history, the political role of geographical and anthropological knowledge and ignorance requires serious reconsideration. In a poll taken in the United States in 1999, for example, it was shown that the more people knew about a country, the less likely they were to support sanctions or military action against that country.[3] Interestingly, the poll was commissioned by Exxon, which at that time, with all of its oil interests, was developing a campaign for the lifting of U.S. economic sanctions against Iran, which had been imposed after the hostage crisis and revolution of 1979. The dubious origin of this poll information reinforces the point that geographical knowledge has political implications, in this case for the state of public opinion, since Exxon clearly understood that changing the qualities of that geographical knowledge can have political effects. Part of the reason President Reagan got into so much difficulty over the illegal covert operations the United States sponsored in Central America, and the so-called Iran-Contra scandal, was that so many church groups in the United States had links to religious organizations in Central America (from Moravians to Catholics) and therefore knew that much of the insurgency there was about the popular search for social justice (with liberation theology at its root) and not a mere offshoot of Cuban communism, as the Reagan administration maintained. The State Department, for its part, was fond at that time of using maps that showed a red tide of Cuban-inspired revolution creeping northward from Nicaragua to threaten Texas (of all places!). The manipulation of maps to create a sense of threat from outside is a legendary tool for political propaganda. From this it would seem that elite groups, themselves supposedly well informed, might prefer a population to remain geographically and anthropologically ignorant and therefore easily manipulable. But elite groups themselves often make decisions on the basis of incredibly simplistic and often downright erroneous geographical and anthropological suppositions. When the full story of the Iraq War is told, it will almost certainly become clear that those (based in the Pentagon) who made the key decisions to start and implement the war had no idea what they were likely to encounter on the ground and blithely overruled all those within government (in the State Department, in particular) who at least had some inklings of what the problems on the ground were likely to be like. President Bush, in particular, seems to have been far too preoccupied with his role as an agent of God's intelligent design on earth to pay any mind whatsoever to grubby geographical or anthropological details. If he registered the difference between Sunnis and Shias at all, he seems to have believed that it was analogous to the difference between Methodists and Baptists in Texas.[4]

Oversimplifications of this sort are not uncommon. Blair's foreign policy adviser Robert Cooper, for example, provided a simplified geopolitical vision of the world in which he classified states into three broad types: premodern, modern, and postmodern.[5] Postmodern states are those willing to submerge their national interest in pursuit of constructive international collaborations within a cosmopolitan universal rule of law administered through effective international institutions (such as the International Criminal Court, the WTO, and the United Nations). The modern state, by way of contrast, ruthlessly pursues its own narrow national interest in competition with, and at the expense of, other states within the interstate system, sometimes in such a barbaric manner (think of Libya and Iraq of yore) as to deserve the title of a "rogue" state. Premodern states are those that have yet to impose an adequate rule of law internally, whose institutions and political structures are so weak and shaky that they fall apart in the face of the mildest difficulties. There is still, Cooper argued, an enormous job to be done (including influence exercised by civilized external powers) in bringing such "failed" states into the framework of a workable interstate system. Cooper is here repeating, of course, the simplistic nineteenth-century distinctions between civilized, barbarian, and savage societies (though with more respectable wording). The civilized postmodern states (such as those that have constituted the European Union) are charged with the heavy historical burden of bringing both the savage premodern states (like Afghanistan and the Congo) and barbarous modern states (like China and Iran) into a civilized (postmodern) world. Cosmopolitanism, for Blair, was the appropriate philosophical stance for a postmodern version of imperialism, with its doctrines of universal human rights in the foreground (as he indicated in his speech to the U.S. Congress). Geopolitical simplifications of the Cooper sort are occasionally useful, but far more often than not they turn out to be grossly misleading. That for so many other analysts the nation-state is no longer an adequate conceptual anchor for any kind of cosmopolitanism escaped Cooper's (and presumably Blair's) attention. And then there is the acute problem of how to fit actual states into such neat boxes. How do we categorize the U.S. posture when it seems to vacillate between rogue state and modern state with occasional intimations (when advantageous) of a supposedly civilized postmodernity? But then it turns out that that is the way that most states are, even those within the European Union that provide the model for Cooper's definition of postmodern states. France and Britain, after all, are hardly models of subservience to ideals of international law, even though they readily evoke such law when it is in their interest to do so.

Geographical and anthropological knowledge therefore plays a very important political role, and from this it follows that struggles over the qualities of that information are integral to the political process itself. This is particularly true in the case of environmental politics, where much of the battle is fought over exactly what are the appropriate and truthful representations of the geographical and anthropological facts. In the long history of mega-dam projects supported by the World Bank, the bank was in the habit of picturing such projects as pristine and shining gifts of modernity to grateful backward rural populations who could now look forward to rural electrification, flood control, and irrigation possibilities for commercial agriculture. Opponents of such projects typically tabulated the wholesale displacements of populations, the disruptions of indigenous rights and ways of living, habitat destruction and loss of biodiversity, commercial impositions, and unwanted transformations in social relations, at the same time as they pointed out that the lucrative contracts for building the dams benefited multinational corporations more than local inhabitants. In the face of such rhetoric, the World Bank found itself obliged to withdraw from funding, for example, the huge Narmada Dam project in India (in which the late lamented Enron corporation was involved) against the will or even knowledge of most local inhabitants. The World Bank has now largely ceased to fund mega-dam projects.[6] We are currently exposed to similar controversies in which the nature of the geographical and anthropological information turns out to be critical to the forms of political judgment and economic action. Is global warming occurring, and with what effects and where (if not in my back yard, then who cares?)? How much of it is due to human action, and who is chiefly to blame? What can and should be done about it, and who will benefit or lose most from remedial policies? Where and in what form will the major impacts fall? A vast array of specialists from the scientific community has been mobilized to provide answers to these questions, and the nature of the answers is critical for politics. The problem is that this then opens up the prospect for the science to become, as it is said, "a fig leaf for policy," which then explains why political forces mobilized within the Bush administration spent so much time trying either to doctor the science or to discredit it, when it pointed to unpalatable conclusions for certain corporate interests (primarily in the energy and transportation sectors).[7]

Even when unpalatable conclusions about global warming or global poverty become inescapable, the dominant response is to seek remedies within the framework of a universal theory of market freedoms and private property rights, supplemented by a hefty dose of imperial politics to protect dominant power structures. The global poverty problem will be solved, it is said, by the extension of private property rights and microcredit institutions everywhere, no matter what the anthropological or geographical circumstances or consequences (from Lima to Bangladesh and Cairo). An international trading system in pollution rights, plus a new wave of market-led technological innovation, will solve all environmental problems everywhere (this was and is Al Gore's main promarket and pro–venture capitalist contribution to the debate on global warming). But here, then, is the paradox, for it is the main political powers, led by the United States and the European Union, that pontificate so freely on the importance of the universal principles of liberty and freedom (of the market) while imposing carbon sequestration forestation projects on impoverished countries that in effect have little choice but to accept them, while exporting arms (a trade that Blair and the "postmodern" European Union—Belgium in the lead—did nothing to discourage), barbaric forms of counter-insurgency training (a U.S. specialty), and benevolent forms of aid (dispensed through market mechanisms and often tied to particular commercial interests in donor countries) to many of the modern and premodern states. The lucrative contemporary arms trade into Africa, largely paid for by the loot of that continent's natural resources, is an appalling form of contemporary neocolonial violence conducted in the name of the free market that makes John Stuart Mill's paternalistic liberalism toward British imperial rule in nineteenth-century India look positively benign.

The question is how many of these projects and so-called solutions to, say, the global poverty or global warming problem fail out of plain geographical and anthropological ignorance. The history of economic development projects dispensed by the United States and the European powers since World War II (and the "war" against global poverty has been going on intermittently ever since then), is littered with examples of grandiose schemes that failed miserably because of a misreading of the geographical and anthropological circumstances (one of the best documented is the ill-fated "ground-nut scheme" that the British colonial authorities launched in East Africa in the 1950s). The World Bank has, if the truth be known, a huge dossier of such failed projects in its archives. But in some sense failure does not matter, because the real issue of, for example, a program launched around environmental sustainability has nothing to do with the environment, any more than an antipoverty program has to do with poverty. The central purpose is to hold together the universal principles upon which liberal, neoliberal, and some version of the Blairite version of cosmopolitanism is based, in order to sustain the social power relations that are reproduced so effectively through such arrangements. Any good (and admittedly, the good results can occasionally be substantial) that arises from such projects in terms of reversal of environmental degradations or diminution of poverty is purely incidental. Even the launching of a substantial program of redistribution of wealth through institutional reforms and the construction of welfare arrangements in the United States after the disastrous experience of the 1930s had—as President Franklin D. Roosevelt, for one, well understood—more to do with saving capitalism from itself than with improving the lot of the American people. It follows that foreknowledge of the geographical and anthropological conditionalities that may lead to success or failure does not matter too much, either, because the definition of success or failure has nothing much to do with what happens to people on the ground. From the viewpoint of the Halliburton company, for example, the Iraq war has been a great success. The war on poverty, made so much of in the U.N. Millennium project now shaped under the supposedly benevolent intellectual leadership of Jeffrey Sachs, is charged with the impossible task of curing global poverty without in any way touching the global processes of accumulation of wealth.

Small wonder, then, that there is so little incentive within the sciences and the social sciences (let alone within the media or in those arenas where public opinion is shaped) to place anthropological and geographical knowledges in the "propaedeutic" position that Kant thought they should in principle occupy. At best, the geographical and anthropological conditions are introduced to explain the particular failure of this or that project in a particular place and time (while always leaving the universal principles unscathed, off limits to criticism). But proponents as well as opponents of the universal theories invariably find themselves obliged to comment in some way on the anthropological and geographical "conditions of applicability" if not "conditions of possibility" for their own arguments. Martha Nussbaum, as we saw, asserts categorically that some new educational strategy in geography, anthropology, and ecology is needed for her cosmopolitanism to work, but she refrains from inquiring into what such an educational strategy might entail. David Held inserts local "situatedness" and "hermeneutical complexity" into his Kantian cosmopolitan frame, but then passes on as if nothing significant is implied thereby. S. Benhabib sees nothing wrong with admitting a great deal of latitude to local interpretations of universal ethical principles, but apparently this in no way interferes with how the universal principles are to be articulated. Ulrich Beck, for his part, reassures us that the spatial issue is all worked out (though his commentary is simplistic beyond belief) and unproblematically supports a universal theory of global individualized human rights, at the same time as he worries that the cosmopolitanism of time badly needs to be addressed. U. Mehta, while vociferously opposing the universalisms of liberalism, says, without justification, that no one has specified what spatial theory is about, and goes on to embrace Burke and Heidegger (problematic figures both) as providing the necessary answers. Thomas Friedman, of course, just assumes the world is flat and horizontally networked (for rich entrepreneurs) and that the realities of unflatness (for the rest) is just a passing phase, an unfortunate local manifestation of cultural backwardness that will surely pass. Jeffrey Sachs is emphatic that the systemic theories of development economics are fine in themselves but cannot be applied without "a commitment to be thoroughly steeped in the history, ethnography, politics and economics of any place where the professional advisor is working."[8] Parenthetically we might note that-Sachs knew little or nothing about these facts when he involved himself in the disastrous policy of "shock therapy" neoliberalization imposed upon a Russian economy in total turmoil in the 1990s. He has since denied any responsibility for what happened there. But then this is also standard practice. When something works because of special anthropological and geographical conditions, then it is claimed as a triumph for universal theory; if it fails, it is explained away by appeal to exactly those same conditions. When the developmental economies of East and Southeast Asia were chalking up remarkable growth figures in the 1990s, for example, they were depicted by the World Bank as triumphs of neoliberalism lubricated by local Asian values of networking (which the rest of us should consider emulating, as Friedman continues to urge upon us, as a universal principle), but when they crashed in 1997–98 they were universally scorned as examples of crony Asian capitalism that had so violated the tried-and-true principles of neoliberal individualism as to require the ministrations of the IMF to bring them back to good health.

An uncomfortable impression arises out of all this. The facts of anthropology and geography (to which we should also add history), rather than being viewed as systematic conditions of possibility for all other forms of knowing, are being opportunistically appealed to in order to discredit unfavored or promote favored universal positions. This strategy can work successfully precisely because of the inherent positionality, which Kant detected but could not act upon, of geographical and anthropological knowledges in relation to all other ways of knowing. It also happens to be convenient that the facts of geography, anthropology, and history can be mustered so specifically as to be hard to refute. While the general theory would suggest one outcome, the particularities in this place and time are so special and so strange as to generate something entirely different. In this way the principles of the general theory, like the standard "structural adjustment" prescriptions of the IMF (to say nothing of all the standard teaching in the social sciences), can endlessly be protected against refutation at the same time as the failures can be plausibly explained away as local aberrations. The anthropological, historical, and geographical circumstances, the argument seems to go, did not properly collaborate with the universal rationalities of the theory. Bush was right to lead the world into a freedom struggle against tyranny in Afghanistan and Iraq (no one, after all, is in favor of tyranny except tyrants), but the locals did not collaborate properly and live up to rational expectations. They were so irrational, in fact, that everyone from John Locke to Adam Smith and John Stuart Mill could be invoked to justify their being placed under the yoke of some version of imperial tutelage until they became mature enough to recognize tyranny as evil.

Any resultant incentive from this dismal history to treat geography and anthropology as foundational is blunted by two major barriers. First, it would undermine the capacity for selective opportunism and thereby remove the mask that so conveniently and effectively conceals and protects the particularities of the class or ethnic nationalist power hiding behind the noble universal principles. Second, when theorists have ventured very far in this direction, they find the insertion of geographical and anthropological perspectives disruptive for how the universal theory actually works. The mere introduction of spatiality (let alone environmental dynamics and the politics of place formation) into economic theory, for example, has a powerfully disruptive effect upon its foundational propositions. In 1957, T. Koopmans and A. Beckman published an article that threw "serious doubt on the possibility of sustaining an efficient locational distribution of activities through a price system." The "decisive difficulty," Koopmans reported, is that the "dependence of one man's [locational] decision criterion on other men's decisions appears to leave no room for efficient price-guided allocation." Throw spatiality into the hopper of economic reasoning, and the whole logic falls apart because prices cannot do their proper work of coordinating activities in an efficient and optimal manner. Koopmans and Beckman were so distressed by the result that they delayed publication for several years.[9] Koopmans got his Nobel Prize, and most economists have cheerfully avoided the paradox ever since. Only recently did Paul Krugman return to the question in order to offer at least a partial mathematical solution. But that solution is neither complete nor foundational, and in any case it is marginalized within economics as a special kind of geographical applicability precisely because of its troubling implications. Given the hegemony of economic thinking, it is passing strange that a discipline that cannot incorporate raw spatiality (surely a universal conditionality of all economic activity), let alone real geography or anthropology, into its fundamental propositions, and which still cannot adequately explain geographical differences in the wealth of nations (except by crude versions of geographical determinism), has such a profoundly influential position in our knowledge structures, over public policy as well as in the media. That this theoretical apparatus ends up obscuring the class character of capitalist accumulation through market exchange is not entirely accidental.

This acute difficulty of incorporating spatiality into general theory is not confined to economics. Consider the work of a leading political theorist like William Connolly.[10] His laudable radical intent is to critique what he considers the false universals of political theory (such as rational choice) that protect concentrated political power (particularly within the state). He introduces spatiality into his argument as a vehicle to achieve this goal precisely because, as Koopmans had found earlier, the introduction of spatiality is disruptive of received wisdom. He uses spatiality strategically to attack the universals and argue for "a more cosmopolitan, multidimensional imagination of democracy that distributes democratic energies and identifications across multiple sites." But when faced with defining what "a more multiplicitous spatialization of democratic energies" might mean, he says little about any kind of material geography or anthropology and merely reviews what other political theorists have had to say about space (which is not much) and territory, concluding that it is impossible to identify theoretically "the *place* that might, if not supplant loyalty to the state, compete with it so that sometimes a new 'we' finds itself bestowing allegiance on constituencies and aspirations in ways that contest the state's monopoly over political allegiance." Connolly accepts the disruptive consequences for political theory in general (and Kant's cosmopolitanism in particular) of rapidly shifting spatialities, but sees this primarily as an opportunity to argue for a new kind of "rhizomatic" and "fragmented" cosmopolitanism in which the Internet figures large as a vehicle for democratic possibility. To complete his project Connolly needs some sense of how spatialities and geographies (the actual places he is looking for) are actively produced and with what anthropological consequences. He appeals to a general principle of "time-space compression" as a disruptive force, but fails to register that "speed-up" in modern culture has been and continues to be produced by a capitalist-military alliance, exacerbated by the revolution in financial powers as a means to preserve and enhance specific class and territorial powers. The Internet has no liberatory potential whatsoever for the billion or so wage workers who, according to the World Bank, are struggling to eke out an existence on less than a dollar a day. Exactly at the point where tangible geographical and anthropological knowledges are essential Connolly's political theorizing breaks off. We get no further with key concepts of "site," "spatiality," "speed," "territory," and "place" than their use as convenient metaphors to deservedly disrupt received wisdoms (rational choice theory in particular) within political science.

M. Shapiro, to take another example from political theory, runs into similar difficulties. He sets out to explore the Kantian ethics of hospitality in the midst of global difference. Kant, he points out, "envisioned a world in which an enlarged ethic of hospitality would diminish the significance of the bordered world." The problem was that Kant did so in a way that "effaces much of the difference that the Kantian ethics of global hospitality is designed to appreciate." In particular, Kant, by taking a bounded view of space (my formulation, not Shapiro's) and treating the state as the only relevant institution, could not attend to internal differences (of religion, ethnicity, or merely lifestyle preferences) within states: "Because Kant's moral map enclosed states as abstract 'societies of men,' he lacked a sensitivity to peoples and nations that were not organized in the form of states. Kant's practical map is strictly geopolitical, recognizing no nations that are not also states. . . . Recognizing a plurality of 'islands,' Kant sought a means for creating a peaceful milieu, a tranquil sea within which these islands could become a harmonious archipelago. 'Peace,' for Kant is, therefore, primarily a relationship between state entities. Although he advocated a hegemony-resisting form of republican governance within states, his notion of war did not recognize contested terrains—for example, the struggles between settlers and indigenous peoples—within states." [11]

The problem, Shapiro correctly suggests, is to reconcile Kant's cosmopolitanism with anthropological and geographical differences that are far more complex than a system of nation-states. But instead of investigating the problem through geography and anthropology, Shapiro merely resorts to a self-referential study of the variety of spatial, geographical, and territorial metaphors deployed by the usual philosophical suspects (Derrida, Foucault, and Lyotard—though, interestingly, Deleuze and Guattari get passed over). This leaves to one side the active terrain of production of space and of real geographies and anthropologies (as if the only thing that matters is getting the metaphors right, rather than investigating the material processes whereby human populations get together or get disaggregated and differentiated). Had Shapiro read Kant's Geography, he might also have worried more about Kant's recorded "sensitivities" to people and places. As it is, Shapiro's account is learned, and interestingly so, precisely because it recognizes the potential significance of anthropological and geographical conditionalities, but it is sadly deficient in understanding the contingencies that arise "from the interactions of space and discourse" within the contemporary political economy of globalization.

The blurring of the boundaries between anthropology and history achieved by the subaltern studies group in India might offer a friendlier terrain upon which to address these issues. Their insistence on seeking to reveal history from below, as it occurs in actual places through individual lives irrespective of class or culture, does indeed yield important insights. But while their handling of history shows a good deal of skill and depth, their treatment of spatiality and geography is peculiarly wooden. S. Deshpande, working in the contemporary version of this tradition, provides an instructive example.[12] He investigates the relations between globalization, conceptions of the Indian nation, and the construction of "Hindu-ness" (or "Hindutva") as a locus of distinctive identity and meaning across the Indian subcontinent. He sees the history of these relations as "closely and crucially intertwined with a geography," though it also has a class character. Nehru's secular developmental model depended, for example, upon a "privileged pan-Indian elite that could, by and large, afford to cut loose its regional moorings." It entailed a distinctive spatial logic (the history of which "has yet to be written") of "multi-dimensional relations of domination established along the inter-regional, rural-urban, and city-megacity axes." A distinctive social geography was superimposed upon the Indian national space. But this spawned a variety of regional-ethnic oppositional movements. Hindutva, as invoked by the BJP Hindu nationalist party, exploits "the ideological vulnerability of the placeless universalism of the Nehruvian nation-space" and seeks "to rekindle a personalised commitment to particular places that are nevertheless embedded within the abstract social space of hindutva." Hindutva appeals to what Deshpande calls "the sedimented banalities of neighbourliness—the long-term, live-in intimacy of residential relationships among persons and families and between them and their local environment." Deshpande's terms are interesting; it is the *banality* of mundane, everyday local experiences in the streets and residential areas that defines truths that acquire the status of "self-evident common sense." This forms the basis for a politics (including pathological expressions of intercommunal violence) that is far removed from Kant's cosmopolitanism. The "banalities" of local geographical loyalties disrupt the cosmopolitan ideal of Nehruvian developmentalism (just as spatialities disrupt the grand harmonies of neoclassical economic or rational choice theories).

This seems a productive line of inquiry until Deshpande looks for some way to better understand the role of spatiality. "One way of understanding spatial strategies," he writes, "is to think of them as ideological practices involved in the construction of heterotopias." Spatial strategies "attempt to tie an imagined space to a real place in such a way that these ties also bind people to particular identities and to the political/practical consequences they entail."[13] The formulation is superficially attractive because it at least opens up a consideration of how spaces and places are actually produced. Invocation of Foucault's concept of heterotopia also has theoretical cachet. But this conceptual move ends up flattening a potentially rich geographical argument into an absolute Kantian space whose wooden banality is no better than the "sedimented banalities of neighborliness" that it interprets. The full implications of heterotopia crucially depend, Deshpande discovers, upon "the context of its mobilisation for some larger than everyday activity or campaign" (that is, it is dependent upon some nonlocal source of power). Nehru had his steel mills, and Hindutva has its symbolic centers and places. Both are equally heterotopic sites. And so what? Is there no better theoretical handle to deal with actual geography and the complexities of spatiality than Foucault's wooden version of absolute spaces?

In the face of such difficulties some thinkers have understandably chosen to reject cosmopolitanism and to dismantle Kantian universals into local, contingent, and purely place-based communitarian meanings. Michael Walzer, for example, takes this path in formulating a "radically particularist" theory of justice. Senses of justice, a universal principle, can and do vary greatly across space, he argues, even from neighborhood to neighborhood. Such differences often become a manifest source of serious political and juridical conflict. "Local justice" (Jon Elster's term) is a fact of geographical as well as institutional life and one that deserves close attention. Like Kant's concession to local laws, this seems to pose an intractable dilemma. We are caught between a relativism that suggests "that for each cultural group there is some theory of justice that captures its ethical intuitions" and "moral universals" that may be just as unpalatable even if they can be defined. But because justice (as Walzer argues) may be "rooted in the distinct understandings of places, honors, jobs, things of all sorts, that constitute a shared way of life," it does not follow, as Walzer asserts, that "to override those understandings is (always) to act unjustly."[14] The cosmopolitan temptation is, of course, to revert to Zeno's dream of a "well-ordered and philosophical community" where we should not be "divided from one another by local schemes of justice," but regard all human beings as "fellow citizens." Walzer's communitarian reply is equally utopian, however, since it rests on a belief in "my community right or wrong" without any clear idea of the geographical and anthropological processes that might make something called "community" a possible (let alone coherent) entity of political judgment and of economic action in the first place.

Such abstract communitarian arguments—often produced in direct opposition to neoliberal, liberal, and cosmopolitan universals—invariably end up assuming (tacitly rather than explicitly) a geographical world divided into a mosaic of cultures or communities understood as a series of what Anthony Appiah condemns as "closed territorial boxes." They fail to note how places and localized ways of life are relationally constructed by a variety of intersecting socio-ecological processes occurring at quite different spatio-temporal scales. No attention is paid in this communitarian political theory to the actual historical-geographical processes of place and community construction. To ignore these processes and build a particularist theory of local justice with respect to places and cultures as embodied *things* located in a fixed, absolute space is to advocate a fetishistic politics that would try (fortunately, against all odds) to permanently freeze existing geographical structures of places and their social norms of justice. When the communitarian boxes close, exclusions invariably follow. The effect would be as dysfunctional as it would be oppressive. Compared to multiple authoritarian and even neofascist forms of localized social regulation, Kant's cosmopolitanism as a norm for intervention in an unsatisfactory and violent world of geographical difference appears positively liberatory. The problem for Walzer lies in his failure to examine how "local and particular solidarities" are actually formed and how they work. Take away the presumption of closed boxes, and Walzer's theory has no clear geographical or anthropological base. Reimpose the closed boxes, and the repressions start.

In reflecting on a set of essays on cosmopolitics, the anthropologist James Clifford, a long-time critic of studying cultures as if they are a series of closed boxes, returned somewhat to his own anthropological roots and came up with the term "discrepant cosmopolitanisms" as the most satisfactory description of his own ambiguous stance toward the word. While he accepts that we live in an increasingly cosmopolitan world, he could not forget that "people have, for many centuries, constructed their sense of belonging, their notions of home, of spiritual and bodily power and freedom, along a continuum of sociospatial attachments. These extend from local valleys and neighborhoods to denser urban sites of encounter and relative anonymity, from national communities tied to a territory to affiliations across borders and oceans. In these diverse contact zones, people sustain critical, non-absolutist strategies for survival and action in a world where space is always already invaded. These competences can be redeemed under a sign of hope as 'discrepant cosmopolitanisms.' But it is a chastened hope associated more with survival and the ability to articulate locally meaningful, relational futures than with transformation at a systemic level."[15]

But the search for "locally meaningful, relational futures" brings us back to Mehta and Edmund Burke. Burke did not deny the possibility of conversations between "mature individuals" (shades of Kant) who could agree upon common policies based upon experiences that were local and particular in character. Burke even envisaged the possibility of systemic transformations arising out of such conversations. "To be attached to the subdivision, to love the little platoon we belong to in society," he wrote, "is the first principle (the germ as it were) of public affections. It is the first link in the series by which we proceed towards a love to our country and to mankind."[16] Far from being hostile to cosmopolitanism, Anthony Appiah concludes, Burke "posits the culminating value of universalism, that overarching love of humanity; that's how love of the little platoon is justified, as a first step along the path." Envisaged here is the possibility of some kind of "rooted cosmopolitanism," and this is what Appiah celebrates so emphatically.[17] It roughly seems to accord with the sentiments expressed in Clifford's formulation of "discrepant cosmopolitanisms" and parallels in some ways the more subversive argument for a "globalization from below," based either in place-based revolutionary politics of the sort that the anthropologist Arturo Escobar supports or the "subaltern cosmopolitanism" put forward by de Sousa Santos.

All these "adjectival cosmopolitanisms," as we might call them, have in common the idea of somehow combining respect for local differences with compelling universal principles. From such a standpoint, local patriotism rooted in the geographies of actual places and cosmopolitanism are not necessarily at odds. Rather, they have the potential, as Richard Falk also, somewhat surprisingly, maintains, to "share a common commitment to refashioning conditions for the humane state, the humane region, and, depending on the success of transnational social forces, a decent inclusive globalism."[18] Unlike the postcolonial critics of John Stuart Mill, however, Appiah can take Mill's theory as one pillar of his cosmopolitanism because it can be merged, he says, with the specifics of existing local cultural traditions (in his case, that of the Asante). The "rooted cosmopolitanism" and the "cosmopolitan patriotism" he seeks to defend are openly and unashamedly rooted in local loyalties (that is, in some version of the anthropological and geographical facts) and form the basis for a global cosmopolitanism of negotiated difference. This cosmopolitanism "is not the name for a dialogue among static closed cultures, each of which is internally homogeneous and different from all the others: not a celebration of the beauty of a collection of closed boxes." Appiah thus seeks to evade the charge of any narrowly based communitarian politics. He searches for what Clifford called "the ability to articulate locally meaningful, relational futures." "Localism is," he argues, "an instrument to achieve universal ideals, universal goals," and on this basis it is possible to construct "a form of universalism that is sensitive to the ways in which historical context may shape the significance of a practice."[19] This double grounding (in both universals and particulars), he argues, makes possible a truly "liberal cosmopolitanism." There was, therefore, nothing wrong with both Locke and Smith grounding their liberalism in their own local worlds because that is what all liberals do everywhere. What counts is precisely the fact that they can do so everywhere across the globe while negotiating local differences.

But then there is the problem of how local histories and cultural traditions are to be understood. His father's pride in Asante tradition, Appiah suggests, was just as important as his father's British education and admiration for John Stuart Mill in grounding his universal conception of respect for and dignity of the individual as a basic human right against the arbitrariness of colonial and postcolonial state power. But Appiah also suggests that private property rights are necessary to escape from conditions of poverty, and in so doing he happily sets aside "traditional" Asante practices and beliefs concerning common property rights. Appiah's claim to the mantle of Asante cultural history is highly selective, as well as seductive, evidence as to his own cultural authenticity, and conveniently so. It is not even clear from Appiah's own account whether his father's embrace of liberal human rights doctrine was derived more from Asante cultural tradition or from his experience of struggle within the postcolonial Ghanaian state. When we look more closely at where Appiah ends up, we see the construction of an apologia for the extension of liberal (not Asante) doctrines. At the core lies respect for individual human rights and the free development of individuality (as Mill depicted it), supplemented by tolerance toward diverse social, religious, and cultural practices, values, and beliefs.

The great lesson of anthropology, according to Appiah, is that "when the stranger is no longer imaginary, but real and present, sharing a human social life, you may like or dislike him, you may agree or disagree; but, if it is what you both want, then you can make sense of each other in the end."[20] This capacity for making sense of each other, for setting up conversations between mature individuals who are willing to lay aside stereotypical representations of each other, plays the central role in Appiah's "rooted cosmopolitanism." But unfortunately, this fails to touch the core of contemporary forms of neoliberal capitalism, even as it offers a shining path out of religious bigotry (of the sort that Osama bin Laden and Christian fundamentalists compose) and the petty hatreds that identity politics both highlights and strives to combat. Appiah's proposals could possibly smooth out the conflicts that derive from cultural and religious differences. But they would do so at the price of ignoring the political-economic inequalities that capitalism typically foments (exacerbated under neoliberalization). In effect, Appiah ends up supporting the liberal and neoliberal imperialist practices that reproduce class inequalities, while soothing our nerves with respect to multicultural differences. His proposals occupy center stage in a longstanding conversation in the United States about identities, diversity, differences, and all manner of discriminations, a conversation that addresses everything under the sun, as Walter Benn Michaels points out in *The Trouble with Diversity*, except the central difference that really matters: class power and its associated social inequalities.[21] Treating others with respect costs nothing, Michaels notes, but the redistribution of real income and of political power does.

Nothing that Appiah proposes has anything to say about the immense concentrations of wealth that have in recent years been amassed on Wall Street, except to imply that we should be prepared to tolerate that difference, too.

But within Appiah's superficially rooted cosmopolitanism lurks a far deeper and more complicated history of place-based and territorialized identifications, with nationalism in the forefront politically and the phenomenology of place taking a central position philosophically. With respect to the latter, the imposing figure of Heidegger (who, as Mehta claims, is "very Burkean") looms large. Heidegger's attachment to "dwelling" and "place," coupled with his thorough rejection of all forms of cosmopolitanism (capitalist, socialist, modernist), seem to place him in polar opposition to Kantian ethics, while giving a substantial philosophical and phenomenological foundation for place-based theories of morality. And Heidegger attracts at least as much attention as Kant among the scholarly elite. The battle between those two philosophical titans and their intellectual legacies will doubtless rage for the next millennium in much the same way that the founders of Greek philosophy (both Kant and Heidegger drew heavily for inspiration on different strains of pre-Socratic thought) defined major intellectual schisms in the past. But can Heidegger give a metaphysical foundation, a philosophical voice, to the stubborn particularities of Kant's Geography?

Heidegger's work is, however, distinctly odd in one respect. The phenomenological experience of objects, places, spaces, time, and cultures (languages and myths) makes "place" the "first of all things" and "the locale of the truth of being."[22] Heidegger is the preeminent theorist of that fundamental geographical concept we refer to by the word *place*. Yet Heidegger never writes about actual places. Though his affiliations with the Germanic cultural and linguistic tradition are evident, and his postwar texts in particular (such as *Building, Dwelling, Thinking*) were oriented to the practical problem of how to establish a more solid sense of place in a world of massive destruction, he fails to connect his abstracted metaphysical conceptions to the material circumstances of any particular lived geography let alone any specific urban design. The most famous exception is his invocation of the traditional Black Forest farmstead as a site of "dwelling" and "being" in the world. But his presentation is romanticized. Furthermore, the conditions he describes are not material qualities of the contemporary world, and this particular *heimat* (as Germans call their dwelling-place) is not something to which he or we can return. There is no real geographical or anthropological content to his writing. This has left his followers struggling with the question of how to define the "authentic" qualities of "real places" and what the "rootedness" of morality or of a work of art might mean—in short, how to give more tangible meaning to Heidegger's abstractions through actual place-building. We also have to struggle to comprehend Heidegger's earlier support for National Socialist ideology (and its active political practices) and his failure ever to offer any clear renunciation of that connection. What do such cultural and political attachments have to do with his philosophical arguments about "dwelling" in "place"?

It was Hannah Arendt, whose abiding attachment to Heidegger also proved a puzzle, who coined the phrase "the banality of evil" as she watched the Eichmann trial in Israel.[23] The connections here may seem far-fetched or even bizarre (though no more so than the intimacy of the Arendt-Heidegger relationship). For what if Arendt's characterization of evil has some subterranean connection to the banalities of "dwelling," of "place," and of "*heimat*" as social constructs essential to the human condition? What if Deshpande's "sedimented banalities of neighborliness" are so fundamental to the human condition (as even Foucault ended up acknowledging of space) that they form the preconditions—the Kantian propaedeutic—for all knowledge of and action in the world (including the actions of an Eichmann)? Such a possibility gets evaded in contemporary discussions of cosmopolitanism. Appiah avoids any mention of Heidegger, as well as any reference to those who have developed theories of place and rootedness based on Heideggerian phenomenology. Heidegger rates only one entry in Cheah and Robbins's *Cosmopolitics,* even though the frequent appeals to some sort of "rooted" cosmopolitanism are loud and recurrent throughout the book. But the one entry for Heidegger, in the chapter by Jonathan Ree, is telling: "nationalism is not overcome through mere internationalism; it is rather expanded and elevated thereby into a system." That thought leads Ree to comment on "a fateful slippage in Kant's transition over the years from the idea of cosmopolitanism to that of perpetual peace. In the process the shining ideal of world citizenship was reduced to a grudging concession that we ought always to allow foreigners to travel among us unmolested, provided they do not stay around too long—an obligation Kant derived from a 'right all men have . . . founded upon common possession of the surface of the earth, whose spherical form obliges them to suffer others to subsist contiguous to them.' Apart from this depressing reflection on human sociability, *Perpetual Peace* allows cosmopolitan rights to be swallowed up again by the old patriotisms they were originally meant to supplant."[24]

The evident rootedness of peoples in places draws us rather awkwardly back to Kant's actual geographical world characterized by folly and aggression, childish vanity and destructiveness—the world of prejudice that cosmopolitanism must counteract or actively suppress in the name of human progress. It takes but a small step then to see geographies and spatialities (and local loyalties) not only as disrupting order and rational universal discourse, but as potentially undermining universal morality and goodness, much as they undermine the basic foundational propositions of economic theory. They become, as with Kant's Geography, the fount of all prejudice, aggression, and evil (culminating in that of the Eichmann sort). Is this why Bush got away so easily with banal simplifications about an "axis of evil" in the same way that Reagan could so easily slip into a language of "evil empires," while both repeatedly emphasized universal values of liberty and freedom? Heidegger's uncompromising honesty takes us precisely to the metaphysical root of what these particular "evils" (both intellectually and politically) might be about. Iraq, East Timor, Rwanda-Burundi, Darfur, and, of course, the Holocaust tell us what they might mean on the ground.

But this cannot be the whole story. Heidegger certainly did not believe himself to be peddling the metaphysics of inherent evil. His acolytes would find unacceptable the equation of the banality of evil with his metaphysics. From this perspective, the evil (if such it is) arises out of the dreadful cosmopolitan habit of demonizing spaces, places, and whole populations as somehow "outside the project" (of market freedoms, of the rule of law, of modernity, of a certain vision of democracy, of civilized values, of international socialism). What if Heidegger is right in insisting that cosmopolitanism is always rooted and situated? This is what Burke presumed, and it is the position that Appiah now fiercely defends. Isaiah Berlin, for his part, was prepared to see Kant as "an unfamiliar source of nationalism," going on to remark how the Kantian ideal of autonomy of the will, when blended with the doctrines of Herder and Rousseau, "led to terrible explosions" and "pathological" forms of nationalism.[25] The peculiar version of U.S. cosmopolitanism then makes sense. It is based, says T. Brennan, on "an Americanism distinct from patriotism yet also jealously supportive of an American imperial myth about the portable ethos of the United States as an idea and (with some modifications) an honorable longing."[26] Was this not the logic that President Bush articulated in his speech on the first anniversary of the terrorist attacks of September 11? But the myth cannot be sustained without emphatic denunciations and demonizations of "evil empires" and resistant spaces—"axes of evil"—or even problematic spaces (such as Pakistan) where forces of good and evil seem to be locked in never-ending battle.

This tension points to an intellectual impasse in our dominant representations. An awful symmetry defines the two positions. And the symmetry is secured because we cannot deal with "the banality of evil" (as manifest in the particular barbarisms encountered in East Timor, Rwanda-Burundi, or Yugoslavia, and intercommunal violence in the Middle East, in South and Southeast Asia, or even in our own cities, such as Los Angeles and Paris) because, in turn, we cannot understand and deal with geographical and anthropological difference itself. When we do confront it, the banality of the formulations boggles the mind. Nussbaum, for example, inveighs against the collapse of values and the indifference to cosmopolitan goals in the United States: "The state of things in very many parts of the world gives reason for pessimism; when, two hundred years after the publication of Kant's hopeful treatise, we see so many regions falling prey to ethnic and religious and racial conflict; when we find that the very values of equality, personhood and human rights that Kant defended, and indeed the Enlightenment itself, are derided in some quarters as mere ethnocentric vestiges of Western imperialism; when, in a general way, we see so much more hatred and aggression around us than respect and love."[27]

How easy it is to justify (as does Ulrich Beck) from this perspective those NATO bombs on Serbia as a grand effort to eradicate a particular geographical evil in the name of Kantian ethics. It is even possible to support State Department threats against Serb authorities for crimes against humanity, while supporting the U.S. refusal to sign the international convention against such crimes in order to protect Henry Kissinger and his innumerable colleagues from indictment. And are we not all obliged and grateful to President Bush for leading the noble struggle to rid us of evil in Iraq, for leading the great struggle to bring liberty, freedom, and democracy to the world? This is the point where we need to follow Kant into the nether regions of his Geography and Anthropology and there, perhaps, expose the wrong-headed metaphysical foundation given to that geographical perspective by Heidegger. The only way out of the impasse, the only way to break the awful symmetry around which politics has rotated so fearfully for two centuries or more, is to press for that "revival of the science of geography" that will not only "create that unity of knowledge without which all learning remains only piece-work" but also better equip us to deal with the palpable but seemingly intractable problem of the banality of geographical evils on the ground.

So how, then, are geographical, anthropological, and ecological knowledges constituted, and what relation should they have to the noble universal theories that we typically espouse and all too often act upon with the usual complement of disastrous failures? Unfortunately, there is no adequate framework of historical geographical and anthropological knowledge begging and striving to be incorporated into all other forms of knowing. These fields of study are, for a variety of reasons, a terrible mess when it comes to providing a coherent and substantial answer to the grand question that Nussbaum posed but did not resolve. The reasons for this mess are multiple. While there are, as we shall see, critical elements within the particular disciplinary frames of geography and anthropology that could contribute to such an intellectual project, geography in particular has far too often functioned and continues to function as a mere handmaid to state power, imperialist politics, and corporate interests. Anthropology, while it has stronger roots in the Enlightenment tradition of critical engagement, is not immune to such charges either (as shown by its involvement in counter-insurgency practices in Latin America and Southeast Asia in the 1960s, and by the recent revelations of the involvement of some anthropologists in military activities in Iraq). Although some individual geographers (beginning with Alexander von Humboldt) and anthropologists (beginning with Kant and Herder) have worked assiduously on matters of great import, the main body of materials that has been accumulated and assembled within each of these disciplinary frames is incoherent and anecdotal rather than systematic.[28] The seeming ordinariness if not banality of geographical descriptions, for example, fails to inspire deep philosophical reflection, even as it conceals, as I hope to show, basic problems of understanding. Had Heidegger spent time describing actual banal geographies as examples of how we might better dwell, then we might not read him with the same attention and respect. And then there is the problem of how we are to understand the geographical racisms and ethnic prejudices of Kant's actual geographical writings and the repeated failures of theorists of all stripes to confront the banal problematics of materialist geographies, ecologies, and anthropologies, as opposed to delighting in the conveniently disruptive metaphors of spatiality. The conventional response is to maintain respect for Kant by shearing off his geographical writings as aberrant, unfortunate, and irrelevant to his philosophical contributions, much as we accept that Heidegger can be the preeminent theorist of place without ever actually writing about one.

Finally, we also have to recognize that if geographical and anthropological understandings do indeed occupy a "propaedeutic" position in relation to all other forms of knowing, then those other forms of knowing internalize secret ways in which they incorporate geographical and anthropological understandings into their own statements. The implication is that geography and anthropology cannot be isolated disciplines in their own right that contribute to how other disciplines construe the world, because they are forms of knowledge that flow everywhere even as we pretend to ignore their explicit forms. From this it also follows that geography is too important to be left to geographers, and anthropology is too important to be left to anthropologists. The contrary is also true, for no forms of knowledge can work without explicit, tacit, or secret suppositions about the geographical and anthropological world in which they operate, any more than the major institutions of our social order—whether the state and the military, the security apparatus and public health, corporations, the IMF and the World Bank, the NGOs and the trade unions, the Vatican and the United Nations, militant and revolutionary movements—can operate as if they are outside of geographical and anthropological conditionalities. If geography and anthropology describe the conditions of possibility of all forms of thinking (including, as Foucault recognized, the whole of Kant's philosophy) and of action, of being and becoming in the world, then we surely need to get beyond the banalities and learn more about how such conditions of possibility are actually constituted.

Part Two
Geographical Knowledges

Chaper Six
Geographical Reason

If the devil all too often lies in the geographical details when it comes to either the unintended consequences or the willful use of noble universal principles of freedom, justice, and liberty for nefarious purposes of localized exploitation and domination, then we should pay very careful attention to how geographical knowledges are produced and used. Their seeming banality, furthermore, makes it seem as if there is little or no point in interrogating the obvious, when it turns out that this obviousness is a mask for something far more problematic. The ruses of geographical reason are far more sophisticated and complicated than those of history. So what, then, is geographical reason all about?

I begin with what those who have called themselves geographers say about what they do and how they think geographical knowledge might best be understood. At a talk given to the U.S.–based National Council on Geographic Education in November 1963, William Pattison usefully identified what he called "The Four Traditions of Geography." His thesis was that American geographers "had established a broad consistency" in their work by interweaving these traditions in their practices. The traditions, he pointed out, are "all of great age and have passed into American geography as parts of a general legacy of Western thought." Furthermore, he asserted (though without advancing any evidence), these principles are "shared today by geographers of other nations." The four traditions he identified were "(1) a spatial tradition, (2) an area studies tradition, (3) a man-land tradition and (4) an earth science tradition."[1]

The spatial tradition, emphasizing the importance of location, distances, direction, and spatial patterns in the organization of political and economic life, went back at least to the Greeks. It was codified in the *Geographia* of Ptolemy in the second century C.E. and achieved particular historical expression in the development of cartography and mapmaking (a topic since exhaustively covered in the magnificent *History of Cartography* initiated by David Woodward and J. B. Harley).[2] This tradition acquired additional authority from Kant's view of geography as a specialized spatial science, dealing exclusively with spatial ordering, separate from history. Armed with geometry as a distinctive language, this kind of geography could and often did aspire to the status of a mathematically based science. Transport networks, river networks, social networks could all be brought together under the aegis of the mathematics of network analysis, for example.

The area studies tradition, traced back to Strabo's monumental *Geography* (a political tract "addressed to the statesmen of Augustan Rome," evidently as an aid to better governance), focused on the nature of places, their differentiation, and, hence, upon their unique qualities. The uniqueness derived as much from history as from location. The qualitative nature of places and their peoples (their culture or, as Kant preferred to describe it in his Anthropology, their "national or local character") had, however to be approached nomothetically through an idiographic method seemingly at odds with the scientific pretensions of geography as a spatial science. Regional and area studies have always formed one pillar in geographical work, and in recent years the fascination with the concept of "place" has given this tradition new life.

The man-land tradition, which goes back at least to Hippocrates' work *On Airs, Waters and Places,* has long sought to clarify the question (which Kant also regarded as central) of "man's" position in the natural order. While the answers to that question have been extraordinarily diverse—varying from God's intelligent design (apparently espoused by President Bush) through environmental determinism to a secular ideology of human mastery over nature—the tradition of "man-land" studies has long been a powerful presence within the discipline. At the time when Pattison was writing, for example, the landmark volumes of a Wennergren-financed symposium (which brought together geographers and anthropologists, as well as philosophers and historians), *Man's Role in Changing the Face of the Earth,* established a significant benchmark of reflection that has lasted until today. The early history of this tradition in Western thought is comprehensively recounted in Clarence Glacken's monumental *Traces on the Rhodian Shore.*[3]Lately, this tradition has strengthened and diversified significantly in response to rising concerns over environmental issues.

But the earth sciences tradition, Pattison observed, "confronts one with a paradox." The idea of a comprehensive and distinctive discipline of physical geography, which Kant failed so miserably to construct, has faded, as specialized earth sciences have emerged, such as geology, climatology, meteorology, hydrology, oceanography, vulcanology, paleontology, geomorphology, and the like. The sciences of ecology, botany, and forestry have likewise flourished as independent specialized sciences. Physical geographers contribute to this general earth science effort, though only, it must be said, in a minor way. This tradition is not, therefore, central, and geographers themselves have sometimes sought (unsuccessfully) to exclude it. But the umbilical cord that links geographers with the earth and biological sciences is hard to cut. Not only did the discipline of geography originate in association with them (geology in particular), but it also continues to sustain its institutional position by branching out into, or being absorbed by, more broadly conceived environmental science programs. Geographers cannot, in any case, do without some aspects of earth and ecological sciences if they are to pursue their interests in "man-land" relationships and even area studies with any depth and rigor.

Pattison closed by peremptorily concluding that these four traditions, "though distinct in logic are joined in action." He hoped, furthermore, that geography would be better able to secure both its "inner unity and outer intelligibility" through "a widened willingness to conceive of and discuss the field in terms of these traditions."

Most geographers would, I suspect, recognize Pattison's descriptions of the different traditions (naïvely given though they are) as a general representation of the fields of knowledge (together with overlaps) with which they and their colleagues typically engage. But the unities are not always easy to spot in the actual practices of geographers. Fragmentations are everywhere in evidence. A "discipline" that simultaneously embraces geographical information systems, paleo-ecology, and desert geomorphologies, as well as urban political economy, postmodernist and queer spatial theory, and the cultural aesthetics of landscape, obviously has an identity problem. The presumption that there is some singular and settled way of understanding a unified academic field of knowledge called "geography," or that there is some as-yet-to-be discovered "essentialist" definition of its subject matter, has always been suspect. Whenever some group of geographers has attempted to impose such an essentialist definition (as the area studies specialists did in the United States after World War II and the spatial theorists tried to do in the 1960s in the English-speaking world), the results have been disastrous. Pattison is therefore right to insist that the plurality of perspectives within the discipline should be considered a source of strength rather than of weakness.

But Pattison's eclectic account of the four traditions united under the magic sign of synthesis unfortunately glosses over serious difficulties. To begin with, the four traditions are not easily conjoined since they presuppose, on the surface at least, radically different epistemologies and demand very different standards of validation. In the case of the first three traditions, Pattison tacitly treats the concepts of space, place, and environment as both foundational and fundamental without subjecting them to any critical scrutiny or even attempting any systematic elaboration of their possible range of meanings (they are all, as we shall see, extremely complicated terms). The half-hearted attempt to treat the earth sciences as inherently geographical though outside the discipline per se appears particularly problematic. But it is also indicative. If we examine how the concepts of space, place, and environment function more generally in knowledge construction, we find they are by no means unique to the discipline of geography. These concepts (in some form or other) play critical roles in almost every discipline, from ecology and biology to anthropology, sociology, and political science. They are widely appealed to in the humanities also. One can argue that this is necessarily so, because foundational and universal concepts of this sort articulate, as Kant and Foucault quite properly understood, "the conditions of possibility" of all other forms of knowledge. They are omnipresent in all academic disciplines because no discipline can do without them. How professional geographers use and deploy them then becomes a relatively minor question. But an examination of how these concepts work in other disciplines suggests that they acquire quite different meanings in different settings. This is the true paradox that Pattison hints at, but fails to analyze, in the case of the environmental sciences.

But the matter has to be pressed further. There is a significant difference between geographical knowledges held in the various branches of academia and the geographical knowledges that function in different institutional settings (such as state apparatuses, the World Bank, the Vatican, the media, the CIA, the public at large, the military, NGOs, the tourist industry, multinational corporations, financial institutions). The tension between geography as a distinctive discipline and geography as a way of assembling, using, and understanding knowledge of a certain sort in a variety of institutional settings is palpable.[4] Geographical knowledges are widely dispersed throughout society, and they deserve to be understood in their own right. Different institutions, furthermore, demand and themselves create radically different kinds of geographical knowledge. The tourist industry, for example, does not highlight the geography of social distress or of contagious diseases in its brochures, and in its zeal to persuade us to buy its products and services it actively produces all manner of imaginary and fantasy geographies of the mind that have nothing necessarily to do with what exists upon the ground. One important outcome of activities of this sort is that only a very small portion of the geographical knowledges available and actively in use in society is found within the discipline of geography or, for that matter, within the academy more generally. A "critical sociology" of all of these forms of knowing is therefore required if we are to understand their role in managing, sustaining, and transforming the socio-ecological order. This has to be the focus when we seek to instill a proper education in matters geographical in relation to the pursuit of distinctive cosmopolitan projects. The putative field of "critical geography" studies that arose during the 1970s and which now sees itself in alliance with critical theory more generally is one arena where such studies might be pursued. Professional geographers, by reflecting carefully upon how the "conditions of possibility" of geographical knowledge operate within their own works, may be in position to contribute (as indeed some of them have done) to the wider question of the role of geographical knowledges in sustaining or transforming a given socio-ecological order. A critical examination of how geographical knowledges were mobilized in the causes of imperialism or colonial administration, and as an adjunct to military strategy, has been a significant endeavor in recent years.[5]

Pattison was, I think, correct to identify the first three traditions and their foundational concepts of space, place, and environment as constituting the conceptual core of all geographical knowledges. He was also quite correct to point out that these traditions are longstanding, but wrong to confine their provenance to Western thought. There is abundant evidence from the historical, anthropological, and geographical record that the art of spatial orientation (including its symbolic uses and techniques of representation, such as cognitive if not actual mapmaking), to take just one example, has been fundamental to all forms of human social organization. We need then to ask: in what ways do these foundational geographical concepts enter in as conditions of possibility for all forms of knowing? Geographers, it must be said, have not been particularly assiduous in answering this question. Nor have they been very active in exploring the epistemological status of their foundational concepts. To be sure, there have been phases of controversy over concepts such as "region" (are they real, waiting to be discovered by scientific inquiry, or mere intellectual constructs through which we conveniently aggregate data about the world?) and "the environment" (is it a causative and determinant agent, or merely a passive condition of human action?). And there was a brief phase of intense controversy over whether the Kantian definition of geography as an exclusively spatial science was appropriate.[6] But it is hard to avoid the conclusion that most practicing geographers have complacently accepted the banal and obvious view of their own academic terrain and happily worked away within its inherent limitations. Geographers have the interesting habit of asking questions of major import and trivializing the answers. Not much insight is to be gained, therefore, from any deep engagement with the history of geographical thought in the narrow sense of documenting what geographers themselves have to say—though, as Glacken shows in his monumental work on the history of environmental thought, there is much to be gained from an examination of what all manner of thinkers have to say about human action in the natural order.

There is, however, a broader way to understand the role that geographical knowledges might play, and that is to examine their historical significance in past social orders as well as in processes of social and ecological change. The long process of commercial expansion that has been with us since at least 1492 if not before (and which we now refer to as "globalization") depended, for example, upon the accumulation of certain kinds of geographical knowledge. This was as true for the Renaissance (when mapping of the world was crucial to the project of human command over it) as it is today. Reciprocally, geographical understandings have affected the paths of political-economic development and environmental transformation (through, for example, the recognition of environmental constraints, the identification of new resources and commercial opportunities, understandings of cultural diversity, or the promotion of utopian plans for new cities and towns). Even if the knowledge is erroneous, substantial unintended consequences can follow. The Portuguese in their early explorations sought, among other things, an imagined Christian kingdom of Prester John located on the other side of Islam. The effects on global history of this erroneous geographical idea were substantial. Ebenezer

Howard erroneously believed that economic and social ills could be cured by adequate town planning (a specific kind of spatial determinism), with significant consequences for processes of urbanization that sought to instantiate that belief. How, then, does this dialectical relationship between political-economic and socio-ecological change, on the one hand, and geographical knowledges, on the other, actually work?

The need to answer such a question remains as pressing as ever. The most recent phase of globalization has, as we have seen, been powered by a neoliberal, free market agenda in which privatization and the opening up of markets worldwide to entrepreneurial and multinational capitalism have become a dominant moving force backed by the military and commercial power of the United States. With the collapse of the Berlin Wall, the triumph of the free market seemed complete worldwide. Highly mobile finance capital has become more dominant, at the same time as revolutions in transport, communications, and information technologies have broken down many spatial barriers. Geographical structures and relations have been profoundly altered. The seemingly fixed geographical configuration of political-economic powers has become fluid. The result has been reterritorialization of the world and uneven geographical developments of all sorts (increasing social and geographical inequalities of wealth and power, patchwork quilts of political instability, a resurgence of local nationalisms, localized environmental stresses). Geographical differences have become more, rather than less, significant because highly mobile capital is in a position both to shape them and to take advantage of them. In addition, geopolitical stresses and tensions (even regional wars) are as widespread as ever. As a result, many of the major institutions of global capitalism (the IMF, the World Bank, the G7) have had to adjust their views and rebuild their geographical vision. But they have also encountered a rising tide of criticism (from some mainstream economists, such as Stiglitz and Sachs, as wells as from the NGOs, the churches, to say nothing of the street protesters in Seattle, Washington, Bangkok, Melbourne, and Genoa) of the soulless commercialism of multinational capitalism, its injustices, and its insensitivity to local cultural and other geographical differences. The problem of applying universal concepts of freedom, justice, need, and dignity across the variegated spaces and complex geographies of cultural and political-economic divergence has no easy solution. This brings us back to the initial question: how are we to understand the complex relationship between universal claims about rights, property, freedom, democracy, and the market, and the geographical particularities with which the world abounds? One condition of possibility of finding an answer to that question rests upon an exploration of how key geographical concepts work. And the triumvirate of concepts—space, place, and environment—that constitutes the core of geographical reason—no matter whether in a tribal council, the World Bank, a corporate boardroom, or a neighborhood association—is the place to start. Therefore, we now turn to a deeper elaboration of these concepts. In so doing we need also to be mindful of Pattison's closing question: in what ways can these different conceptual realms, seemingly so logically different from each other, be conjoined in action?

Chapter Seven
Spacetime and the World

The word *space* internalizes multiple meanings. Confusions arise because different meanings get conflated in inadmissible ways. Sorting out these confusions is essential to the clarification of all manner of substantive issues. Alfred North Whitehead claimed, for example, that "it is hardly more than a pardonable exaggeration to say that the determination of the meaning of nature reduces itself principally to the discussion of the character of time and the character of space."[1] I would likewise claim that many of the key terms we use to characterize the world around us—such as *city, state, community, neighborhood, ecosystem* and *region*—cannot properly be understood without a prior consideration of the character of both time and space. It is in this sense that I believe Kant was correct to regard a proper knowledge of geography—in this instance, the proper characterization of space and time—as a necessary precondition as well as the ultimate endpoint of all forms of human enquiry.

In what follows, I outline a view of space in relation to time that draws in the first instance upon my own practical work on issues of urbanization and uneven geographical development at a variety of scales (from imperialism to social relations in the city). This view has also been shaped by a partial reading of the long history of philosophical debate on the nature of space and time, as well as by scrutinizing the more recent inquiries of many geographers, anthropologists, sociologists, and literary theorists on the subject.[2]

The summary framework to which I appeal operates across two dimensions. On the first, we encounter three distinctive ways of understanding space and time: absolute, relative, and relational. Across the second dimension, we encounter another three definitions (most notably argued for by Lefebvre): space as materially sensed, conceptualized, and lived. I shall go on to argue that space is constituted by the integration of all these definitions. These different ways of understanding space must be kept in dialectical tension with each other if we are to understand how concepts of space and time condition our possibilities, as Kant would put it, to understand the world around us.

The First Dimension

Absolute space is fixed and immovable. This is the space of Newton and Descartes. Space is understood as a preexisting, immovable, continuous, and unchanging framework (most easily visualized as a grid) within which distinctive objects can be clearly identified, and events and processes accurately described. It is initially understood as empty of matter. This is the space to which Euclidian geometry could most easily be adapted. It is amenable to standardized measurement and open to calculation. It is the space of cadastral mapping, Newtonian mechanics, and its derivative engineering practices. It is a primary space of individuation—*res extensa,* as Descartes put it. Individual persons and things, for example, can clearly be identified in terms of the unique location they  occupy in absolute space and time. No other person can be exactly in your or my space at a given time. Location in absolute space and time is, therefore, the means to identify the individuality and uniqueness of persons, things, and processes. Distinctive places, for example, can be identified (named) by their unique location on a map. Within this conception, measurement and calculability thrive. When Descartes's engineer looked upon the world with a sense of mastery, it was a world of absolute space (and time) from which all uncertainties and ambiguities could in principle be banished and in which human calculation could uninhibitedly flourish. Socially, absolute space is the exclusionary space of private property in land and other bounded entities (such as states, administrative units, city plans, and urban grids). Bounded spaces can be conceptualized as containers of power. Space of this sort is clearly distinguishable from time. Spatial ordering is one thing. Absolute time unfolding on a linear line stretching to an infinite future is another. History, from this perspective, has to be construed as distinct from geography. This was, as we have seen, Kant's view, so although he departed from Newton in grounding knowledge of space and time in the intuition of the synthetic a priori, he followed the Newtonian separations of space and time in practice.

Relative space is mainly associated with the name of Albert Einstein and the non-Euclidean geometries that began to be constructed most systematically in the nineteenth century.[3] This is preeminently the space of *processes and motion*. Space cannot here be understood separately from time. History and geography cannot be separated. All geography is historical geography, and all history is geographical history. This mandates an important shift of language from absolute space *and* absolute time to the hyphenated concept of relative space-time. The relative space-time of transportation relations and of commodity and monetary circulation looks and is very different from the absolute spaces of private property. The uniqueness of location and individuation defined by bounded territories in absolute space gives way to a multiplicity of locations that are equidistant from, say, some central city location in terms of time it takes to move to and from that location. Relative identity is multiple rather than singular. Many people can be in the same place relative to me, and I can be in exactly the same place as many other people relative to someone else. We can create completely different maps of relative locations by differentiating between distances measured in terms of cost, time, or modal split (car, bicycle, or skateboard), and we can even disrupt spatial continuities by looking at networks and topological relations (the optimal route for the postman delivering mail, or the airline system operating through key hubs). We know, given the differential frictions of distance encountered on the earth's surface, that the shortest distance (measured in terms of time, cost, energy expended) between two points is not necessarily given by the way the legendary crow flies. Furthermore, the standpoint of the observer plays a critical role in establishing perspectives. The typical New Yorker's view of the world, as the famous Steinberg cartoon suggests, fades very fast as one thinks about the lands to the west of the Hudson River or east of Long Island.

All of this relativization does not necessarily reduce or eliminate the capacity for individuation or control, but it does indicate that special rules and laws are required for the particular phenomena and processes under consideration. Measurability and calculability become more complicated. There are multiple geometries from which to choose. The spatial frame varies according to what is relativized and by whom. When Gauss first established the rules of a non-Euclidean spherical geometry to deal with the problems of surveying accurately upon the curved surface of the earth, he also affirmed Euler's assertion that a perfectly scaled map of any portion of the earth's surface is impossible. If maps accurately represent directions, then they falsify areas (Greenland looks larger than India on the Mercator map). Each map projection tells its relative truth, even though it is mathematically correct and objective. Einstein took the argument further by pointing out that all forms of measurement depended upon the frame of reference of the observer. The idea of simultaneity in the physical universe, he taught us, has to be abandoned. It was, of course, Einstein's achievement to come up with exact means to examine such phenomena as the curvature of space when examining temporal processes operating at the speed of light.[4]

Difficulties do arise, however, as we seek to integrate understandings from different fields into some more unified endeavor. The spatio-temporal frame adequate to represent energy flows within and through ecological systems may not be compatible with that appropriate to represent capital flows through global financial markets. It is hard to put the rapidly changing spatio-temporal rhythms of capital accumulation into the same space-time framework as that required to understand global climate change. Such disjunctions, though difficult to work across, are not necessarily a disadvantage, provided we recognize them for what they are. Comparisons between different spatio-temporal frameworks (as is also the case in the selection of map projection) can illuminate problems of political choice. Do we choose a map projection centered on New York, London, or Sydney, and why is the northern hemisphere always represented as being "on top"? Do we favor a spatio-temporal frame appropriate to follow financial flows or that of the ecological processes they would and frequently do disrupt? When the second Bush administration refused for eight years to deal with global climate change problems because to do so might disrupt the economy, it tacitly evinced a preference for one spatio-temporal framework (the flow of capital as well as the electoral cycle, for example) over another. Relative space-time frameworks are not necessarily stable, either. New technologies of transport and communications have historically and geographically transformed spatio-temporal relations. Relative distances of social interaction and communication between New York, London, and Paris have changed radically over time. Relative locations have shifted, sometimes rapidly, as a result.[5]

The idea that processes produce their own space and time is fundamental to the relational conception. This idea is most often associated theoretically with the name of Leibniz who, in a famous series of letters to Clarke (effectively a stand-in for Newton), objected vociferously to the absolute view so central to Newton's theories.[6] Leibniz's primary objection was theological. Newton made it seem as if God were inside a preexisting space and time, rather the maker of space-time through the creation of matter. The absolute view diminished God's stature. Our contemporary version of this controversy would ask whether the supposed big bang origin of the universe occurred in space and time or whether it was the creation of space-time.

In the relational view, matter and processes do not exist *in* space-time or even affect it (as in the case of relative space-time). Space and time are internalized within matter and process. Whitehead argued, for example, that "the fundamental order of ideas is first a world of things in relation, then the space whose fundamental entities are defined by means of those relations and whose properties are deduced from the nature of these relations." It is impossible to disentangle space from time. They fuse into spacetime (the hyphen disappears). Memories and dreams are the stuff of such a fusion. How can we understand things, events, processes in terms of the relational spacetime they produce? Identifications and individuation become problematic, if not seemingly impossible. Relational spacetime implies, furthermore, the idea of internal relations, and this, as B. Ollman has long argued, is fundamental to dialectical modes of analysis.[7] An event, process, or thing cannot be understood by appeal to what exists only at some point. It (the event, process, or thing) crystallizes out of a field of flows into what Whitehead calls either "an event" or "a permanence." But in so doing "it" internalizes everything going on around it within that field of flows, in past, present, and even future. Many individuals assembled in a room to consider political strategies, for example, bring to their discussion within that absolute space a vast array of past experiences, memories, and dreams accumulated directly or indirectly (through reading, for example) from their engagements with the world, as well as a wide array of anticipations and hopes about the future. Under the relational view disparate influences flow from everywhere to everywhere else. These influences can, at least momentarily, congeal to form "monads" (Leibniz's preferred term), or "events" or "permanences" at identifiable "moments" (in Whitehead's terms). Identity here means something quite different from the sense we have of it from absolute space or even in relative space-time. It becomes open, fluid, multiple, and indeterminate.

Identities become, in short, "immaterial but objective." But that is how we live day by day.

The implications of this argument are far-reaching. For example, the conception that time (and history) is the domain of masculinity and that space (geography) is the domain of femininity—made much of in some of the feminist literature—rests, as E. Grosz for one openly acknowledges, on accepting the Cartesian view of space and time as both absolute and separable.[8] How we understand masculine-feminine relations changes dramatically as we move through the relative to the relational understanding of spacetime. This is so, as Whitehead argues, because the gender power relation precedes the production of spacetime under the relational interpretation. If, therefore, space has indeed become the domain of femininity and history that of masculinity, it would simply be because the gender power relations have made it so. I seriously doubt the utility of this kind of simplistic distinction, however, because the historical geography of gender relations has produced far more nuanced spatio-temporalities than this in almost all social orders that I have encountered or read about. The relational view of spacetime also generates entirely different understandings of the concept of "place" compared to the territorial closures and exclusions that can so easily be manufactured out of absolute conceptions. Edward Casey, as we shall see in chapter 8, rests his whole argument for the priority of "place" over "space" on a profound objection to the emptiness of space presupposed in the Cartesian/Kantian absolute view.[9] His objections dissolve when confronted with relational interpretations. And if, as Whitehead maintains, all conceptions of nature arise out of our understandings of space and time, then our whole understanding of the socio-ecological dialectic, as well as our understanding of place, is directly implicated in how we formulate our understandings of space and time.

What can this possibly mean for everyday understandings and practices? Consider a few examples where the relational conception makes intuitive sense. If we ask, along with Whitehead, what is the time and space of a thought or a memory, then we are hard pressed to find a material answer. We cannot find thoughts or memories by dissecting someone's brain. They seem to fly around in our heads without themselves taking material form, although an active brain obviously exists as a material enabling structure that supports the processes of thinking and memorizing. But if the thoughts and memories are themselves immaterial, fluid, and unstable, they can and often do have solid material and hence objective consequences when they animate action.

In relational spacetime, direct measurement is problematic, if not impossible. But why should we believe that spacetime only exists if it is quantifiable and measurable? Dreams and memories cannot be dismissed as irrelevant because we cannot quantify and measure their spacetime. The inability of positivism, empiricism, and traditional materialism to evolve adequate understandings of spatial and temporal concepts beyond those that can be measured has long been a serious limitation on thinking through the role of spacetime. Relational conceptions bring us to the point where mathematics, poetry, and music merge, where dreams, daydreams, memories, and fantasies flourish. That, from a scientific (as opposed to aesthetic) viewpoint, is anathema to those of a narrow positivist or simple materialist bent. The problem is to find adequate representations for the immaterial spatio-temporality of, say, social and power relations. Kant, as we have seen, recognized the dilemma in a shadowy form. Though absolute space was characterized as real and independent of matter in the Newtonian scheme of things, there was no way to come up with an independent material measure of it outside of the matter and the processes it contained. Kant here tried to build a bridge between Newton and Leibniz by incorporating the concept of space within the theory of aesthetic judgment and the synthetic a priori. In so doing, Kant encountered some horrendously difficult contradictions.[10] Kant clearly failed to recognize the potential power of Leibniz's relational conception. Leibniz's return to popularity and significance, not only as the guru of cyberspace but also as a foundational thinker with respect to more dialectical approaches to mind-brain issues and quantum theoretical formulations, signals a return toward relational views. Many contemporary thinkers go beyond absolute and relative concepts and their more easily measurable qualities, as well as beyond the Kantian compromise. But the relational terrain is a challenging and difficult terrain to cultivate successfully. Einstein, for one, could never accept it and so denied quantum theory until the end. Alfred North Whitehead did much to advance the relational view in science.[11] David Bohm's explorations of quantum theory also focus heavily on relational thinking. G. Deleuze made much of these ideas in reflections on baroque architecture and the mathematics of the fold, drawing inspiration from Leibniz and Spinoza.[12] Together with Guattari, Deleuze charted some very interesting relational paths of analysis in texts like *A Thousand Plateaus*. Relational conceptions have recently entered into the political arena, particularly through the work of Arne Naess on deep ecology and through T. Negri's recent writings on empire and the multitude; both of these authors, it should be noted, draw heavily upon the relational thinking of Spinoza rather than upon Leibniz.[13] And A. Badiou's theorization of "the event" as fundamental to our understandings has led him to a particular kind of political critique.[14]

But why and how would I, as a working geographer, find the relational mode of approaching spacetime useful? The answer is quite simply that there are certain topics, such as the political role of collective memories in urban processes, that can be approached only in this way. I cannot box collective memories in some absolute space (clearly situate them on a grid or a map), nor can I understand their circulation according to the rules, however sophisticated, of circulation and diffusion of ideas in relative spacetime. I cannot understand much of what Walter Benjamin does in his Arcades project without appealing to relational ideas about the spacetime of memory. I cannot even understand the idea of the city without situating it in relational terms. If, furthermore, I ask the question, of what the Basilica of Sacré Coeur in Paris, Tiananmen Square in Beijing, or "Ground Zero" in Manhattan *means*, then I cannot come to a full answer without invoking relationalities.[15] And that entails coming to terms with the things, events, processes, and socio-ecological relations that have produced those places in spacetime.

So is space (space-time and spacetime) absolute, relative, or relational? I simply don't know whether there is an ontological answer to that question. In my own work I think of it as all three. I reached that conclusion thirty years ago and I have found no particular reason (nor heard any arguments) to make me change my mind. This is what I then wrote:

> space is neither absolute, relative or relational in itself, but it can become one or all simultaneously depending on the circumstances. The problem of the proper conceptualization of space is resolved through human practice with respect to it. In other words, there are no philosophical answers to philosophical questions that arise over the nature of space—the answers lie in human practice. The question "what is space?" is therefore replaced by the question "how is it that different human practices create and make use of different conceptualizations of space?" The property relationship, for example, creates absolute spaces within which monopoly control can operate. The movement of people, goods, services, and information takes place in a relative space because it takes money, time, energy, and the like to overcome the friction of distance. Parcels of land also capture benefits because they contain relationships with other

> parcels . . . in the form of rent relational space comes into its own as an important aspect of human social practice.[16]

Are there rules for deciding when and where one spatial frame is preferable to another? Or is the choice arbitrary, subject to the whims of human practice? The decision to use one or other conception certainly depends on the nature of the phenomena under investigation or the political objective in mind. The absolute conception may be perfectly adequate for determining narrow issues of property boundaries and border determinations for a state apparatus (indeed, it was no accident that the absolute view came into prominence, if not dominance, around the time the Treaty of Westphalia of 1648 set up the system of European sovereign states), but it helps me not a whit with the question of what is Tiananmen Square, Ground Zero, or the Basilica of Sacré Coeur. Conversely, state apparatuses obsessed with identities, control, and surveillance turn again and again to the absolute conceptions of space and time as central to their mission of effective governance and control, thereby imposing absolute conceptions on much that is or could be either relative or relational. I therefore find it helpful—if only as an internal check—to sketch in justifications for the choice of an absolute, relative, or relational frame of reference. Furthermore, I have sometimes presumed in my practices that there is some hierarchy at work: that relational space can embrace the relative and the absolute, relative space can embrace the absolute, but absolute space is just absolute and that is that. But I do not recommend this view as a working principle, let alone try to defend it theoretically. I find it far more interesting in principle to keep the three concepts in dialectical tension with each other and to constantly think through the interplay among them. Ground Zero is an absolute space at the same time as it is located in relative space-time and has relational positionalities.

From this I derive the first preliminary determination: the three conceptions of absolute, relative, and relational need to be held in dialectical tension with each other if we are to understand space as a condition of possibility of all other forms of knowing.

The Second (Lefebvrian) Dimension

H. Lefebvre constructs a quite different way of understanding spatiality in terms of human practices. He derives (almost certainly drawing upon

Cassirer's distinctions among organic, perceptual, and symbolic spaces, though, as is often the case in French intellectual circles, without acknowledgment) a tripartite division of material space (space as experienced through our sense perceptions), the representation of space (space as conceived), and spaces of representation (space as lived). The second set of terms (those placed within parentheses) are not identical to the first, but in what follows I shall largely ignore that problem. I will pay most attention to the bracketed meanings, since these refer concretely to human behavior and social practices.[17]

Material space is, for us humans, the world of our sense perceptions, as these arise out of the material circumstances of our lives: for this reason it can be called the perceptual space of primary experience mediated through human practices. We touch things and processes, feel them, see them, smell them, hear them, and infer the nature of space from those experiences. How we represent this world of experienced sense perceptions is, however, an entirely different matter. We use abstract representations (words, graphs, maps, diagrams, pictures, geometry, and other mathematical formulations) to represent space as we perceive it. In so doing we deploy concepts, codes, and abstractions. The correspondence between the material space of sense perceptions and its representation is always open to question and frequently fraught with dangerous illusions. But Lefebvre, along with other Marxists like W. Benjamin, insists that we also have imaginations, fears, emotions, psychologies, fantasies, and dreams. What Lefebvre calls, rather awkwardly, spaces of representation refers to the way we humans live—physically, affectively, and emotionally—in and through the spaces we encounter. Venturing down a dark street at night we may feel either fearful or adventurous. One person may welcome open space as a terrain of liberty while another, a victim of agoraphobia, may feel so insecure as to experience a panic attack. Some people welcome open borders for immigrants, while others want to keep them tightly shut for security reasons. A geographer like Yi-fu Tuan has focused much of his work on cultural and personal divergences in how space is lived.[18]

The way we live in space cannot be predicted from material stimuli and sense perceptions or even from its manner of representation. But this does not mean that the three dimensions are disconnected. Lefebvre keeps them in a dialectical tension. Mutual and reciprocal influences flow freely between them. The way a space is represented and conceptualized, for example, may affect (though not in easily predictable ways) how the space is lived in and even materially sensed. If I have just read a horror story or Freud, then my feelings about venturing down that dark corridor-like street will surely be affected. Furthermore, my physical experience may be heightened (my senses may be "on edge," as we say) precisely because I am living in that space in a particular state of fear or anticipation. Conversely, the strange spatio-temporality of a dream, a fantasy, a hidden longing, or a lost memory, or even a peculiar thrill or tingle of fear as I walk down a street, may lead me to seek out conceptualizations and representations that can convey something of what I have lived to others. The artist Edvard Münch may have had a nightmare of some sort. Passing through a series of conceptualizations and codes of representation, he produced a material object, the painting called *The Scream,* open to the material sense experience of others. We look at this thing—the painting—and get some feeling of what it might have been like to live that moment in that way. The physical and material experience of looking at the spatial ordering of the painting is mediated by representations in such a way as to help us understand the immateriality of a state of mind. I suspect that the continuing fascination with Velázquez's painting called *Las Meniñas* (a fascination that led Picasso to undertake endless variations on its themes and Foucault to use it as a foundational starting point for reflection in *The Order of Things*) is due to the way its spatial ordering within the absolute space of the pictorial frame conveys some sense of the shifting sands of changing social power relations in that place and time. This is certainly the manner in which T. J. Clark interprets the rising tide of hostile responses to Courbet's famous painting *Burial at Ornans* as it progressed from the provinces toward Paris where the rentier landed class were all too familiar with and fearful of the nature of the class relations it portrayed.[19]

The spaces and times of representation that envelop and surround us as we go about our daily lives likewise affect both our direct sensory experiences and the way we interpret and understand representations. We may not even notice the material qualities of spatial orderings incorporated into daily life because we adhere to unexamined routines. Yet through those daily material routines of everyday life we absorb a certain sense of how spatial representations work and build up certain spaces of representation for ourselves (such as the visceral sense of security in a familiar neighborhood or the sense of being "at home"). We only notice when something appears radically out of place. It is the dialectical relation between the categories that really counts, even though it is useful for purposes of understanding to crystallize each element out as a distinctive moment to the experience of space and time.

Many contemporary artists, making use of multimedia and kinetic techniques, create experiential spaces in which several modes of experiencing space-time combine. Here, for example, is how Judith Barry's contribution to the Third Berlin Biennial for Contemporary Art is described in the catalogue:

> In her experimental works, video artist Judith Barry investigates the use, construction and complex interaction of private and public spaces, media, society, and genders. The themes of her installations and theoretical writings position themselves in a field of observation that addresses historical memory, mass communication, and perception. In a realm between the viewer's imagination and media-generated architecture, she creates imaginary spaces, alienated depictions of profane reality. . . . In the work *Voice Off* . . . the viewer penetrates the claustrophobic crampedness of the exhibition space, goes deeper into the work, and, forced to move through the installation, experiences not only cinematic but also cinemaesthetic impressions. The divided projection space offers the possibility of making contact with different voices. The use and hearing of voices as a driving force, and the intensity of the psychic tension—especially on the male side of the projection,—conveys the inherent strength of this intangible and ephemeral object. The voices demonstrate for spectators how one can change through them, how one tries to take control of them and the loss one feels when they are no longer heard.

Barry, the catalogue concludes, "stages aesthetic spaces of transit that leave the ambivalence between seduction and reflection unresolved."[20]

From this description we see how we need to take our understanding of space and time to an even deeper level. There is much here that refers back to the distinctions between absolute space and time (the cramped physical structure of the exhibit), relative space-time (the sequential motion of the visitor through the space), and relational spacetime (the memories, the voices, the psychic tension, the intangibility and ephemerality, as well as the claustrophobia). Yet we cannot let go of the Lefebvrian categories either. The constructed spaces have material and sensual, conceptual and lived dimensions.

A Structural Representation

Reflection on the description of Barry's work leads me to take a speculative leap in how best to construe the multidimensionality of space and time. Consider, then, how matters look when we put the threefold division of absolute, relative, and relational space-time (spacetime) in direct relation to the tripartite division of sensed, conceptualized, and lived. The result is a three-by-three matrix (fig. 1). The points of intersection within the matrix suggest different modalities of understanding the meanings of space, space-time, and spacetime. Unfortunately, a matrix mode of representation is restrictive because it depicts an absolute space only. Since I am also resorting to a representational practice (conceptualization), I cannot do justice to space as materially sensed or lived, either. The matrix therefore has limited revelatory power. If it is treated as a fixed classification that constitutes all there is, then my project will come to naught. I find it helpful, however, to consider the combinations that arise at different intersections within the matrix as a way to jump-start the analysis. Reading across or down the matrix yields complex combinations of meanings. Confining oneself to just one modality of thinking becomes impossible. Actions in absolute space end up making sense only in relational terms, for example. The rigidities of the matrix can be surpassed only by placing all the categories and their combinations in dialectical tension. Let me illustrate.

FIGURE 1

	SPACES OF MATERIAL PRACTICE (EXPERIENCED)	REPRESENTATIONS OF SPACE (CONCEIVED)	SPACES OF REPRESENTATION (LIVED)
ABSOLUTE SPACE AND TIME (NEWTON /DESCARTES/KANT)	@	@	@
RELATIVE SPACE-TIME (EINSTEIN)	!@!	!@!	!@!
RELATIONAL SPACETIME (LEIBNIZ)	K?!@!?K	K?!@!?K	K?!@!?K

In what space or spacetime is the site known as "Ground Zero" in Manhattan located, and how does this affect our understanding of that site and of what should be built there? It is, plainly, an absolute physical space, and someone holds the property rights to it. It stands to be materially reconstructed as a distinctive thing. There is much discussion about retaining walls and load-bearing capacities. Engineering calculations (informed by Newtonian mechanics) and competing architectural designs (representations) are submitted. Aesthetic judgments on how the space, once turned into a material artifact of some sort, might be lived in by those who visit it or work there are also influential considerations. Only after it is built will we get some sense of how people might live in that space. The problem is to so arrange the physical space as to produce an emotive affect while matching certain expectations (commercial as well as emotive and aesthetic) as to how the space might be experienced. Once constructed, the experience of the space may be mediated by representational forms (such as guide books, museums, and plans) that help us interpret the intended meanings of the reconstructed site. But moving dialectically across the dimension of absolute space alone is much less rewarding than the insights that come from appealing to the other spatio-temporal frames. Capitalist developers are keenly aware of the relative location of the site and judge its prospects for commercial development according to a logic of exchange relations and the flows of people, commodities, and capital that relate to it and give the site its potential commercial and speculative value. Its centrality and proximity to the command and control functions of Wall Street are important attributes, and if transportation access can be improved in the course of reconstruction, then so much the better, since this can only add to future land and property values. For the developers, the site does not merely exist *in* relative space-time: the re-engineering of the site offers the prospect of transforming relative space-time so as to enhance the commercial value of the absolute spaces (by improving access to airports, for example). The temporal horizon is then dominated by considerations of the amortization rate and the interest/discount rate applying to fixed capital investments in the built environment.

But there would almost certainly be popular objections, led by the families of those killed at that site, to thinking and building only in these absolute or relative space-time terms. Whatever is built at this site has to say something about individual and collective memory. Memory is immaterial but objective and hence relational. There will likely also be pressures to say something about the meanings of community and nation, as well as about future possibilities (perhaps even a prospect of eternal truths). Nor could the site ignore the issue of relational spatial connectivity to the rest of the world. Can something experienced as a local and personal tragedy be reconciled with an understanding of the international forces that were so powerfully condensed within those few shattering moments in a particular place? Will we get to feel in that space the widespread resentment in the rest of the world toward the way U.S. hegemony was so selfishly being exercised throughout the 1980s and 1990s? Will we get to know that the Reagan administration played a key role in creating and supporting the Taliban in Afghanistan in order to undermine the Soviet occupation and that Osama bin-Laden turned from being an ally of the United States into an enemy because of U.S. support for the corrupt regime in Saudi Arabia? Or will we only learn of cowardly, alien, and evil "others" out there who hated the United States and sought to destroy it because of all it stood for in terms of liberty and freedom? The relational spatio-temporality of the event and the site can be exhumed with enough dedicated digging. But the manner of its representation and of its materialization is uncertain. The outcome will clearly depend upon political struggle. And the fiercest battles will have to be fought over what relational spacetime the rebuilding will invoke, what it will project as a symbol to the world. Governor Pataki, for example, in canceling the plans for a Freedom Museum there on the grounds that at some time in the future an exhibit critical of U.S. policies might be mounted, mandated that nothing should be placed at the site that could ever be offensive to the memory of those who died there. His intent was to refuse any and all expression of criticism of U.S. military and financial engagements with the world. Capitalist developers would not be averse to combining their mundane commercial concerns with inspiring symbolic statements (emphasizing the power and indestructibility of the political-economic system of global capitalism that received such a body blow on September 11, 2001) by erecting, say, a towering phallic symbol that spells defiance. They seek their own distinctive expressive power in relational spacetime. But there are all manner of other relationalities to be explored. What will we know about those who attacked, and how far will we connect? The site is and will have a relational presence in the world, no matter what is built there, and it is important to reflect on how this "presencing" works: will it be lived as a symbol of U.S. arrogance or as a sign of global compassion, reconciliation, and understanding? Taking up such matters requires that we embrace a relational conception of what the absolute space of Ground Zero is all about. And that, it turns out, is where the most interesting and contested meanings lie.

The Space and Time of Marxian Theory

This general framework provides a beginning point for the integration of concepts of space and time into all segments of literary and social theory. Let me illustrate how it works in relation to Marxian theory in particular. Marx is a relational thinker. In revolutionary situations, such as that of 1848, he worried, for example, that the past as memory might weigh like a nightmare on the brain of the living. He went on to pose the key political question: how might a revolutionary poetry of the future be constructed in the then and there?[21] He also pleaded with Cabet not to take his communist-minded followers to the New World. There, Marx averred, the Icarians would only replant the attitudes and beliefs internalized from the experience of the old. They should, Marx advised, stay as good communists in Europe and fight for a revolutionary transformation in that space, even though there was always the danger that a revolution made in "our little corner of the world" would fall victim to the global forces ranged around it.[22]

In the works of Marxists like E. P. Thompson, R. Williams, and others, we find different levels of appreciation of spatio-temporality.[23] In Williams's novel *People of the Black Mountains*, for example, the relationality of spacetime is central. Williams uses it to bind the narrative together, directly emphasizing the different ways of knowing that come with different senses of spacetime: "If lives and places were being seriously sought, a powerful attachment to lives and to places was entirely demanded. The polystyrene model and its textual and theoretical equivalents remained different from the substance they reconstructed and simulated. . . . At his books and maps in the library, or in the house in the valley, there was a common history which could be translated anywhere, in a community of evidence and rational enquiry. Yet he had only to move on the mountains for a different kind of mind to assert itself; stubbornly native and local, yet reaching beyond to a wider common flow, where touch and breadth replaced record and analysis; not history as narrative but stories as lives." [24]

For Williams the relationality comes alive when walking on the mountains. It centers a completely different sensibility and feeling than that constructed from the archive. While it is stubbornly local, it reaches beyond to a wider common flow and thereby bridges the gap between geography and locality, on the one hand, and cosmopolitan concerns and some sense of our species being, on the other. These were exactly the sentiments of Elisée Reclus, a famous nineteenth-century anarchist geographer.[25] Interestingly, it is only in his novels that Williams seems able to get at this problem. How then can the broader perspectives I have outlined on the dialectics of space and spacetime become more closely integrated into our reading, interpretation, and use of Marxian theory? Let me lay aside all concern for caveats and nuances in order to present an argument in the starkest possible terms.

In the first chapter of *Capital*, Marx introduces three key concepts of use value, exchange value, and value. Everything that pertains to use value lies in the province of absolute space and time. Individual workers, machines, commodities, factories, roads, houses, actual labor processes, expenditures of energy, and the like can all be individuated, described, and understood in themselves within the Newtonian frame of absolute space and time. This is the domain of physical calculability and rational mathematical modeling of production systems, input-output structures, and systematic planning. Everything that pertains to exchange value lies, in the first instance, in relative space-time because exchange entails movements of commodities, money, capital, labor power, and people over time and space. It is the circulation, the perpetual motion, that counts. Exchange, as Marx observes, therefore breaks through all barriers of (absolute) space and time.[26] It perpetually reshapes the geographical and temporal coordinates within which we live our daily lives. It gives different meaning to the use values we command in absolute space. With the advent of money, this "breaking through" defines an even grander and more fluid universe of exchange relations across the relative space-time of the world market (understood not as a thing but as continuous movement and interaction). The circulation and accumulation of capital occurs, in short, in the first instance in a relative space-time that is itself perpetually subject to change through the ability to move in space-time. But this is the world of a posteriori valuations, of speculative ventures, and the anarchy of market coordinations.

Value is, however, a relational concept. Its referent is, therefore, relational spacetime. Value, Marx states (somewhat surprisingly), is immaterial but objective. "Not an atom of matter enters into the objectivity of commodities as values."[27] As a consequence, value does not "stalk about with a label describing what it is," but hides its relationality within the fetishism of commodities. The only way we can approach it is through that peculiar world in which material relations are established between people (we relate to each other through what we produce and trade) and social relations are constructed between things (prices are set for what we produce and trade). Values are, in short, social relations, and these are always immaterial but objective. They are impossible to measure except by way of their effects (try measuring any social relation of power directly, and you always fail). Value, according to Marx, internalizes the whole historical geography of innumerable labor processes set up in the world market. Many are surprised to find that Marx's most fundamental concept is "immaterial but objective," given the way he is usually depicted as a materialist for whom anything immaterial would be anathema. But he roundly condemns the materialism of those scientists who cannot incorporate history (and, I would add, geography) into their understandings. This relational definition of value renders moot if not misplaced all those attempts to come up with some direct and essentialist measure of it. I repeat: social relations can only ever be measured by their effects. Yet, value can be represented both in the relative space-time of exchange and the absolute space and time of use values. This is what money does.

If my characterization of the Marxian categories is correct, then this shows no priority can be accorded to any one spatio-temporal frame. The three spatio-temporal frames must be kept in dialectical tension with each other in exactly the same way that use value, exchange value, and value dialectically intertwine within the Marxian theory. There would, for example, be no value in relational spacetime without myriad concrete labors constructed in absolute spaces and times (for example, in the factory during the working day). Nor would value emerge as an immaterial but objective power without the innumerable acts of exchange, the continuous circulation processes, that weld together the global market in relative spacetime. Value is, then, a social relation that internalizes the whole history and geography of concrete labors in the world market. It is expressive of the social (primarily but not exclusively class) relations of capitalism constructed on the world stage. It is crucial to mark the temporality involved, not only because of the significance of past "dead" labor (fixed capital, including that embedded in built environments), but also because of all the traces of the history of proletarianization, of primitive accumulation, of technological developments that are internalized within the value form. Above all, we have to acknowledge the "historical and moral elements" that always enter into the determination of the value of the commodity labor power.[28] We then see Marx's theory working in a particular way. The spinner and weaver embed value (that is, abstract labor as a relational determination that has no material measure) in the cloth by performing concrete labor in an absolute space and time. The objective power of the value relation is registered when they are forced to give up making the cloth and the factory falls silent because conditions in the world market are such as to make this activity in that particular absolute space and time valueless. While all this may seem obvious, the failure to acknowledge the interplay among the different spatio-temporal frames in Marxian theory often produces conceptual confusion. Much discussion of so-called "global-local relations" has become a conceptual muddle, for example, because of the inability to understand the different spatio-temporalities involved.[29] We cannot say that the value relation *causes* the factory to close down, as if it is some external abstract force. It is the changing concrete conditions of labor in the absolute spaces of Chinese factories that, when mediated through exchange processes in relative space-time across the world market, transform value as an abstract social relation in such a way as to bring a concrete labor process in the Mexican factory to closure. A popular term like *globalization* functions relationally in exactly this way, even as it disguises the value form and its reference to class relations. If we ask: "where is globalization?" we can give no immediate material answer.

We can see this dialectic at work in Marx's understanding of how money comes to represent value. A particular use value—gold—is produced in a particular way in a particular place and time. Through exchange in relative space-time that particular commodity, by virtue of its qualities of consistency and permanence, begins to take on the role of a money commodity (other commodities, such as silver, copper, or cowrie shells could do the job equally well). Its use value is that it stay permanently in circulation within the relative space-time sphere of exchange value. To function more effectively as a means to circulate commodities, relational symbols of money (coins, paper money, and monies of account) are constructed. Money becomes a relational form that nevertheless retains its position in relative space-time as well as in absolute space and time (the coin I have in my pocket). But its presence in these three spheres centers a whole series of contradictions between the universal and the local, the symbolic and the tangible, the functional and the transcendental. Marx analyzed these contradictions in a particular place and time, but we still live these contradictions today, though in very different ways. How do we understand the symbolic forms of global money on the world market (the symbols that cover the financial pages of our newspapers) in relation to the coins we carry in our pockets? In what ways are the contradictions that Marx warned us might be the source of financial and monetary crises still with us, indeed, even more emphatically so now than when Marx wrote?

So far, I have largely confined attention to a dialectical reading of Marxian theory down the lefthand column of the matrix. What happens when I start to read across the matrix, instead? The materiality of use values and concrete labors in the factory is obvious enough when we examine the laborer's social practices and sensory experiences in absolute space and time. But how should this be represented and conceived? Physical descriptions are easy to produce, but the social relations (themselves not directly visible or measurable) under which the work is performed are critical also. Within capitalism the wage laborer can be conceptualized (second column) as a producer of surplus value for the capitalist, and this can be represented as a relation of exploitation. This implies that the labor process is lived (third column) as alienation. Alienated subjects are likely to be, the argument goes, revolutionary subjects. Under different social relations—for example, those of socialism or anarchism—work could be lived as creative satisfaction and conceptualized as self-realization through collective endeavors. It may not even have to change materially in order to be reconceptualized and lived in a quite different way. This was, after all, Lenin's hope when he advocated the adoption of Fordism in Soviet factories. Fourier, for his part, thought that work should be about play and the expression of desire and should be lived as sublime joy; for that to happen, he believed, the material qualities of work processes would need to be radically restructured.

At this point we have to acknowledge a variety of competing possibilities. In his book *Manufacturing Consent,* for example, M. Burawoy found that the workers in the factory he studied did not generally experience work as alienation.[30] This arose because they smothered the idea of exploitation by turning the workplace into a site for role- and game-playing (Fourier-style) The labor process was performed by the workers in such a way as to permit them to live the process in a nonalienated way. There are obvious advantages for capital in this, since unalienated workers often work more efficiently and are unlikely to act as revolutionary subjects. And, we have to admit, if there is no prospect of any radical revolutionary change, workers might just as well try to live their lives in an unalienated way and have as much fun as they can while they are about it. Capitalists have sometimes promoted measures, such as calisthenics, quality circles, and the like, to try to reduce alienation and to emphasize incorporation (the Japanese were particularly notable for this). They have also produced alternative conceptualizations that emphasize the rewards of hard work and produce ideologies to negate the theory of exploitation. While the Marxian theory of exploitation may be formally correct, therefore, it does not always or necessarily translate into alienation and revolution. Much depends on how the labor process is conceptualized. Part of class struggle is about driving home the significance of exploitation as the proper conceptualization of how concrete labors are accomplished under capitalist social relations. Again, it is the dialectical tension among the material, the conceived, and the lived that really matters. If we treat the tensions in a mechanical way, then we are lost.

Now let me range widely (and perhaps wildly) across the whole matrix to see what can be gained when we think dialectically across its various combinations. Consider, for example, a category such as class consciousness. In what space and time can it be found, and how can it be articulated across the spatio-temporal matrix in ways that lead to fruitful results? Let me suggest in the first instance that it resides primarily in the conceptualized relational space of Marxian theory, that it must therefore be regarded as immaterial and universal. But for that conception to have meaning it must be both relationally lived (be part of our emotive and affective being in the world) at the same time as it operates as an objective force for change in particular (that is, absolute) spaces and times. In order for this to be so, workers have to internalize class consciousness in their lived being and find ways to put that sense of what ought to be into motion across relative space-time. But only when the presence of a class movement is registered in the absolute space and time of streets, factories, corporate headquarters, and the like can the movement register a direct materiality. This even applies at the level of protest. No one really understood what the antiglobalization movement stood for until bodies appeared on the streets of Seattle at a certain time.

But who can say what workers' dreams and beliefs are actually about? Rancière, for example, provides a good deal of substantive evidence that workers' dreams, and hence aspirations, in the 1830s and 1840s in France were far from what many Marxist labor historians have inferred from a study of their material circumstances.[31] They longed, he says, for respect and dignity, for partnership with capital, not its revolutionary overthrow. We can, of course, dispute Rancière's findings, but the world of utopian dreams is a complicated world, and we cannot make automatic presumptions as to how it may be constituted. But we can say with certainty that only when those dreams are converted into an active force do these immaterial longings and desires take on objective powers. And for that to happen requires a dialectical movement across and through the whole matrix of spatio-temporal positionings. Blockages can be thrown up at any point. Hegemonic neoliberal representations of market exchange as both efficient and just create barriers to reconstructions of actual labor processes, because that conception of the market, if accepted, leads people to live their lives as if anything and everything wrong is their own individual responsibility and as if the only answer to any problem lies in strengthening existing or developing new markets (such as in pollution credits). Transformations in spatial and temporal relations through technological innovations alter identities and political subjectivities at the same time as they shift terrains across which the circulation of capital and labor can occur. Time horizons of capital circulation shift with the discount rate, which is in turn sensitive to the circulation of speculative capital in financial markets. The effects are registered in the absolute spaces of neighborhoods (as in the dramatic neighborhood concentrations of foreclosures, largely in African American areas, in U.S. cities during the sub-prime mortgage crisis of 2007), factories, shopping malls, and entertainment centers. But to accept the market logic is to interpret what happens as both inevitable and just, precisely because the market is predominantly (though erroneously) conceptualized as the harbinger and guardian of individual freedoms.

Dynamics

Any absolute form of spatial representation, such as a matrix, has inherent limits. At the heart of Leibniz's relational conception lies the idea that matter and process define space and time. This poses the question: what are the processes at work within the matrix itself? If there are multiple processes, can there be multiple spatio-temporal worlds and multiple matrices? While Leibniz appealed to dreams and fairy stories to demonstrate the possible existence of many spacetime worlds, he considered that God in His wisdom had chosen in practice only one: spacetimes were harmonized with each other by God's embrace of "the principle of sufficient reason." Whitehead, eschewing theology, conceded the possibility that different processes might produce different spacetimes but held that differences were fortunately small. Different spacetimes became "cogredient" (interwoven and consistent) with each other, at least in the physical world. This presumption cannot be (fortunately or unfortunately) sustained in the realm of social practices. Harmony and cogredience here give way to antagonism, opposition, conflict, and contradiction. Capitalism's spacetime is not at all consistent or cogredient with the spacetime of ancient cosmologies or even that of human reproduction (as illustrated, for example, in Harevens's compelling description of the contrast between industrial and family times in the twentieth-century United States). We therefore have to concede, in the first instance, a chaos of different spatio-temporalities attaching to different processes and the very real possibility of huge breaks and disjunctions between them. On this point the anthropological, geographical, and historical evidence is conclusive. The spacetime worlds of the medieval monk, the Nuer, the Ashanti, the Salteaux Indians, the inhabitants of Gawa, and the Wall Street financier are radically different from each other.[32] The spacetime worlds of the homeless, the welfare recipients, the day laborers, the schoolteachers, and the financiers in New York City likewise differ, as is indeed also the case with Mexican, Haitian, Bangladeshi, Korean, and Filipino immigrants living in the same city. The Wall Street financier may operate in one spacetime at work and in another when he goes home and thinks of how soon he might retire and go fishing. His trophy wife will construct a quite different spacetime world and, not being enamored of fishing, will doubtless ultimately demand alimony to live in it. Corporate capital may insist upon a rate of exploitation of a renewable resource (such as a fish population) in ways so inconsistent with the rate of its reproduction that the resource is destroyed.

How, then, are we to make sense of the innumerable and seemingly inconsistent spatio-temporalities that coexist within our social world? There are two answers to this question. The first says we simply cannot arbitrarily impose order upon this chaos and that the chaos is part of the ferment out of which new configurations of social life are perpetually being constructed. This is the picture that seemingly emerges, for example, in D. Moore's examination of intersecting spatio-temporalities in the Kaerezi district of Zimbabwe, where "situated struggles produced an *entangled landscape* in which multiple spatialities, temporalities and power relations combine: rainmaking and chiefly rule; colonial ranch and postcolonial settlements scheme; site-specific land claims and discourses of national liberation; ancestral inheritance and racialized dispossession. Entanglement suggests knots, gnarls and adhesions rather than smooth surfaces; an inextricable interweave that ensnares; a compromising relationship that challenges while making withdrawal difficult if not impossible."[33]

The second view says that while there is plenty of chaos and contradiction, social life in a particular social formation ultimately becomes so ordered as to render one particular configuration of spatio-temporality both dominant (socially imposed as a disciplinary apparatus) and hegemonic (internalized within our very being, often without our realizing it). Different spatio-temporalities, within a particular social formation, tend, therefore, to become cogredient—interwoven and interconnected with each other—in the ways that Whitehead envisages. But not totally so. Resistance and dissent within a social formation may be registered as a longing and desire (sometimes converted into an active struggle) to construct and adhere to some alternative spatio-temporality: the ecological movement is often particularly explicit on this point as it seeks to hold back the spatio-temporalities of capital accumulation in the name of preserving ecological processes (for example, the reproduction of habitats and ecological assemblages of a certain sort). In Moore's account a certain cogredience emerges through an exploration of how "localized land rights became articulated through relational histories of nation, regional anticolonial movements, the legacies of imperial projects in southern Africa, and globalized discourses of development, human rights, and social justice." While held together in the net of governmentality, political economic processes, and racialized dispossession, the different forms of spatio-temporality provide resources with which to contest a dominant social order.

I broadly adhere to this second view. But to advance the argument, we must first understand how it was that capitalism's distinctive spacetime (itself dynamic and by no means fixed and static) came for the most part to be accepted (albeit unevenly across space) as a powerful global norm. How this came to be is a story widely told in the transition from feudalism to capitalism.[34] The forcing of cogredience in our contemporary world arises in the first instance out of the dual powers of state apparatuses and of capital. The effect is to impart (and in some instances to impose) a distinctive spatio-temporal order to the circulation and accumulation of capital and to the bureaucratic coordinations necessary for the state to support the infrastructures required for capital accumulation. These impositions have wide-ranging secondary effects. It is not hard to trace the ways, for example, in which a standardized spatio-temporal discipline penetrates into daily life (our eating and sleeping habits, for example). Foucault is therefore right to suggest that general disciplinary apparatuses, as well as those specifically constructed in various institutional settings (hospitals, prisons, schools, factories, homes) together constitute a system of governmentality that operates through specific spatio-temporal orderings. We all tend to internalize a certain normative sense of a hegemonic spatio-temporality as a result. But this process is not free of internal contradictions (as well as external resistances). To begin with, the circulation and accumulation of capital is not a stable process. It is perpetually changing because of the pressures of competition and the disruptions of periodic crises. One mode of resolution of its crisis tendencies is to accelerate circulation processes (speed up production, exchange, and consumption) and to transform space relations (opening new territories and geographical networks for accumulation). The spatio-temporality of capitalism is therefore in perpetual flux. The relative space-time of exchange relations is particularly sensitive to the mediating technologies of movement (chiefly transport and communications). The effect, however, is to reconstitute definitions right across the matrix. The absolute space of the factory, if it continues to exist at all, no longer has the meaning it once did as relative and relational spatio-temporalities shift. The absolute space of the city has to accommodate to the exigencies of rapid shifts in circulation. The predominant scale (and there is now an immense literature on this) at which spatio-temporality is registered also shifts. The time and space of the world market become compressed. The absolute space of the nation-state then acquires a different meaning as the scalars of economic action in relative space-time shift, posing problems for the contemporary definition of sovereignty and citizenship. Events like the global antiwar protests of February 15, 2003, postulate a different kind of relationality (dependent upon a relative space-time world now made more possible by technological shifts in communications). Again, pressures are mobilized on the absolute spaces of territorial powers from a different direction, one that puts constraints upon the idea of territorial sovereignty as the primary container of power. And then there is the issue of resistance and divergence. Not all activities—as Moore, for one, correctly notes—are incorporated into the shifting spatio-temporal logic of capitalist accumulation.

Politics

In her book *Radical Space*, Margaret Kohn sets out to explore the role that space has played in politics. She is particularly interested in the ways space is implicated in the articulation of transformative political projects. This contrasts with the more familiar imaginary, largely derived from Foucault, of space as integral to a disciplinary regime of power. Kohn focuses attention on the way in which subaltern classes, often under adverse conditions, "created political spaces that served as nodal points of public life." She examines how, for example, the creation of "houses of the people" in many European cities at the beginning of the twentieth century served both practically and symbolically to shape the ideals and practices of radical socialist democracy in opposition to the dominant forms of class power. Space, she argues, "affects how individuals and groups perceive their place in the order of things. Spatial configurations naturalize social relations by transforming contingent forms into a permanent landscape that appears immutable rather than open to contestation. By providing a shared background, spatial forms serve the function of integrating individuals into a shared conception of reality. . . . Political spaces facilitate change by creating a distinctive place to develop new identities and practices. The political power of place comes from its ability to link the social, symbolic, and experiential dimensions of space. Transformative politics comes from separating, juxtaposing, and recombining these dimensions."[35]

Like Lefebvre, Kohn accepts that space has corporeal, symbolic, and cognitive dimensions. She pays particular attention to relationality: "The meaning of a space is largely determined by its symbolic valence. A particular place is a way to locate stories, memories and dreams. It connects the past with the present and projects it into the future. A place can capture symbolic significance in different ways: by incorporating architectural allusions in the design, by serving as a backdrop for crucial events, or by positioning itself in opposition to other symbols. Its power is a symptom of the human propensity to think synecdochally; the chamber of labor, like the red flag, comes to stand for socialism or justice. It is a cathexis for transformative desire. The physical environment is political mythology realized, embodied, materialized. It inculcates a set of enduring dispositions that incline agents to act and react in regular ways even in the absence of any explicit rules and constraints."[36]

Kohn is particularly insistent in adumbrating the totality of interrelations. While history remembers the Turin Factory Councils of 1917–18, she complains, it largely ignores the critical role of the Turin Cooperative Alliance. It was through the latter that workers linked "disputes over the control of production to consumption and leisure, building coalitions between workers and potential allies and transforming struggles rooted in daily life into politics." Through these mechanisms, largely articulated through the houses of the people rather than through the factory, workers "created local and regional geographies of power." The house of the people was a "microcosm of the outside world, combining the spheres of consumption, production and social and political life, but in a more just, rational and egalitarian form." It was "both an organization of resistance and the attempt to institute a universal." In short, it housed and gave symbolic meaning to a localized attempt to define a progressive cosmopolitan project.[37]

Though mainly concerned with a particular place (Italy) and time (the period of formation of socialist movements from the 1890s until the late 1920s), Kohn's work offers support for the general nature of the argument I wish to make. It shows how the spaces of politics and the dialectics of space-time are consequential for and formative of activities of struggle, on the part of those seeking to sustain and consolidate their existing power and of the innumerable social groups, factions, and classes ranged against them, seeking alternatives. The possibility of an alternative cosmopolitanism built upon this process is palpably evident. But care is required in articulating such possibilities. Kohn cannot, for example, provide us with prescriptive lessons or a mechanical model to follow. The historical geography of global capitalism has evolved in such a way as to make the spatio-temporal forms of resistance of yesteryear increasingly irrelevant to the current situation. While the houses of the people still exist as instructive historical markers, it would be rank nostalgia to attempt a contemporary reconstruction of their social and political meanings. This is not to say that analogous efforts are redundant. In Italy in our times, for example, feminist activists have built somewhat similar centers as part of a networked organization for political action. It therefore becomes even more important to get the theory of spatio-temporality for this kind of political work right. And on this point Kohn, like many other analysts, wobbles somewhat by being rather too impressed by Foucault's formulation of heterotopia as an appropriate theoretical framework. So let us look more closely at Foucault's formulation of the problem.

Foucault first articulated the idea of heterotopia in *The Order of Things,* published in 1966. He reflected further on its possibilities in a lecture entitled "Of Other Spaces" delivered to architects in 1967. That lecture was never revised for publication (though Foucault did agree to its publication shortly before he died). Extracted by his acolytes as a hidden gem from within his extensive *oeuvre,* the essay on heterotopia has become a means (particularly within postmodernism) whereby the problem of Utopia could be resurrected and simultaneously disrupted. Foucault appealed to heterotopia to escape from the "no place" that is a "placeful" Utopia.

Heterotopia encompass sites where things are "laid, placed and arranged" in ways "so very different from one another that it is impossible to define a common locus beneath them all." This directly challenged rational urban planning practices as understood in the 1960s, along with the utopianism that infused much of the movement of 1968. By studying the history of spaces and understanding their heterogeneity, it became possible to identify absolute spaces in which difference, alterity, and "the other" might flourish or (as with architects) actually be constructed. This idea appears attractive. It allows us to think of the multiple utopian schemes that have come down to us through history as not being mutually exclusive (feminist, anarchist, ecological, and socialist utopian spaces can all coexist as *potentia*). It encourages the idea of what L. Marin calls "spatial plays" to highlight choice, diversity, difference, incongruity, and incommensurability. It enables us to look upon the multiple forms of transgressive behaviors (usually normalized as "deviant") in urban spaces as important and productive. Foucault includes in his list of heterotopic spaces such places as cemeteries, colonies, brothels, and prisons.[38]

Foucault assumes in this piece that heterotopic spaces are somehow outside the dominant social order or that their positioning within that order can be severed, attenuated or, as in the prison, inverted on the inside. They are construed as absolute spaces. Whatever happens within them is then presumed to be subversive and of radical political significance. But there is no particular reason to accept this assumption. Fascists construct and use distinctive spaces, as do Catholics and Protestants (churches), Muslims (mosques), and Jews (synagogues), as bases for their own versions of a universal and in many respects cosmopolitan project. Under Foucault's formulation, the cemetery and the concentration camp, the factory and the shopping mall, Disneyland, churches, Jonestown, militia camps, the open-plan office, New Harmony (Indiana), and gated communities are all sites of alternative ways of doing things and therefore in some sense heterotopic. What appears at first sight as so open by virtue of its multiplicity suddenly appears as banal: an eclectic mess of heterogeneous and different absolute spaces within which anything "different"—however defined—might go on. Ultimately, the whole essay on heterotopia reduces itself to the theme of escape. "The ship is the heterotopia par excellence," wrote Foucault. "In civilizations without boats, dreams dry up, espionage takes the place of adventure and police take the place of pirates." But here the banality of Foucault's concept of heterotopia becomes all too plain. The commercialized cruise ship is indeed a heterotopic site if ever there was one; and what is the critical, liberatory, and emancipatory point of that? Foucault's words could easily form the text of a commercial for Caribbean luxury cruises. His heterotopic excursion ends up being every bit as banal as Kant's Geography. Worse still, the absoluteness of the space confines, pointing to segregation and stasis rather than progressive motion. I am not surprised that he left the essay unpublished. What is surprising is how widely the essay had been taken up as somehow definitive of ways to define liberatory spaces.

Foucault obviously sensed, however, that something or other was important about spatiality, so that he could not let the issue die, either. He later worried, perhaps with a critique of his own concept of heterotopia in mind, at the way "space was treated as the dead, the fixed, the undialectical, the immobile," while "time, on the contrary, was richness fecundity, life, dialectic." Though it points to critique, this very formulation ends up reaffirming his acceptance of the Kantian view that space and time are separable from each other. If "space is fundamental in any form of communal life," he later observed, then space must also be "fundamental in any exercise of power." And in his lectures published as *Security, Territory, Population,* he recognizes the significance of absolute spatial ordering as part of the disciplinary apparatus—what he called governmentality—that emerged in the seventeenth and eighteenth centuries, and the tension between that ordering and the dynamics of circulation of commodities: people, on the one hand, and the structuring of milieu (place and environment), on the other. But by refusing, when interviewed by the editors of the geographical journal *Hérodote,* to elaborate on the material grounding for his arsenal of spatial metaphors, he evades the issue of a geographical knowledge proper to his understandings (even in the face of his use of actual spatial forms, such as panopticons and prisons, to illustrate his themes). Above all, he fails, as I argued in chapter 1, to give tangible meaning to the way space is "fundamental to the exercise of power."[39]

Lefebvre, however, fashioned an alternative view of heterotopia. In *The Urban Revolution,* published in 1968, a year after Foucault's lecture (of which Lefebvre almost certainly learned from his friends in architecture), Lefebvre set out a counter-definition. He understood heterotopias as spaces of difference, of anomie, and of potential transformation, but he embedded them in a dialectical conception of urbanization. He kept the idea of heterotopia in tension with (rather than as an alternative to) isotopy (the accomplished and rationalized spatial order of capitalism and the state), as well as with utopia as expressive desire. Lefebvre well understood that "space [and space-time] changes with the period, sphere, field, and dominant activity" and that it is suffused with "contrasts, oppositions, superpositions and juxtapositions." As a consequence, "the isotopy-heterotopy difference can only be understood dynamically. . . . Anomic groups construct heterotopic spaces, which are eventually reclaimed by the dominant praxis."[40] The differences captured within the heterotopic spaces are not about segregation and separation, but about potentially transformative relations with all other spaces (as in Kohn's examples). The political problem is to find ways to realize their ephemeral potentialities in the face of powerful forces that work to reclaim them for the dominant praxis. The urban women who founded educational institutions like Bryn Mawr College in the late nineteenth century thought of them as places where a distinctively feminist education could go on, but the story of these colleges is very much about their reabsorption as sites for the reproduction of dominant class and gender relations. Lefebvre's invocation of relative and relational meanings (underscored by the very idea of "the production of space") contrasts with Foucault's heavy emphasis upon the concept of absolute space (even as he invokes the relative space-times of circulatory processes). In Lefebvre's hand, the concept of spacetime becomes both dialectical and alive (potentially progressive and regressive), as opposed to dead and fixed.

It is unfortunate that Lefebvre's dialectical conception is not better known, because the frequent appeal to Foucault's static and rather sterile conception of heterotopia (as opposed to Foucault's later and somewhat looser formulations) invariably exercises a baleful and deadening influence on understandings of progressive possibilities. This was the case, as we saw earlier, in Deshpande's investigation of the relations between globalization, conceptions of the Indian nation, and the construction of "Hindu-ness" (or "Hindutva"). Kohn, for her part, narrowly avoids a similar fate by setting Foucault aside in favor of a more robust implicit theory, in which Lefebvre's more dialectical approach has greater purchase. Moore, likewise, takes the Foucauldian insight on how spatiality and power connect in the theory of governmentality and liberates it from its absolute qualities by injecting the Lefebvrian sense of relationalities into his analytic framework.

Perhaps one of the most difficult of all political issues is to get a handle on how relationalities work. The simplest answer, of course, is to "follow the process." This is in effect what Julia Elyachar does in her book *Markets of Dispossession*. She discovers that different processes not only create different relational spatio-temporalities in the lived lives of Cairo's working inhabitants, but also give rise to totally different notions of value. The workshop culture is not about maximizing profitability through competition but about acquiring respect and social standing over a limited spatio-temporal terrain, even if that means passing potentially profitable business on to others. The attempt by the international financial institutions and microcredit institutions to integrate the productivity of these labor processes in the Cairo workshops into the general circulation of capital not only entails a transformation of value structures and the dismantling of mutually supportive social relations, but also creates a "market of dispossession" in which value of one sort is sucked out of one segment of society (primarily through the organization of a credit system) in order to support the rapacious appetite for surplus value of the international financial institutions of capitalism. Resistance to such depredations rests on the articulation of alternative value structures, attached to quite different social relations than those that capitalism typically defines. Marx's value theory is not a normative or universal measure, but a distinctive product of capitalist social relations where the mottoes "time is money" and "moments are the elements of profit" clearly apply. Different value relations arise out of different social relations. When time is no longer equated with money, then a different value theory necessarily arises. Competing spatio-temporalities are in this way inevitably associated with competing ways, as D. Graeber for one well articulates, of understanding value.[41]

The intangibles of myth and memory, morality, ethics, and rights, of affective loyalties to imagined communities and to places, do a great deal of work with far-reaching objective consequences in the dynamics of political struggle. Conceptual political battles fought in this immaterial realm become crucial. To which myth, memory, or affective loyalty do I, or can I, most effectively appeal? This was what Ulrich Beck had in mind when he complained about the lack of understanding of temporality in the second modernity, but he, too, falls into the trap of presuming that Kantian separation of space and time is adequate. The big question is: in what spacetime do morality, ethics, and rights have their being? The answers do not present themselves to us in immediate material form. Nussbaum invites us to construct relational loyalties with everyone living on planet earth. Can this ideal have any material referent? As Kant pointed out, a certain kind of cosmopolitanism necessarily follows on the material spread of trading and commercial relations between peoples. This underpins the bourgeois cosmopolitanism that Marx and Engels evoked in *The Communist*

Manifesto. Yet, as Marx and Engels also concede, there is something positive and constructive about the bourgeois construction of the world market. The question then arises: how can a more far-reaching and progressive cosmopolitan project—such as that of universal communism—be constructed on the ruins of the bourgeois order? Again, is this a mere abstraction, or are there ways to think through how it might take on objective material form by working dialectically through the matrix of spatio-temporalities as it is constituted in particular places and times?

Consider a tangible example. For everyone living in the advanced capitalist world and increasingly beyond, the simple question of where our food comes from and who is involved in its production quickly spirals outward (when we consider all the inputs of energy, machinery, fertilizers, and the like) into millions upon millions of working people in almost every nook and cranny of the world. The bourgeoisie has indeed lent "a cosmopolitan character to all production." Surely, we have some sort of moral or ethical obligation to all those people who sell us our daily bread? The genius of the market system, however, is that it masks social relationships between people behind social relations between things (that is, the transaction in the supermarket). It is not hard to construct a moral as well as a political imperative to go behind what Marx called "the fetishism of commodities" and imagine a relational bond across the whole world of social labor as a central fact that underpins our moral obligations. But what of the moral obligations of the food producers to us? What happens when we suddenly realize what is incorporated in our food supply, in terms of both abhorrent practices and dangerous materials? The lemons and tomatoes that look so luscious, the shrimps that look so tempting, the chicken that is so cheap, and the corn that turns out to have been genetically modified. . . . Suddenly, the politics of food, the issue of food sovereignty, becomes a matter of political agitation and moral as well as material concern.

This is, it seems to me, the tacit moral problem that Marxian value theory poses. On this basis the outlines of a more just version of the cosmopolitan project become visible. But it is exactly on this relational point that Nussbaum fudges the issue. Bush and the neoliberals are, after all, thoroughly behind a programmatic attempt to bring freedom and liberty to the world through the imposition of private property arrangements, free markets, and free trade. But there is no critical heft in Nussbaum's argument to cut through that fetish argument and to recognize that the objective consequences of the pursuit of that immaterial idea, when mediated through the relative space-times of market exchange into the absolute spaces of private ownership and political control, will be greater and greater levels of social inequality and of uneven geographical development. That kind of cosmopolitan project, as we have seen, simply means the restoration of overwhelming class power within the hands of a small global (cosmopolitan?) elite in a few select locations.

It is tempting, in the face of such outcomes, to argue that all cosmopolitan projects are ineffectual or counterproductive from the standpoint of the mass of the population, particularly those living in the deprived and marginalized spaces of the global capitalist economy. But I want to argue strongly against that conclusion. Nussbaum's starting point, for example, seems about as good as any other. The problem is the failure to articulate what appropriate anthropological and geographical understandings are required to fulfill her noble aims and the inability to grasp how the dialectics of spatio-temporalities, when moving from the immateriality of a relational world through the relative space-time of exchange and into the absolute spaces of factories, school, homes, and territories, have all manner of unintended (or in Bush's case, intended) consequences. It is all too easy, as I have shown in Part One, for noble projects and aims to be perverted into the grubby politics of exploitation, inequality, and rank injustice when they touch upon the ground. A better grasp of the dialectics of spacetime, we may conclude, is a necessary precursor—a condition of possibility, as Kant would put it—for any pursuit of the geography of freedom.

Chapter Eight
Places, Regions, Territories

"Place is the first of all things," said Aristotle, and influential twentieth-century philosophers, such as Heidegger and Bachelard, agree. Edward Casey has probably done more than anyone else in recent years to explore the history and contemporary relevance of this idea. He complains forcefully at the priority given to space over place in Enlightenment thought, and in the process he challenges the very foundation of Kant's cosmopolitanism. Kant's paradigmatic statement that "general knowledge must always precede local knowledge," says Casey, "sets the stage—indeed, still holds the stage in many ways—for the idea that space precedes place." In the Kantian view, as we have seen, space is empty, pristine, and innocent, waiting to be divided and compartmentalized into places of distinctive qualities. But, Casey asks, "what if things are the other way round? What if the very idea of space is posterior to that of place, perhaps even derived from it? What if local knowledge . . . precedes knowledge of space?"

The idea that place is foundational and therefore general, and space contingent and particular, is central to phenomenological approaches. Casey, in his learned history of that idea, from the Greeks onward, provides a compelling and impressive genealogy for this line of thought. The turn of the postcolonial critics of liberal cosmopolitanism toward Heidegger then becomes more readily understandable. In effect, they are demanding that "placefulness" take precedence over the emptiness of the pristine space of the "flat earth" presupposed in liberal, neoliberal, and cosmopolitan theory. Casey's argument for such a turn is powerfully made. "To live is to live locally, and to know is first of all to know the places one is in."

Therefore, "local knowledge is at one with the lived experience." Place, "the privileged site of lived experience and daily life," is necessarily at the center of our understandings of the world.[1] Prioritizing abstract generality, as Kant does, over local knowledge is exactly what Burke and others of his ilk object to. Since Heidegger is, as Mehta puts it, "very Burkean," the tables can be turned on liberal and cosmopolitan theory by invoking Heidegger as well as Burke.

The problem with Casey's argument is that he accepts the Cartesian, Newtonian, and Kantian conceptions of absolute space and time as his foil. From that standpoint, place does indeed appear as something subsequently constructed within a space that is empty, fixed, and abstract. Casey's claim that "place" is where space and time come together only makes sense, furthermore, given the Kantian/Newtonian presumption that space is separable from time. Place takes on a quite different meaning when put in the context of relative space-time and relational spacetime (see chapter 7). Relational spacetime starts with matter and process, and is therefore neither empty nor fixed. Furthermore, space and time are not separable in relational spacetime. Spacetimes and places, from this standpoint, are jointly produced out of matter and of process. For this reason, it proved impossible, as we found in chapter 7, to understand relational spacetime without frequent invocation of actual places like New York's Ground Zero and the cultural centers whose political role forms the subject of Kohn's close inquiries.[2] The only interesting question—to which we shall return—is in what ways it might be useful to distinguish between place and spacetime.

The undoubted historical hegemony of the absolute view of space and time has, however, given rise to a long oppositional tradition of thinking about place as distinct from space. This oppositional literature deserves critical scrutiny, bearing in mind that place-based theories of nationalism, national socialism, and fascism have frequently been the epicenter for the most vicious assaults upon cosmopolitanism as well as liberalism. Possibly for this reason, liberals and cosmopolitans tend to ignore the problematics of place altogether or to write about it with undue caution. But that is no solution. The problem of place must be negotiated and not ignored. After all, the lack of roots in (and seeming indifference toward) the material and affective circumstances of everyday life in particular places was a persistent focus of criticism of both cosmopolitanism and liberalism. In response to Nussbaum, for example, Gertrude Himmelfarb argued that Nussbaum had obscured "the givens of life" and that "parents, ancestors, family, race, religion, heritage, history, culture, tradition, community—and nationality" are "not 'accidental' attributes of the individual," but "essential." A. Escobar likewise rejects neoliberalism and developmentalism on the grounds that they can never hope to realize the human potentialities latent in different social groups living their lives in different places and forging their own distinctive cultures. Edmund Burke as we saw, articulated an even more fundamental argument when he wrote: "I cannot stand forward and give praise or blame to any thing which relates to human actions, and human concerns, on a simple view of the object, as it stands stripped of every relation, in all the nakedness and solitude of metaphysical abstraction. Circumstances (which some gentlemen pass for nothing) give in reality to every political principle its distinguishing colour, and discriminating effect. The circumstances are what render every civil and political scheme beneficial or obnoxious to mankind."[3] The only valid cosmopolitanism, according to Anthony Appiah, is, therefore, a "rooted" cosmopolitanism. [4]

But what on earth is a "rooted" cosmopolitanism rooted in? Can patriotism, nationalism, localism, and doctrines of religious, ethnic, gendered, or racial superiorities all equally well pass muster? If a patriotic cosmopolitanism is perfectly acceptable, then why not a nationalist, theocratic, or even fascist cosmopolitanism? The Italian communist leader Antonio Gramsci, for example, considered Catholic cosmopolitanism (with its seat of wisdom in the Vatican) one of his grand enemies. The principled rootedness in local culture that Appiah embraces ends up folding his cosmopolitanism (understood as appreciation and respect for diversity) back into the classic liberalism of individual rights via multiculturalism, conveniently ignoring the recalcitrant and class-bound world of political-economic processes of capital accumulation. Appiah thereby ends up being supportive of an elitist neoliberal social order, spiced with dashes of multiculturalism, while ignoring the class and social inequalities that arise out of and continuously deepen under an individualized free market capitalism. In more recent times the patriarchal and paternalistic qualities of many cosmopolitan theories have also been duly noted. For this reason, many who overtly embrace "pure" cosmopolitanism and the different shades of liberalism prefer to accord no explicit role to rootedness. Open that door, and all manner of unsavory characters come rushing in. But the door keeps flying open. Kant, after all, taught anthropology and geography in the hopes of displacing religious, cosmological, and transcendental concepts of the human subject by a scientific and, at the end of the day, a "rooted" understanding of "man" as an anthropological and geographical species being. Nussbaum accepts (with respect to our child-rearing practices, for example) that "to give one's own sphere special care is justifiable in universalist terms." More recently, she has argued that nation-state formation is a valid way to aggregate toward a more just global order. If, as Ulf Hannerz remarks, "home is not necessarily a place where cosmopolitanism is in exile," then we cannot avoid taking our affective identifications with particular places seriously, even as we seek to embrace an open cosmopolitanism.[5]

If place is defined as that arena in which we, as individuals, live out our daily lives, then there is a banal sense in which local affections and loyalties cannot possibly be seen as inherently opposed to a cosmopolitan or liberal ethic. But, as we have more than once already noted, when it comes to geographical concepts, banality all too often conceals deep problems. The meaning of "place" as a generic concept in relation to cosmopolitanism has therefore lain largely unexamined, at least until recently, leaving the word (and its numerous cognates) to do immense though often hidden work in shaping our representations and conceptual worlds, as well as our practices. Its variegated and sometimes chimerical meanings need, therefore, to be brought into sharper focus. So what might be the role of local loyalties, of the affective social life that circulates in particular places, in relation to cosmopolitan projects? What roles do geographical differentiations and territorial affiliations have to play in all this? How do affective attachments and political loyalties to particular places and territories actually work? What happens when these very real phenomena are inserted into the cosmopolitan calculus or into liberal and neoliberal economic theories?

Ideas of Place, Region, and Territory

Like "space" and "nature", the idea of "place" turns out to be a multilayered and messy geographical concept. To begin with, we use many generic terms, such as *place, region, area, territory,* and *locality,* to identify a distinctive and usually bounded space as if it is a relatively permanent and separable entity endowed with particular and distinctive qualities. A series of cognate descriptive terms, such as *city, village, hamlet, state, fiefdom, administrative district, neighborhood,* and even *community* and *home and hearth,* as well as more technical-sounding determinations, such as *ecosystem, microclimate, topographic region,* or *landscape,* effectively describe some distinctive and coherent assemblage of particular phenomena in a bounded space. The metaphorical usages of *place* are also important—we all know what it means to feel "out of place" or to be "put in our place," and those metaphorical meanings often flow into physical designations, such as being "in the wrong place at the wrong time" or "on the wrong side of the tracks." But the saying that "there is no place like home" signals the role that deep emotions (both positive and negative) might play in shaping our conceptions, identities, and actions. The sense of belonging and not belonging (and hence of identity and otherness) is closely intertwined with ideas about place and territory. *Place* has so many cognates that it seems in itself to require a small indexical dictionary of intersecting meanings.

Geographers, for their part, have traditionally preferred the term *region* to *place* and have sometimes sought to define their discipline around the practices of regional geography (Pattison's "areal tradition" is of this provenance). But, as Raymond Williams notes from a study of literary uses of *region*, there is a "definite tension" within that word "as between a distinct area and a definite part." If the latter, then the question that immediately follows is: a part of what? and to what degree the part is subordinate to some whole. *Regional*, along with *provincial*, "are terms of relative inferiority in relation to an assumed centre." Regional studies are therefore frequently considered less important than, if not intellectually inferior to, the more universal and hence more central studies of liberal or cosmopolitan theory (thus typically placing geography as a discipline in an inferior position within the academy compared to, say, economics). Yet *regional* also "carries implications of a valuably distinctive way of life," thus making "the distinctive virtues of regions the basis for new forms of identity or degrees of self-government." The regional or the local is seen as the site of authenticity and lived meaning.[6] This was the line of thinking taken by the nineteenth-century French regional geographer, Vidal de la Blache, whose ideas influenced the French Annales school of historians (Fernand Braudel's work on the Mediterranean lies in this tradition, for example). This is the path taken by all those interested in vernacular architecture, the power of regional traditions, and the role of place-bound collective memories in grounding our sense of the world. Vidal did not consider regions as given, but as a symbiotic practical achievement of long-maturing human cultural endeavors in given environmental settings. Distinctive regions and places are made and not given. It is, perhaps, for this reason that a renowned architect like Aldo Rossi took Vidal de la Blache as a foundational thinker in his approach to urbanization.[7]

Among geographers, the term *region* as an object of study carries a different set of connotations than the more subjective and phenomenological connotations of *place*. Regions can be identified and described empirically, as spatially distinctive collective phenomena including ways of life that have evolved through human social action over time. Regional geography, for many, entails classifying, on a territorial basis, data about the different modes of life encountered around the globe. The Kantian distinction between geography, as the "outer knowledge" of human activities as part of nature (and describable in terms analogous to Linnean classificatory systems), and anthropology, as the "inner subjectivities" of human beings responding to experience, is here put in motion. The main controversy in geography has been over whether regions actually exist as real entities open to discovery through empirical inquiry or whether they are simply convenient ways of classifying geographical differentiations in phenomena. The Kantian distinction between objective and subjective meanings typically breaks down, however, when it comes to understanding political organization. Insofar as those collective ways of life achieve some kind of structured coherence, so a connection emerges between objective, reified territorial forms of social organization and concepts of affective human affiliations of community, body politic, or nation (the latter including Kant's ideas concerning national character). While regions, states, or nations may appear at one level as mere imagined abstractions, the sense of a territorial bond and of an affective loyalty to it has enormous political significance. At this point the notions of region, state, and nation converge with those of both territory and place, requiring us to reflect somewhat on the complicated histories of both these latter terms.[8]

The term *territory*, for example, has a fraught but illustrative history that illuminates problems with the equally fraught concepts of "place" and "region." Territorializing behavior has long been noted as a feature of the natural world, of course, and primates and human beings are no exceptions, exhibiting both historically and geographically an astonishing range of territorializing behaviors at a variety of scales. Though such behaviors are often interpreted in terms of a logic of competition, they turn out to have a strong collaborative element: signaling a territorial boundary, in the case of robins, for example, signals to other robins that there is no point entering this territory because the food supply there is already spoken for and partially depleted. The naturalness of territorializing behavior (subject to endless studies by biologists and ethnologists) gives rise to the convenient myth of "the territorial imperative," in which it is claimed that all forms of territorializing behavior are simply an expression of this natural urge.[9] The myth is convenient because it naturalizes the very specific forms of territorializing behavior of human beings that arose historically from the seventeenth century on in Europe. The rise of modern state forms, and political claims to state jurisdiction and sovereignty (as exemplified in the Treaty of Westphalia of 1648), coupled with the instantiation of a legal and administrative system of private property rights, amounted to an administrative and institutional revolution in and codification of territorializing behaviors, the primary requirement of which was the construction of territorial forms that were unambiguous, fixed, and secure. This last required unique appeal to the absolute theory of space and time and the invention of practices of representation (mapping and cadastral survey) that confirmed the fixity and lack of ambiguity. From this time onward the dominance of the absolute theory of the state and the relegation of relative and relational dimensions to subsidiary roles was politically assured in Western Europe. This mode of territorializing behavior was later extended to much of the rest of the world through colonizing practices. There was, clearly, nothing natural about this particular form of territorialization or its underpinnings in absolute theories of space and time: it was a social construction and a political achievement. The work of establishing a cohesive relational sense of territorialized national identity, for example, is long, painstaking, and always fragile. It took, as A. Paasi points out in the case of Finland, a whole army of cartographers, cultural producers, historians and political workers to achieve a sense of Finnish national identity throughout the nineteenth century. But it has always been ideologically useful, once such work has been accomplished, to "naturalize" the sense of nationhood by appeal to Newtonian and Cartesian conceptions of territory, coupled with a temporal tale of mythological origins and a genealogy of descent. For all his supposed "modifications" of the grounds for understanding space and time, this was the absolute framework that Kant adopted to explicate his cosmopolitan world order of federated republics, each with its own, distinctive territorial sovereignty.

The result has been, as David Delaney summarizes it, that territory became "a device for simplifying and clarifying something else, such as political authority, cultural identity, individual autonomy, or rights"; "in order to have this effect, territory itself has to be taken as a relatively simple and clear phenomenon"—hence attachment to the absolute theory of space and time. The general consequence was not only to presume that there were clear-cut territorial entities, called states, that could act, enter into relations with each other, go to war, negotiate treaties, and the like, but that these entities had some "natural" and unambiguous being in absolute space and time, and even that competition and war between these entities (as opposed to collaboration) was wholly natural and therefore inevitable. This happened because, as Delaney again notes, once territory becomes "reified and rendered relatively simple and unambiguous," it "does much of our thinking for us and closes off or obscures [relational] questions of power and meaning, ideology and legitimacy, authority and obligation and how worlds of experience are continuously made and remade."[10] To the degree that the idea of "nation" became connected to that of "state," we actually witness a reversal of Casey's complaint about the hegemony of spatial thinking over place-based experience. In the case of Israel, for example, a relational idea (Zionism) was made concrete by territorializing practices of settlement and capturing global financial flows in such a way as to reify and absolutize the Israeli state on the ground as well as on the map of the world in 1948. More generally, Kant's cosmopolitan vision was trumped politically by nationalism , and his vision of an inevitable progression toward perpetual peace between federated republics lost out to geopolitical territorial contestation between naturalized state entities. Many now belatedly realize that this line of thinking falls into what P. Taylor correctly terms "the territorial trap." [11]

By assuming there is nothing ambiguous and insecure about the territoriality of the state, of sovereignty, and of private property, a fictitious world was created that was supposedly unmovable by, say, the complex spatial dynamics of commodity, money, and people exchanges and capital accumulation in relative space-time. It was also supposedly equally immune to the influence of the complex human immaterial relationalities (such as those of sovereignty, loyalties, and the projection of political authority) occurring within relational spacetime. This fixed imagined world becomes the basis for political decision making. For example, once a region is defined and reified politically, it can then become the subject of state economic and social policy with all manner of effects. Once a territory is defined as a state, it can be construed as an active agent, sometimes with disastrous consequences (two world wars, for example, were largely cast in this theoretical frame).

Extensive analysis of the spatio-temporal dynamics of capital accumulation shows, however, a completely different geopolitical dynamic of uneven geographical development, of recurrent "spatial fixes" and persistent processes of deterritorialization and reterritorialization from the eighteenth century onward. Marx and Engels recognized this tension between fixity and motion clearly enough in *The Communist Manifesto,* and by extending this argument to the dynamics of capital accumulation in relative space-time it is possible to show how processes of capital accumulation necessarily internalize a distinctive form of "the territorial imperative" to create a landscape and territorial structures appropriate to its dynamics in a given place and time, only to undermine and completely displace these landscapes and territorial structures at later points in place and time.[12] Subsequently given philosophical respectability under the imprimatur of Deleuze and Guattari's conceptualization of deterritorialization and reterritorialization (an obvious political problem, given the processes of formation of the European Union), this recognition of the fluidity, relationality, and indeterminacy of territoralizing practices and behaviors has steadily displaced the fixed and frozen notions of territories in absolute space and time that formerly dominated.[13] Contemporary discontents with the traditional theory of the state, in fields including international relations, anthropology, history, and cosmopolitan and Marxian theory, derive from the realization that the earlier, damaging fictions concerning state, sovereignty, and private property need to be transformed if a saner and more secure global political order is to be constructed. In the language adopted here, this means integrating the concept of territory into the dialectics of absolute, relative, and relational modes of approach to space and time.

In fact, the history of "territory" as a concept provides a beautiful illustration of how absolute, relative, and relational conceptions of space and time get dialectically integrated in particular ways through material social practices (border and boundary building), representations (cartographic practices), and lived meanings (affective loyalties to the territorial unit of the nation-state). While former dominant practices of imposing absolute definitions may be questioned, the frequently pressing political need for unambiguous definitions (of state borders, for example) does not go away: it has, however, to be put into perspective of the continuous processes of capitalist and other modes of production of relative space-time (through financial and commodity flows and migratory movements) and the pervasive relationalities of global political power and contested moral authority. It is intriguing to note, for example, that the "fortress USA" anti-immigrant and antiglobalization mentality that is now seizing hold politically in the United States seriously contradicts longstanding international policies nominally dedicated to encouraging and facilitating the open spatio-temporal dynamics of capital accumulation in a more borderless world.

How this sharpening tension will be resolved remains to be seen, but the consequences for the future of the United States and of the global political economy will be far-reaching. As it is, state powers continue to emphasize the absolute territoriality of the concept of citizenship, while many immigrant groups—for example, those from Mexico—live their lives in a relational universe in which the border has no affective meaning, even as it poses an increasingly insurmountable physical barrier.

Place, as opposed to territory, is usually defined as the preeminent field of phenomenological experience and inquiry (topics kept at bay in the absolute theory of territory formation and thereby confined to derivative characteristics, such as loyalty to some preformed territorial entity). This phenomenological foundation, as Casey might claim, is what distinguishes his theory of place from contamination by notions (however important in their own right) of territory and region. The latter, while clearly objects of affective loyalties, require, he might claim, quite different methodological approaches from that given by phenomenology if they are to be properly understood. But the distinctions among place, territory, and region are far more porous than Casey and others in the Heideggerian tradition commonly allow. The grounds for regarding these concepts as mutually exclusive are shallow, and there are many points of overlap between them. This becomes particularly evident when we examine another concept, such as landscape. The anthropologist Keith Basso, for example, in his study of the Western Apache, aligns his thinking with that of Casey and Heidegger. He shows how "geographical features have served the people for centuries as indispensable mnemonic pegs on which to hang the moral teachings of their history." The permanence of places in the landscape, coupled with stories told about those places, provides a means to perpetuate a cultural identity: "Apaches view the landscape as the repository of distilled wisdom, a stern but benevolent keeper of tradition, an ever-vigilant ally in the efforts of individuals and whole communities to put into practice a set of standards for social living that are uniquely and distinctively their own. In the world that the Western Apache have constituted for themselves, features of the landscape have become symbols of and for this way of living, the symbols of a culture and the enduring moral character of its people."[14]

We here encounter, in the symbolic dimension, a dialectic between the social and environmental aspects of experience in place and mental attachments to a territorialized landscape. The Apache's inhabited and constructed realm within that territory is invested with moral value. By comprehending their relationships to the physical world in a particular way, the Apache engage in a moral act of imagination that constitutes an understanding of themselves. Losing access to the land (territory) under these conditions is equivalent to being dispossessed of one's identity. Processes of modernization, capital accumulation, and spatial integration are profoundly disruptive of such particular territorialized markers of cultural identity. "As places animate the ideas and feelings of persons who attend to them, these same ideas and feelings animate the places on which attention has been bestowed, and the movements of this process—inwards towards facets of the self, outward towards aspects of the external world, alternately both together—cannot be known in advance." What and how the self knows is a social affair: "deliberately and otherwise, people are forever presenting each other with culturally mediated [relational] images of where and how they dwell. In large ways and small, they are forever performing acts that reproduce and express their own sense of place—and also, inextricably, their own understandings of who and what they are." Hence the perpetual question that strangers often ask: "Where are you from?" It is the inextricable quality of this connection that here resonates so strongly. In making places (such as a home), we make ourselves, and as we remake ourselves, so we perpetually reshape the places we are in, materially, conceptually as well as in how we live within them. This implies that places are not, cannot be, fixed and stable, but are subject to perpetual transformations as conceptions, material practices, and lived experiences change. The dialectic that Basso here invokes is in principle just as compatible with Lefebvre's approach to spatiality as with Heidegger's. But Basso unfortunately looks to the latter for theoretical guidance. He comes dangerously close to replicating Mehta's views on the locale as the singular terrain upon which moral judgment can be founded. So although Basso's descriptions, assembled out of closely observed ethnographic work, fit easily into the matrix of spatio-temporal meanings set out in chapter 7, he is unable to capitalize on the way absolute, relative, and relational meanings dialectically intertwine through spatial material practices, conceptualizations, and, above all, through the evidently achieved lived sense of moral worth and cultural identity. As Moore observes, Basso's sense of place is "cordoned off from translocal knowledge, experience and the multiple spatialities that shape the landscapes of the US Southwest." The result is that place is deemed to have a settled single sense, while "culture becomes a shared system of meaning devoid of situated struggles."[15] Basso's failure to incorporate a Lefebvrian moment of critique and of contestation into his otherwise compelling account poses, therefore, a whole series of difficult problems.

The Relationality of Place

The meaning of a place, both individual and collective, is both powerfully present (absolute) and unstable (relational), dependent on the context in which the place and the human agent are situated. "Cultural practices, social relations, and political economic processes meld with the materiality of milieu, producing place," writes Moore. "Just as multiple spatialities coexist in a single moment within place, so also are experiences of place differentiated across diverse subject positions." The novelist Don DeLillo recounts an interesting example of the tension between absolute and relational meanings in his book *The Names*. Though located in Athens, the narrator long avoided visiting the Acropolis. Seen from afar, the "somber rock" appeared daunting. "The weight and moment of those worked stones promised to make the business of seeing them a complicated one. So much converges there. It's what we have rescued from the madness. Beauty, dignity, order, proportion . . . a white fire of such clarity and precision." But when he finally climbs the rock, he is surprised. "We approach hypnotically, walking on the smooth stones, not watching where we step. It would take a wrenching effort to take our eyes from it. . . . The marble seems to drip with honey, the pale autumnal hue produced by iron oxide in the stone." His sense of the place shifts dramatically: "I walk to the east face of the temple, so much space and openness, lost walls, pediments, roof, a grief for what has escaped containment. And this is what I mainly learned up there, *that the Parthenon was not a thing to study but to feel*. It wasn't aloof, rational, timeless, pure. I couldn't locate the serenity of the place, the logic and steady sense. It wasn't a relic species of dead Greece but part of the living city below it. This was a surprise. I'd thought it was a separate thing, the sacred height, intact in its Doric order. I hadn't expected a human feeling to emerge from the stones but this is what I found, deeper than the art and mathematics embodied in the structure, the optical exactitudes. I found a cry for pity. This is what remains to the mauled stones in their blue surround, this open cry, this voice that we know as our own."[16]

The objective measure (the Kantian exactitudes in absolute space and time) here collides with relational spatio-temporal meaning, but it does so around a particular place. DeLillo makes contact with a wider common flow of the sort that Raymond Williams, as we saw in chapter 7, experienced walking the Black Mountains. This is the way relational spacetime is lived (as Lefebvre would put it) in place, rather than materially experienced and conceptualized in abstraction. Is there, then, something inherent in the qualities of places that brings us to such wider understandings—and, if so, exactly what is it?

It is hard to probe very long in the extensive literature on place without encountering the relationalities of memory and identity. Writes Michel de Certeau, "connecting history to place is the condition of possibility for any social analysis." In his *Poetics of Space*, G. Bachelard puts it this way: "all really inhabited space bears the essence of the notion of home. [Here] memory and imagination remain associated, each one working for their mutual deepening. In the order of values, they both constitute a community of memory and image. Thus the house is not experienced from day to day only, on the thread of a narrative, or in the telling of our own story. Through dreams, the various dwelling places in our lives co-penetrate and retain the treasures of former days. . . . The house is one of the greatest powers of integration for the thoughts, memories and dreams of mankind. . . . Without it, man would be a dispersed being."[17]

But is this sense of place confined to the house as home? And what happens to us over time as we move from one house to another, making and finding a different kind of home in each? And can this mode of thinking be extended to "homeland," or what the Germans refer to as *Heimat*? The latter word, says Edgar Reitz, director of the 1984 film of that name (arguably one of the most important cultural productions of the 1980s), "is always linked to strong feelings, mostly remembrances and longing." It is, comment D. Morley and K. Robbins, "about conserving the 'fundamentals' of culture and identity" and "sustaining cultural boundaries and boundedness."[18] As such, it appears to point solely to an exclusionary politics of a place-bound nationalism, regionalism, and communitarianism, precisely because memories built around places cannot easily be shared with outsiders. The exclusions here are troubling; the threat of exclusionary nationalisms and local fascisms looms large. But memory of the past is also about hope for the future. "There is," says Mary Gordon, "a link between hope and memory. Remembering nothing one cannot hope for anything. And so time means nothing."[19] The preservation or construction of a sense of place is then an active moment in the passage from memory to hope, from past to future. This is, one suspects, why so many people locate the possibility of politics in actual places. Places are sites of collective memories that hold out the prospects for different futures. "Critical regionalism," as it is called in architecture, invoking as it so often does vernacular traditions and icons of place, is considered a basis for a politics of resistance to the homogenizing force of commodity flows and monetization. "Militant particularism," of the sort I have often advocated, seizes upon the qualities of place, reanimates the local bond between the environmental and the social, reactivates collective memories, and seeks to bend the social processes constructing spacetime to a radically different universal purpose. "Imagination," says Bachelard, "separates us from the past as well as from reality: it faces the future." Imagined places, the utopian thoughts and desires of countless peoples, have consequently played a vital role in animating politics.[20]

History and memory in places are quite distinct from one another.[21] History typically establishes a secure narration in absolute time. "To articulate the past historically does not mean to recognize it 'the way it really was,'" writes Benjamin. C. Boyer explains it this way: "memory, as opposed to history, responds more than it records, it bursts upon the scene in an unexpected manner, demanding an alteration of established traditions. Operating only in fragments, memory is an art that connects disparate events; it is formed on the tactics of surprise, ruptures, and overturnings that reveal its true power." Memory of this sort is not only the great destabilizer. "Memory springing from the natural chains of tradition should be like an epiphany, flashing up in ephemeral moments of crisis, searching to exhibit at that particular time the way of the world in order to direct one's pathway toward the future.[22] Time future is fragmentarily illuminated by memory constructed out of time past. Dominant powers therefore go to great lengths to control, coopt, corrupt, stage, deflate, and manage the memory of key events (such as the terrorist attacks of September 11, 2001) by converting them into historical narratives and monumentalizing them in absolute spaces. Keeping the sense of the event alive, saving it from this sort of monumentalization and incorporation into standard history, is, Badiou suggests, crucial to any form of radical politics. If, as Balzac has it, "hope is memory that desires," then it is not hope that guides memory but free-floating memories that generate hope when animated by desire. Though desire in the now is the active agent and the catalyst, memory and event are the key resources and place is "the anchor of memory and meaning."[23]

The worlds of myth, of religion, of collective memory, and of national or regional identity focus on distinctive places (shrines, places of worship, icons, stories, festivals) symbolic of distinctive beliefs, values, imaginaries, and social-institutional practices. These are mobilized in political causes. Many traditional institutions, such as those of church and nation, depend crucially upon the existence of a whole network of symbolic places to secure their power and express their social meaning. What Basso discovered for the Western Apache is a common enough occurrence: wisdom is often supposed to sit in particular places (Mecca, the Vatican, the Federal Reserve Bank). But to suppose that wisdom, as opposed to particular meanings and cultural identifications, actually sits in such places is to suppose too much. What kind of wisdom, after all, sits in Guantanamo Bay, Auschwitz, My Lai, or the Gulag? And while particular meanings and cultural identifications may indeed derive from our relationality to such places, these are not by any means the kinds of meanings and identifications that we might welcome, let alone wish to treat as iconic of our moral sense. Basso assumes without warrant that it is indeed wisdom rather than repressions that sit in the places his informant narrates and that the moral authority that derives from the landscape is comforting rather than confining. Here, however, Heidegger's shadow looms large. For what Heidegger in effect proposes is an essentialist theory of place as dwelling that is a unique source of authentic and real meaning (hence of all real wisdom).

This Heideggerian move is marked, for example, in the concept of *genius loci*. Every place is construed to have an "essence" or a "guardian spirit" that not only gives it its special qualities but also calls forth human behaviors that acknowledge and ultimately reveal those essential qualities. The "existential purpose" of building, architecture, and urban design, says C. Norberg-Schulz, is "to uncover the meanings potentially present in the given environment." This does not mean that places cannot change. "To protect and conserve the *genius loci* in fact means to concretize its essence in ever new historical contexts." Human action perpetually uncovers new possibilities and potentialities, even as it articulates respect for the place's distinctive character. To respect the *genius loci* "means to determine the identity of the place and to interpret it in ever new ways. Only then may we talk about a *living tradition* which makes change meaningful by relating it to a set of locally founded parameters."[24] Freedom is here understood not as arbitrary play, but as creative dialogue between the inherent qualities of places and human aspirations and actions. In this interpretation, the theme of relationality is central. Buildings and places gather together social, symbolic, psychological, biological, and physical meanings so as to constitute the *genius loci*. In so doing they create a particular relational identity from which we draw meaning and definitions of self.

There are clear dangers in this mode of argumentation, not least because the road can all too easily lead toward an exclusionary, place-based fascism. But it does not always do so, and herein lies a conundrum that cries out for critical engagement. To begin with, the *genius loci* concept is vague. If, as Aldo Rossi, for one, insists, the history of our built environment "is always the history of the architecture of ruling classes," and if "monuments" (key elements of memory and identity in urban contexts) are constituted symbolically through various forms of collective activities (not necessarily those of the ruling classes), then the fluidity of meaning that Norberg-Shulz necessarily admits to the concept of place can be taken in a more constructivist vein to mean the exploration of possibilities from radically different political and cultural standpoints. Whose identity and which collectivity of class, belief, or gender, for example, is to dominate particular practices of place construction? And if collective memory is located in places, and if that collective memory is vital to the perpetuation of some repressive social order (or to the visualization of some hoped-for alternative in the future), then all essentialist formulations of the *genius loci* fall away to be replaced by a contested terrain of competing definitions.

This is exactly the move that A. Loukaki makes in her study of competing treatments and visions of the Acropolis over time.[25] Discursive controversies among architects, archaeologists, and art historians over how to understand the *genius loci* here fade before the political power struggle coursing through Greek history. And that contest, as Loukaki shows, is not simply about the proper interpretation of the past, the authenticity of this or that collective memory, but also about all hopes for the future. To release a different imaginary concerning the past is to release a different imaginary as to future possibilities. The *genius loci,* the marked qualities of any place, is open to contestation, both theoretically (as to its meaning) and concretely (as to how to make a particular place). The absence of active political controversy is usually a sign of the domination of some hegemonic power. What makes the site of the Acropolis so interesting is not only the competing claims based on class, national sentiments, and locale, but also the competing claims of outside powers (such as those of Germany, Britain, and the United States). Each power seeks to appropriate the Acropolis for its own particular purpose as a symbol of the origins of Western civilization, rather than to respect it as a living monument embedded in the history of Greek geopolitical and political-economic struggles.

The Acropolis "belongs" simultaneously to radically divergent imagined communities. And the question of to whom it "truly" belongs has no direct theoretical answer: it is determined through political contestation and struggle and, hence, is an unstable determination. A seemingly dead monument is, as Delillo notes, alive with meaning.

The Heideggerian Moment

Behind much of this looms the imposing figure of Heidegger. Some account of his thought is unavoidable, since this is the fount of so much anticosmopolitan thinking. "Place," said Heidegger (echoing Aristotle), "is the locale of the truth of Being." But this locale does not exist outside of a particular world of space-relations: "All distances in time and space are shrinking. . . . Yet the frantic abolition of all distances brings no nearness; for nearness does not consist in shortness of distance. What is least remote from us in point of distance, by virtue of its picture on film or its sound on radio, can remain far from us. What is incalculably far from us in point of distance can be near to us. . . . Everything gets lumped together into uniform distancelessness. . . . What is it that unsettles and thus terrifies? It shows itself and hides itself in the *way* in which everything presences, namely, in the fact that despite all conquest of distances the nearness of things remains absent."[26]

Heidegger fears the loss of identity, the loss of contact with the real sensory world that occurs as the space-time coordinates of social life become unstable through the spread of market relations and rational calculation. "The object-character of technological dominion spreads itself over the earth ever more quickly, ruthlessly, and completely," he complains. As a result, "the humanness of man and the thingness of things dissolve into the calculated market value of a market which not only spans the whole earth as a world market, but also, as the will to will, trades in the nature of Being and thus subjects all beings to the trade of a calculation that dominates most tenaciously in those areas where there is no need of numbers."[27] In attacking the material forces of liberal capitalism and the cosmopolitan spirit of commerce, Heidegger is attacking the very processes that Adam Smith and Kant welcomed as progressive. For Heidegger, the terror produced by the formation of the world market and the consequent dramatic and rapid shifts in space-time relations is omnipresent. Physical nearness no longer brings with it understanding or an ability to appreciate or even appropriate a "thing" (, for that matter, relate to another person) properly.

Heidegger therefore rejects the world market and seeks to uncover the truths of human existence phenomenologically in place. The concept to which he appeals is that of "dwelling." He most famously illustrates this with a description of a Black Forest farmhouse:

> Here the self-sufficiency of the power to let earth and heaven, divinities and mortals enter in simple oneness into things, ordered the house. It places the farm on the wind-sheltered mountain slope looking south, among the meadows close to the spring. It gave it the wide overhanging shingle roof whose proper slope bears up under the burden of snow, and which, reaching deep down, shields the chambers against the storms of the long winter nights. It did not forget the altar corner behind the community table; it made room in its chamber for the hallowed places of childbed and the "tree of the dead'—for that is what they call a coffin there; the Totenbaum—and in this way it designed for the different generations under one roof the character of their journey through time. A craft which, itself sprung from dwelling, still uses its tools and frames as things, built the farmhouse.[28]

Dwelling is the capacity to achieve a spiritual unity (come to terms, for example, with the *genius loci*) between humans and things. From this it follows that "only if we are capable of dwelling, only then can we build." Indeed, commercially constructed buildings "may even deny dwelling its own nature when they are pursued and acquired purely for their own sake." Although there is a narrow sense of homelessness that can perhaps be alleviated simply by building shelter, there is a much deeper crisis of homelessness to be found in the modern world; many people have lost their roots, their connection to homeland. Even those who physically stay in place may become homeless (rootless) through the inroads of modern means of communication, such as radio and television. "The rootedness, the autochthony, of man is threatened today at its core." If we lose the capacity to dwell, Heidegger argues, then we lose our roots and find ourselves cut off from all sources of spiritual nourishment. The impoverishment of existence is incalculable. Heidegger believes that genuine works of art can only flourish when rooted in a native soil. "We are plants which—whether we like to admit it to ourselves or not—must with our roots rise out of the earth in order to bloom in the ether and bear fruit." Deprived of such roots, art is reduced to a meaningless caricature (so much for modernist internationalism). Universal moral judgments are likewise judged empty and inauthentic unless they are similarly rooted. This is the view that Mehta echoes when he points to the way human beings "inherit a mass of predispositions from an unfathomable past bounded by the variations of time and place" and notes that this defines the "integrity and self-understanding from which alone life can be, and is, richly experienced—indeed, from which alone moral action is possible."[29]

Place construction, from this perspective, must be about the recovery of roots and the recovery of the art of dwelling. The myth of an unfathomable past here becomes the problematic key to Heidegger's theory. He focuses on the way in which places "are constructed in our memories and affections through repeated encounters and complex associations." He emphasizes how "place experiences are necessarily time-deepened and memory-qualified." He creates "a new way to speak about and care for our human nature and environment," so that "love of place and the earth are scarcely sentimental extras to be indulged only when all technical and material problems have been resolved. They are part of being in the world and prior, therefore, to all technical matters." [30] Heidegger reverses the priority traditionally given to space over place in the Kantian scheme of things. Spaces "receive their being from locations and not from space," or, as Casey puts it, "space and time are contained in places rather than places in them."[31] The active production and making of space therefore occurs through building and dwelling. The inspiration that H. Lefebvre drew from Heidegger in constructing his theory of the production of space then becomes clear. Lefebvre, however, transforms the Heideggerian concept of "dwelling" into "habiting," in order to free it of mythical and metaphysical presumptions. He likewise transforms Heidegger's fears of the frantic shrinking of distances into a constructive critique of what he calls the "abstract space" of capitalism and the state, and introduces a class element into the counter-politics of production of alternative spaces.[32] What for Heidegger leads to withdrawal into the phenomeonology of place generates in Lefebvre the spirit of a counter-attack to produce alternative and more humane spaces and places. Lefebvre takes up the relational theory of space and place, and gives it a more explicit political meaning.

But Heidegger also laments the loss of an intimate and authentic relation to nature. This has inspired a tradition of place-based environmentalist politics. "By reviving a sense of place," Heideggerians say, "we may be able to reactivate the care of the environment." A "reawakened sense of beauty of local places may fuel a deeply spiritual concern for the preservation of the ecological diversity and uniqueness of each place." This faith is not only found in the theological literature. It is also strongly evident in bioregionalist, communitarian, and anarcho-socialist forms of ecological politics. Place is, therefore, the preferred terrain of much environmental politics.[33] Some of the fiercest movements of opposition to liberal and neoliberal capitalism arise out of struggles to preserve valued environmental qualities (not only natural but also built environments) in particular places.

There are, however, difficulties with these arguments. Heidegger's prescriptions are notoriously abstract and vague. For example, what might the conditions of "authentic dwelling" be in a highly industrialized, modernist, and capitalist world? We cannot turn back to the Black Forest farmhouse (even Heidegger recognized that), but what else might we turn to? Nostalgia for some imagined past is no panacea. The issue of authenticity (rootedness) of the experience of place (and nature in place) is a peculiarly modern preoccupation. "A truly rooted community," notes Yi-Fu Tuan, "may have shrines and monuments, but it is unlikely to have museums and societies for the preservation of the past."[34] The conscious effort to evoke an "authentic" sense of place and of the past is a very contemporary preoccupation. It even becomes a selling point for developers and community boosters, a source of monopoly rent for capitalist entrepreneurs promising to deliver authentic community and a harmonious relation to nature. Heidegger's own formulations seem to be predicated upon an opposition to a world of commodification, modernization, globalization, and time-space compression (though some believe they were more explicitly directed toward a critique of the largely U.S.–inspired modernist reconstruction of West Germany after 1945). He provides no examples of what it might really mean to dwell authentically in our actual contemporary conditions of existence, and herein lies an acute danger. The quest for authenticity is, it turns out, itself a modern value, and it stands to be subverted by the market provision of constructed authenticity, invented traditions, and a commercialized heritage culture. This was the ultimate fate of Wordsworth's romanticism as he shifted from writing poems romanticizing closeness to nature in his beloved Lake District, to writing commercial tour guides to this place.[35] The final victory of capitalist modernity is not the disappearance of the nonmodern world, but its artificial preservation and reconstruction, as much in Heideggerian theory as in actual cultural practices.

But the problems run far deeper than this. Who, for example, are these "mortals" who, along with earth and heaven and divinities, enter into the "simple oneness of things"? Heidegger's conception of species being (he never uses the term) is strictly limited to a person, whose only existence is given over to the search for authenticity and personal self-realization through learning to dwell in harmony with the earth, heaven, and divinities. Cultural variation (along with all language and art) is an output and not an input into that quest. To read a work in the Heideggerian mold is to encounter a world of no prior class distinctions, no hierarchical structures of social power, no complex bodies politic and social institutions, and, of course, no market valuations and coordinations, no military-industrial technologies, and certainly no dynamics of capital accumulation through uneven geographical development. Actually existing materialist history and geography, including an earth that has been radically transformed, if not ravaged, by human action over millennia, is washed away in the make-believe Heideggerian universe that withdraws from the practicalities of daily life in order to offer a critique of where we now are in terms of our social, cultural, and natural relations. Heideggerianism trades upon the undoubted capacity of human beings to sense moments of harmony, peace, and spiritual serenity, if not sublime joy, in particular places at particular times and to develop deep attachments to the places where they live, but it then goes on to suppose that this is all that is relevant to people's lives. The problem, of course, is that if the market system, along with monetary valuations, contemporary technologies (organizational as well as materialist), and capital accumulation, were all to disappear tomorrow, and if all the bankers of the world suddenly committed themselves to the Heideggerian project, then most of those capable of reading this book and many more besides would die of starvation within a few weeks. The Heideggerian conception of "mortals" is every bit as abstract and as rootless as that of the liberal subject, though with radically different ambitions: not to achieve self-realization through the accumulation of property, wealth, and power, but to do so through learning to dwell.

The supposed connection between ecological sentiments and place likewise deserves critical scrutiny. The penchant for regarding place as a privileged if not exclusive locus of ecological sensitivity rests on the human body as "the measure of all things" in an unmediated and very direct way. Sensory interaction between the body and its environs can certainly carry with it a wide range of psychic as well as social insights and meanings. But the intimacy of many place-based accounts—Thoreau's famous and influential exploration of Walden being the classic example—yields only limited knowledge of ecological processes operating at a small scale. This is insufficient to understand broader socio-ecological processes (global warming or stratospheric ozone depletions cannot be directly detected by phenomenological means). Insofar as "alienation from nature" is thought to be (and there is a huge gap between being thought to be and actually being so) a widespread phenomenon in contemporary society, then the temptation is to treat specific places (increasingly preserved as wilderness, for example) as the loci of a supposedly unalienated direct sensory interaction with nature (ecotourism trades on this). The result is to fetishize both nature and the human body, the Self and the realms of human sensation, as special places, as the locus of all being in the world. And while there are ways, such as those proposed in the "deep ecology" of Arne Naess, to turn this into a global and universal standpoint, the leap of faith from personal experience to empathy with the whole of nature is colossal. Yet this is the leap of faith—often recounted as an epiphany—that many deep ecologists and environmental ethicists make. But there are deep reasons to be skeptical of the omniscient view, adopted even by the nineteenth-century anarchist geographer Elisée Reclus, that "humanity is nature becoming conscious of itself" and that we, and only we, can realize the deep harmonies of nature's plan through wise interventions.[36]

Heidegger's claim (and note that this is a claim and not a proven fact of life) that the authenticity of dwelling and of rootedness is being destroyed by the spread of technology, rationalism, mass production, and mass values has been influential with many of those concerned to articulate a critical understanding of place under capitalism. Ted Relph, for example, holds that place is being systematically destroyed, rendered inauthentic or even "placeless" by the sheer organizational power and depth of penetration of the market and of capital. Unfortunately, this line of thinking cannot avoid descending into a pervasive elitism. Some people can claim the status of authenticity by virtue of their capacity to dwell in real places, it is said, while the rest of us—the majority—live empty and soulless lives in a "placeless" world. The mark of this kind of elitism, of course, is that it has nothing necessarily to do with class in the capitalist or even traditional sense and can even take opposition to capitalist modernity and market valuations as its political stance. The virtue of authenticity is more often than not accorded to those living simple lives close to the land, capable of absorbing the wisdom that, according to Basso, supposedly sits in places. The response is a politics of place construction that is then held up as the way forward to the promised land of an authentic existence and of an unalienated relation to nature and to others. "The only political vision that offers any hope of salvation," writes Kirkpatrick Sale, "is one based on an understanding of, a rootedness in, a deep commitment to, and a resacralization of, *place*." In his popular *Geography of Nowhere*, R. Kunstler likewise lambastes capitalist developers and their all-too-easily duped clients for permitting an urbanization process that embraces the crass shopping mall and a suburbanite culture that is soulless, faceless, and therefore "placeless."[37] But unfortunately, Kunstler looks no further for an alternative than the "new urbanism" preached by developer architects (such as Duany), with its equally false concept of a "community of living" and an ersatz "closeness to nature" (landscaped design) as an antidote. Placefulness becomes a construction of profitable enterprise.

Yet there is also something positive and progressive in what Heidegger has to offer, particularly from the standpoint of critique of the existing order. What many subsequent writers have drawn from him—and this includes Lefebvre—is the possibility of resistance, outright rejection of and active opposition to any simple capitalist, market-based (or modernist) logic of place and space construction. The increasing penetration of technological rationality, commodification and market values, and capital accumulation into social life, together with time-space compression, provokes resistances. The search for some "authentic" sense of community and for an unalienated relation to nature among many radical and ecological movements is one cutting edge of resistance. Place, Escobar argues, is not only *the* locus of resistance to a globalizing capitalism but, more plausibly, a site from which alternatives can be actively sought and incipiently constructed. This is where the search for the true realm of freedom can begin.[38] The key difference between Lefebvre and Escobar, is that the former conceptualizes the problem in terms of the production of space, while the latter construes it in terms of the production of new ways of living in place. And therein lies a difference that has, as we shall see, significant political implications.

Open and Closed Places

Contemporary writers who insist on the priority of place over space typically declare that they do not construe places as exclusionary, as culturally homogeneous "closed boxes" (as Appiah puts it). They position themselves this way, one suspects, because they are all too aware of the dangers of exclusionary nationalisms and local fascisms. The places they envisage are therefore depicted as open and diverse. Place must, Casey declares, be porous toward the outside and diverse to the point of "wildness" on the inside. Why they must be so (as opposed to why we might struggle to make them so) is, however, unclear. Places have to be understood, Casey says, as "both concrete and relational."[39] But this, too, poses the question: relational to what? In effect, he here escapes the logic of closed boxes in absolute space (Foucault's heterotopias) by invoking a relational idea of place (closer to Lefebvre's dialectical conception of heterotopia). This is not an unfamiliar ruse. It has suffused much of the thinking about place in recent years. D. Massey, for example, correctly challenges the essentialist Heideggerian idea that place is definable in terms of internal histories, timeless identities, or fixed boundaries. "The identities of places are always unfixed, contested and multiple," she writes, "and the particularity of any place is, in these terms, constructed not by placing boundaries around it and defining its identity through counter-position to the other that lies beyond, but precisely (in part) through the specificity of the mix of links and interconnections to that 'beyond.' Places viewed in this way are open and porous." If there is any uniqueness to place, she says, then it is always hybrid, arising out of "the particular mix of social relations."[40]

Such formulations sacrifice much of what the concept of place was originally designed to capture—the unique qualities and character of some segment of the earth's surface and the coalescence of human activities into some sort of distinctive structured coherence. A. Dirlik, having sympathetically reviewed a plethora of arguments for openness and porosity, comes back in the end to the idea that place must also be understood as concrete and bounded, because the purely relational formulations become too "diaphanous." Massey, he writes, is "over zealous" in "dissociating place from fixed location." "Porosity of boundaries is not the same as abolition of boundaries." If everything is totally open, then "there is nothing special about place after all." Dirlik here identifies the underlying problem. While it is conventional, he argues, to construe place and space as opposed but interrelated terms, the transformation of place "may be inconceivable without a simultaneous transformation of space, because place and space, while analytically distinct, are nevertheless linked in intimate ways."[41]

But how are they linked? The problem, which we encountered at the very outset, is that we cannot understand the concept of place (or region or territory) without understanding space. Casey's Kantian conception of absolute and empty space underlies his particular theory of place, and it is from this confined conception that he seeks to break free by reversing the charges, as it were. "Rather than being the minion of an absolute space and time, place is the master of their shared matrix," he writes.[42] But, as we also saw in chapter 7, it is impossible to articulate a full understanding of relational spacetime without invoking ideas about place as both "concrete and relational" in the way Casey proposes. This brings us to the crux of the ontological problem. The way in which place is understood shifts as we change our conceptions of space and time. Whitehead, working directly with a relational theory of spacetime, provides the most satisfying answer to what a relational theory of place would look like. He construes "places" as "entities" that achieve relative stability for a time in their bounding and in their internal ordering of processes. Such entities he calls "permanences." These permanences come to occupy a piece of space in an exclusive way (for a time) and thereby define a place—their place—for a time. The process of place formation (including that of bounding and internal ordering) is, therefore, a process of carving out "permanences" from a flow of processes that simultaneously create a distinctive kind of spatio-temporality.[43] Financial flows define new spatio-temporalities but also rest on the creation of distinctive physical markets in places like Wall Street, Chicago, or the City of London. These distinctive places are marked by exclusions: only certain people are allowed on the trading floor of the stock exchange, for example. This "carving out" of distinctive places entails the activities of bounding, of building markers of exclusion such as fences and walls, and of establishing an internal ordering of space relations, but then also involves bringing places into relation to a wider world by making bridges and doors, establishing communication links, projecting images of reputation, and the like. Boundaries and borders, like reputations, are not given but made. But the "permanences"—no matter how solid they may seem—are not eternal. They are always subject to time as "perpetual perishing" (as Whitehead puts it). Places are, in short, always contingent on the relational processes that create, sustain, and dissolve them. The coexistence of "multiple spatialities" in places undermines any simple, unitary sense of place. Nevertheless, at the end of the day, the emphasis has to be upon the bounded entity or "permanence," the distinctive shape, form, and internal ordering a particular place acquires, the attributes and distinctive qualities it evinces, and the consequences that derive for socio-ecological processes that sustain and evolve life within and around that permanence. While it is true, as Moore, for one, insists, that "within one place, social actors become subjected to multiple matrices of power," and that the qualities of place are perpetually contested, this does not mean that there is no hegemonic configuration of relations through which we experience and define the places we encounter. It is in this spirit that Cindi Katz proposes the construction of "countertopographies" that offer a "multifaceted way of theorizing the connectedness of vastly different places made artifactually discrete by virtue of history and geography but which also reproduce themselves differently amidst the common political-economic and sociocultural processes they experience." Construing relations between space and place in this fashion permits, she claims, the analysis of particular issues "in and across place," at the same time as it inspires the creation of a "different kind of politics, one in which crossing space and 'jumping scale' are obligatory rather than overlooked."[44]

Place formation is not, furthermore, neutral with respect to the production of spatio-temporality. Cities crystallize out as "permanences" (absolute spaces with an internal ordering) within the flows of trade (relative space-time), but they then become foci of innovative activities and new global imaginaries (relationalities) that transform the spatio-temporal forms and the socio-ecological dynamics going on around them. The Hanseatic League, initially centered on Lubeck, grew into a trading network of well over one hundred emergent cities (each bounded and internally ordered in some way). The activities of the league created a new spatio-temporality to political-economic life from Novgorod to London in the fourteenth and fifteenth centuries. The shifting global network of interurban flows of finance capital in our own era, facilitated by the new information technologies and powered by new kinds of markets (based on financial innovations encompassing securitization and credit and currency derivatives) in distinctive places in New York, Chicago, London, and Frankfurt, has destabilized older spatio-temporalities of political-economic and social life, and created new impulses of urbanization worldwide (in Shanghai, Mumbai, or Sydney). The production of space, in short, proceeds alongside of, as well as *through*, the production of places. Interplace competition produces in turn new spatio-temporalities.[45] Uncovering the dialectical character of this space-place connection is crucial.

This can be systematized by referring back to the matrix of concepts of space and time (see fig. 1 in chapter 7). Places plainly have material, conceptual, and lived dimensions of the sort that Lefebvre describes. They can likewise be considered as absolute (bounded, fixed, and named), relative (interconnected and interactive through myriad flows), and relational (internalizing forces, powers, influences, and meanings from elsewhere). If we ask: what is the place called "Paris"? then the answer will vary according to where we situate ourselves within the different dimensions of this matrix of possibilities. The sheer physicality of Paris is experienced in the absolute spaces of work, reproduction, leisure, and the search for pleasure. These absolute spaces can be represented in innumerable ways (chiefly but not exclusively through cartographies), and an archive of such conceptions (both past and present) can be preserved. We inhabit these absolute spaces in a variety of psychic states (pleasure, fear, lassitude). This may provoke reconceptualizations—as in poetry and literature—followed perhaps by new architectural initiatives (first conceived as cartographic plans) to reengineer the absolute physical spaces of the city in ways more in accord with our felt wants, needs, and desires. In designating the city as an absolute Cartesian space, we fix its administrative cartographic form and set up principles of internal ordering. Its absoluteness may be physically signaled by ramparts, boundaries, and a city wall, while its internal ordering may reflect class, ethnic, and racial divisions, as well as differentiations deriving from divisions of labor.

As an entity in relative space-time, Paris takes on the character of some kind of "permanence," an evolving receptacle open to the whirling currents of global flows of goods and services, of people, commodities, money, information, cultural values, and capital in motion. The inhabitants of the city engage with these flows through physical, material practices and encounters in particular locations that are themselves always "in process" (under threat, for example, of urban renewal). These relations can be conceptualized in flow charts and diagrams, in data of inputs and outputs, in concepts such as "the metabolism of the city." We seek ways to represent the city as speed, spectacle, motion, and movement. We live in states of exhilaration or exhaustion, resignation or resistance, as the case may be, as we rush hither and thither within and beyond the city. Reconceptualizing Paris as a city of motion in fantastic works of art may lead to attempts to distill architectural plans to rebuild the permanence of the city in ways that both reflect and animate the flows (this is the kind of architecture that Hadid seeks but invariably fails to produce, as she concretizes her work in absolute spatial terms).

Finally, the relationality of Paris can only be experienced through the materiality of dominant processes and effects. These processes are not only material. We recognize, for example, the importance of the urban spectacle, of the symbols of Paris's reputation as we walk the streets (the Eiffel Tower, Notre Dame, and other iconic sites or the burned-out hulks of cars that litter the suburbs of discontent). Relationalities are conceptualized in an evocative language of repute that is projected throughout the rest of the world (beckoning to those in search of artistic liberty or political freedoms, to tourists in search of culture and romance, and repelling those appalled by Paris's oppressive colonial history and the continuing racism so blatantly manifest there). Paris is projected as "the city of light," as "romance in springtime," but also as the city of revolutionary excess, of tumbrils and guillotines, and of immigrant discontent and racist oppressions. Paris can be lived as memory, generating sensations of intense pleasure or pain for an Iraqi doctor caught in the bombing of Baghdad. It can be fantasized, from near or from afar, without ever setting foot in the place, as an object of desire or of disdain. It can be reconceptualized in artistic or in literary forms (as Manet did in his paintings and as Charles Dickens did in *A Tale of Two Cities*). As a result of encounters with these conceptualizations, we recognize new iconic sites as we walk the streets, dream new fantasies of an urban utopia. We may even seek to put these fantasies to work in an effort to reengineer the absolute spaces of Paris, as Le Corbusier once sought to do, more to our heart's desire.

Almost everyone who attempts to theorize place starts at one point within the matrix of spatio-temporal possibilities, only to shift somewhere else when they attempt to unravel the rich complexity of the idea. Casey, having accepted the absolute Kantian definition of space and time at the outset, ends up introducing relationality into his concept of place in order to render it more dynamic. Had he started out with a relational concept of spacetime, he would have created a non-Aristotelian theory of place that resembled that of Whitehead. Instead, he has to liberate place from absolute spatiality by proclaiming it to be porous to the outside and wild on the inside! Norberg-Shulz, having started from what seems like a fixed and essentialist definition of the *genius loci*, subsequently liberates it from stasis and permanence by, in effect, recognizing with Rossi that even myths can change their meaning and their purchase over time. Heidegger, though "stubbornly local" (as Williams puts it), understands that places and things (like bridges) create spaces, and that places take on their character through relationalities established in space-time. While he refuses the broader common flow given by commerce, communication technologies, and modernity, Heidegger invokes a sense of that wider common flow by appeal to the worlds of myth and religion from which Kant had sought to free the concept of place. Dirlik, having evinced a certain sympathy with Massey's relative and relational formulations, gently reminds her that uniqueness in the absolute dimension cannot be ignored. Foucault, restlessly trapped in the absolute spaces of his Kantianism, fantasizes a relational escapist vision of liberty and freedom to explore difference and unconstrained otherness behind the prison walls or on the pirate ship. Deleuze, freed from Kantian historicity by the figure of the schizoid personality and from absolute spaces by the Leibnizian relational idea of the fold, nevertheless grounds his key philosophical ruminations concerning deterritorialization and reterritorialization (which can be understood as processes of place-formation) on the isolated and absolutist metaphor of the desert island.[46] No one, it seems, can ever occupy only one point in the matrix of spatio-temporalities. Everyone who begins at some point finds herself or himself drawn into an unavoidable dance of the dialectic across the terrain of complementary spatio-temporalities. From this standpoint those who proclaim, with Aristotle, that there is some essentialist theory of place, that "place is the first of all things," or who hold, with Heidegger, that "place is the locale of the truth of being" (though not of becoming!) are plainly mistaken. The only concept of place that makes sense is one that sees it as a contingent, dynamic, and influential "permanence," while being integrally contained within the processes that create, sustain, and dissolve all regions, places, and spacetimes into complex configurations.

The Politics of Place

So where does this analysis leave us, with respect to the thesis dear to the hearts of many within the alternative globalization movement: that place is not only the locale of the truth of being but also the key locus of consciousness formation and organization against the predatory and destructive forces of a universalizing and abstracted neoliberal capitalism? The groundwork for an answer to this question was laid in chapter 7, where Margaret Kohn was approvingly cited as saying that "political spaces facilitate change by creating a distinctive place to develop new identities and practices. The political power of place comes from the ability of popular forces to link the social, symbolic, and experiential dimensions of space" into a transformative politics.[47] But from Lefebvre we also derived the salutary warning that the heterotopic spaces constructed by anomic groups are likely at some point "to be reclaimed by the dominant praxis" and that the production of space and place is shot through at every moment with the dynamics of indeterminate social struggles whose outcomes depend upon the shifting currents of power relations between social groups. Into this cauldron of social struggles we also must insert the charged fact that much of the envisioning of political alternatives rests either upon a utopian vision of a different kind of yet-to-be-constructed, perfectly harmonious place or upon some version of place-based communitarian theory and praxis as an appropriate and adequate answer to the pursuit of the good life.

To discuss the politics of place is therefore to enter into a terrain of debate that is fraught and frequently marked by misconceptions. It is said, for example, that I think working-class movements are ineluctably confined to place and that I am hostile to place-based politics because it inevitably becomes exclusionary and reactionary.[48] What I actually said was that there is a long history of working-class and popular movements successfully commanding places, only to be defeated by bourgeois forces that seem to be more adept at commanding space. This is what happened in Paris in 1848 and 1871, in Seattle in 1918, and in Tucumán in 1968, and we have in recent times seen revolutionary movements in Chile and Nicaragua (and the list goes on and on) that have lost out in this way. The answer, of course, is that working-class and popular movements have to pay more attention to geopolitical and universal strategies (as did the First International and as elements within the World Social Forum are currently doing). If they do not do this, then they are more vulnerable to suppression from the outside. The international labor movement is currently no match for the international powers of finance capital. This imbalance is not inevitable, but progressive movements have to grapple directly with this problem. Place, I have argued, is always a crucial basis for progressive and emancipatory movements. In *Spaces of Hope*, for example, I took it as a crucial mediating factor in the movement from the foundational moment in which the personal is political through the organization of local solidarities in particular places to a more universal politics of rights and justice.[49] The model is parallel to that proposed by the Stoics as well as by Marx and Engels in *The Communist Manifesto*. Here is how Nussbaum describes the Stoic position: "They suggest that we think of ourselves not as devoid of local affiliations, but as surrounded with a series of concentric circles. The first one encircles the self, the next takes in the immediate family, then follows the extended family, then, in order, neighbors or local groups, fellow city-dwellers, and fellow countrymen. . . . Outside all these circles is the largest one, humanity as a whole. Our task as citizens of the world will be to 'draw the circles somehow toward the center,' . . . making all human beings more like our fellow city-dwellers . . . [as we] give the circle that defines our humanity special attention and respect."[50]

All circles must, says Nussbaum, be accorded proper respect. The model that Marx and Engels proposed (possibly drawing upon the Stoics, since Epicurus was the focus of Marx's dissertation) started with the alienated individual worker, passed through the formation of collective solidarities, first in the factory and then in the city region,then shifted scale to the pursuit of nation-state power, finally ending up with the call for workers of the world to unite around their common humanity.[51] All of these "moments" or circles of struggle must be kept in dialectical tension with each other. A universal politics that cannot link back to the way the personal is political or to collective solidarities achieved in particular places would become hollowed out, if not repressive. Furthermore, what makes good political or ecological sense at one scale does not necessarily work well at another. The chronic local smog problem of London (or of the Ohio River Valley) in the 1950s was resolved by building tall smokestack power stations that deposited acid rain all over Scandinavia (or New England). A local solution produced a regional problem. Conversely, decentralization of political power to the local level all too often turns out, under neoliberal rules, to be a superb means to gain or maintain centralized class control and monopoly power. My theory of place-based politics derives from this overall conception.

The foundational point is that there can be no universal politics without an adequate place-based politics. In taking up Raymond Williams's conception of militant particularism, furthermore, I suggested that local politics is in practice nearly always the grounding for some kind of qualified universalism.[52] All politics is, as the old adage has it, local politics. Problems arise when the dialectic between the moments gets lost, when politics gets stuck in the local, such that this becomes an end in itself. At this point the reactionary and exclusionary dangers loom large. And if I have warned too explicitly of such dangers, and thereby offended the sensibilities of those who like to romance the local to death, I have done so because I see far too many examples of local, even neighborhood, fascism and exclusionism, of anti-immigrant and gated-community fervor, of "not in my back yard" politics, and the like. If we do not pay close attention to how something potentially progressive can so easily turn reactionary, then we lose sight of the grander political possibilities that always attach to mobilizing the power of place as a moment in the search for the geography of freedom.

Consider, for example, the politics of place-bound communitarian solutions. Distinctive communities are painstakingly built in place by social practices that often include the exercise of authoritarian powers and conformist restrictions. Such places can never remain entirely open, as Dirlik for one ends up acknowledging. An achieved "community" is an enclosed absolute space (irrespective of scale or even frontier definitions), within which certain rules of social engagement prevail. To enter into that bounded space (and the activity of bounding is crucial in itself) is to enter into a space of rules (both tacit and explicit) that one acknowledges, respects, and obeys (either voluntarily or through some sort of compulsion). The construction of "community" entails the production of such a place. The rules are open to subversion or overt challenge (as is the bounding), but this then challenges the very existence of community as a "relative permanence," which in turn will likely spark defensive resistance on the part of at least some inhabitants. Communities are, therefore, contested terrains. Under contemporary conditions of neoliberal hegemony, they are rarely stable for long.

It is not always easy to define the difference between a progressive communitarian politics of place, and the exclusionary and authoritarian practices of, say, homeowner associations defending their property against speculators, developers, and in-migration of "people of the wrong sort." Amitai Etzioni, a leading proponent of the new communitarianism, actively supports, for example, the principle of closed and gated communities as a progressive contribution to the organization of social life. For the privileged, community often means securing and enhancing privileges and a way of life already gained. For the underprivileged, it all too often means "controlling their own slum" (but at least it is "their" slum) as a residual space. The communitarian solution goes nowhere in relation to hegemonic neoliberal practices, except to challenge ethical individualism through small-scale collective solidarities that often turn out to be more protective of individual private property rights and values than generative of new kinds of social relations.[53]

Place formation under neoliberalism is, like the production of space, an active process. It is against this background that prospects for an alternative, place-based resistance to neoliberalism have to be engaged. The circulation and accumulation of capital destabilizes the "permanences" of places and regions, if only because money power destroys all other kinds of community so that it itself becomes the community. Phenomena like urban growth, changing regional divisions of labor, deindustrialization, gentrification, regional class alliance formation, and the like are products of this process. Place-making and the production of uneven geographical development go hand in hand.[54] But the circulation and accumulation of capital are not the only process that matters. Consider, for example, the circulation of energy through socio-ecological systems, the circulation of cultural impulses and information, the shifting dynamics of geopolitical power relations, the conflicting identities (nationalist, ethnic, racial, gendered) that arise relationally and clash (often violently) through place formation in absolute space. The contestation over places (the construction of boundaries, barriers, walls, and policed borders) is an omnipresent feature of our world. How people associate and construct collectivities and communities (sometimes but not always within bounded territories) varies enormously, as do the organizational forms (rhizomatic or hierarchical, centralized or decentralized, democratic or authoritarian) and the specific aims (by no means confined to political-economic ends). How power is amassed in, and how it circulates within and between, collectivities and particular territorial forms of political organization also matters, since it is against the background of such processes that alternative possibilities come into being. The very instability of places and the perpetual disruptions of community mean there are always open spaces for oppositional politics to arise and even to flourish. The instability and uncontrollability of relational connections render impossible completely successful repressive totalitarian controls.. A space can always be opened up in which people come together to define ways of relating and of valuing that depart from neoliberal monetized norms.

While mobilizing the "power of place" is a vital aspect of political action, there is always the danger of fetishizing this moment. The politics of localism and parochialism is no answer to the universal repressions of neoliberal exploitation and accumulation by dispossession. And this is so precisely because of the intimate relation between spaces and places. Distinctive places do indeed form key sites for individual encounters through which commonalities and solidarities can be established between individuals, such that counter-hegemonic movements against a dominant order can be articulated. From such sites it is "possible to mobilize participants for political projects" that transcend "parochial concerns while still preserving accountability to the base." And, over time, the density of enduring social, economic, and political ties in places (from neighborhoods to regions and to states) provides "a pragmatic anchor for political activity." The problem, of course, is that this anchor can prove a drag upon movement unless it is supplemented by the kind of "inspired" politics that C. Katz envisages, a politics that is prepared to both cross space and jump scales. [55]

Even then, it is important to recognize that this process cuts a variety of ways depending upon ideological orientation and particular political objectives. This is the way that Christianity built its base, as did socialism. Reactionary fascism, the BJP in India, and the progressive civil rights movement in the United States all mobilized the power of place as a means to pursue their political agendas. Furthermore, contestation and struggle over who controls the power of place is everywhere apparent. The rise of fascism in Italy in the 1920s, as in Chile after 1973, was accompanied by a total destruction of the places and spaces in which the left was organized and the substitution of an alternative territorial organization of political control to sustain power. Authoritarian mayors in U.S. cities have traditionally organized places—ward systems—into a territorialized political machine to maintain their position, and they have sought to destroy alternative place-based forms of political organization. All political, social, and religious movements use place-building territorial strategies to achieve their goals. The geographies of freedom and of authoritarian repressions go hand in hand in their resort to territorial strategies of place-building. It is no more possible to escape the logic of territoriality and place-building than it is to escape politics.

Place-based community entails a delicate relation between fluid spatiotemporal processes (both relative and relational) and relatively permanent rules of belonging and association constructed in absolute space (like the those formally imposed by the nation-state). The tangible struggle to define its limits and range (sometimes even territories and borders), and to create and sustain its rules and institutions through collective powers such as constitutional forms, political parties, the churches, the unions, neighborhood organizations, local governments, and the like, has proven central to the pursuit of alternatives to the selfishness of personalized market individualism presupposed in neoliberal and liberal theories. The problem is that although community "in itself" has meaning as part of a broader politics, community "for itself" almost invariably degenerates into regressive exclusions and fragmentations (what some would call negative heterotopias of spatial form). To emphasize that danger is not to propose that all place-based forms of political organizing are inevitably reactionary.

Anarchists, particularly of the social variety, are deeply interested in place construction even as they abjure that particular territorial form of place construction called the state. Murray Bookchin, for example, advocates the creation of "a humanly scaled self-governing municipality freely and confederally associated with other humanly scaled, self governing municipalities." This "anarchic vision of decentralized communities, united in free confederations or networks for coordinating the communities of a region, reflects the traditional ideals of a participatory democracy in a modern radical context." Furthermore, "an ecological community would municipalize its economy and join with other municipalities in integrating its resources into a regional confederal system. Land, factories and workshops would be controlled by the popular assemblies of free communities, not by a nation-state or worker producers who might very well develop a proprietory interest in them."[56] Bookchin is proposing a particular form of place construction to displace the nation-state. His formulation actually ranges across the matrix of spatio-temporal forms in interesting ways. His vision of municipal associationism begins at the absolute territorial level with local assemblies of equally endowed individuals, shifts to the relative space-time dimension through the networks of regional assemblies, and expresses relationality through the "common flow" idea that everyone, everywhere, should sense their solidarity with everyone else by living a life of nonhierarchical social relations in municipal associations that cultivate an intimate relation with nature.

The geographical theory of place tells us that Bookchin's proposals cannot avoid encountering all the paradoxes and contradictions that arise in all forms of place construction (including that of the nation-state). How will the reifications of this anarchist ideal actually work on the ground in absolute space and time? Will the self-governing municipalities be bounded, fenced in, and guarded from outside marauders? What principles of membership/citizenship will apply, and how will the exit and entry of members be regulated (if at all)? How will the power structures that inevitably form at higher scales (the regional confederal assemblies) actually work, and how can the danger that decentralization can assure the perpetuation of hidden forms of centralized power be avoided? "If the whole society were to be organized as a confederation of autonomous municipalities," Iris Marion Young comments, "what would prevent the development of large-scale inequality and injustice among communities, and thereby the oppression of individuals who do not live in the more privileged and more powerful communities?"[57] To this I would add another difficulty: how would a world of 6 billion or more people living in this way protect biodiversity in, say, tropical rainforests? Bookchin is aware of many of these questions and does his best to answer some of them in his numerous writings without, unfortunately, providing altogether convincing answers.

What geographical theory teaches is that all forms of place construction, no matter whether organized by socialists, autonomistas, social anarchists, religious groups, city corporations, developers, or dictators, face similar foundational questions. A geographical theory of place poses these questions head on and so helps us avoid the more egregious blunders of well-intentioned alternative forms of place construction. Place-making according to conscious design, as evidenced, with all its faults, by the utopian tradition, is one of our greatest powers. It is also one of our unavoidable tasks. How it is integrated as a constructive rather than disruptive moment into cosmopolitan projects therefore becomes of crucial significance, a condition of possibility for human emancipation.

Chapter Nine
The Nature of Environment

Jared Diamond's book *Guns, Germs, and Steel,* with its portentous subtitle "The Fates of Human Societies," has sold well over a million copies since it was first published in 1997. As of October 2006, when it finally fell off the list, it had been among the *New York Times* top twenty best sellers for 205 weeks. "History," Diamond argues in the book, "followed different courses for different peoples because of differences among peoples' environments, not because of biological differences among peoples themselves." Geography, he argues, is the "primary cause" that operates through the "proximate causes" of food production, animal husbandry, metallurgy (technology), disease regimes, and language. The question of geography's role (as opposed to genetic endowments) in shaping human histories is, for Diamond, a materialist scientific question. He mobilizes both his own credentials (from molecular physiology, evolutionary biology, and biogeography) and wide-ranging scientific information (culled from archaeology, anthropology, epidemiology, linguistics, behavioral ecology, and the history of science and technology) in the search for answers. Diamond aims to provide a unified and synthetic account, a materialist scientific history, "on a par with acknowledged historical sciences such as astronomy, geology and evolutionary biology."[1] He also writes in popular and readily accessible scientific terms.

Diamond's is the kind of "popular propaedeutic" work that Kant might have written if only he had known how. It lays out the geographical "conditions of possibility" of human history and therefore seems to provide the perfect secular answer to the question of what kind of geographical knowledge is required to properly ground our understanding of our species being and human social evolution. Diamond claims not to be an environmental determinist in the strict sense of that term. "Without human inventiveness, all of us today would still be cutting our meat with stone tools and eating it raw, like our ancestors of a million years ago. All human societies contain inventive people. It's just that some environments provide more starting materials, and more favorable conditions for utilizing inventions, than do other environments."[2] How he reconciles this closing statement with the opening insistence on geography as a prime cause is somewhat of a mystery. The first part of the book provides a compelling account of the ecological conditions that facilitated the domestication of plant and animal species. The argument is simple: relatively few plant and animal species were suited for domestication; of those that were, some were far more nutritious and amenable to domestication than others; and the geographical distribution of the species was strictly limited by environmental constraints to nine small areas of the globe. The initial wave of plant and animal domestication around 8000 B.C.E. therefore occurred in these few favored locations. Of these, one, the Fertile Crescent, was more favorable than the others. Diamond skillfully uses his evidence to describe agricultural origins and, incidentally, to showcase his scientific credentials. While commentators have pointed out errors and voiced criticisms, Diamond's account of the initial wave of plant and animal domestication is probably as good as any other that we have. But the thesis of environmental causation within which he frames his account is nowhere demonstrated. The most that can be inferred is that appropriate environmental conditions were a necessary but by no means sufficient "condition of possibility" for domestication to occur in the places that it did.

The environment-as-cause thesis becomes even more problematic as the book moves forward in time. Current geographical inequalities in economic development and in the global distribution of wealth, Diamond argues, are largely explicable in terms of the initial environmental conditions that gave rise to domestication. If this is true, then racial differences and human genetic endowments do not explain the current disparities in the wealth of nations. But this also means that Western colonial and imperialist practices, in themselves, have little or nothing to do with the sorry state of, say, contemporary African development. A predatory capitalism engaging in ruthless resource extraction from Africa pales into insignificance compared to the dead weight of Africa's environmental legacy. The well-documented history in which the fragile fertility of the tropical and subtropical soils in Africa was destroyed within one generation of colonial rule passes unremarked, as does the earlier shadowy history of a thriving decentralized rice agriculture in West Africa that was destroyed by the slave traders (though the techniques of rice cultivation lived on, as the slaves brought them to the Carolinas to found a thriving rice plantation agriculture for the benefit of their white masters). The damning histories of Belgian colonial rapine of the Congo and the violent repression of the Ogoni peoples in the Niger delta in the name of big oil do not figure in Diamond's account because it is the "hand of history's course at 8000 BC [that] lies heavily upon us."[3] The ghost of King Leopold of Belgium and the current directors of Shell Oil will doubtless appreciate being let so lightly off the hook. And Diamond's tale must be comforting news—reassuring and untroubling—to many Americans who cheerfully consume a third of the world's resources (some from Africa) while taking little or no responsibility for the consequences of such profligacy on the ground. No wonder the book is consumed with such gusto in the United States.

So how, then, does Diamond navigate across the 10,000 years between the initial wave of plant and animal domestication (about which he may well be correct) and the current state of social inequality and uneven geographical development within the global economy (about which he is dead wrong)? Plainly, the world has not stood still, and some of the initial areas of plant and animal domestication (such as the Tigris-Euphrates crescent, which today is Iraq) are hardly models of advanced development compared to northwest Europe, Japan, or the United States where no domestication occurred. Some of the human groups that pursued domestication were more advantaged than others, says Diamond. The Fertile Crescent, for example, had a particularly nutritious food source (wheat is better than sorghum) and a large enough area suited to its cultivation to support a large population with a food surplus to support other activities. Initial advantages of this sort permitted the development of technologies, germs, literacy skills, and military hardware that allowed these particular groups to spread outward "at the expense of other groups, until either the latter groups became replaced or everyone came to share the new advantages."[4] Competition between and conquest of human groups lies at the root of this process (there is no role here for cosmopolitan collaborations of the limited Kantian sort, or even of subtle processes of cultural transmission, though there is more than a hint of a covert theory of Kant's "species being" in which human groups always seek domination of others). Imperial practices, wars, and conquests are absorbed (scientifically naturalized) in Diamond's account into Darwinian struggles between human groups for growth and survival, but those who had the initial advantage win out. Political-economic choices have no fundamental role in this dog-eat-dog world.

Geographical conditions (presented mainly in terms of a fixed and unchanging spatial ordering of physical qualities), furthermore, guided migratory movements and the spatial diffusion of innovations. In this the axes of the continents played a crucial role, since latitudinal movements of crop regimes along the climatic belts is easier than movement across them (thus Africa and the Americas, where some initial plant and animal domestication occurred, were disadvantaged because north-south movements across the climatic belts are far more difficult). This same condition affects the diffusion of technologies and literacy (though why the climatic belts mattered in these instances is obscure). Eurasia, where the geographical and ecological barriers to movement were supposedly minimal, was therefore able to seize the advantage and develop the technologies and ultimately the guns (and to foment the germs) that facilitated conquest everywhere else. If we look back to the Fertile Crescent as *the* origin, then, it is because the geographical paths of diffusion outward were easiest from there (particularly after the productive capacities of the original hearth were exhausted by overuse, which interestingly appeals to human predilections rather than environmental causation as an explanation). Ultimately, these advantages permitted a few Spanish conquistadors to conquer a military force of many thousands in the Americas. Europe's confused physical geography also felicitously prevented the development of any centralized state power (a negative attribute in these neoliberal times, in spite of the contemporary evidence from China), and this fostered more competition (supposedly a positive attribute, of course) and, hence, more innovation in Europe than elsewhere. In these ways, the initial "civilizational" breakthroughs in one selected hearth of plant and animal domestication spread unevenly around the world along broadly predictable geographical pathways. Bringing us up to date, Diamond even wonders "whether nuclear weapons will proliferate around the world by the same often-violent process." [5]

Compared to the first part of the book, the evidence advanced for the subsequent argument is speculative and shallow. To construct such a macro account of human history over 10,000 years in 200 pages obviously demands a high level of generalization and abstraction, but in this instance scientific method of any sort gives way to crude guess-work and wishful thinking. The maps deployed are of an absolute sort (recall the distinction made in chapter 7 and presented in fig. 1 in that chapter), and Diamond makes no attempt to take up the radical shifts in relative space-time produced by innovations in transport and communications that have characterized human historical geography. His account is only believable, one suspects, because the reader carries over the scientific authority established in the first part of the book to the second. Consider, for example, his comparative exploration of the fates of China and Europe, both of which should have benefited from lateral movement of innovations from the key area of initial domestication (Diamond ignores entirely the barrier of the Tibetan/Himalayan traverse). Eyeballing maps, Diamond notes that Europe's coastline is much more indented and fragmented than China's and posits this as the explanation for China's "chronic unity and Europe's chronic disunity."[6] A grossly simplified representation based on maps of a certain scale in absolute space is given causal power in relation to material social practices and history on the ground. China's loss of political and technological preeminence (as well as its failure to pursue early possibilities of overseas exploration and discovery) is attributed to excessive centralization of state power because of its straight coastline. This is the crassest form of spatial determinism. The argument is easy to ridicule. Eyeballing the coastlines of the United States and China suggests the United States should be even more centralized than China. Deng clearly forgot about China's coastline when he decentralized power to provinces, municipalities, and even villages after 1978 and hence launched China on its astonishing process of economic and technological development. Excessive bureaucratic centralization within any state or imperial apparatus sometimes (but only sometimes) has negative consequences for innovation and growth. On this point, Diamond follows the standard liberal and neoliberal dogma that excessive state control is always bad (ignoring the fact that bureaucratized and authoritarian states, such as Japan, South Korea, Singapore, Taiwan, and now China, have dominated the growth curves in contemporary capitalism for many years and that the United States is hardly a model of non–state intervention in the economy in key areas such as military technologies). This "finding" about the dangers of excessive state centralization brought Diamond glowing reviews from Bill Gates and put him close to the Microsoft engineers (fortunately the coastline around Seattle is indented enough to sustain their efforts to monopolize the software world). What Gates and Deng have in common, however, is the discovery that appropriately organized decentralization can be one of the most effective vehicles for highly centralized control. The emphasis here has to be on the meaning of "appropriately organized," because chaotic decentralization of the sort that occurred in Russia after 1989 did not work, except for the seven oligarchs who emerged to take control of much of the economy (assembling immense personal wealth in the process). Chaotic decentralization is a chronic problem in many parts of Africa, though local elites often do very well out of it. Appropriately organized decentralization is a political-organizational choice that has nothing to do with coastlines. In his afterword to a later edition Diamond recognizes the problem of "optimal" fragmentation in a way that loses all connection with his postulate of spatial shape in absolute space as an explanation for political organization.[7] His assertions on the causal effects of coastlines have absolutely no plausibility, let alone any "scientific" basis. They are, in short, nonsense.

The economist Jeffrey Sachs—an influential adviser to the United Nations—tells a very different but similarly environmentally loaded story about China's rising economic power in his best-selling book *The End of Poverty*. Compared to Russia and Eastern Europe, it was China's "very different geography, geopolitics, and demography," rather than "a difference of policy choices," that gave it an advantage after the end of communism. China's large coastline, Sachs argues, "supported its export-led growth, whereas the Soviet Union and Eastern Europe did not have the benefit of large coastlines and the resulting low-cost access to international trade."[8] The thesis that lack of access to navigable water was the problem for Russia is convenient, since Sachs played a very important role in administering the market-based "shock therapy" to the former Soviet Union that had such disastrous economic and social consequences in the early 1990s. (We could conclude from this that the main advantage in China's case was that Sachs had no influence over policy there, while Russia will have to wait upon global warming to open up its Arctic coastline before it can develop.) But the big problem for China, Sachs goes on to argue, is not its homogeneity (as Diamond supposes), but its geographical diversity, particularly the north-south divide and, even more important, an east-west differential based on distance from navigable water. This echoes Sachs's more general principles of geographical determination: using seemingly sophisticated statistical techniques, he shows that almost all the variation in the level of economic development of the world's states can be explained by physical distance measured from the equator and from navigable water.[9] More expansively, he suggests that "geographical advantages might include access to key natural resources, access to the coastline and sea—navigable rivers, proximity to other successful economies, advantageous conditions for agriculture, advantageous conditions for human health." He also follows Diamond, though somewhat more cautiously, by suggesting that agricultural and health technologies could spread more easily within ecological zones defined by climatic belts rather than across them. In their analyses, both Sachs and Diamond forget, however, that spatial associations between different phenomena (for example, between the spatial distribution of cows and of pastureland, or of straight coastlines and centralized power) are no proof of causation. They also both use absolute measures of space, location, and environmental (mainly climatic) conditions as if they are unproblematic. The relativity of space-time is of little consequence, while relationality apparently has for them no meaning at all.

Interestingly, Sachs later on in the same book offers a very different account of China's historical geography, based on the good neoliberal mythology, also advanced by Diamond, that centralized power is inimical to economic development. "What made the centralized state possible in China," writes Sachs (in an account that grossly oversimplifies China's complex historical-geographical evolution), "was a vast subcontinental scale society of villages. The villages themselves looked a lot like each other across a very wide space: they were rice-growing communities of hundreds of millions of people, living in hundreds of thousands of villages, with common economic and cultural characteristics. In such a homogeneous setting, a centralized administrative strategy flourished, with orders going down from the top, percolating through various levels, and reaching the endpoints in communities very similar in their basic internal organization."[10] The achievements of the centralized state that emerged on this basis (and Sachs cheerfully lays aside all the geographical north-south and east-west variation that he had earlier invoked as crucial) were, he says, remarkable, but economic development of the Western European sort, "where political and thus economic power was always decentralized," was impossible (no matter what the regime). The centralized Chinese state was "not compatible with the dynamism of a decentralized and diverse market economy and market-based society, which depends on migration, multiple bases of power and wealth, and regional diversity." China's contemporary economic success arises, he then goes on to tell us, because of "the empowerment of provincial and local governments to experiment at their levels by allowing for diversity, creating a more complex division of labor and enabling mobility." The willingness of the Chinese centralized state to decentralize, to experiment, and "to see what works" has been crucial, making policy choices (a determinant that Sachs had earlier denied) rather than an accessible coastline the principal explanation of the rapidity of growth.[11]

What is odd about both of these popular and influential accounts by Diamond and Sachs is that the role of geography (always understood as some aspect of the physical environment including the fixed spatial ordering of the land) slips in and out of the argument as an explanatory and sometimes as an active causal agent in disconcerting ways. While physical geographical condition is frequently appealed to (in true Kantian fashion) as the "condition of possibility" of everything else, the actual dynamics described invariably entail human agency (such as human innovative capacities, technologies, and intergroup competition in Diamond's case and market versus state behaviors and policy choices in Sachs's case). The result is to propel developments in ways outside of direct or even indirect environmental controls, unless we are prepared, as Diamond urges, to suppose some deep and hidden connection to events 10,000 years ago, which is in principle no different from tracing contemporary global inequalities back to the big bang origin of the universe.

But the effect of attributing global inequalities to the effects of geography, construed as physical environmental and locational conditions, rather than to, say, market forces, policy choices, and imperialist practices changes radically how we think of political possibilities. If policy choices are trumped by coastline determinism (as in Sachs's initial formulation), then why bother about policies? This turns out to be a longstanding trick. It also has popular resonance, as illustrated by an article in the journal *Foreign Policy* entitled "A Case of Bad Latitude: Why Geography Causes Poverty," in which the thesis of environmental causation of global inequalities is boldly stated and then supported by the usual academic references. The Reverend Thomas Malthus long ago explained poverty and unemployment in terms of natural proclivities for human beings to procreate versus natural resource constraints, thereby denying the feasibility of rationalist and egalitarian/socialist solutions because of natural barriers. David Ricardo appealed to diminishing returns in agriculture to explain the inevitability of capitalist crises, leading Marx to comment scathingly that "when faced with a crisis Ricardo takes refuge in organic chemistry." Ricardo could thus avoid any discussion of the inherent contradictions and class inequalities engendered by free market capitalism as an explanation for capitalism's instabilities.[12] Furthermore, the myth that centralized state control is inimical to human development merely has to be asserted in these neoliberal times in order to be accepted without an iota of scientific justification (whereas to assert the opposite is to incur intense skepticism, followed by demands for rigorous scientific and empirical proofs). In the case of China, the environmentalist proposition that the supposed excessive centralization of power there arises out of environmental conditions has a long history. Karl Wittfogel, starting out as a Marxist materialist in the 1930s, argued for the necessity of a centralized state bureaucracy to control the massive irrigation works required to survive in that environment, and on this basis he advanced a universal thesis (elements of which can also be found in Marx) of an "Asiatic mode of production" (or even more generally, a "hydraulic society") characterized by "oriental despotism" as its primary political form.[13] Rain-fed agriculture in Western Europe, in contrast, supposedly created the conditions for individual liberty, decentralized democracy, and a market society (which makes the rise of fascism in Europe inexplicable, since there is no evidence it stopped raining—though much of Spain is pretty arid, so maybe this does explain Franco). Wittfogel thus turned historical materialism into a certain kind of historical-geographical materialism by viewing physical environmental conditions (nature) as the bedrock upon which all forms of human activity depended. Diamond just looks at the shape of coastlines, and Sachs (in one of his versions) focuses on climatic conditions and accessibility to navigable water.

There is one other curious angle to this debate over whether or not geography matters. Daron Acemoglu, winner in 2005 of the prestigious John Bates Clark award for the most promising economist under forty, has made his reputation in part by disputing both Diamond's and Sachs's arguments, proving that global inequalities have little to do with geographic, climatic, and ecological factors, and everything to do with institutions. Since the geographical factors (spatial locations and climatic belts) have remained fairly constant since 1500, he argues, they cannot possibly explain the considerable shifts that have occurred in global wealth distribution since that time. The "historical evidence suggests that European colonialism not only disrupted the social organization of a large number of countries, but in fact led to the establishment of extractive institutions in previously prosperous areas and to the development of institutions of private property in previously poor areas." The result was "a reversal in the relative [wealth] rankings among countries affected by European colonialism," particularly during the nineteenth century, such that impoverished and relatively empty areas (like the United States, Canada, and Australia) became wealthier, while the previously wealthy, high-population-density countries (like India, China, Indonesia, and Bolivia) all became poorer under a regime of extractive institutions.[14] His measure of wealth, interestingly, rests on degree of urbanization (itself, surely, a geographical phenomenon) though later versions of this argument have rested on more conventional income and wealth estimates. The poorer countries that won out were, not surprisingly, those that encouraged investment by establishing strong private property rights regimes.

This huge shift in the geography of global wealth since 1500 is totally and conveniently ignored in Diamond's potted history, and it would indeed be hard to come up with any explanation of it in the geographical terms to which Diamond appeals. While Acemoglu's concern to shift the terrain of debate about global poverty from geography, about which we can supposedly do very little, to social and political questions is laudable, and while it is also helpful to have colonial and imperialist extractive practices brought back into the forefront of discussion, the categorical distinctions Acemoglu deploys are as seriously wrongheaded as those used by Diamond. To begin with, the assertion that geography has not changed much since 1500 is plainly in error. It denies, without even caring to assess the evidence, that the massive ecological transformations that have occurred since 1492—the deforestation (by sheep and goats) and land clearances, the soil erosion that destroyed much of the agricultural capacity of Mexico and Africa, the land degradation and invasions by foreign species, the desertification and rapid shifts in international trade in agricultural commodities, therapid pace of urbanization—have had anything to do with the shifts in inequality. Even more dramatic is the failure to recognize that it is the relative space-time of transport and communications that is the relevant measure of distance and location, rather than the simple physical distances of absolute space to which Acemoglu appeals. The latter have indeed remained constant, but the former have changed drastically. And it is noteworthy that the most radical transformations in relative space relations occurred in the nineteenth century (steamships and railroads), just when what Acemoglu calls "the great reversal" in the distribution of wealth mainly occurred. But this points to a deeper difficulty, because Acemoglu also assumes that institutions (such as those of the state) are not geographical affairs and that considerations of geography are separable from institutions, when institutions are in fact "produced spaces of social relations of a more or less durable sort. In the most obvious sense they are territorializations—territories of control and surveillance, terrains of jurisdiction, and domains of organization and administration."[15] To imply that the state (local or national), for example, is not a geographical phenomenon and then to represent the state's extractive institutions as if they have no geographical grounding is plainly wrong. Many of our key institutions (state, military, religious, educational) are actively produced through the creation of particular places, spaces, and environmental qualities (new geographies). The military have their barracks, the priests their churches, the educators their schools and universities, and so on. Investments in physical and social infrastructures go hand in hand with institution building. Conversely, the production of spaces (the building of the railroads that revolutionized relative space relations in the nineteenth century) and of places (cities), and the environmental transformations that humans have wrought across the earth's surface since the fifteenth century, have depended heavily upon the formation of institutions, such as those of the state and of finance. Acemoglu incorrectly postulates a dichotomous world in which a supposedly static geography (understood as an absolute space of location and fixed climatic belts) starkly contrasts with dynamic social institutions. Of course, the former, depicted from the outset as the fixed, the dead, and the undialectical—as Foucault complained of all traditional Kantian formulations—fails to generate change compared to the latter. But the dichotomy is completely false: the production of space and radical transformations of nature and of geography are engineered through human institutions and the organization of labor, through territorializations and deterritorializations (as in Africa in 1885), new technologies (designed, for example, to overcome the frictions of distance), and the emergence of completely new ways of life. In effect, all that Acemoglu does is to prove what he has already assumed to be true: that geography (erroneously construed as an immutable physical condition) is passive and not active in human affairs.

We must not ignore the politics of these arguments. Attributing our ills to natural environmental causes and fixed spatial orderings, about which we can supposedly do little or nothing, rather than to societal malfunctioning, about which we can take strong action, makes a huge difference in how we might understand, feel responsible for, and attempt to confront global inequalities and political repressions. And even if, as Sachs argues, it is possible to do something about the disease regimes associated with tropical climates (cheap mosquito netting for the poor), the policy invoked evades entirely the political and economic origins of much of the poverty that bedevils the global South. On these counts Diamond's text, Malthusian arguments, and, to a lesser degree, Sachs's proposals for confronting the problem of global poverty are deeply troubling. If this is the kind of geography to be inserted into a cosmopolitan project, then we are, I submit, in deep difficulty. Acemoglu's reversal of the argument is, given the choice, obviously to be preferred, but he merely ends up compounding the problem by appealing to a definition of "geography" that is profoundly misleading. The extensive debate that flourishes these days within economics and political science over the "geography" versus "institutions" question, pays absolutely no mind to the growing trend within science in general to abandon the Cartesian/Kantian framework that grounds the dichotomy between physical geography (nature) and social institutions (culture).[16] The transformations since the sixteenth century in space-time relations, place building, the organization of territorial and regional structures, and environmental conditions collectively amount to a massive reshaping of the world's geography. It is astonishing to find that none of this gets registered in the economics or political science literature.

Environmental Determinisms

Diamond and Sachs have revived a long tradition of assertion of geographical and environmental influences upon human action. Bizarrely represented in Kant's fumbling Geography, this tradition goes back at least to the Greeks. Clarence Glacken's monumental *Traces on the Rhodian Shore* provides us with a comprehensive account of how this idea of environmental influences weaves in and out in Western thought with other traditions that highlight either the idea of "man's domination of nature" or a nature-human-heavenly continuum ordered according to some God-given intelligent design with human beings occupying the pinnacle, close to God, within a "great chain of being" (a medieval idea that evangelical Christians and President Bush seem intent on reviving). Montesquieu and Rousseau, for example, frequently invoked environmental influences on human behavior and at times turned downright deterministic (Montesquieu held that islands produce conditions for individual liberties, and Rousseau, that desert climates give rise to monotheism and absolutist forms of government).[17] Ellen Churchill Semple, a student of the German geographer Friedrich Ratzel, is probably Anglo-American geography's most famous representative of the deterministic line of thinking. In *Influences of Geographical Environment*, published in 1911, she wrote:

> Man is a product of the earth's surface. This means not merely that he is a child of the earth, dust of her dust; but that the earth has mothered him, fed him, set him tasks, directed his thoughts, confronted him with difficulties that have strengthened his body and sharpened his wits, given him his problems of navigation or irrigation, and at the same time whispered hints for their solution. She has entered into his bone and tissue, into his mind and soul. On the mountains she has given him leg muscles of iron to climb the slope, along the coast she has left these weak and flabby, but given him instead vigorous development of chest and arm to handle his paddle or oar. In the river valley she attaches him to the fertile soil, circumscribes his ideas and ambitions by a dull round of calm, exacting duties, narrows his outlook to the cramped horizon of the farm. Up on the windswept plateaux, in the boundless stretch of the grasslands and the waterless tracts of the desert, where he roams with his flocks from pasture to pasture and oasis to oasis, where life knows much hardship but escapes the grind of drudgery, where the watching of grazing herds give him leisure for contemplation, and the wide-ranging life of a big horizon, his ideas take on a certain gigantic simplicity; religion becomes monotheism, God becomes one unrivalled like the sand of the desert and the grass of the steppe, stretching on and on without break or change. Chewing over and over the cud of his simple belief as the one food of his unfed mind, his faith becomes fanaticism; his big special ideas, born of that regular ceaseless wandering, outgrow the land that bred them and bear their legitimate fruit in wide imperial conquests.[18]

The gendering of the passage is remarkable, but this reflects a long tradition that opposes mother earth (geography) to father time (history). Francis Bacon held unreservedly that the domination of nature by man was strictly equivalent to men dominating capricious and wayward women (which explains much of what Shakespeare was doing in *The Taming of the Shrew*). But also interesting is the wide array of physical environmental features to which Semple appeals. This illustrates a certain advantage that environmental determinists enjoy, since for every detectable variation in human social organization or historical transformation, there is bound to be some unique physical environmental feature (climatic, physiographic, and so forth) that can be associated with it. If association is taken as proof, then the thesis of environmental determination becomes irrefutable. Notice, therefore, how elements of Semple's reasoning are reproduced by Sachs (all those monotonous villages in the river valleys of China) and Diamond

(China's straight coastline and imperial conquests by people that "outgrew the land that bred them"). The mode of argumentation in the second part of Diamond's book flips from one kind of environmental association to another, and Sachs invokes coastlines when convenient and policy choices when he wants. The opportunistic environmental determinism of the second part of Diamond's book contrasts with the more singular and systematic theory laid out in the first part, for which he deserves some credit. In practice, the more singular and systematic the theory, the more productive it is, and the more easily we can evaluate and refute it. Ellsworth Huntington, for example, in a series of books published from 1925 to 1950, sought to reduce all forms of environmental influence to climatic determinations. Climatic determinism has a long history that stretches from the Greeks to the present day (Sachs relies heavily though not exclusively upon it, for example, and even the eminent nineteenth-century economist Alfred Marshall took it as axiomatic). Huntington went to great lengths to carefully investigate the nature of climatic variation and in so doing furthered the development of accurate climatic classification (an activity that went back to the pioneering work of Köppen in the nineteenth century). The trouble was that Huntington's climatic data became the basis for asserting the superiority of the temperate climates and the white populations of European descent that populated them. When he attempted to define the climatic conditions most conducive to intellectual activity and produced a map where the optimal location fell suspiciously close to Harvard, where he taught for many years (though there was another outlier in Edinburgh), his whole enterprise looked so self-serving as to be ridiculous. But his broader findings certainly had great relevance to understanding questions of agricultural productivity, and it would be hard to deny, given the appalling experience of the 1930s "Dustbowl" in the United States, that the overextension of agricultural practices into regions of high drought risk had something to do with the social disaster that followed. The mass migration from Oklahoma and Kansas to California commemorated in Steinbeck's epic novel *The Grapes of Wrath* was in part a response to climatic events, though in Steinbeck's novel, as well as in actual history, it was a combination of drought conditions and mechanized agribusiness, backed by the bankers' drive to foreclose on mortgaged lands, that drove the Okies out.[19] An analogous case in recent times would be to attribute the disaster in New Orleans in 2005 solely to hurricane Katrina, as if socio-political and economic circumstances had nothing to do with events. There is, it turns out, no such thing as a purely "natural" disaster.[20]

One of the more celebrated instances of geographical determinism in action arose around the work of the geographer Griffith Taylor who, in the 1920s, strongly objected on environmental grounds to the political plans for population expansion through massive immigration into Australia. Using well-grounded scientific data on climatic, hydrological, and soil conditions, Taylor drew up detailed and quite accurate maps to argue that there were strict environmental limits to the distribution and density of population achievable within the country. His concluding map of what might be possible in the way of population density and distribution by the year 2000 remarkably predicts the current patterns. In the 1920s, however, a promethean technological triumphalism combined with a white racist colonial settler mentality to promote an image of a new Australia of teeming millions to rival the United States. In this context Taylor's writings created such a furor of opposition in the popular press that he was hounded out of Sydney University and indeed out of the country; he went to Canada where he later promoted the idea of "stop and go determinism." While it is possible, he conceded, for human societies to stray from environmental determinations, in the long run we are bound to succumb to the inevitability of environmental limits and controls.[21] This is the stance taken by many contemporary environmentalists. That Taylor's predictions for Australian settlement broadly conform to later realities would seem to support his theoretical stance. This would imply, however, that the dynamics of what became energy-intensive and fossil fuel–based forms of urbanization and the shifting evolution of Australia's position within the international division of labor, of trading relations and migratory streams (to mention just a few elements that have produced the present geographical distributions), can be attributed to environmental causes—or, less dramatically, that they were somehow all contained within environmentally imposed constraints. If Taylor and, by extension, Diamond and Sachs were scientifically serious in their environmentalism, they should be able to identify the processes whereby the environmental conditionalities (which undoubtedly exist and which can never be ignored as necessary conditions) play an active rather than passive role in the outcomes to be explained. Correlations and associations can be suggestive (as, for example, in the case of smoking and lung cancer or in the case of stomach cancers and water supply qualities), but until actual mechanisms and processes of production are identified, environmental determinations remain entirely speculative, and environmental limits remain contingent rather than determinant. In Diamond's case, for example, there is no attempt to show the mechanisms whereby coastlines have effects on political organization.

There is a continuum of argument moving from strict environmental determinism (with a few grains of human initiative at the center) to total freedom of human action (within an aura of light environmental constraints). Taylor's theory of stop-and-go determinism, for example, morphs into the idea of challenge and response in Arnold Toynbee's magnum opus *The Study of Civilization*. Toynbee's idea was simple enough: distinctive geographical environments pose different challenges, but the responses depend on differential human capacities and powers (such as human "character" of the sort that Kant invokes or the policy choices that Sachs mentions in one of his versions of China's development). Toynbee proves his thesis by noting different responses to similar environmental conditions but, as Oscar Spate points out, the way Toynbee specifies "similar" leaves much to be desired. To suggest that the Nile and the Rio Grande are similar riverine environments and that, therefore, the differences in human development between them are explicable in terms of differential human response is wildly off the mark when the physical differences between the two river valleys are subjected to even casual scrutiny.[22] But here, again, we encounter the problem of deciding exactly what the environmental difference is that makes a difference to human action.

At the other end of the spectrum lies an entirely different school of thought, called "possibilist," a term derived largely from the French historian Lucien Febvre who most famously stated in 1910 that "there are no necessities, but everywhere possibilities; and man as master of these possibilities is the judge of their use." The causal arrow here gets reversed. "Man dominates nature" and shapes her (and in the past the relation has usually been spelled out in this gendered fashion) to his will. Francis Bacon and Descartes thus celebrated "man's" potential to dominate nature through science, engineering, and technology. This promethean argument rarely holds that absolutely anything is possible. But it does insist that what humans do depends fundamentally on technologies, cost, finance, human organization, cultural preferences, and the like. It is always, as the geographer Isaiah Bowman once quipped, possible to move mountains, but first you need to launch a bond issue.[23] Within the Marxist tradition there are abundant expressions of a promethean and productivist approach to the world, and these carried over, with some disastrous consequences, to actual practices in the Stalinist phase of Soviet development. They even affected scientific inquiry, in the lamentable Lysenko affair in which for some forty years Soviet agronomy was imprisoned in the false dogma that acquired characteristics could be inherited (a view that Lefebvre, then a member of the French communist party, refused to endorse). Whether it is accurate to derive this promethean viewpoint from Marx's own writings is, however, a matter of contemporary contention. Other forms of possibilism are more restrained. The French geographer Vidal de la Blache, for example, recognized that the distinctive regional landscapes of France (from Brittany to Burgundy) were human constructions, but he saw the process of their emergence as one in which human action ultimately converged upon a distinctive regional personality, a harmonic symbiosis of human action with natural possibilities. Distinctive regions are not given but carved out of nature by human action.[24] At times, this comes close to being a regional version of the *genius loci* idea encountered in chapter 7: human action reveals the essential and inherent qualities of the natural world. Regional landscapes and city forms are construed, as it were, as works of art wrought by years of patient human artifice.

This benign view contrasts, however, with an extensive literature bemoaning unintended consequences. This point was made as long ago as 1864, by that extraordinary pioneer in the study of the historical geography of environmental change, George Perkins Marsh. Marsh recognized that it was often hard to distinguish between anthropogenic and naturally occurring changes in the environment, but regarded it as "certain that man has done much to mould the form of the earth's surface." Much of the geography we now confront is the product of human activities (an idea totally foreign to both Diamond and Acemoglu). While these changes were by no means always destructive to human interests, we too often forget that the earth is given to us "for usufruct alone, not for consumption, still less for profligate waste" (even Margaret Thatcher voiced a similar opinion, though in her case it turned out to be good cover to close down the coal mines and smash the Miner's Union that had long anchored the British labor movement). Human action turns "the harmonies of nature" into "discords," said Marsh. Intentional changes pale "in comparison with the contingent and unsought results which have flowed from them" with all manner of destructive consequences.[25] Engels made the same point: "Let us not, however, flatter ourselves overmuch on account of our human victories over nature. For each such victory nature takes its revenge on us. Each victory, it is true, in the first place brings about the results we expected, but in the second and third places it has quite different, unforseen effects which only too often cancel the first. . . . Thus at every step we are reminded that we by no means rule over nature like a conqueror over a foreign people, like someone standing outside of nature—but that we, with flesh, blood and brain, belong to nature, and exist in its midst, and that all our mastery of it consists in the fact that we have the advantage over all other creatures of being able to learn its laws and apply them correctly."[26]

Societies may strive to create ecological conditions and environmental niches for themselves conducive to their own survival, but they cannot do so without bringing about unintended ecological consequences. Not all of these turn out to be universally bad from the standpoint of supporting human activity (there are parts of the world, such as Siberia, that may benefit from global warming through increased agricultural productivity, while other zones, such as the U.S. Midwest, may suffer considerably). But it is hard to see that the possibility of cheaper trans-Arctic shipping routes (yielding Russia the coastline that Sachs believes essential to its development) will offset the global impacts of sea level rises of a meter or more.

The gamut of opinion therefore runs from environmental determinism through stop-and-go determinism, and challenge and response, to the human domination of nature, only to double back on itself by collapsing into usually woeful accounts of unintended consequences and nature's revenge. The so-called Frankfurt School of social scientists, one of whose most influential members in the 1960s was Herbert Marcuse, further argued that the domination of nature inevitably entails the domination of other human beings and even of human nature itself.[27] But nearly all these positions have in common the idea that there is a clear analytic separation to be made between "man" and "culture," on the one hand, and "nature," "environment," and even "geography," on the other. Differences of opinion exist concerning the direction of the causal arrow and the degree of reciprocal interactions and feedbacks involved. But the Cartesian/Kantian dichotomies between facts and values, things and mental constructs, the physical and immaterial worlds, carry over to the idea of a never-ending struggle between "man" and "nature," and the presumption of some sort of causal interactions between these independent entities. The Kantian separation of geography from anthropology then makes sense; the former is the study of man in the system of nature, buffeted and tossed around in a sea of natural forces that drive social orders hither and thither, while the latter is a study of how human beings as active subjects have made themselves, forged character out of natural temperaments (as Kant put it), and overcome the deficiencies of their original environmental condition to move toward a regional symbiosis (as in Vidal de la Blache's discussion of the production of regionality) or even toward a cosmopolitan rationality in the reshaping of both social and natural relations (Ulrich Beck's utopian dream).

All interpretations of the relation to nature require, therefore, serious critical scrutiny, not only concerning their cogency and "truth value," but also for their political and ideological implications. The praise heaped upon Diamond's text by influential political figures and the book's success (it has been made into a PBS television mini-series)is as much a political problem as a question of scientific veracity. While environmentalist (or, for that matter genetic, racist, or culturalist) readings cannot be dismissed simply because of their discomforting political implications, or because they offend some deeply cherished ideological beliefs, the eager political embrace and promotion of Diamond's text in certain powerful quarters should alert us to a key political problem: how do we know when our relation to nature and to environmental conditions is a key determinant of our actions? So where do we begin a critical analysis and how should we proceed?

The Natural Order of Things

Words like *nature* and *environment*, with which the idea of "geography" is so closely associated, are, like *space* and *place*, contested, controversial, and full of multiple meanings. "Nature," Raymond Williams famously pointed out, "contains, though often unnoticed, an extraordinary amount of human history . . . both complicated and changing, as other ideas and experiences change."[28] The "unnoticed" aspect of this poses particular difficulties, because it is hard to spot what Arthur Lovejoy calls the "incompletely explicit *assumptions*, or more or less *unconscious mental habits*, operating in the thought of an individual or generation," but which define "the dominant intellectual tendencies of an age." Unnoticed shifts in meaning, of the sort that Diamond's text produces, can have wide-ranging political and environmental consequences precisely because they become incorporated into policies and actions: "It is largely because of their ambiguities that mere words are capable of independent action as forces in history. A term, a phrase, a formula, which gains currency or acceptance because one of its meanings, or of the thoughts which it suggests, is congenial to the prevalent beliefs, the standards of value, the tastes of a certain age, may help to alter beliefs, standards of value, and tastes, because other meanings or suggested implications not clearly distinguished by those who employ it, gradually become the dominant elements of signification. The word 'nature,' it need hardly be said, is the most extraordinary example of this."[29]

Contemporary struggles over the meaning of *nature* are more than mere semantics. If, as even Marx acknowledged, our mental conceptions of the world translate into material forces that shape human history and geography, then struggles over the meanings of this word become, as Kate Soper shows in *What Is Nature?* a leading edge of political and cultural conflict. [30]

The word *environment* is equally contentious, but for somewhat different reasons. Environment is whatever surrounds or, to be more precise, whatever exists in the surroundings of some being that is *relevant* to the state of that being at a particular moment. Plainly, the spatial "situatedness" of a being and its internal conditions and needs have as much to say about the definition of *environment* as the surrounding conditions themselves, while the criteria of relevance vary widely and are conditional upon location in complex configurations of spatio-temporality. Business leaders worry about the political and legal environment, politicians worry about the economic environment, city dwellers worry about the social environment, and, doubtless, criminals worry about the environment of law enforcement, and polluters worry about the regulatory environment. Each and every one of us is situated in an "environment" (though often only temporarily, since we travel) and all of us therefore have some sense of what "environmental issues" might be about. When we connect the terms *nature* and *environment* to formulate a concept of "the natural" or "geographical" environment, as Diamond and Sachs do, then we find ourselves doubling up on all the ambiguities to the point where obfuscations rather than clarifications can all too easily ensue. This problem is chronically manifest in the innumerable and often conflicting ways in which a popularly acceptable and seemingly neutral concept such as "sustainability" gets framed and interpreted within environmental debates. But the confusions and ambiguities also create openings, and it is therefore possible, as A. Lovejoy suggests, for critical engagements to produce new possibilities of thinking and of action. The outcomes are not necessarily benevolent or progressive, and they are by no means easily compatible with a moral commitment to cosmopolitanism. If, for example, Diamond's version of appropriate geographical knowledge is correct, then Martha Nussbaum's capabilities approach to global justice requires as a precondition that we first lift the heavy hand of that history of 10,000 years ago that weighs so heavily upon us.

The approach to the question of nature from the Enlightenment onward was largely to regard it as whatever was both external to and a universal condition of possibility for human action.[31] Although I will later dispute this view, it is true that much of our contemporary knowledge of nature is derived from this conceit. From it come long-lasting binary distinctions between nature and culture, mind and matter, the natural and the artificial, and equally long-running disputes over nature versus nurture, facts versus values, the human domination of nature versus environmental or genetic determinism, and the like. Since much of our valuable knowledge of "nature's laws" derives from this approach, and since the disputes and distinctions this knowledge generates continue to inform our commonsense views, then it becomes important to say something about the status of this knowledge and the concept of nature to which it gives rise. To dispute its foundation is not to deny the important insights into natural law that have been gained. The Newtonian and Cartesian mechanical view of the world presumes, however, that space and time are absolute, and, as Whitehead argues, once this exclusive presumption is made, then a very particular construction of "nature" follows. The absolute version of space and time facilitates mensurability and calculability, and underpins the elaboration of technologies and practices that are, among other things, superbly adapted to building bridges with the same mechanical efficiency as the military technologies that have been developed to knock them down. The absolute view underpins a model of explanation in which discoverable entities (individuated in absolute space and time) function as causal agents, provoking measurable effects on other entities and so giving rise to larger configurations (much as human individuals are considered ontologically prior to the creation of something called society). While figures like Leibniz disputed this Newtonian/Cartesian view, the trend was to see God as the supreme engineer, a watchmaker who eventually had to play no other role than to wind up the mechanism of the universe. The Cartesian engineer was a rational calculator, a neutral observer, a grand architect who could dominate the world with "next to God-like" precision.

By viewing nature as a universal condition of possibility for all human activity, Enlightenment science constructed nature in a way that was consistent with liberal theory (as most obviously evidenced in the relation between John Locke and Newton). The world and everything in it had to be flattened, homogenized, and reduced conceptually (as Thomas Friedman does), if not physically, to fit the absolutisms of Newtonian and Cartesian science. Everything the grand Cartesian engineer encountered had to be made cogredient and compossible (as Whitehead would put it). Nature was most easily universalized under the sign of private property rights, commodification, and market exchange, such that access to its component parts could be bought and sold at will, and its storehouse raided and plundered for anything and everything that was of utility to the fulfillment of human wants, needs, and desires. Nature was considered, as Heidegger later bitterly complained, as nothing more than one vast gasoline station. The consequences of a nascent entrepreneurial capitalism that could latch on to such understandings and the technologies they allowed were enormous. The whole of the socio-ecological world could be and was dramatically transformed as a result.

The problem with such a science is that it is both fragmented and reductionist. It works best in closed and bounded systems constituted by interactive parts (clearly defined entities, which accounts for the reliance upon the theory of absolute space and time) whose behavior determines the behavior of the bounded whole. Such a science cannot cope very easily with open systems or relative space-time processes (although it ultimately learned to do so in both instances through radical reconfigurations of the mathematics of calculability, resort to non-Euclidean geometries, systems and complexity theories, and the like), and to this day it struggles to comprehend relationalities. The greatest danger arises when valid findings for the structure and dynamics occurring in such a hermetically sealed, closed-system world get projected onto other terrains. "The weak points in the abstract materialism of natural science, a materialism that excludes history and its process," writes Marx in a cutting commentary that surely applies to Diamond, "are at once evident from the abstract and ideological conceptions of its spokesmen, whenever they venture beyond the bounds of their own speciality."[32] In the history of social Darwinism, and in the current resort to genetic determinism or chaos theory, we likewise encounter the dangers that arise when nonspecialists take up established natural law concepts and treat them as universal truths. There are, for example, those who interpret current environmental difficulties solely in terms of the increasing entropy specified in the second law of thermodynamics.[33] Within closed physical systems energy dissipates over time. The problem is that if this were the only law that mattered in our universe, then the big bang would never have happened and the evolutionary process on planet earth (including the whole history of civilization), characterized by greater and greater (though admittedly localized) concentrations of energy, could not have occurred. This does not detract from the analysis that points out that the energy stored within the earth through biological processes over eons is being rapidly dissipated by a rampant capitalism, that the stored energy of the carboniferous age (coal) was the basis of capitalist industrialization in the nineteenth century, while that of the cretaceous (oil and natural gas) moved to the fore in the latter half of the twentieth century, leaving a big question mark over what the stores of exploitable energy will look like by the end of the twenty-first century. But if trees and crustaceans can store energy, then so can we. The technical problems may be huge, but it is still the case that the immense quantities of stored energy currently being used annually amount to less than 5 percent of the annual energy budget available to us directly from the sun. Until the sun burns out, that source of energy will always be with us and is potentially usable. The idea that we should regulate our lives solely around the singular and iron limits of the second law of thermodynamics is as ludicrous a proposition as that we should accept the thesis that our behavior is dictated by our genes.

That the second law of thermodynamics is in deep contradiction with that other major achievement of natural science, the Darwinian theory of evolution, is clearly recognized in Prigogine and Stengers's book *Order Out of Chaos*, and they struggle mightily to reconcile the two through the application of probabilistic theory. Levins and Lewontin, in contrast, see no option except to abandon Cartesianism altogether for a more dialectical form of argument in which space and time take on relational and relative as well as absolute meanings. Given the arguments laid out in chapter 7 concerning space and time, it should be obvious, to invoke Whitehead's observation once more, that the Newtonian/Cartesian conception of science, while a magnificent achievement in many respects and still fully applicable when it comes to building bridges and knocking them down, is far too limited to support any complete definition of what constitutes nature even from within the realm of the natural sciences. But who says that the natural sciences have a lock on the definition of nature? The sciences build models of certain aspects of nature for certain purposes. These models have changed dramatically in their scope and placement, and in their formal language over time (for example, the shift from deterministic to probabilistic mathematics or from Euclidean to non-Euclidean geometries). Great "paradigm shifts" (as we now refer to them after Thomas Kuhn's famous work *The Structure of Scientific Revolutions*, first published in 1962) have occurred from time to time within the sciences;

there has also been an increasing recognition of the social, political, and cultural foundations of the scientific enterprise that brings into question the supposed neutrality and pure objectivity of the scientist as observer.[34] Metaphors drawn from social life, for example, have played a crucial role in scientific inquiry (as Darwin's appeal to Malthus's population theories famously illustrated). "Nature" is therefore subject to heterogeneous and often rapidly shifting meanings within and across the so-called natural sciences. It is also shot through at almost every turn with all manner of social connotations.

None of this invalidates the scientific enterprise, nor does it detract from the astonishing advances that have been made in our understandings of "nature's laws." But it does insert a certain note of caution into our inferences from scientific findings to appropriate social meanings. What happens, for example, when Beck's idealistic human rights cosmopolitanism is put up against contemporary findings from human genetics, and how do we respond socially and politically to the discovery of the genetic bases of certain diseases and extend that idea to beliefs concerning the genetic bases of human aggression, violence, and predatory instincts? Is it cooperation and mutual aid (as Kropotkin believed) that is coded into our genes, or competitive entrepreneurialism and the struggle for dominance (as social Darwinists typically argue)?

Species Being and the Human Order of Things

If the concept of nature is heterogeneous, unstable, and controversial even from within the perspectives of the natural sciences, then the concept of human nature is even more so. Fields such as genetics, neurobiology, or evolutionary psychology touch directly on our understandings of human endowments, and powers, and in the process render highly porous older Cartesian dichotomies between mind and brain, biological needs and moral imperatives. The thorny problem of our species being, which Kant left lingering in an uncomfortable duality between the geographical perspective (it is given by and within nature) and the anthropological (it is constructed out of human creativity), is perpetually with us. Whatever the perspective, the idea that we can pursue, as Nussbaum and Held suppose, some moral imperative toward a cosmopolitan existence in the absence of any understanding of the social ramifications of our biological being seems absurd. Yet this is what they, and indeed most practitioners within the social sciences and the humanities do. The reluctance to engage is understandable, since the uncertainties that attach to any conception of the nature of human nature make any excursus on to this terrain fraught with many dangers (religious and political as well as scientific) and characterized by not a little acrimony. The general result is a total avoidance of any serious discussion of the nature of our species being in almost all renditions of liberal, neoliberal and cosmopolitan theories.

The one person in recent years who has cheerfully thrown down the gauntlet on these issues is E. O. Wilson. In shaping the field called sociobiology in the 1970s, Wilson stirred up fierce opposition (particularly from the left), and he continues to provoke accusations of biological determinism in his most recent, and again widely read, work *Consilience*. The work is, in my view, flawed by the conjoining of two self-limiting beliefs. First is his absolute faith (and he readily concedes it is a faith) in reductionism. "All tangible phenomena, from the birth of stars to the working of social institutions, are based on material processes that are ultimately reducible, however long and tortuous the sequences, to the laws of physics."[35] The second is his deep attachment to a causal model of explanation. It is "the thread of connecting causal explanations" that makes it possible to move "back through the behavioral sciences to biology, chemistry, and finally physics."[36] This formal attachment to causality sits uneasily with his critique and partial rejection of the Newtonian/Cartesian dichotomies (particularly that of mind and brain) and his firm rejection of logical positivism as a framework of understanding. Wilson also embraces the absolutism of Cartesian and Kantian constructions of space and time (and this, as Whitehead would observe, plainly affects his concept of nature). The absolute theory underpins, in turn, his appeal to causal chain explanations. But Wilson has a wide-ranging knowledge of contemporary biological sciences, and we can learn a lot from him as he sets out to inject those findings into our understanding of both nature and human nature. His savage attack upon the social sciences for the "banality" of their conceptions concerning the biological foundations of human species being has to be taken seriously even though it is often a caricature. His political stance has, however, shifted in recent years toward an environmental alarmism concerned over how we, as a species, have become a geophysical and evolutionary force such that "genetic evolution is about to become conscious and volitional, and usher in a new epoch in the history of life."[37] This leads him toward advocacy for an environmental ethic, thus aligning him with radical environmentalism. His fierce critique of the "pietistic and selfish libertarianism into which much of the American conservative movement has lately descended" and of the "myopia" of the economists has also helped assuage some of the more vociferous objections to his biological reductionism.

Reductionism is not wrong in principle, and those who use the term *reductionist* to dismiss arguments as inadmissible are plainly in error. But reduction does need to be carefully demonstrated. Wilson, like Marx, thinks that the only truly scientific method is one that moves from the materialist base (in Marx's case, the organization of human labor practices, and for Wilson, the laws of physics) to a "predictive synthesis" of everything else (including culture, art, law, language, politics). But Wilson's substantive work and the innumerable examples he sets out indicate that such a form of reductionism is an impossible dream. The problem derives in part from the exponential increase in complexity, but another factor is that the branching choices become infinite when it comes to genetic modifications, let alone cultural adaptations, which makes it impossible to predict one outcome rather than another. In practice, both Marx and Wilson recognize that it is far easier to move in the other direction, and discern the "earthly core" (as Marx puts it) of, say, religious beliefs in material labor practices (Marx) or in the laws of physics (Wilson).[38] The search for an unattainable predictive synthesis of the sort that Wilson has in mind has, however, led to very important discoveries and, like the idea of utopia, this performs a useful function.

Wilson places great emphasis on the importance of understanding relations across and between different temporal and spatial scales (defined in absolute terms). Within biology, the steps run from macro to micro, through "evolutionary biology, ecology, organismic biology, cellular biology, molecular biology, and biochemistry." Considerable difficulties, Wilson admits, stand in the way of making these systems of knowledge "consilient" with each other. "The degree of consilience can be measured by the degree to which the principles of each division can be telescoped into those of the others."[39] Wilson gives enough examples where this can fruitfully be done to make a plausible case for this kind of reductionism, at least among the biological sciences. But to telescope the findings of microbiology into those of evolution is not the same as saying that evolutionary processes are caused by or even explicable through molecular biology or biochemistry. I can telescope the findings on the genetic origins of physical handicaps in humans into an understanding of how an event like the "Special Olympics" comes about, but the latter cannot be causally attributed to genetics. Diamond's work on domestication (generously praised by

Wilson, presumably because he only read the first half of his book and did not get to the sillier stuff about coastline determinism) can be telescoped into our investigations on contemporary global inequalities but cannot be used to explain them. The problem is that Wilson (unlike Marx, who avoids causal reasoning and turns to dialectics) equates telescoping with causation, and this equation creates the difficulties.

When Wilson presses the details of his case, however, he shifts from a tightly controlled reductionism to a softer theory of epigenesis, by which he means "the development of an organism under the joint influence of heredity and environment." Culture is increasingly significant in shaping environments. His argument, then, runs as follows: genes prescribe epigenetic rules, but culture helps determine which of the prescribing genes survive and multiply; the successful new genes alter the epigenetic rules, and these in turn change the direction and effectiveness of the channels of cultural acquisition. Genes and culture coevolve, but in a way that allows culture a shaping role: "The nature of the genetic leash and the role of culture can be better understood as follows. Certain cultural norms also survive and reproduce better than competing norms, causing culture to evolve in a track parallel to and usually much faster than genetic evolution. The quicker the pace of cultural evolution, the looser the connection between genes and culture, although the connection is never completely broken. Culture allows a rapid adjustment to change in the environment through finely tuned adaptations invented and transmitted without corresponding precise genetic prescription. In this respect human beings differ fundamentally from all other animal species."[40]

This comes close, as we shall see, to a dialectical mode of argumentation in which genes (heredity) and culture (environment) make up what Wilson calls a "coevolutionary circle." He then goes on to state that "there is nothing contradictory in saying that culture arises from human action while human action arises from culture."[41] But Wilson cannot bring himself to abandon the causal model. He persistently reasserts its power even as its hold loosens. As the human species becomes a more powerful geophysical and evolutionary force, capable of engineering immense environmental transformations, the causal role of genetic imperatives appears more and more remote. Human cultural behavior needs, he says, to be consciously controlled if humanity, and the nature that supports it, is to survive in an adequate state. The confusions in this argument are rampant. The upshot is that "human nature is still an elusive concept because our understanding of the epigenetic rules composing it is rudimentary."[42]

Wilson's injunction that we pay careful attention to questions of spatial and temporal scale and of the problems that arise as we move across and between them is well taken. There is a troubling trend in the social sciences to treat the particular spatial and temporal scale at which a particular cohort of researchers is working as the only valid scale for analysis. This creates its own forms of reductionism, such that, for example, some anthropologists, geographers, and sociologists take the local ethnographic or regional cultural scale as the true fount of all understandings. In a way, this choice of scale is understandable, since at this scale the intricacies of cultural difference become most readily identifiable, and as a result immensely illuminating and informative work has been produced on cultural differentiation at this scale. A problem arises, however, when it is then inferred that the only way to understand imperialism or neoliberalism is by working through the messiness of local ethnographic details. Since these never provide neat reflections of the larger argument, then, it is presumed, the macro-formulations of imperialism or neoliberalism (largely cast in political-economic and geopolitical rather than cultural terms) must be wrong.[43] Conversely, that it is difficult to assess through local studies alone the significance of the vast quantities of surplus liquidity sloshing around the world in financial markets (financing mergers and acquisitions, pushing global interest rates to all-time lows, and sparking speculative building booms or massive periodic crises that seriously disrupt the daily lives of millions of people in Argentina, Indonesiaand now the United States) cannot be used to dismiss the informative work carried out at local scales (particularly with respect to cultural forms of response to economic crises) as irrelevant or in some way subservient to the larger story. The tendency to privilege one scale against all others would not be so problematic if it did not carry over politically, as it does in the work of an anthropologist like Escobar and the geographers who jointly publish under the name of Gibson-Graham, resulting in claims that the unique place and perspective from which politics is possible is the locality (place) where the unique "truth of being" resides.[44] The task, as Wilson correctly defines it, is to work across different scales (as the Stoics implied, as Marx and Engels suggested, and as I proposed in *Spaces of Hope*) and to find ways to "telescope in" the political insights and energies that can be amassed at one scale into political insights and action at another. But as Neil Smith, among others, has pointed out many times, we have yet to come up with satisfactory or agreed-upon ways to do this.[45]

The Dialectics of Nature

Is there some other way to meet Wilson's objections and realize his goals, other than by a causal Cartesian reductionism? We can find alternatives either in process-based philosophy, of the sort that Whitehead articulated, or in dialectics. The latter is by far the most controversial, in part because any talk of dialectics immediately conjures up images of a closed and hermetic system of reasoning, of Hegel, of Marx, and, even worse, of the horrors of dialectical materialism as foisted on the world by Stalin. But there are, as Roy Bhaskar points out, many different forms of dialectical reasoning, and to jettison them all by reference to one aberrant strain is totally unwarranted.[46] This makes it imperative to spell out the form of dialectics that is being embraced. There have always been alternative ways of thinking of the nature-human relation other than in terms of a mutually exclusive distinction and causal relations. Spinoza, for one, provided a philosophical and ethical argument based on a refusal of such a distinction (and Spinoza's influence is felt in contemporary deep ecology, as well as in the work of Negri, Deleuze, and many other thinkers). In the 1930s several of those within the so-called Frankfurt School pushed toward more dialectical formulations in their inquiries into nature and human nature.[47] Christopher Caudwell, also writing around that time, saw this relation to nature as

> a double process—the environmentalisation of organized men, beginning all the human values—language, science, art, religion, consciousness; and the humanisation of nature, begetting the material change in nature and man's own greater understanding of reality. Thus the development of humanity is not the increasing separation of man from a "state of nature." It is man's increasing interpenetration with nature. History is not, as the bourgeois supposes, the story of man in himself, or of human "nature" . . . but the story of the increasing interpenetration of nature by man as a result of his struggle with it. It is the story of economic production. The story of man is not the story of increasing subjection of man's freedom and individuality to organization in order to cope with nature, but his growth of freedom and individuality through organization. . . . History is the study of the object-subject relation of men-nature, and not of either separately.[48]

The kind of history that Caudwell proposes is radically different from Diamond's. Three things stand out. First, the boundary between "culture" and "nature" is porous and becomes even more so over time. Nature and society are not separate and opposed realms but internal relations within a dynamic unity of a larger totality (this was the conception to which Wilson leaned when considering the coevolutionary circle of epigenesis). Caudwell dissolves the Cartesian/Kantian dichotomies through an examination of economic production and reproduction. It is, therefore, not only meaningful but essential, as Neil Smith insists, to look closely at "the production of nature," in exactly the same way that Lefebvre conceptualizes the production of space.[49] Human beings have, through their laboring activities, played an increasingly important part in the production of nature and of environment (a fact Wilson concedes and worries about). This means conceptualizing a socio-ecological world that is actively being shaped and reshaped by a wide array of intersecting socio-ecological processes (some but not all of which are intimately expressive of human activities and desires) operating at different scales. The processes, flows, and relations that create, sustain, or dissolve the socio-ecological world must be the focus of inquiry. The geographical environment of 8000 B.C.E. has since been radically transformed (not least by human action) into something utterly different from what it was during the first stumbling steps toward plant and animal domestication (itself a clear moment when human action actively produced aspects of nature through, for example, breeding practices, as well as land modification and the use of fire).

Furthermore, the Lefebvrian dialectic among material practices (physical economic production), conceptualizations of nature (such as those given in the sciences, philosophy, and the arts), and lived consciousness of the world ("all human values," as Caudwell calls them) must be actively engaged. "The cosmos of our culture is a different environment from the cosmos of the [ancient] Egyptian" because the material practices, the conceptualizations, and the way we live the relationality to nature have been radically transformed, along with the material environment itself, over both space and time. Third, the growth of individuality and freedom (the transformation of social relations) is achieved through forms of organization that interact and interpenetrate rather than separate out from nature. The idea that humanity has become increasingly alienated or even liberated from a nature to which it was once intimately attached is, Caudwell insists, downright wrong. There is an increasing interpenetration and deepening of the bond between the human and the natural over time. We are now, as Neil Smith puts it, involved in the "financialization and commodification of nature 'all the way down,'" as property rights are claimed over genetic materials and biological processes, and new chemical and genetic combinations (such as genetically modified foods) are brought into being. The results, as the history of everything from agricultural clearances to anthropogenic climate change shows, are as extensive as they are problematic.[50] Genetic engineering, which poses such immense ethical questions, now, for example, puts humanity in a position to purposively intervene in the very roots of the evolutionary process rather than doing so through the slow processes of genetic modification that earlier occurred: plant and animal breeding practices or the gradual environmental transformations that created favorable habitats for new species to emerge. Meanwhile, more and more aspects of the environment are merged with the circulation of capital as property rights regimes and market exchanges (like carbon trading) are imposed upon them.

Caudwell prefigures the view that animates what I call "historical geographical materialism." This view is, as B. Braun notes, radically anti-Aristotelian.[51] Aristotle held that the world is made up of distinct and autonomous things (such as places), each with its own essence. Dialectics and process-based philosophies (such as that of Whitehead) jointly hold, by way of contrast, that "elements, things, structures and systems do not exist outside of or prior to the processes, flows, and relations that create, sustain, or undermine them." Things have no unchanging essence because, as Whitehead once succinctly put it, "reality is the process." Or, as Levins and Lewontin insist, heterogeneity is everywhere, and "change is a characteristic of all systems and all aspects of all systems."[52] There is, therefore, no solid, independent "external nature" we can appeal to as an authority (as Malthus and Semple do) or wage war against (as the prometheans do) or interact harmoniously with (as ecological utopians do). Nature and society are internal relations within the dynamics of a larger socio-ecological totality.

Putting that relation back into the analysis generates a completely different kind of historical geography from that which Diamond proposes. W. Cronon provides us with an example of what such an alternative might look like in *Changes in the Land*. He depicts a New England environment at the time of colonial settlement that was the product of more than 10,000 years of Indian occupation and forest use (promoting, through burning, the forest edge conditions that favored species diversity). The colonizers misread this nature as pristine, virginal, natural, rich, and underutilized by indigenous peoples. The implantation of European institutions of governance and property rights (coupled with distinctively European aspirations toward accumulation of wealth) wrought an ecological transformation of such enormity that indigenous populations were deprived of their habitat and therefore their livelihood. The destruction of the nature that the Indians had constructed out of their own social relations meant the destruction of their culture. The changes in and on the land made it impossible to sustain a nomadic and highly flexible indigenous mode of production and reproduction. In reflecting on this process, Cronon sets out the dialectical principles that animate his account (principles totally absent from Diamond's work but hinted at in Wilson's theory of epigenesis). A proper ecological history "begins by assuming a dynamic and changing relationship between environment and culture, one as apt to produce contradictions as continuities. Moreover, it assumes that the interactions of the two are dialectical. Environment may initially shape the range of choices available to a people at a given moment but then culture reshapes environment responding to those choices, the reshaped environment presents a new set of possibilities for cultural reproduction, thus setting up a new cycle of mutual determination. Changes in the way people create and re-create their livelihood must be analyzed in terms of change not only in their *social relations* but in their *ecological* ones as well."[53]

Dialectics of this sort constitute an entirely different approach from that enshrined in the Cartesian/Kantian dichotomous view of the world. It centers Marx's relational, process-based, and dynamic way of thinking, as well as the tradition of Spinoza, Leibniz, and many others. It has now been accepted as foundational in David Bohm's interpretations of quantum theory, the approach of Maurice Wilkins to microbiology, and that of Levins and Lewontin to biology more generally. The contemporary neurosciences, even E. O. Wilson is forced to concede, have dispensed entirely with the "mind and matter" distinction and now formulate research in relational terms. Relational thinking has, furthermore, entered into politics directly through the "deep ecology" of Arne Naess (inspired by his studies of Spinoza) and the formulations of Michael Hardt and Toni Negri in *Empire* (likewise inspired by Spinoza).[54] This suggests that a widespread oppositional culture is emerging from traditional ways (as contemporaneously exemplified by the causal analysis of Diamond and Sachs) of talking about nature and environment. Ecological theorizing, across the political spectrum, is now pervaded by a far more dialectical approach.

The Dialectics of Socio-ecological Transformations

Is there, then, any more systematic way to construct a dialectical approach to the dynamics of socio-ecological transformations? To answer this question requires that we come to terms with both the proper dialectical method and the substantive questions that need to be addressed. The substantive questions have long been in play. Consider, for example, the published proceedings of the Wennergren symposium "Man's Role in Changing the Face of the Earth."[55] The symposium, held in 1955, was an attempt by anthropologists and geographers with help from, among others, earth scientists, philosophers, historians, planners, and theologians, to explore the anthropological and geographical foundations for understanding the historical geography of global environmental transformations as influenced by human activities. It was the most systematic attempt up to that time, one that in many respects has yet to be superseded, to answer Kant's call for a systematic examination of the geographical and anthropological conditions of possibility for understanding the world around us. The theme is the coevolution of nature and culture (with emphasis upon the latter). There is much here, therefore, that comes close to the spirit of Wilson's demand for a theory of epigenesis, without Wilson's insistence on driving everything back to the genetic if not microphysical levels (pretty much an impossible idea back in 1955). But, as might be expected, the view of culture set out in these volumes goes way beyond Wilson's, for it acknowledges the power and importance of myths of origins, of religion, of symbolic practices and beliefs in defining how different human societies have seen themselves in relation to the natural world. There is a clear recognition that the Newtonian/Cartesian world view transformed our way of thinking from what Herbert Gutkind called an "I-Thou" relational view into an alienated and depersonalized "I-It" objective view (thus anticipating Carolyn Merchant's feminist thesis in *The Death of Nature*, as engineered by the revolutionary empiricism of Francis Bacon). Wilson's argument that the natural leash over cultural evolution has slackened over time and that the scale of human influence has dramatically increased to the point where we have become a major evolutionary force is presciently articulated. That we needed to become more conscious and responsible with respect to future evolutionary directions was of great concern more than fifty years ago, as it is repeatedly asserted in our own times.

There is a great deal to criticize in the Wennergren volumes. There is a stunning absence of any concern for critical social and political questions, such as those of gender (not a single woman contributed to the symposium), racism, colonialism, and the continuing practices of imperialism. The dynamics of the Cold War, struggles for national self-determination, let alone anything as tendentious as the crisis-prone character of capitalism and the imperatives of global capitalist expansion, did not rate a mention. This was, after all, 1955, when McCarthyism was rampant in the United States with censorious (often self-imposed) ramifications even in the hallowed halls of Princeton. There was, as a result, an overemphasis upon supposedly objective scientific and empirical enquiry into the state of the world's environments, although Lewis Mumford, who had strong roots in the anarchist tradition of Kropotkin via the work of the urbanist Patrick Geddes, did manage to sound the alarm at what he saw as the disastrous trajectory of contemporary urbanization. In the absence of much direct political critique, many contributors then (as now) took refuge in the abstractions of aesthetics and ethics to voice their concerns over what they saw as a profligate and uncaring approach to natural relations. But what stands out more positively in retrospect is the range of substantive themes and relationalities with which many of the contributors were prepared to engage. It is salutary, for example, to read the theologian Teilhard de Chardin's commentaries on "the revolution in the very process of evolution" wrought by human activity, describing the "irresistible totalization" then being imposed by the powerful forces of science, and noting also how "mankind has suddenly become compressional and converging" (anticipating my later arguments concerning time-space compression). The onus for conscious change, he argues, rests on the human power of "reflexive invention" (shades of Ulrich Beck on reflexive modernity as a core cosmopolitan value). The architect/planner E. A. Gutkind focuses on how our sense and vision of the world has changed dramatically as air travel (and aerial photography) became available to us. This was far more than a technological breakthrough: it entailed a fundamental and far-reaching revolution in our cultural perspective on the world (much as space travel, satellite monitoring, and remote sensing have done for us in more recent times). Clarence Glacken examined the immense variety of discourses about nature, pointing to the shifting history and often conflicting cosmologies and opinions about our place in the natural order. He closed with a plea that cultural and environmental histories not go their separate ways but recognize their integral relation (epigenesis). Alexander Spoehr, in a short and pithy piece, persuasively argued that so-called "natural" resources were technical, economic, and cultural appraisals of elements in nature useful to a particular social order and its dominant classes (anticipating somewhat contemporary social constructionism). Lewis Mumford insisted that urbanization be seen as an integral part of natural history (presaging my own view that "there is nothing unnatural about New York City").

Others insisted that the histories and cultural mores of peasant societies must be seen as ecological as well as social and cultural phenomena. As befitted a symposium dedicated to reviving the spirit of George Perkins Marsh, there was much written about the unintended consequences of human actions and the risks that attached thereto. Carl Sauer and others made much of how the use of fire had early on dramatically altered the landscapes of the world in unintended ways. While each author tended to plow particular and sometimes unduly narrow furrows, the collective impact of the volumes was far more than the sum of its parts. It amounted, in effect, to an accounting of the then adequacies and inadequacies of anthropology and geography as foundational "propaedeutic" disciplines for understanding the environmental historical geography of planet earth. The pious hope, best articulated by the "Burkean" geographer Carl Sauer, was that it would also be the staging ground for the construction of political-ecological alternatives. We should, he said, cast aside our concern for the comforts and displays of the flesh and create "an ethic and an aesthetic under which man, practicing moderation, may indeed pass on to posterity a good Earth."[56]

The Method of Moments

The participants in the symposium returned again and again to the idea of the transformation of nature through human practices and the implications of those transformations for human life. This, of course, is the central proposition upon which Marx hangs his dialectical approach to socio-ecological relations. "Man opposes himself to Nature as one of her own forces, setting in motion arms and legs, head and hands, the natural forces of his body, in order to appropriate Nature's productions in a form adapted to his own wants. By thus acting on the external world and changing it, he at the same time changes his own nature." The question of what kind of transformed natural world human beings produce and inhabit cannot be divorced, according to Marx's formulation, from the question of what kind of human society emerges. This is the core of Marx's dialectical reconstruction of how the socio-ecological totality works. It is a core constructed from the human standpoint, of course, but as far as Marx was concerned, that was the only possible standpoint we, as human beings, could have. What makes our labor exclusively human is that we dream up our projects before we realize them in practice. "What separates the worst of architects from the best of bees," says Marx, is "that the architect erects a structure in imagination before realizing it upon the ground."[57] A utopian moment, when we become conscious of this core dialectic and fight conceptually and intellectually over alternatives, is as inevitable as it is critical in defining how the dialectical relation between human action and the natural world unfolds.

This simple dialectical and relational view underpins the general argument I have made at length elsewhere: that all political and social projects are ecological projects, and vice versa.[58] But such an approach requires deeper elaboration if we are to realize its full potentiality. Marx provides us with a powerful clue as to how to do this. In comparing his method to that of Darwin's evolutionism in the natural sciences, and in one of those rare moments when he offered some guide as to what his "scientific" version of historical materialism was really all about, he wrote that "technology discloses man's mode of dealing with Nature, and the process of production by which he sustains his life, and thereby also lays bare the mode of formation of his social relations, and of the mental conceptions that flow from them."[59] The formulation in this passage is cryptic, but read through the lenses of dialectical and process philosophy, it opens up a rich terrain for theoretical elaboration. There are, he in effect suggests, six distinctive and identifiable "moments" (as Whitehead would term them) revolving around the organization of the human labor process. Let us consider each of these moments in turn.

1. By *technology*, Marx means not only the hardware (the tools, machinery, fixed capital equipment, and the actual physical infrastructures for production and consumption) but also the software (the programming and incorporation of knowledge, intelligence, and, in our times, science into machines and production activities more generally) and the distinctive organizational forms assumed (including corporate and bureaucratic management structures, as well as the more obvious forms of cooperation and the division of labor backed by scientific management). By all of these means, the productivity of human labor stands to be enhanced.[60]

2. *Nature* in the first instance refers to the whole immensely variegated and diversified world of phenomena and processes, always to some degree unstable and in perpetual flux (and therefore characterized by a dynamism all its own), that surrounds us in its pristine condition (sometimes referred to as "first nature"). This nature is increasingly modified, channeled, and reordered by human action over time to form a "second nature" that directly or indirectly bears the marks of human action with both intended

and unintended consequences. Human beings, like all other organisms, are part of nature and as such are "active subjects transforming nature according to its laws."[61] The only difference from other organisms—and on this point both Marx and Wilson agree—is that human beings can engage in this process consciously, knowledgeably, and reflexively. This is what distinguishes the worst of architects from the best of bees.

3. The *activity of production* refers to the labor process by which available raw materials are transformed into items of utility for us. Under capitalism, these labor processes are also required to produce surplus value (profit) for the capitalist, not only through the production of goods and services for direct use and consumption, but also through the production of means of production (intermediate goods and technological hardware), symbolic forms (books and art objects, religious and cultural icons, cathedrals, palaces and temples of finance, learning, state and class power, and the like), physical infrastructures (agrarian landscapes and whole cities as resource systems), spaces of transport and communications, and all those transformations in the land that produce uneven geographical developments and regionally differentiated landscapes. The labor processes required to produce and maintain spaces, places, and built environments also fall under this heading.

4. The *sustenance of daily life* refers to the daily processes, both social and ecological, through which individuals and social groups reproduce themselves and their social relations through working, consuming, living, engaging in sexual relations, reproducing, communicating, and sensually/existentially engaging with the world. This entails an account of our individual and collective embeddedness in the ongoing web of socio-ecological life—what Gramsci refers to as the "practical activity" of "the man in the mass," Lefebvre refers to as "everyday life," Braudel calls "material life," and Habermas depicts as "the lifeworld." This sphere also incorporates what some feminists conceptualize as social reproduction.[61] Long neglected in Marxian theory, this became a critical field within which questions of gender relations and sexual orientation in relation to processes of social reproduction could be more fully explored and integrated into general theory.[62]

5. *Social relations* occur between individuals and social groups as these are constituted into networks, hierarchies, and institutional arrangements (within corporate and state administrations, bureaucracies, and military apparatuses). While Marx focuses primarily on class relations, plainly these social relations are complex and frequently unstable, incorporat-

ing also reproductive units (family and kinship structures) and groupings structured around gender and sexual orientation, racial identifications, religious and linguistic affiliations, place-bound and political loyalties (as nationals or as citizens and subjects), and the like. Gender and racialized distinctions have clearly played an enormous role in the dynamics of capital accumulation, both locally and globally, and it is therefore impossible to take the class character of labor exploitation or dispossession without considering the whole complex field of social relations through which that class relation is constructed.[63]

6. *Mental conceptions of the world* refer not only to how individuals think on a day-to-day basis but to the whole inherited arsenal of language, concepts, and stored symbolic, cultural, religious, ethical, scientific, and ideological meanings and aesthetic and moral judgments. These affect how the world is represented and conceptualized, and therefore lived, interpreted, and acted upon by particular people in particular social situations and in particular places at particular times. The vast heterogeneity and diversity of these ways of thinking and knowing, and the innumerable lines of dispute and conflict over adequate ways of understanding and acting in the world (highly sensitive to social situatedness in terms of class, gender, subalternity, and the like), guarantee not only a remarkable amount of conflictual intellectual activity, but also a capacity for thought experimentation that has powerful reverberations across all the other moments. Mental conceptions are always subject to reality checks in the worlds of social relations, production systems, everyday life, and technologies, and in the encounter with natural law.

Many of these six distinctive moments were invoked in the Wenner-gren symposium. Spoehr, for example, cites nature, technologies, mental conceptions, social relations, and the activities of production in his definition of natural resources. So-called "natural disasters" have since been analyzed in much the same way to emphasize their social, technologically mediated, and conceptually framed qualities. How, then, are we to conceptualize the relations among these six moments? In placing technology at the head of the list, Marx seems to give some support to the version of Marxism (most clearly laid out in G. A. Cohen's *Karl Marx's Theory of History: A Defense* and accepted by Thomas Friedman) that says technologies—or the "productive forces," as they are usually referred to in the Marxist tradition—are determinate.[64] But Marx actually speaks of technology "disclosing" and "revealing," rather than causing. Technologies are interlinked with and internalize effects from all the other moments. The software aspects, for example, clearly overlap with the moment of mental conceptions, while social relations are fundamentally implicated in organizational forms (such as those of the division of labor). The hardware has to be produced, and technologies always entail a mobilization of natural forces according to natural law. In a parallel way technological changes generate and communicate transformative impulses into, for example, social relations, daily life, and mental conceptions, which in turn reverberate back into the technological moment. We have to conceptualize, therefore, a continuous process of conflictual transformation in and between all the moments, including that of nature itself. This is what I shall refer to as Marx's "method of moments." It is most clearly outlined in the *Grundrisse* as follows: "individual moments" within the totality "determine each other internally and search for each other externally; but . . . they may or may not find each other, balance each other, correspond to each other. The inner necessity of moments which belong together, and their indifferent, independent existence towards one another, are already a foundation of contradictions."[65]

For illustrative purposes, let us focus upon the technological moment. The perpetual search for new technologies is mainly impelled, in our world, by geopolitical rivalries over military superiority and intercapitalist competition for economic advantage. Those who capture superior technologies are more likely to come out ahead in competitive situations. These longstanding social pressures have produced a fetish belief, a blind faith, in new technologies as a possible answer to every difficult question (notice, for example, how frequently in recent times the answer to environmental problems such as global warming is said to lie in new technologies). Technological innovation, as Marx long ago noted, becomes a business in itself, feeding on this fetish belief, driven onward under the social and political relations of capitalism and imperialism.[66] The role that new technologies play, for good or bad, in our evolutionary dynamic (particularly through production and consumption systems, rapid changes in the relation to nature, and changes in human nature itself) is, therefore, a by-product of our dominant social relations (capitalist and militarist) and their accompanying mental conceptions. Technology is not some free-floating *deus ex machina* that haphazardly evolves in the rough and tumble of diverse human endeavors or through the singular efforts of mythical figures, be it Prometheus or the creative entrepreneur. It arises out of the chaotic ferment of interactions in and around all the other moments, impelled forward by fetish beliefs that arise in part out of the coercive laws of geopolitical and economic competition.

But then consider how our mental conceptions of the world depend upon our ability to see, to measure, to calibrate with the help of telescopes and microscopes, of X-rays and CAT scanners, and how all this technological capacity has helped change our understanding of (and the identity to be attributed to) the human body in relation to its environment (the cosmos). We, in the advanced capitalist world, recalibrate our daily lives around such technologies as automobiles, mobile phones, and BlackBerries (to say nothing of how we adapt to the organizational forms of corporations and bureaucracies), all the while creating new technological demands to deal with the daily frustrations and contradictions (gridlock in our cities produces a call for congestion pricing, which will require the implementation of new technologies of monitoring and surveillance). To what degree, D. Haraway asks in her celebrated manifesto on the subject, has human nature morphed into a cyborg nature through our rapidly involving engagements with new technologies?[67] But then look back through the other end of the telescope, and consider why it was that someone in a certain time and place had the mental conception that there was something important that could be seen in a particular way, and found a material and social situation with lens grinders and metalworkers, as well as patrons willing to support and appreciate (often in the face of social antagonism and opposition) the development of a new way of seeing with the aid of telescopes and microscopes. And then consider how capitalists, obsessed with the competitive need and desire to accelerate and expand the terrain of capital circulation, seek out and instantaneously adopt technologies (for example, cell phones) that facilitate speed-up and the diminution of spatial barriers to movement, in preference to exploring other technologies that relate to rest and stasis.

The evident existence of autonomous and fetishistic forces defining the technological moment does not imply the determinacy of that moment in relation to all the others. There is, it turns out, a long history of selecting one or other of these six moments as *the* determinant force. This occurs because every one of the moments internalizes autonomous forces for change that have widespread ramifications across the other moments. These impacts are easily tracked, leaving the impression of a prime moving force at work. Prioritizing the moment of nature (within which there is abundant and overwhelming evidence for autonomous shifts) gives us environmental determinism (though rarely in total isolation from the other moments, as Diamond's "soft form" of environmental determinism demonstrates). There are those (like Gutkind in the Wennergren symposium) who put the autonomy of ideas and mental conceptions in the vanguard of all change, even without invoking the Hegelian idealism to which Marx objected. But Marx did not deny the autonomy of the "mental moment," agreeing that ideas could be a material force in making history. Marx also famously wrote that "all history is the history of class struggle," which bolsters the case for putting contentious social relations of class (or of gender, race, and religion) in the driving seat of history. There is a very strong tradition among some Marxists of taking this line of class relations as the ultimate determinant, a view also held by some anarchists and autonomistas who believe this is the main determinant of social change. Some feminists prefer to prioritize gender relations as the prime moving force, while other analysts, as represented in the popular tract by P. Hawken, suggest that autonomous impulses arising out of daily life and processes of social reproduction, out of the lifeworld of particular places, do, can, or will play a determinate role in socio-ecological evolution.[68]

None of these deterministic readings works. Even in Diamond's case, the first part of his book, which does work reasonably well, tacitly involves not the simple geographical causation he claims, but a dialectical movement, a coevolution, in which technological innovations, new forms of social relations, and new mental conceptions of the world (symbolic learning systems) come together with particular natural circumstances in a mutually supportive way. The only proper way to proceed, therefore, is to see and keep each of the "moments" in dialectical tension with all of the others. At one curious moment in his text, Diamond almost acknowledges as much: he suddenly shifts his language from environmental causation to that of an "autocatalytic process" of evolutionary change, described as "one that catalyzes itself in a positive feedback cycle, going faster and faster once it is started. This amounts to an invocation of process philosophy rather than cause and effect! But this is not surprising since it would be relatively easy to take the most plausible part of Diamond's account of agricultural origins in the Fertile Crescent and recast it in the theoretical framework of "moments" in a process of coevolution. The most insightful work on our evolving and coevolving relation to nature in recent times, such as Haraway's brilliant analysis in *Primate Visions: Gender, Race and Nature in the World of Modern Science*, has come from exploring the cross-dialectical relations among, if not all, then some of these six moments.[69] When confronted with economic or environmental crises, for example, we have to focus on the dynamic interrelations among the six moments, even as we recognize there are certain asymmetries among them. Mental conceptions concerning environmental probity, for example, pass for naught until materialized, say, as new technologies in production and as radical reconfigurations in the conduct of daily life (as environmentalists frequently and frustratedly note). Technological innovations remain empty of meaning (as Chinese history again and again showed) until they are adopted and diffused through the worlds of production and consumption, and neither of those can change without transformations in social relations and mental conceptions that make the new technologies acceptable to daily life, as well as politically and legally sanctioned (a tricky matter when it comes to interventions in human sexuality and reproduction). In specific historical and geographical conjunctures, the uneven tensions and asymmetries among the different moments may influence the overall direction of transformations within the socio-ecological totality. In one place and time technological change may seem to be in the vanguard while the other moments either lag behind or become active loci of refusal and resistance, and at another moment, revolutions in social relations or in daily life may come to the fore. Mental conceptions and utopian ideas frequently stretch far beyond what any of the other moments can bear, but in other instances ideas do become a leading force for change, at least for a while in a particular place.

We cannot, therefore, ever reduce one moment to a simple refraction of the others. Mutations in the natural order that produced the smallpox and syphilis germs that wrought such demographic havoc with indigenous populations in the past, and the HIV/AIDS and West Nile viruses, the avian flu, and the SARS that have posed direct problems to global health in recent years, were not direct products of human action. But these mutations posed immense problems for the reproduction of daily life, for our mental conceptions as well as for social relations and production processes, while calling forth immediate demands for technological responses. Yet we cannot presume even in this case that the seemingly autonomous mutations bear no trace of human influence. The extreme density of human populations and activities in, say, the Pearl River Delta in China creates a perfect habitat for the emergence of all manner of new pathogens, as seems to have been the case in ancient Mesopotamia, as Diamond notes. Nor is the nature of the responses across the moments determinate in advance: it matters whether HIV/AIDS is represented in our mental conceptions as God's retribution for the evil of homosexuality or as a mutational accident with enormous social consequences. Movements that arise around the reproduction of daily life (for example, questions of sexual identity and preference) in particular places likewise look to the production of new technologies, demand new social relations and mental conceptions, and imply a different relation to nature. The transformation of the totality cannot occur without transformations across all six interpenetrating moments. There is no automatic response that sets a predictable (let alone deterministic) pattern of interaction between the moments. The qualities immanent within the socio-ecological totality do not move it inexorably toward some teleological end. The evolution is contingent and not determined in advance.

The six moments taken together do not, under this reading, constitute a tightly organized totality of the Hegelian sort, in which each moment is so tightly bound as an internal relation of all the others that there is no liberty or autonomy of movement. Marx's "method of moments" leads to a theory of coevolving ecological moments within what Lefebvre would call an "ensemble" or Deleuze an "assemblage" of interactive processes. Lefebvre imagines this process as inextricably related to the production of space (an idea that Neil Smith unfolds in *Uneven Development* as an explicit relation between the production and transformation of nature and the production of space). Deleuze sees it in terms of processes of territorialization and deterritorialization. He defines an assemblage, for example, as "a multiplicity that is made up of heterogeneous terms"—what I refer to as moments—"and which establishes liaisons, relations between them. . . . Thus the assemblage's only unity is that of a co-functioning: it is a symbiosis, a 'sympathy.' It is never filiations which are important, but alliances, alloys: these are not successions, lines of descent but contagions, epidemics, the wind."[70] The assemblage, says Deleuze in a passage that helps connect the production of place with the idea of an assemblage, "has both *territorial* sides, or reterritorialized sides, which stabilize it, and cutting edges of *deterritorialization*, which carry it away."[71]

Marx's treatment of the assemblage of socio-ecological moments can in this way be brought to bear on processes of place formation. Put the other way round, we cannot understand processes of place formation, dissolution, and renewal without examining the bounded interplay between the six socio-ecological moments. This is how I think of the processes of city formation and urban evolution. Interestingly, when we look back at some of the best forms of historical regional geography, such as that produced by Vidal de la Blache, what we see is a way of understanding the production of regionality through a coevolution, over space and time, of the moments that Marx defines.

How are we to reconcile this way of thinking with the proposition that the labor process lies at the core of the dialectical relation to nature? Marx firmly believed that the labor process—the meshing of social relations and productive forces in the transformation of nature—was the real economic foundation upon which there arose a legal and political superstructure, and corresponding forms of social consciousness. "Arising from," it should be noted, does not necessarily denote "determined by." But Marx then went on to say that "it is not the consciousness of men that determines their existence, but their social existence that determines their consciousness."[72] Marx seems here to deny any autonomy to our mental conceptions. That ideas are not the ultimate determinant (as Hegel and the idealists supposed) is entirely consistent with the framework of moments that we have been elucidating, but the denial of any autonomy at all to mental conceptions is not. This denial is, furthermore, contradicted by Marx's key metaphor of the architect who, unlike the bee, erects a structure in imagination before materializing it on the ground. Marx elsewhere acknowledges that ideas can become a material force in historical change (otherwise, why would he bother to write out his own ideas so eloquently?) We should therefore reject the proposition that mental conceptions lack any autonomy as a manifestation of Marx's overzealous quest for an impossible (but often fruitful) reductionism and of his correct concern to refute Hegelian idealism. Mental conceptions and their associated cultural transformations have a creative but not determinate role within the socio-ecological system of moments.

But Marx also argues, in this same passage, that changes in the economic foundation lead eventually to the transformation of the whole immense superstructure. This reductionist statement (and, recall, not all reductionism can be ruled out automatically as illegitimate) is immediately modified by saying that "it is always necessary to distinguish between the material transformation of the economic conditions of production, which can be determined with the precision of natural science and the legal, political, religious, artistic or philosophic—in short ideological forms in which men become conscious of this conflict and fight it out."[73] One interpretation of this formulation is entirely consistent with the theory of moments. The forms in which individuals and social groups become conscious of conflict and fight it out (in the realm of mental conceptions, for example) are relational and therefore immaterial, but how these struggles are resolved has objective consequences in the world of practices. The mechanical causal model of relations between base and superstructure that is sometimes propounded must be dissolved into a dialectic of interactive and internalizing relations between the six moments. But the only objective point in the socio-ecological evolutionary process where we can physically measure impacts and find out where we are is that of the physical transformation of nature through human labor. The parallel here is with Marx's concept of capital as value (an immaterial but objective social relation) in motion that takes the physical forms of purchased commodities (labor power and means of production), production processes, commodities for market, and, finally, money (understood as a material representation of the immateriality of value). Only at the money point is it possible to know whether the capitalist has gained surplus value (measured materially as money profit) or not. But it is one thing to gain a materialist measure of where we are in the relation to nature or in the accumulation of capital ("with the precision of natural science") and quite another to figure out how we got there. And that "how we got there" entails all manner of peculiarities including, for example, moving dialectically across all six of the moments that Marx identifies. Marx's materialist point, which is well taken in this instance, is that if we end up in a relation to nature that is materially obnoxious or physically dangerous to us (famines, ozone holes, toxic pollutants, global warming)—or in a relation to the circulation of capital that is measurably unprofitable—then something in "the whole immense superstructure"—or, as I would prefer it, "across all moments"—has to change, be it social relations, mental conceptions, everyday life, legal and political institutions, technologies, or the relation to nature. The method of moments earlier outlined is in no way violated under this conception. The material measure of the relation to nature does provide a solid baseline for judgment, and this seems to introduce a certain asymmetry into how relations among the moments unfold. We cannot, in short, eat and drink ideas, and our material reproduction as species beings within nature has to recognize that elemental fact, even as we freely acknowledge that our species being is about far more than just eating and drinking. But at the heart of all these dialectical interactions among the different moments, at the core of the process of coevolution, lies the foundational question of the organization of human labor, because it is through the material activities of laboring that the crucial relation to nature unfolds. Any project that does not confront the question of who has the power to organize human labor and to what purposes and why is missing the central point. Not to address that point is to condemn ourselves to a peripheral politics that merely seeks to regulate our relations to nature in a way that does not interfere with current practices of capital accumulation on a global scale.

So what kind of geographical and ecological knowledge is required for the adequate formulation of a cosmopolitan project? And what, more specifically, is our conception of the human-nature relation? The answer is a dialectical, process-based, and interactive approach to world historical geography, of the sort that Cronon practices, Lewontin preaches, Marx theorizes through the dialectical method of moments, and Whitehead pushes forward in his process-based philosophy of nature. This is the essence of the historical geographical materialism that must be incorporated into any cosmopolitan project if that project is to have any chance of success. Any conception of alternatives, furthermore, has to answer the questions of what kind of daily life, what kind of relation to nature, which social relations, what production processes, and what kinds of mental conceptions and technologies will be adequate to meet human wants, needs, and desires. Any strategy for change has to consider how to coevolve changes across all the moments. This is as true for place construction as for the transformative activities that constitute the socio-ecological dialectic and the modes and mannerisms of the production of spatio-temporalities. Revolutions that move away from the existing state of things do so by moving across the dialectics of these integral moments.[74] A revolutionary geographical theory has to incorporate such a dialectical understanding into its very heart. So is there, then, something we can call "geographical theory"? And if so, what is it all about?

Epilogue

GEOGRAPHICAL THEORY AND THE RUSES OF GEOGRAPHICAL REASON

We are now in a position to return to the question that Martha Nussbaum left open: what kind of geographical, anthropological, and ecological knowledge would be required to adequately ground a liberatory cosmopolitan politics? W. Pattison's definition of the different traditions of geographical inquiry opened up the way to a critical engagement with three foundational concepts that underpin all forms of geographical knowledge—space, place, and environment. Within the discipline of geography, the tendency has been to treat these three conceptual realms separately. The spatial is generally viewed as systematic, mathematical (geometrical), and amenable to the scientific study of spatial order (with time relegated to the study of comparative statics); the regional (place) as nomothetic, unique, time-deepened, and more susceptible to humanistic and hermeneutical treatments; and the environmental, while susceptible to hermeneutic and literary treatments, as the scientific study of temporal dynamics of climatic, geomorphological, and other changes on the land in the evolutionary tradition of the earth sciences. Such conventional geographical knowledge structures, even when not openly deployed (as they all too frequently are) in support of state power, capital accumulation, and imperialistic and military practices, plainly cannot ground the critical perspectives required for a liberatory cosmopolitan education, let alone confront the innumerable ruses of geographical reason that from Kant onward have permitted noble universal principles to be paralleled by devilishly distressing geographical details and disruptions. Pattison's suggestion that all three perspectives might come together in practical work was more a hopeful gesture than a systemic conclusion.

In chapters 7, 8, and 9, however, we frequently encountered situations where, once the Kantian and positivist frames were abandoned, it was both possible and necessary to see these three conceptual fields of space, place, and environment not only as interrelated but also as potentially integral to each other. If Alfred North Whitehead is only partially correct to say, for example, that "the determination of the meaning of nature reduces itself principally to the discussion of the character of time and the character of space," and if it is also impossible, as A. Dirlik and C. Katz insist, to specify the meaning, definition, and qualities of place outside of an understanding of space and time, then unification of the three conceptual fields is not only possible but unavoidable. This conceptual unification, I claim, defines a proper core for a geographical theory that can work as a "condition of possibility" for all other forms of knowing, at the same time as it sheds critical light on the dangerous but hidden ruses of geographical reason. The question is: by what means might a unification of these three conceptual fields be achieved?

The three conceptual fields are, recall:

1. *Environment,* understood in terms of the dynamic interrelations (the co-evolution) among the six moments that make up the socio-ecological dialectic—technologies, the relation to an evolving nature, production and consumption processes, shifting social relations, changing mental conceptions, and the reproduction of daily life
2. *Spatio-temporality,* understood in terms of the dialectic of absolute, relative, and relational space-times as these intersect with material socio-spatial practices, competing conceptualizations and representations, and radically different modes of living space-time.
3. *Place* and *region,* understood as the human construction, maintenance, and dissolution of distinctive and meaningful entities as "relative permanences" in the geographical landscape (territorialized assemblages such as neighborhoods, cities, and economic and cultural regions) at a variety of scales (local, regional, national, and so forth).

The intersecting forces perpetually reshaping the historical geography of social life on earth can be reduced theoretically to processes of production of spaces, places, and environments. This reduction requires deployment of a process-based philosophy and the application of dialectical methods of both representation and inquiry. Only then can a unified field of knowledge called "geographical theory" be articulated.

Most of the hegemonic social theories (including historical materialism) that have shaped dominant interpretations and political practices (at the popular as well as at the academic level) over the last three hundred years, in the advanced capitalist world and beyond, have paid little or no critical attention to how the production of spaces, places, and environments might impinge upon thought and action. In practice, we almost everywhere find tacit assumptions about the nature of space and time, the cohesion of places (the nation-state), and the idea of what is or is not given by nature. The problem is that these geographical concepts are deployed uncritically and in an ad hoc manner, without any consideration of the importance of the geographical assumptions in shaping modes of thought and action. The effect is like trying to navigate the world with any old map, no matter how arbitrary or erroneous it may be.[1] Serious errors of interpretation (of the sort that Jared Diamond commits) and equally serious mistakes in policy and politics (of the sort that Jeffrey Sachs and Thomas Friedman continue to be responsible for) owe a lot, I suggest, to this failure to acknowledge, let alone understand the significance of, the geographical knowledge deployed. The ruses of geographical reason operate unchallenged.

The geographical theory I am here advocating permits critical examination of how notions of space-time, place, and socio-ecological relations play out in all fields of endeavor. It explicates what happens, for example, to economic theory, to Nussbaum's cosmopolitanism, to communist internationalism, and to neoliberalism, as well as to abstract theories of biopolitics, feminism, and the various forms of identity politics, when the full force of geographical theory is explicitly applied to examine their hidden geographical presuppositions. When the claims to universal truths incorporated into such theorizations are held up to geographical scrutiny, they are, as we have seen, invariably found wanting. Since the main objections to these theories and their claims to universality focus on their lack of material grounding and the "deracinated" nature of their founding concepts, the incorporation of geographical theory should provide an antidote to such objections. But the result of such an encounter is often to so transform these theories as to render them unrecognizable. I shall illustrate this through consideration of two foundational but contested terms in the history of the social sciences as well as in liberal, neoliberal, and cosmopolitan theories: the "individual" and the "state." The selection of these two terms is particularly significant, given their interconnectedness and Foucault's compelling account of how "the modern sovereign state and the modern autonomous individual [have codetermined] each other's emergence."[2] In what follows it will become clear that the "co-determination" of which Foucault speaks can best if not uniquely be understood in terms of geographical theory.

The Individual

The practice of "individuation" has long been a topic of philosophical reflection and of argumentation. Applied to human populations, this practice defines a concept of the individual that plays an important role, not only in the formulation of social and socio-ecological theories and administrative practices, but also in ideologies and perceptions that ground personal behaviors and actions. How I think of my individuality has important implications for my actions in and expectations of the world. In recent years, the topic of individuation has become more contentious, as poststructural engagements with identity politics, an increasing concern with fluidity and indeterminacy (in queer theory, for example), and a shift of focus from structures to processes and narratives have become more common. These shifts have had demonstrable practical effects in everyday life and in the making of political claims. For example, what were once considered clear census categories in the United States concerning race and ethnicity have increasingly come to be seen as unanswerable questions. Even economics has increasingly turned to behavioral theories and psychology in order to understand more clearly what individuals actually do (as opposed to what fictional economically rational individuals are supposed to do). Individuation is not, therefore, a stable practice, and its historical geography needs to be investigated and elucidated. My narrower concern here, however, is with how the individual might be understood in the light of geographical theory.

Imagine that a conquering force takes control of a well-defined territory (like an island) and exercises power over an indigenous population. The conqueror wants to have a full and adequate inventory of the lands and an account of the people under his control in order to impose a system of taxation upon them, based upon their landholding, to pay for maintenance of his army and the expenses of his royal household and his numerous retainers. To what representation of space and time would he appeal in order to complete such a task? The answer is obvious: the absolute theory of space and time permits the clear identification of landholdings and provides unambiguous locational addresses to which inhabitants can be assigned. This is the tacit theory that underlay the production of the famous Doomsday Survey that William the Conqueror imposed upon Britain after the Norman Conquest of 1066. This is what the British state later systematized in the seventeenth-century land-mapping exercises, and this theoretical spatial framework underpinned the birth of the science of political economy through the work of William Petty in the land survey of Ireland around that time. Understandably, colonial administrations (such as the British in India) and settler regimes (such as that of the United States with its various forms of Homestead Acts) have appealed to this particular aspect of spatial theory ever since. The political institutions of a property-owning democracy, with its associated practices of individuation that underpin everything from citizenship and voting to taxation, depend exclusively upon this way of understanding space and time. To have "no fixed address" in such a system is, for example, a serious problem.

There is, we see from this example, a strong connection between the exercise of a certain kind of political power and practices of individuation that rest upon a particular way of understanding space and time. Those of us who live under such a regime of political power tend to think that the absolute theory of space and time is natural, foundational, and perhaps the only theory of space and time there is. Placing these specific practices of individuation within the matrix of spatio-temporal possibilities outlined in chapter 7, however, suggests that this is only one out of several possibilities. The definition of the individual looks quite different when the dialectic of absolute, relative, and relational spatio-temporalities is invoked. Whereas my unique identity is firmly located in absolute space and time, my changing positionality relative to, say, flows of money and commodities, production systems and labor processes, or the basic metabolic biological processes that sustain life produces a relativized individual identity that is tangible but not unique. Identities are multiple, shifting, and insecure (I can be a rich man today and a poor one tomorrow; today I bask in the sun, and tomorrow I catch cold in the freezing rain). My movements in relative space-time (movements that actually help to construct, albeit only in a minor way, relative space-time configurations) make it hard to fix my address in any clear and unambiguous way. My life is not confined to a fixed address. Why should I not have some sorts of citizen's rights while moving or wherever I happen to be? The immaterial spatial relationalities that I internalize from, say, some sense of solidarity or empathy with the victims of the Iraq War, some tragedy such as the Asian tsunami, or more vaguely from a sense of belonging to something (a nation, the category of "woman" or "worker," the whole of humanity, the whole of nature, or a deity) provides an entirely different relational way of defining who I am. Though immaterial, these allegiances have objective consequences for how I act and think in the world, as well as for how others view me. How I respond to abstract invocations, furthermore, such as a triumphal nationalism, a fatwah from Iranian mullahs, or threats such as those of climate change or terrorism is a relational problem, and these relationalities are fluid, multiple, and indeterminate. They are nonetheless important and powerful for all that, since the individual identities constructed around these relationalities have objective, even if unstable, consequences (look at how the Bush administration mobilized a relational fear of an abstract terror to its own advantage for several years). We here encounter also the politics of moments when, as W. Benjamin puts it, memories can flash up unpredictably at moments of danger.[3] Only in this way can we understand the madness of crowds, the spectacle of revolution, emotive surges of public opinion (sometimes sparked by a single event, such as Rosa Parks's refusal to go to the back of the bus or that astonishing manifestation of global public opinion in the worldwide marches of February 15, 2003, to try to stop the Iraq War), or the actions of individuals who live next door to each other for many years in a mutually helpful and friendly mode and then suddenly kill each other in a frenzy of ethnic or religious hatred. Only in the relational mode can moral cosmopolitan perspectives of the Nussbaum sort take root and immaterial demands for cosmopolitan governance become objective.

Geographical theory insists that the individual does not exist outside the complex dimensionalities of space and time. The neighbors who suddenly kill each other may do so in absolute space and time, but they act out of immaterial relational motivations in the relative spaces of their spatio-temporal encounters.

Now consider the other dimension to the matrix of spatio-temporalities. The political battles fought over representations and conceptualizations, as well as over how space and time are lived, are just as important, as Lefebvre insists, as those waged in the fields of material social practices. Relationally, individuals may live their lives affirmatively and happily as patriotic citizens, as secure members of some "imagined community" (of the sort that Benedict Anderson attributes to the idea of nation), and they may represent themselves to the world as law-abiding and obedient subjects owing fealty to some greater socio-spatial power (such as state or nation).[4] Or they may represent themselves (or find themselves represented) as classical liberal subjects, independent and autonomous agents supposedly endowed (sometimes against their will, as happened to Iraqis under the occupation) with legal and juridical status and rights in ways that supersede all other forms of authority even as they recognize their interdependency with others through market exchange. They may then represent themselves in relative space-time as freely mobile geographical agents both willing and able to take advantage of or even promote new patterns of commodity and money flows. Or they may see themselves as passive victims of recession, deindustrialization, and the predatory activities of the financiers as capital flows away from the space where they are located.

Who individuals are is contingent not only upon how space and time are understood, both by themselves and by everyone else, but also upon how spatio-temporal relations are themselves being shaped and perpetually reshaped by macro-processes, such as the spread of cartographic techniques of representation from the Renaissance onward, the contemporary evolution of capital flows within the global financial trading system, or the socio-ecological metabolic processes that facilitate human reproduction more generally. If these latter processes internalize and rest upon, as they invariably do, social distinctions of some sort—as, for example, those of gender and race—then it follows that the spatio-temporality produced is itself gendered and racialized. This elemental and obvious fact explains why so many feminist theorists appeal so often to relational theories of spatio-temporality to substantiate their arguments, and why those who seek to understand the oppressions of racialized immigrant populations find themselves forced to question the spatio-temporal framing of legal concepts such as citizenship. The danger, however, is that by rendering the relational approach to spatio-temporality hegemonic and reducing the absolute to an epiphenomenon, the practical aspects of liberatory politics get diminished or even lost. P. Bourdieu's approach to spatio-temporality in his *Outline of a Theory of Practice* is so helpfulbecause he manages to put relational meanings among the Berbers into a dialectical relation with the absolute spaces of fields, houses, and even rooms in houses across phases of absolute time as defined by the calendar.[5]

Nor can individuals be considered as isolated from and outside of the socio-ecological dialectic and ongoing activities of place formation and re-formation. Their positionality in relation to nature, production systems, social relations, technologies, and mental conceptions, as these impinge upon everyday life, is perpetually shifting, as are the contexts of their feelings, sensitivities, and practical engagements. If, in short, the geographical theory I am proposing is correct, then the whole question of what constitutes an "individual" has to be reconceptualized in radically different ways from those typically set out in the simple Kantian/Cartesian logic that undergirds liberal, neoliberal, and most of the legalistic versions of cosmopolitan theory (such as those that treat individual human rights and citizenship as central).

Geographical theory unravels the spatio-temporal integument, and therefore the place-based and environmental constructions of how the "individual" might best be understood. It sheds detailed light on how, as Kant quaintly put it, temperament becomes character and with what consequences. The dialectics of geographical situatedness within the spatio-temporal matrix frames who individuals are and how, where, and when they can act. Furthermore, this situatedness is not a constant but something that is itself always shifting, sometimes rapidly so, with the ongoing production of space, place, and nature. This is the sort of systematic frame that geographical theory places around how to understand individual identity and agency. Instead of being presupposed abstractly, the individual has to be discovered, defined, and elucidated from all these angles through the application of appropriate research protocols.

Some may argue that to conceptualize the individual as always geographically situated in this way is to so confine individual action that real freedom and liberty become meaningless prospects. To this I say that the abstracted, isolated, and deracinated individual presupposed in liberal and neoliberal political theory and in Kantian cosmopolitanism is a chimera that is bound to lead to disillusionment and despair. It leads directly, for example, into all the contradictions that characterize Bush's rhetoric on liberty and freedom in relation to Guantanamo Bay and to the shocking oddity of J. S. Mill's liberal defense of imperial rule over India. Consider, for example, Locke's definition of the individual that prefaces Robert Nozick's approving argument in *Anarchy, State and Utopia*.[6] Individuals in the state of nature are construed to be in "a state of perfect freedom to order their actions and dispose of their possessions and persons as they think fit, within the bounds of the law of nature, without asking leave or dependency upon the will of any other man." Note here how the concept of the isolated individual is ineluctably connected to distinctively and exclusively bourgeois ideals of liberty and freedom of the sort that ground much political debate in our own times (see Bush's speeches that we examined in the prologue)—a connection that Marx, for one, spotted right away and subjected to a powerful critique when he noted that Robinson Crusoe, even when displaced to a desert island, organized his life around the principles of a "true-born Briton." Civil society evolves, according to Locke, only because some people transgress the rule that "no one ought to harm another in his life, health, liberty or possessions," and this leads those offended against to exact retribution. The state is necessary to modulate such retribution and to prevent the descent into the perpetual violence of revenge killings. Behind this formulation lies the idea of the individual as an entirely autonomous being in absolute space and time. From the standpoint of geographical theory, this is both a ludicrous conception and a dangerous illusion, since it conveys an idea of individual autonomy and absolute individual agency that cannot possibly exist. Even Adam Smith recognized the illusory qualities of this formulation, but he then went on to justify acting on it on the equally dangerous and illusory grounds that it redounded to the benefit of society as a whole if everyone acted as if they were free, autonomous, and unencumbered individual agents, even when they clearly were not.

One of Foucault's great achievements in his theory of governmentality is to show the nefarious consequences that follow when individuals internalize such illusions. The political practices that evolved mainly in Europe from the sixteenth century onward and which have become even more deeply inscribed in many of our psyches ever since, systematically deny real freedoms, while leaving the illusion of their existence intact. In so doing, Foucault in effect elaborates upon Marx's key insight in *On the Jewish Question*: "Where the political state has attained its true development, man—not only in thought, in consciousness, but in reality, in life—leads a twofold life . . . life in the political community, in which he considers himself a communal being, and life in civil society in which he acts as a private individual, regards other men as means, degrades himself into a means, and becomes the plaything of alien powers. . . . Here, where he regards himself as a real individual, and is so regarded by others, he is a fictitious phenomenon. In the state, on the other hand, where man is regarded as a species being, he is the imaginary member of an illusionary sovereignty, is deprived of his real individual life and endowed with an unreal universality."[7]

Geographical theory goes even further than Foucault and Marx, however, and exposes how one of the key repressive characteristics of governmentality and its associated political economy is to confine our understanding of space and time to its absolute dimensions, since only through such a diminished theory of space and time can "free" liberal individuals (and the properties they own) be clearly and unambiguously defined, demarcated, numbered, located, taxed, and, of course, governed and controlled. The production of individualized and atomized citizens is constitutive with the rise of a certain form of state power. A strong correlation exists between the hegemony of the absolute theory of space and time and the assumption of absolute bourgeois administrative power. The contemporary United States is an exemplary case of what happens to that power when individuals increasingly take the Lockean fictions to heart, only then to find themselves defending the absoluteness of their spaces (their bodies, their properties, and even collectively, as all the gated communities and the contemporary surge of anti-immigrant fervor so clearly illustrate). Foucault's failure to liberate himself from the Kantian absolute conception of space (as embodied in his concept of heterotopia) unfortunately kept him imprisoned within the very governmentality he sought to overthrow. The absolute theory of space and time has, therefore, been dominant in our thinking ever since the Enlightenment for a very good reason. The rise of the modern state and the modern form of capitalism depended crucially upon the hegemony of this absolute theory of space and time for the proper functioning of their disciplinary apparatuses. The doctrine of progress, which separates Kant's cosmopolitanism from that of the Stoics, likewise depends upon an absolute conception of time. It is hardly surprising, therefore, that relative and relational understandings of space and time (a common feature of premodern cosmologies and epistemologies) have, until recently, been treated either as special issues or as oddities, particularly in the realm of a social theory that is complicit with bourgeois power. The inability of most economists and political scientists to think outside the box of absolute space and time distorts their understandings of the world in debilitating ways.

The geographical theory of the individual allows us to critique and break with this hegemony. It envisages a person burdened and materially bound by the shackles of his or her geographical integuments and social and relational position. Read almost any ethnography, and you are likely to encounter a concept of individuation radically at odds with the Lockean vision. These ethnographies build up a conception of individuals through a careful reconstruction of social practices, representations, and the ways lives are lived in particular historical and geographical situations in tacit or sometimes explicit opposition to the liberal, neoliberal, and cosmopolitical fictions. These individuals are already initiated into and geographically enlightened by their own experience of making and being made by changing space and spatio-temporal relations, place building, and active involvement in environmental transformations. As Michel de Certeau points out, we even make space by walking in the city.[8] But, sadly, many of these ethnographic works fail to theorize their own conclusions to the point of founding an alternative social scientific approach to knowledge, to bring the propaedeutics of geography, anthropology, and ecology into their proper position within the overall schema of our understandings. From this follows a failure to recognize that our task is not simply to understand our geography, our anthropology, and our ecology, but also to change them in constructive and emancipatory ways. We have to recognize that individuals are inherently endowed with the capacity to break out of the confines of their own geographical, anthropological, and ecological constraints. Real politics is always, in short, about "people out of place." The production of alternative geographies is not only a necessary precondition but also a privileged constructive means for radical social change.

Relationalities can never be controlled (which is why state and capitalist power abhors them). But relationalities are always problematic. To whom we are loyal, for example, is not an easy determination (an issue that Raymond Williams frequently addressed in novel form, particularly in his book *Loyalties*).[9] Once agreed upon, strong loyalties can be politically decisive. Relationalities, though immaterial, are therefore far from free-floating. When they crystallize out into fixed patterns of belief and political alignment, they constitute power nexuses of enormous significance. Accepted dogmas (such as the hierarchical views of racial superiorities of the sort that Kant relayed or the paternalism that Mill presumed) can be both dangerous and damaging in their objective consequences. Interestingly, the postcolonial theorists took up Burke's appeal to the facts of geography to counter the invidious consequences of applying the universals of liberalism in a paternalistic way to the Indian case, but unfortunately they turned for answers toward Heidegger's unduly exclusionary (and equally universalistic) theory of place (on the false Aristotelian principle that "place is the first of all things").[10] The problem for cosmopolitanism of the sort envisaged by Held, Beck, Appiah, Nussbaum, and others is that it is still grounded in the abstracted liberal and Kantian concept of the individual person as an actor (even when, as in Nussbaum's case, the animating cosmopolitan principle takes relational form).

Freedom and liberatory politics cannot be pursued, we may conclude, without active human agents individually or collectively producing new spaces and spatio-temporalities, making and remaking places materially as well as in a different image, and producing a new second nature and thereby revolutionizing their socio-ecological and environmental relations.[11] The production of space here means not only making things in absolute space and time, but building and using relative spaces—as well as struggling to internalize (either individually or collectively) the immaterial and relational connections and solidarities in space-time that can liberate us as well as others. Clearly, the starting point of this is some sense of what the individual must be liberated from (and Marx's comment that human freedom begins when the realm of material necessity and physical dependency is left behind is a suggestive beginning). But this liberatory process can never take place outside of space and time, outside of place making, and without engagement with the dialectics of socio-natural relations.

The geographical theory of the "individual" exposes the fictional mistakes of other theoretical systems, and this is no minor achievement for, as Marx once pointed out, often the only answer to an erroneous question is to question the question. It is helpful to reveal, for example, the constraining effect of assuming that the absolute theory of space and time is all there is on a wide range of social issues (such as immigration law). But geographical theory cannot by itself answer any grand questions (analytical or political) as to preferred forms of liberatory politics (for example, what migration policies are desirable). It does, however, lay out the "conditions of possibility" for finding adequate answers. In particular, it insists upon the banal point that the concept of a deracinated, placeless, and environmentally unconstrained individual generates profoundly misleading theoretical propositions that put a seemingly insurmountable practical barrier to the formulation of an active democratic politics. The abstracted concept of the individual (or of any cognate concept, such as the body) leaves us, as Margaret Thatcher liked to say, with no alternative to neoliberal politics. But at this point the question of the relation between the individual and the state moves center stage in the analysis.

State Theories

The concept of the state, like that of the individual, always has been and continues to be problematic and contentious in social theory. An approach to understanding the state through geographical theory sheds some light on how and why. Some social scientists have in recent times become so impatient with the concept that they propose to dispense with it. In other instances, intense and rancorous debates—such as that which took place among Marxists in the 1970s over the relations between class, state, and economy—peter out from sheer exhaustion, leaving behind, in that particular case, the seemingly unsatisfactory conclusion that the state is both a fetish illusion (a mask for class power) and an organized political force in its own right. In more recent times the debate has shifted onto somewhat different terrain. Consider, for example, two major contributions from Philip Abrams and Timothy Mitchell.

"The state," writes Abrams, "conceived of as a substantial entity separate from society has proved a remarkably elusive object of analysis."[12] We have, he suggests, been trapped "by a reification which in itself seriously obstructs the effective study of a number of problems about political power." This reification locates the state as an entity in absolute space and time, to the exclusion of any other kind of spatio-temporality. Behind all the inadmissible reifications (particularly those that view the state as an entity endowed with active causal powers), Abrams notes, lies "a managed construction of belief about the state," such that the "idea of the state has a significant political reality." He therefore proposes that we "abandon the state as a material object of study, whether concrete or abstract, while continuing to take the idea of the state extremely seriously." The state may be an illusion or a misrepresentation, but it is nevertheless a social fact. In effect, Abrams here invokes relational understandings. The state is a myth that "makes the abstract concrete" and makes "the non-existent exist." It "starts its life as an implicit construct, it is then reified—as the res publica, the public reification, no less—and acquires an overt symbolic identity progressively divorced from practice as an illusory account of practice." Here a dialectical relation is tacitly invoked between relational and absolute understandings. The state is, therefore, "not the reality which stands behind the mask of political practice. It is itself the mask which prevents our seeing political practice as it is." It is "an ideological project," and "an exercise in legitimation" that "seeks to elicit support or tolerance of the insupportable and intolerable by presenting them as something other than themselves, namely legitimate, disinterested domination." It is a way of binding subjects "into their own subjection." As such it is, as Marx said of the commodity, a "fetish construct." It masks and fixes the fluidity and instabilities in socio-spatial relations in hard-edged territorialized institutional forms.

The task of the social theorist is to demystify that fetish. This entails a study of how the "state-idea" has been "projected, purveyed and variously believed in, in different societies at different times." It also entails, and Abrams regrettably buries the point, establishing the nature of the conflictual social relations and material social practices that lie behind the production of this state-idea. Abrams does accept, however, Ralph Miliband's view of the "state system" defined as "a cluster of institutions of political and executive control and their key personnel, the 'state elite': the government, the administration, the military and police, the judicial branch, sub-central governments and parliamentary assemblies." But he has nothing to say about the geographical configurations assumed by such institutional arrangements (such as the military in their barracks or even the construction of territorial jurisdictions). He also finds "promising" Nicos Poulantzas's view of the state as a "site" or "place" where a certain contradictory unity can be achieved, but misses out on the opportunity to apply any theory of place construction to the argument, even though he does ask the key question: "what sort of place is it?" (Yet another example of major thinkers invoking a key geographical concept—place—without interrogating its meaning or considering its possibilities as they move on to examine supposedly more important problems.) Abrams then concedes the possibility (having urged us earlier to abandon the study of the state as a material object) that "an empirically accessible object of study is brought into being which, if studied aright, will reveal to us the modalities of domination within given social systems." The state can exist as a reified entity in absolute space and time, but—and here I put my own gloss on Abrams's account—it must be considered as a fetish object in much the same way Marx treats of the commodity. It really exists (it becomes reified), but as "a material relation between persons and a social relation between things." Abrams almost certainly refrained from invoking the idea of fetishism, since that was one aspect of the Marxist debate on the state that Abrams was clearly concerned to leave behind.

What Abrams implicitly ends up with, however, is a shadowy and partial version of what a geographical theory of the state reveals directly. If we take the spatio-temporal being of the state as crucial to its definition (and what state can claim to be outside of space and time?), then it must be construed as the outcome of a distinctive process of place formation. And place formation, as we have seen, cannot be understood without examining how the dialectical unity of absolute, relative, and relational spatio-temporalities gets constructed (internalizing, as Poulantzas correctly surmises, all manner of contradictions). Nor can we consider it as outside the ongoing dynamics of socio-ecological transformations. The problem with Abrams's formulation then becomes apparent. His presumption that the materiality of the state arises out of the reification of a social relation and an idea may have it the wrong way round. Perhaps the concrete material practices of bounding and place making led human beings to construct the state as a representation, as an idea, and then to live that idea in a certain way and consolidate their practices of state reification around that idea. Geographical theory suggests that it the dialectical movement of concrete practices in absolute space and time in relation to relative and relational space-times almost certainly was and continues to be involved in state formation and maintenance.

Timothy Mitchell takes Abrams's argument even further (though in some respects from the opposite direction), and in so doing he comes closer to touching on the dialectics of state formation seen from a more geographical perspective. To begin with, he merges "the state idea and the state system" as "two aspects of the same process."[13] Like Abrams, he considers that our analytic task is not "to clarify such distinctions but to historicize them." In particular, we need to know how the boundaries between state, society, and economy have been conceptualized historically (and, I would add, geographically across the space of the globe). The state is not only a subjective belief, but "a representation reproduced in everyday visible forms, such as the language of legal practice, the architecture of public buildings, the wearing of military uniforms, or the marking or policing of frontiers." So while the state may be a "ghost-like abstraction" endowed with "disciplinary powers" (in the way Foucault envisaged), it is "continually reproduced" (and thereby reified) in tangible materialist ways. We need therefore to discover the historical process whereby "disciplinary powers are somehow consolidated into the territorially-based institutionally structured order of the modern state." Like Abrams, Mitchell sees the state as a fetish object, as "a screen (that of sovereignty and right) superimposed on the real power of discipline." So although the state, in Foucault's words, "is no more than a composite reality and mythicized abstraction," it "takes on the appearance of a structure." The state, in Mitchell's gloss, is "an effect produced by the organized partitioning of space, the regular distribution of bodies, exact timing, the coordination of movement, the combining of elements, the endless repetition, all of which are particular practices." These practices make the state real. They reify it. We should therefore examine the state "not as an actual structure, but as the powerful, apparently metaphysical effect of practices that make such structures appear to exist."

One of the state's chief characteristics, for example, is the physical frontier. "By establishing a territorial boundary to enclose a population and exercise an absolute control of movement across it, governmental powers define and help constitute a national entity." But "setting up and policing a frontier involves a variety of fairly modern social practices—continuous barbed wire fencing, passports, immigration laws, inspections, currency control, and so on." Through such mundane and banal practices, "most of them unknown two hundred or even one hundred years ago," the nation-state is manufactured as "an almost transcendental entity," as a "nonmaterial totality that seems to exist apart from the material world of society." The state, in other words, achieves a presence in relational spacetime by way of its material effects. Mitchell goes on to argue (citing both Poulantzas and Foucault in support) that "both the factory regime and the power of the state are aspects of the modern reordering of space, time, and personhood and the production of the new effects of abstraction and subjectivity." In short, the restructuring of space and time that occurred during the rise of capitalism (though for some reason Mitchell avoids putting things this way) produced both the factory and the state as distinctive entities. "Rather than deriving the forms of the state from the logic of capital accumulation and the organization of production relations"—as the Marxists had tried to do in the 1970s—Mitchell prefers to see both capital and the state "as aspects of a common process of abstraction."[14]

Exactly what this process of abstraction is, where it came from, and why it occurred remains as elusive in Mitchell's account (lest it be simply the imposition of absolute conceptions of space and time as a condition of state governmentality and the unambiguous construction of notions of territoriality) as does the question of the social relations and processes that underlie the creation of the state-idea in the first place. But the content of the state-idea has not remained constant over time. And much of the contemporary debate—and an important ingredient in cosmopolitics—concerns precisely whether the process has gone so far as to render the concept of the state otiose (as in Ulrich Beck's formulations) if not entirely irrelevant. Mitchell does not go this far, but he does point to past transformations. He claims—erroneously, in my view—that "the idea of an economy as a self-contained dynamic totality, separate from other economies and subject to intervention, adjustment and management by an externally situated state could not have been imagined within the terms of nineteenth century political economy" (an odd statement given the formulations of List and the German Historical School) and that "the economy" came to refer to "the structure or totality of relations of production, circulation and consumption within a given geographical space" only in the 1920s and 1930s. What was new, he says, "was the notion that the interrelation of these processes formed a space or object that was self-contained, subject to its own internal dynamics, and liable to 'external' impulses or interventions that created reverberations throughout the self-contained object."

The state became the basis of data collection, and both the state and the national economy were brought into existence by virtue of statistical representation. But this mutual identification occurred far earlier than Mitchell allows (indeed, elements of such a representation go back at least to the mercantilist period, as evidenced in Thomas Mun's tract "England's Treasure by Foreign Trade," published in 1664, and William Petty's statistical inquiry into Ireland's economy around the same time that defined the emerging field of national—and it was national—political economy). The state also emerged as a crucial regulator of national currencies (the quality of the national coinage being so crucial that Isaac Newton was called upon to preside over the King's Mint for a while, where hewould send those found guilty of clipping the coinage to the Tyburn gallows) from the seventeenth century onward. The only heresy worthy of capital punishment was no longer defined by God but by Mammon. But Mitchell's general point is surely correct: "the most important thing imagined to stand outside the economy was the one considered most capable of affecting or altering it—the state." There was a coevolution between the conception of the state and that of the national economy, in exactly the same way as the conceptions of the individual and the state arose integrally with each other.

The malleability of the social practices that reify both the state as a tangible object and our sense of it as a container of power is also worthy of note. Passports, first introduced during the Napoleonic Wars, gradually disappeared during the nineteenth century. Before 1914, Stefan Zweig recalled of his pre–World War I global travels, "the frontiers were nothing but symbolic lines which one crossed with as little thought as when one crosses the Meridian of Greenwich."[15] The analogy is telling, however, since the establishment of a spatial organization of time zones was of crucial significance to the organized efficiency of capitalism and the interstate system at the beginning of the twentieth century. After the 1914–18 war, the passport requirement tightened to the point where we now would find the idea of open frontiers impossibly strange if not appallingly dangerous, even as we cross them with increasing frequency. Yet, curiously, as new distinctions between state and economy emerged in the world of representations, "so-called economic processes and institutions became increasingly difficult to distinguish in practice from those of government or the state."[16] Central banks and state agencies came to straddle the supposed divide between state and economy just as, say, state educational activities and welfare provision straddle the divide between state and civil society. While the state appears as an abstraction, Mitchell concludes, we must nevertheless address it "as an effect of mundane processes of spatial organization, temporal arrangement, functional specification, supervision and surveillance and representation that create the appearance of a world fundamentally divided into state and society or state and economy." In my view, of course, it is the circulation of capital that is the hidden driver behind the "mundane processes" that Mitchell identifies, precisely because, as I have shown elsewhere, if the state did not already exist in some form or other the circulation of capital in space and time would have to create some kind of territorial organization very much like one.[17]

Mitchell's presentation—as might be expected of someone who has long experience of testing Foucauldian ways of thinking against colonial practices in Egypt—is sensitive to spatial determinations. The immaterial but objective qualities of the state are frequently invoked. This places the state firmly in relational spacetime, with all sorts of lines of possibility of analysis in terms of the linkage to the absolute domains of space and time. To begin with, we need to know the dominant social processes and social relations (of gender and class, for example) that set up the relationalities of the state-idea and set the stage for specific forms of reification in absolute space and time. Consider, furthermore, the role of the relation to nature, of environmental (both built and so-called natural) imagery, and of history and collective memory in providing substance to the idea of national solidarities within reified state forms. What is the role of wilderness, the frontier, Mount Rushmore, or the Lincoln Memorial, for example, in defining that exceptionalist sense of the U.S. state and nation to which all U.S. statesmen so frequently appeal (with all manner of objective consequences)? The image of a nation is heavily dependent on how the socio-ecological dialectic has been reworked, conceptually as well as physically, within a state's borders over a long period of time (the German forests, the French *pays*, the Scottish glens, and so on). Mitchell is also very attentive to how the immaterial but objective qualities of the state are tangibly materialized in absolute space and time as barriers, borders, and a variety of other material social practices (often of a ritualistic and symbolic nature). These practices reify the state as a real material entity and give it the appearance, as Abrams would put it, of a coherent structure. The Lefebvrian dimension also creeps in, because the sheer power of representational practices clearly affects material social practices and how we live the relationality of the state.

The dialectical nature of the relations between these different aspects of spatio-temporality is lightly hinted at in Mitchell's work, but it is not hard to expand upon it. In the domain of representation, for example, the long history of cartographic practices has played a central role in reifying the state.[18] It is hard to take seriously Abrams's proposition that states do not exist as material entities, when every map of the world clearly defines and names them so. The militarized fence that separates much of Mexico from the United States or, even more heinously, the wall being built to separate Israeli from Palestinian territory, are very tangible things that exist in absolute space, as are the barriers and booths we encounter at every international airport, through which we may or may not pass at the discretion of some immigration authority. Borders are, to be sure, social constructions, but when turned into elaborate physical fortifications, they render moot the dismissal of the materiality of the state as an inadmissible reification. We cannot, of course, understand these reifications without also unpacking the relationality of the state as an idea, but this is precisely the point about insisting upon the dialectical relations within the matrix of spatio-temporalities and the practice of place making that provides one crucial anchor to geographical theory. But the point on which Abrams, Mitchell, and I agree is that the specific historical geography of all this has to be recounted and that the presumption that the state either embodies some universal and unchanging essence or truth (that can be empirically uncovered or acted upon) or is a simple and unproblematic empirical object of observation has to be discarded. In retrospect, it is astonishing to note how much of conventional social theory as well as political practice was corralled within the unexamined territorial frame of the nation-state (this was true of even progressive formulations, such as that of C. Wright Mills in *The Sociological Imagination*).

So how, then, does geographical theory look upon the state? Consider the following fictional tale. A king rules his kingdom in a benevolent style. One day invading colonial powers present themselves at his court and ask him to define where his kingdom begins and ends. The king says he has no idea. The astonished colonialists say that cannot be so. How can he tell who his subjects are if he cannot define the territoriality of his kingdom?

The king explains that his subjects are defined not by residency in a fixed territory but by fealty to him. They can be located anywhere. Sometimes when he does things of which some of his subjects disapprove, they shift their loyalty to someone else. The number of his subjects willing to pay taxes to him increases with his reputation for good works and his image as a charismatic, wise, and benevolent ruler. And he is not above asserting mythological origins of his power and a privileged relationship to deities whom he alone can persuade to smile fondly on the fates of his believing loyal subjects. The kingdom works very well without any fixed territorial boundaries. It is relationally and relatively defined, but has no clear definition in absolute space and time. The colonial powers, in conflict with one another, insist upon drawing maps to delineate their spheres of influence and insist that the king do likewise. The king's subjects are now defined by residence in a territory defined by Cartesian mapmakers in absolute space and time. The king no longer has to persuade his subjects by good works and wise rule, because the borders are sealed. He can set up systems of control and surveillance within his territory and extract taxes by force of arms (kindly supplied, at a price, by the colonial powers). Completely different powers of domination arise out of the shift from a relational to an absolute definition. This may sound somewhat farfetched but it is not too far from what happened to the kingdom once called Siam (now Thailand).[19]

Viewed from the standpoint of "subjects" of the state, however, this sort of scenario takes on a far more serious tone. N. De Genova, for example, in his study of Mexican migrants in Chicago, found it necessary to deploy "a critical transnational perspective in order to dislodge some of the dominant spatial ideologies that undergird a prevalent common sense about the naturalized difference between the United States and Mexico, as well as between the United States and Latin America more generally." Through the lens of what he calls "Mexican Chicago," he seeks "to render an orthodox spatial knowledge about the relation of Mexican migrants to the U.S. national-state more accountable to a regime of spatial power and inequality." He insists, for example, in situating Mexicans in Chicago in relative space-time as "migrants" in motion rather than as "immigrants" in place. He furthermore accepts their own sense of spatial relationality to "a spatial topography of the Americas" that is "intrinsically racialized" and continuously reracialized to produce "the unequal social relations through which global capital, nation-states, and transnational labor, together in the contradictions of struggle, unevenly produce the particular localities where 'globalization' takes place." The effect is to undermine "the epistemological stability of the U.S. nation-state as a presupposition," at the same time as the very meaning of the Mexicanness of Mexican Chicago signifies a permanent disruption of the space of the U.S. nation-state and embodies the vital possibility of something truly new, a radically different social formation." What happens, he asks, when Chicago is seen as a place produced by Mexicans? These relationalities exist in a deep conflict with the absolute frame of space and time and the "irreducible spatial discontinuity between the United State and Mexico" imposed as a racialized and increasingly impenetrable border to a migrant stream that more and more confronts the border in terms of illegality. The place called Mexican Chicago "is better understood as a spatial conjuncture of *social relations* that thus comprises innumerable places. It is a conjuncture, furthermore, constituted through the everyday social relations and meaningful practices that comprise the intersection of a transnational labor migration, capitalist enterprises, and the U.S. nation-state." The fields of knowledge production called Latin American and Chicano studies are themselves organized, De Genova insists, so as to occlude rather than to illuminate the complexities of the situation and the radical possibilities for creating any kind of new social formation.[20]

I have, in this account, superimposed some of my own geographical theoretical categories of space-time onto De Genova's work, in order to illustrate how solidly researched and decolonized ethnographic accounts typically produce a knowledge structure akin to that which I am here seeking to establish directly. That this can be so easily done derives, of course, from De Genova's indebtedness to Lefebvre's formulations on the production of space. But that Latin American and Chicano studies—two fields in which anti-imperialist and emancipatory politicsis deeply embedded—are judged by an otherwise sympathetic researcher to be lacking in conceptual precision because of their erroneous spatial specifications says a great deal about the problem of getting the Kantian propaedeutic right.

Accounts of this sort pose the question as to what the world might be like were the spatiality of the state constructed along relational lines rather than according to Cartesian/Kantian spatial rationality. That the emergence of the latter as hegemonic had something to do with the rise of the joint disciplinary powers of capital and the state, as Mitchell suggests (though then denies), is in itself an important proposition. But even here there are some oddities illustrative of a broader issue. For example, the U.S. Supreme Court, faced with the challenge that capitalists might not have full-fledged rights to trade in Puerto Rico unless Puerto Ricans had equivalent rights to live in the United States, decided in 1904 that "while in an international sense Puerto Rico was not a foreign country, it was foreign to the United States in a domestic sense." And it is, of course, from this kind of reasoning that another and even more sinister liminal space, such as Guantanamo Bay (outside of any U.S. court jurisdiction but inside the U.S. state for other purposes), could be brought into being.[21]

The parallel between the geographical theory of state formation and the disciplinary apparatus imposed upon individual identities through the hegemony of the absolute theory of space and time here becomes crucial. The modern state could not be what it is without having at hand a simple principle to identify and individuate the population over which control, surveillance, and dominance are going to be exercised, for it was, as Foucault points out, population rather than territory that became the primary focus of state formation and administration. "Seeing like a state," as James Scott notes, entails in the first instance imagining an absolute grid of territorial identifications of places, people, and property rights that can be surveyed, surveilled, and controlled. And it was, furthermore, through the aggregate of atomized individuals that the national economy was in turn defined, sparking all manner of economic theories—liberalism being the prime example—of state management and intervention. That the dominance of an absolute theory of spatio-temporality is a "condition of possibility" for the perpetuation of capitalist and state powers is undeniable. Such domination does not entail the erasure of other forms of spatio-temporality (it never can). To say that the absolute form is hegemonic is to indicate a situation in which relational meanings, such as nationalism, are for the most part confined within the container of a singular absolute territorial definition. Sovereignty, as S. Benhabib points out, is a relational concept, but it takes on much of its specific meaning by the way it is corralled within an increasing dysfunctional notion of the nation-state as a distinctive entity in absolute space and time. The problem is that the "terrain we are traveling on—the world society of states—has changed," but "our normative map has not."[22] What is so interesting about Abrams's, Mitchell's, De Genova's, and Benhabib's writings is that they signal a breakdown of the Cartesian/Kantian hegemony and a reversal in which relative and relational conceptions come to the fore. Interestingly, within Europe, as the absolute boundaries disappear and barriers to personal mobility are reduced, so relational meanings and loyalties reemerge as more salient to personal identifications. That so many people prefer to stay in place even with open borders says a great deal about the power of certain relational attachments and meanings over people's choices. That nationalist antagonisms continue to flourish within the open space of the European Union testifies to the power and significance of relational definitions.

This poses the problem of what happens when we recognize the state as a contingent concept, which has no meaning over and above the diverse processes (in relative and relational space-time) that produce and reproduce it. On the one hand, this liberates us to rethink the relation between space and power (which Foucault identifies but cannot unpack) in all its plenitude. But on the other hand, this poses a signal danger because, as we have seen in earlier chapters, geographical concepts, such as territory or location, often stand in for something else and in so doing occlude rather than illuminate the contradictory socio-ecological functioning of our world. There is, as M. Sparke points out, no point in displacing deracinated universal concepts by what he calls an "anemic geography" of gross simplifications (such as the effect of coastlines or axes of evil). This is why it became so important to construct a geographical theory that is itself rigorous and complete enough to capture the complexities of contemporary life. Sparke illustrates through his careful critique how far and how deep such "anemic geographies" have penetrated into social and literary thought. "Geographical concept-metaphors," he writes, "such as Bhabha's 'location,' Appadurai's 'scapes,' Hardt and Negri's 'smooth space,' and Laclau and Mouffe's 'terrains,' 'fields,' 'areas,' 'frontiers,' 'boundaries,' 'planes,' 'positions,' 'regions,' and so on," are nothing more than "so many anemic geographies that cover over the palimpsest of unfinished and worldly geographical struggles."[23] Mitchell's consolidation of the territorial nation-state as an "almost transcendent entity" is likewise a manifestation of an "anemic geography" because it presupposes a preexisting territorial bond between state and nation (a bond that both Sparke and De Genova destabilize). With such luminaries as Bhabha, Appadurai, Hardt and Negri, Laclau and Mouffe, and Mitchell held to critical account for their "anemic geographies," it becomes even more urgent to define that geographical theory which can get behind the innumerable ruses of geographical reason that flow so uninhibitedly in their otherwise learned analyses. The point, as Sparke and I would agree, is not to suggest that we geographers are in some unique position to exercise judgment (for geographers are just as likely to produce "anemic geographies" as anyone else). A collective endeavor of critical inquiry from all manner of perspectives is needed to get the geographical propaedeutic right. Even then, it should be absolutely clear that an adequate knowledge of geographical theory, of how spaces, places, and environments get produced and with what consequences, is only ever a necessary and never a sufficient condition for political emancipation and that even then lopsided forms of theorizing can be just as problematic as no theory at all.

There is, for example, a danger of casting our spatial conceptions in purely or even predominantly relational terms. If the state is first and foremost construed as an immaterial social relation and therefore only a political idea, then it is all too easy to succumb to the fantasy that the state can be disappeared in spite of all its ugly reifications on the ground, merely by refraining from thinking it. This way of "conceptualizing the state into oblivion" (as R. Trouillot calls it) is longstanding but has undergone a singular revival in recent years.[24] Hardt and Negri abolish the state by conceptual fiat as irrelevant in their best-selling book *Empire*. This procedure is not confined to the state, either. Thomas Friedman likewise flattens the world to promote his neoliberal vision. Margaret Thatcher thought to rid herself of all the recalcitrant forms of civil society by brazenly asserting that there is "no such thing as society, only individual men and women and their families." Conversely, some of the more ardent advocates of civil society politics deny the relevance of the state simply by a wave of their discursive wands. In recent years even "capitalism" has been disappeared by discursive fiat (is this what Mitchell is doing?), leaving many workers around the world mystified as to the primary source of their oppression.[25]

But there is one further crucial insight to be had from exploring a geographical theory of the state. If we view the state as a specific kind of place construction, as Abrams (following Poulantzas) suggests we should, then everything that is involved in the theory of place—in relation to the production of space and of nature—needs to be brought to bear on understanding what the state not only has been and now is but what it might become. We can no longer regard the state as some ideal type or unchanging essence. Rather, we must view it as a fluid outcome of processes of place construction in which the different moments of the relation to nature, production processes, social relations, technologies, mental conceptions of the world, and the structures of daily life intersect within a bordered world (a territorialized assemblage) to make a fluid entity into a solid "permanence" of social power. From this standpoint some rigid political oppositions start to dissolve (much as they do in the works of Sparke and De Genova). For example, the antistatism that founds much of anarchist politics has to be called into question. Anarchists, particularly of the social variety, are deeply interested in place construction. M. Bookchin's vision, as we have seen, of "a humanly scaled self-governing municipality freely and confederally associated with other humanly scaled, self governing municipalities" is exemplary of an "anarchic vision of decentralized communities, united in free confederations or networks for coordinating the communities of a region, [that] reflects the traditional ideals of a participatory democracy in a modern radical context."[26] Bookchin is proposing a particular form of place construction to displace the nation-state, but he cannot avoid encountering all of the paradoxes and contradictions that arise in all forms of place construction, no matter whether organized by autonomistas, social anarchists, Maoists, city corporations, developers, or dictators. While the "withering away" of a particular kind of place-formation called the modern capitalist state may be a worthwhile project, the withering away of all forms of place-construction is inconceivable. Geographical theory not only helps dissolve false oppositions, such as that between state and civil society, but also helps release political energies and the political imagination to examine afresh the whole issue of the most adequate form of territorial organization of human societies to meet specific socio-ecological aims. It poses key questions head on and so helps us avoid the more egregious blunders of place construction while identifying the requisite tools to reconstruct places in an entirely different image. The mere concept of a Mexican Chicago is, for example, one place to start, as is the view that nothing short of a radical geographical reconfiguration of our urban systems is needed if we are to do anything serious about energy use and climate change.

Constructing Geographies

Writings of the Abrams and Mitchell sort betoken a crisis of place construction in the contemporary world system, one in which a narrow absolute definition of a place dubbed a state makes less and less sense. This crisis is rendered explicit in the work of Sparke and De Genova. Under the rules of geographical theory, this crisis in place formation is simultaneously a crisis of spatio-temporality as well as of socio-ecological relations. For states as entities to go to war with each other becomes irrelevant because if they do, as in Iraq, they immediately find themselves embroiled in complicated relational rather than simple territorial struggles. The Iraq invasion was, among other things, an example of U.S. political and military leaders thinking in terms of a spatio-temporal structure that was anachronistic, that is, absolute. The parallel with Kern's account of the outbreak of World War I, when statesmen failed to notice that a new spatio-temporal order had emerged and so failed to prevent the headlong rush into war, is only too exact.[27] Around 1910, wrote Lefebvre in retrospect, "a certain space was shattered." This was "the space of common sense, of knowledge, of social practice, of political power, a space hitherto enshrined in everyday discourse, just as in abstract thought, as the environment of and channel for communication. . . . Euclidean and perspectivist space have disappeared as systems of reference, along with other common places such as town, history, paternity, the tonal system in music, traditional morality and so forth." This was the moment that Yeats recorded in his famous and these days oft-cited lines: "things fall apart; the center cannot hold." This was the era of which James Joyce later wrote, "I hear the ruin of all space, shattered glass and toppling masonry, and time one livid final flame." In this context the Viennese artist Gustav Klimt, desperately seeking "for orientation in a world without secure coordinates," shifted his representations of space and substance "from the naturalistically solid through the impressionistically fluid to the abstract and geometrically static."[28] This was the shattering world that was put back together in absolute terms by the Treaty of Versailles, only to be shattered again, most symbolically by the break-up of the state of Yugoslavia, offspring of Versailles, in the 1990s.[29]

After 2001, Rumsfeld, Cheney, and Wolfowitz persuaded Bush to a political and military strategy that failed to acknowledge the new spatio-temporal and socio-ecological order that came into being after 1990 or so. Not only did they commit a major categorical mistake in attacking a relational problem (called terrorism) in crude absolute terms, but they also failed to see how the rapidly shifting dynamics of geo-economic power and socio-ecological relations was radically altering geopolitical relations on the world stage (four important instances being the end of the Cold War, the rise of China as an economic power, the consolidation of much of Europe around a single currency, and the pressures emanating from a raft of global ecological problems). The seemingly solid reifications of states constructed in earlier times came under stress and in some instances actively dissolved (as in the cases of the former Soviet Union and Yugoslavia). Responses that sought to strengthen the older reifications (by, for example, erecting fences along borders and creating barriers to open movement) appeared more and more politically pressing just when they became more and more futile in the face of burgeoning practices of neoliberal free trade, hypermobility of everything (including people), the shifts in relative space-time relations accomplished through revolutions in transport and communications, and the plain fact that so-called negative externalities (pollution and environmental degradation problems or new diseases like HIV/AIDS) do not stop at state boundaries. Political struggles have been displaced from the fixed territorialities of the absolute to unstable relational realms that cannot easily be controlled, patrolled, and disciplined. Deterritorialization and reterritorialization within the global economy have resulted.

While this situation holds out the promise of freedom from those prior disciplinary constraints (including those over individuals) historically and geographically exercised by capital and the state in absolute space and time (and this increase in freedom is surely to be welcomed), it also poses the dangers of overwhelming instabilities, clashing fealties, disruptive memories, multiple loyalties, and cascading violence. Reterritorialization, as we have seen in the former Yugoslavia and East Timor, is not necessarily a peaceful process (though, with the exception of Chechnya, it was surprisingly pacific in the case of the former Soviet Union). In the face of this, we now see a revival of attempts to reconstruct a disciplinary world order. But it is clear that raw militaristic domination of the U.S. imperial sort is bound to fail and that the collective power of NATO cannot prevail even in Afghanistan. While a balance of power between regional centers mediated through coördinating institutions has a better chance of success, the rapid relative shifts in transport and communications, coupled with rising tides of nationalism, regionalism, and competition for basic resources (energy in particular), put the prospect of any steady-state equilibrium in geopolitical power relations at a low level of probability at the very moment when the socio-ecological and spatio-temporal crisis in place formation (for example, urbanization) is rapidly deepening. Against this, a global system of cosmopolitan governance and ethics, based on a federation of independent states (as Kant envisaged) seems more attractive, but it is disturbing to see the idea of the state, construed and reified as an absolute entity (and so depicted on the map of the world), being brought back in as a crucial stabilizer. Nussbaum's surprising (though very Kantian) rehabilitation of the traditional nation-state and Appiah's insistence upon a rooted cosmopolitanism are indicators of this trend. Such a questionable response is to some degree understandable when it seems as if the main left alternative in active play is some form of global antistatist anarchism (with some of its roots in the libertarian side of neoliberalism).

The geographical theoretical question is therefore this: what is the space and time of the contemporary state, and what kind of place called a state is it now possible and desirable to construct? In examining this, the theory of spatio-temporalities and of place formation earlier outlined provides a point of departure. The absolute qualities of the state, as these have formed historically and geographically, are not hard to document and to critique. We know them well even as some of them weaken. In the realm of material social practices, there are physical borders to be negotiated, while in the sphere of representation cartography continues to play a vital role in supporting the illusion of the state as a clear-cut entity in absolute space and time. The map of the world divided into states that emerged from the sixteenth century onward is still with us, and these representations have been made real by cadastral surveying and the translation of cartographic representations into physical borders on the ground through the kinds of practices that Mitchell describes. Within such physical territorial frames, it became important to build relational solidarities, through the invocation or construction of collective founding myths and cultural forms that celebrated the idea of nation. The Treaty of Westphalia that set up the European state system could not have functioned without such materializations and reifications, nor could notions of state sovereignty be defined in the form we now know them without also building relational solidarities, albeit within the absolutist territorialized frame. But, by the same token, clashes over state sovereignty and interstate wars would not have taken the form they did, absent such reifications and their parallel lived relationalities of identity, loyalty, and fealty to the state. Wars were, in effect, material manifestations of that state fetishism of "material relations between peoples and social relations between things." States went to war with each other as if they were (or their rulers imagined they were) distinctive social entities endowed with powers and vulnerable to threats (what can it possibly mean to say that the security interests of this or that country are under threat?). But it was only under these fictional but reified conditions that the Kantian cosmopolitan proposition concerning the right to hospitality when crossing borders could also arise. Kant's vision of a world federation of independent republics (or, for that matter, Bookchin's vision of a confederation of self-governing municipalities) is grounded solely in absolute space and time. How the absoluteness is lived (as security, confinement, governmentality, domination, exclusion, or exile) also becomes a critical historical and geographical question.

But what of the relative positionality of the state? The porosity of state borders with respect to money, commodity, and people flows, as well as flows of information and cultural habits (to say nothing of physical processes of circulation of air and water), perpetually undermines the idea of the state as a sealed entity, forcing the various state apparatuses to negotiate with other state apparatuses and entities over conditions of circulation and exchange that perpetually escape absolute controls. Tariffs and trade agreements, diplomatic missions and alliances, negotiated flows and staged cultural exchanges, and sharing agreements and joint responsibilities toward, say, air and water pollution or excessive resource extractions postulate the state as a geopolitical and geo-economic fact in the uncontrolled and unstable relative space-time of the world market and of the global ecosystem. Cross-border institutional arrangements arise that put limits on absolute sovereignty but also tempt or in some cases even impel imperialist practices. If, as Woodrow Wilson noted, the U.S. state has to follow exchange value wherever the merchant and financier may go, and then subsequently deploy its powers—diplomatic, military, moral, and economic—to assist if not lead the commercial assault upon other places and states, then struggles over positionality in relative space-time move to the fore as a guiding if not formative aspect of what states must become. States are, in effect, increasingly defined through the machinations of interstate struggles in relative space-time.

The relational idea of the state (and even more so the relational idea of the nation) may get converted into thing-like terms (in absolute space and time). But the state may then become a nexus of social cohesion with all manner of material, cultural, and social effects. The dialectical relation between different spatio-temporalities works both ways (as Mitchell implies in his discussion of how the state becomes a transcendental and immaterial object). Within the territorial Cartesian frame that British imperial rule imposed on India, for example, a nationalist movement subsequently elucidated and constructed powerful myths of nationhood from the nineteenth century onward. These Hindu myths served to consolidate the sense of territorial bonding between a great diversity of peoples and gave a powerful sense of what the Indian state (originally defined by an outside colonial power) could be as both a meaningful entity and as an object of veneration, affection, and fealty for indigenous populations. The effect of partition in 1947 seems to have consolidated such nationalist feelings in many parts of the subcontinent, thus enabling the Indian state to appear as a coherent structure. This permitted centralized power to consolidate and function in a situation of intense, uneven geographical development as well as linguistic, economic, and cultural diversity. Relationalities subsequently worked to consolidate the new territorial division known as the Indian state, for which, at least according to S. Kaviraj, there continues to be popular respect in most (though not all) parts of India in spite of all of the obvious failings on the ground.[30] In effect, a certain kind of relationality is constructed in the service of consolidating that absolute disciplinary power of the state that in turn creates a condition of possibility for capitalism to function within a certain field of constraints and supports. In those spaces of India, such as the northeastern states, where relationalities have not been successfully implanted, then zones of violent conflict emerge (such as the Naxalite movement and its successors). While Nicos Poulantzas erroneously erects such phenomena into a theoretical principle by narrowly defining the state as a contradictory site of social cohesion, he was not wrong to identify this as one of the more common outcomes of the process of place building that has underlain the construction of actual nation-states in recent times. That the absolute power of the state can also hinder rather than facilitate free forms of capitalist development is also easily demonstrated (as in the case of India before neoliberalization).

But relationalities are unstable. One major criticism of the Bush administration is that it has so undermined the image of the United States as a beacon of liberty and freedom, and so diminished the moral authority of the United States on the world stage, that the United States as a political entity is no longer capable of projecting the same symbolic power and thereby exercising the global leadership it once had. The internal divisions generated between, for example, so-called "red" and "blue" states highlight internal contradictions at the expense of social cohesion (though not, it should be noted, in a way that hinders capital accumulation). Image, moral authority, nationalism, and social cohesion are relational (immaterial) terms, and the astonishing speed with which they can change is well illustrated by the case of the United States. When Guantanamo Bay and Abu Ghraib, rather than the Statue of Liberty, become the symbol of what the U.S. state stands for, then something very important has happened in the immaterial relational realm that must have wide-ranging objective consequences. The election of Barack Obama to the presidency of the United States will almost certainly have a major impact upon the moral authority of the United States throughout much of the rest of the world (which is probably why so many segments of corporate capital supported him). The astonishing rapidity with which seemingly solidaritous states can disintegrate also speaks to the inherent instability of relational notions of loyalty and belonging.

The state, viewed from the standpoint of geographical theory, is a dialectically constituted construct, a "relative permanence" caught between absolute, relative, and relational definitions, between material social practices, representations, and ways of living. It is the outcome of distinctive processes of place making caught up in an interactive politics of territorialization. The dialectics of socio-ecological change, operating across and through the diverse moments of technologies (of administration and governance in particular), mental conceptions, social relations (both of class and bureaucratic hierarchies), productive apparatuses within a fictive national economy, relations to nature, and the politics of daily life, underpins contingent and geographically uneven processes of evolution of state apparatuses. The dialectics of the various moments within the assemblage of the state unfolds within a framework of internal and external, uneven geographical developments only partially sealed in by state borders. While the state appears as a coherent entity endowed with an autonomy of action (in relation to the economy and civil society, as well as to other states), the state is always a contingent being (thing, concept, idea, and image), an internal relation within some greater whole, subsumed under the conditions of possibility of its geographical situation, perpetually subject to destabilization.

Geographical theory has relevance far beyond the critical examination of definitions of the individual and the state. Concepts such as city, region, neighborhood, and community can all be similarly elaborated upon. In exactly the same way that the concept of the state has been questioned these last thirty years, so has the concept of the city (even to the point where some analysts, as with the state, want to abolish the use of the term to describe any kind of material entity, though most would concede it should be kept alive as an idea). Conversely, communitarianism as a political theory in the absence of geographical theory makes absolutely no sense, even as political theorists like Putnam and political philosophers like Walzer struggle to articulate their conclusions without it. Geographical theory explains why such sentiments arise, but then resurrects the concept of the community or the city, on a par with that of the state, as a much more complicated geographical term. When, for example, Victor Hugo, in voluntary exile in the Channel Islands during the imperial rule of Louis Bonaparte, was asked if he missed Paris, he simply replied that "Paris is an idea" (thus invoking his positive internalization of a relational conception of Paris that he always carried with him), but that he had "always loathed the Rue de Rivoli" (thereby signaling his objections to the absolute spatial form then being imposed upon Paris by Haussmann).[31] We all, I think, can appreciate what Hugo meant.

Liberating Spaces

The short answer to Nussbaum's question, we may conclude, is that geographical theory has to be incorporated as a foundational part of any curriculum designed to support moves toward a more adequate form of cosmopolitanism. Liberating ourselves, for example, from the narrow confines of that absolute theory of space and time which grounds bourgeois authoritarianism is a vital first step toward freeing up our conceptual world, and so helping to define a broader terrain of "conditions of possibility" for progressive action. A profounder appreciation of how place construction and the socio-ecological dialectic work is likewise a necessary precondition for more thoughtful explorations of alternatives that go beyond the vulgar antistatism that characterizes a goodly portion of the contemporary left. Critical engagement with foundational concepts of social and legal theory can also reveal much. The secret geographical chains—the ruses of geographical reason—that bind our imaginations and our capacities for action are both powerful and subtle (in part because they are so obvious and banal). Such barriers to a more realistic pursuit of greater conceptual freedom must be dismantled.

But the recent questioning of concepts such as "individual," "state" and "city" signals, in addition to the cascading interest in theories of relationality throughout the social sciences and the humanities, a general crisis of spatio-temporality, of place construction, and of socio-ecological relations within the global order that needs to be confronted directly and understood for what it is. This is the central question for geographical theory to address and for social theory to embrace. Failure to recognize its significance both within academia as well as in the corridors of power is intellectually inexcusable and politically dangerous. This immediately poses the question of the nature and form of the dominant socio-ecological processes involved in place construction or, put another way, who (individuals or collectivities) has the power and influence to so shape relational meanings and relative positionalities as to bring into being (reify) a particular kind of place upon the ground in absolute space and time? The consequences of such reifications for how we live our daily lives and construct our own futures are profound.

This leads us, finally, into the murky realms of actually existing left politics in general. What is remarkable in these times is the hegemony on the left of some version of relational politics. This is shown by the popularity of texts such as Hardt and Negri's *Empire*, by the strong impact of John Holloway's *Changing the World without Taking Power*, and by the writings of a "new wave" of radical philosophers, such as Badiou, Rancière, and Žižek, together with the popularity of relational thinkers such as Benjamin and Deleuze.[32] There are, of course, marked differences between these thinkers, but what they all have in common is a certain fidelity (as Badiou would put it) to "the event," the "moment," and the prioritization of process over the concreteness of things (*becoming* is all, says Holloway, and *being* is nothing; while Badiou, in the absence of contemporary events of any note, resorts simply to the purely relational idea of fidelity to the fidelity as the core of contemporary political possibilities, though in his most recent formulations he argues for fidelity to "the communist hypothesis").[33]

This relational positioning is undoubtedly liberating in fundamental ways. For example, it permits Badiou to construct devastating critiques of contemporary political practices and Holloway to emphasize the power of doing, the salience of process, and the political power of labor to transform the world. But critical geographical theory would indicate that the pure prioritization of the relational (particularly when coupled solely with the Lefebvrian notion of "the lived") is profoundly mistaken. It leads right back into that narcissistic, self-preoccupied world that Carl Schorske so effectively describes in fin-de-siècle Vienna, in which transcendence trumps actual political engagement, let alone the concrete issues of political organization and strategies.[34] The insights and inspirations derived from relational thinking may be fundamental, but they remain politically irrelevant until they can be reconnected to the way human beings relate and conduct their daily lives through material practices in the absolute spaces and times of, say, urban life and through the relative space-times of all forms of exchange (social, cultural, and ecological, as well as economic). The relational critique of absolute forms (such as the state) may be entirely justified, but the solution to the problem cannot be to "conceptualize the state into oblivion" or, as Holloway does, to treat every completed thing as a reification from which we are by definition alienated and which, therefore, should not even be considered as relevant to political struggle.

In this way, Holloway wishes away all the tangible problems that arise in the production of spaces, places, and nature, thereby producing a theoretical framework that is every bit as deracinated and abstract as that conceived of in Locke's liberalism. To take his ideas literally would mean, for example, paying no mind whatsoever to what kind of urbanization we actually build around us. Put simply, walls, doors, and bridges matter, and how they are configured makes a lot of difference to how we live our lives. While "urbanization without cities" (to cite a Murray Bookchin title) may sound a good idea as a counter to the alienations of contemporary capitalist urbanization, it does not resolve the problem of how to make tangible the urban geography of our emancipatory dreams. Furthermore, to be dismissive of all forms of organization, institutionalization, and territorialization (including the much maligned state as a specific but distinctly malleable kind of geographical construction) as somehow either irrelevant or inherently repressive is to cut off the routes to any kind of ameliorative, let alone revolutionary, political practice. It is, I must emphasize, the dialectical movement across and through the different dimensionalities of space-time (absolute, relative and relational) and the intersecting moments (of technologies, social relations, processes in nature, mental conceptions, production [labor] processes, and everyday life) entailed in environmental transformations that really count in the theory of place construction. To refuse the practice of that dialectic by ignoring it is to refuse to confront "the conditions of possibility" for a truly transformative revolutionary politics. While it is possible to reaffirm the "communist hypothesis" ideally, as does Badiou, it is also possible to do so through a thoroughly grounded historical geographical materialism, as I have sought to show in a new introduction to *The Communist Manifesto*.[35]

The bourgeoisie, as Marx and Engels so convincingly show, arrived at its own distinctive form of cosmopolitanism (now represented by the frequent flier corporate and business elite, the global accountants and consultants, the employees of international institutions, professional and technological elites, and the like) by revolutionizing the geography of capital accumulation. It built radically new relative spaces of transport and communications, facilitating rapid motion of commodities, money, and people, around a relational form of labor value (represented by the various money forms). It created new places that carry ancient names like Beijing, London, Rome, New York, Cairo, and Frankfurt, as well as relatively new places, such as Singapore, Mumbai, Shanghai, Durban, Saõ Paulo, Los Angeles, Shenzhen, Dubai, and the like. The bourgeoisie produced spaces and places in its own image and according to its own distinctive needs and in so doing launched a socio-environmental transformation of planet earth (both intended and unintended) that is simply astounding to contemplate. We live in a totally different geographical world from that which existed 500 years ago. Everyone has been and still is forced to adapt to these rapidly changing space relations, place constructions, and environmental transformations, all the while striving to construct counter-spaces and –places, the better to cope or to actively resist. Cosmopolitanism of the contemporary bourgeois sort was not, therefore, simply an idea that arose out of nothing. Rather, it was an ideology that arose out of these multiple geographical transformations that began as long ago as 1492 if not before. The rise of an alternative, oppositional, and far more egalitarian cosmopolitanism likewise demands that attention be paid to the prior transformations in the geographical conditions of possibility for such political ideals not only to be realized but even to be fully formulated. If a subaltern insurgent cosmopolitanism is to take hold, it must contemplate no less a radical transformation in its geography than that which the bourgeoisie collectively accomplished.

To understand geographical theory in all its fullness is, undoubtedly, a daunting intellectual task. But, as the great nineteenth-century geographer Elisée Reclus wrote in an open letter to his anarchist comrades toward the end of his life: "Great enthusiasm and dedication to the point of risking one's life are not the only ways of serving a cause. The conscious revolutionary is not only a person of feeling, but also one of reason, to whom every effort to promote justice and solidarity rests on precise knowledge and on a comprehensive understanding of history, sociology and biology" as well as the geography to which he had dedicated so much of his life's work.[36] Or, as Locke, Kant, and Nussbaum might all agree to put it, without an adequate knowledge of geography, not only will we fail to understand the world around us and undermine our cosmopolitan quest for universal justice: we will forego all possibility of revolutionary politics for a relational dream-world of narcissistic transcendentalism, of perpetually unfulfilled desire, at the very moment when "spaces of hope" are opening up all around us for the taking and the making. If our geography has been made and remade again and again by human endeavor, then it can be remade yet again to accord more fully with our political ambitions.

Notes

Prologue

1. G. W. Bush, "Securing Freedom's Triumph," *New York Times*, 11 September 2002, A33.
2. T. Blair, Speech to U.S. Congress, 18 July 2003, "History Will Forgive Us"; available online at: http://politics.guardian.co.uk/speeches/story/0,11126,1008150,00.html
3. G. W. Bush, "Both Our Nations Serve the Cause of Freedom," *New York Times*, 20 November 2003, A14.
4. G. W. Bush, "Acceptance Speech to Convention Delegates in New York," *New York Times*, 3 September 2004, P4; "The Inaugural Address: The Best Hope for Peace in Our World Is the Expansion of Freedom in All the World," *New York Times*, 21 January 2005, A12–13.
5. D. Brooks, "Ideals and Reality," *New York Times*, 22 January 2005, A15.
6. Cited in N. Chomsky, *On Power and Ideology* (Boston: South End Press, 1990), 14.
7. N. Smith, *The Endgame of Globalization* (New York: Routledge, 2005).
8. M. Foucault, "What Is Enlightenment?" in *The Foucault Reader*, ed. P. Rabinow (Harmondsworth, Middlesex, England: Penguin, 1984), 45.
9. Smith, *Endgame of Globalization*, 30–31.
10. Bush, "Securing Freedom's Triumph."
11. J. Sachs, *The End of Poverty: Economic Possibilities for Our Time* (New York: Penguin, 2005), 80–81.
12. S. Benhabib, *The Rights of Others: Aliens, Residents and Citizens* (Cambridge: Cambridge University Press, 2004), 16, 44.
13. The critical perspective can be found in N. Chomsky, *The New Military Humanism: Lessons from Kosovo* (Monroe, Maine: Common Courage Press, 1999).

U. Beck, *Cosmopolitan Vision* (Cambridge: Polity Press, 2006), 127–29, takes a far more pragmatic view of it, though rather less supportive than in initial comments.

14. M. Nussbaum et al., *For Love of Country: Debating the Limits of Patriotism* (Boston: Beacon Press, 1996), 11–12.
15. I. Kant, cited in J. May, *Kant's Concept of Geography and Its Relation to Recent Geographical Thought* (Toronto: University of Toronto Press, 1970), v.
16. N. Smith, *American Empire: Roosevelt's Geographer and the Prelude to Globalization* (Berkeley: University of California Press, 2003), 18.
17. J. Locke, cited in May, *Kant's Concept of Geography*, 135.

1. Kant's Anthropology and Geography

1. I. Kant, *Kant: Political Writings* (Cambridge: Cambridge University Press, 1991), 107–8.
2. Kant, cited in S. Benhabib, *The Rights of Others: Aliens, Residents and Citizens* (Cambridge: Cambridge University Press, 2004), 27.
3. Benhabib, *Rights of Others*.
4. Ibid., p. 33.
5. R. Bolin, "Immanuel Kant's *Physical Geography*," trans. and annotated by R. L. Bolin, master's thesis, Department of Geography, Indiana University, 1968; I. Kant, *Geographie (Physiche Geographie)* (Paris: Bibliotheque Philosophique, 1999); J. May, *Kant's Concept of Geography and Its Relation to Recent Geographical Thought* (Toronto: University of Toronto Press, 1970).
6. An English version of Kant's Geography, translated by Olaf Reinhardt, will shortly be published in the Cambridge University Press series, The Complete Edition of Kant's Works in Translation, and will be accompanied by a volume of critical commentaries, edited by Stuart Elden and Eduardo Mendietta, to be published by SUNY Press in 2009.
7. May, *Kant's Concept of Geography*, 132–36.
8. Kant, cited in May, *Kant's Concept of Geography*, 137; Kant, cited in F. Van de Pitte, "Introduction," in I. Kant, *Anthropology from a Pragmatic Point of View* (The Hague: Martinus Nijhoff, 1974), xiii; See also J. Zammito, *Kant, Herder, and the Birth of Anthropology* (Chicago: University of Chicago Press, 2000).
9. M. Foucault, *Introduction to Kant's Anthropology*, ed. Robert Nigro (Los Angeles: Semiotext(e), 2008), 33.
10. M. Foucault, "Commentary of Kant's Anthropology from a Pragmatic Point of View," trans. Arianna Bove, http://www.generation-online.org/p/fpfoucault1.htm; A. Allen, "Foucault and Enlightenment: A Critical Reappraisal," *Constellations*, 10, no.2 (2003): 180–98.
11. M. Nussbaum, "Kant and Stoic Cosmopolitanism," *Journal of Political Philosophy* 5 (1997): 1–25, especially 8.
12. I. Kant, "An Answer to the Question: 'What is Enlightenment,'" in Kant, *Political*

Writings; Kant, *Anthropology from a Pragmatic Point of View* (The Hague: Martinus Nijhoff, 1974), 249–51.

13. Kant, *Anthropology*, 203.
14. P. Cheah and B. Robbins, eds., *Cosmopolitics: Thinking and Feeling Beyond the Nation* (Minneapolis: University of Minnesota Press, 1998).
15. K. Marx, *Capital*, vol. 3 (New York: Penguin, 1981), 958–59.
16. Kant, *Anthropology*, 96.
17. Ibid., 225.
18. Foucault, "What Is Enlightenment?"
19. R-P. Droit, "Kant et les Fournis du Congo," *Le Monde*, 5 February, 1999.
20. Kant, *Geographie*, 223 (my translation from the French); May, *Kant's Concept of Geography*, 66.
21. E. Thompson, *The Making of the English Working Class* (Harmondsworth, Middlesex, England: Penguin, 1968); L. Barzini, *The Italians* (New York: Athenaeum, 1967); T. Zeldin, *The French* (New York: Vintage, 1984); P. Anderson, *English Questions* (London: Verso, 1992).
22. J. Rawls, *The Law of Peoples with The Idea of Public Reason Revisited* (Cambridge, Mass.: Harvard University Press, 1999); M. Walzer, *Spheres of Justice* (Oxford: Blackwell, 1983).
23. Droit, "Kant et les Fournis du Congo."
24. S. Elden, *Mapping the Present: Heidegger, Foucault and the Project of a Spatial History* (London: Continuum, 2001).
25. C. Glacken, *Traces on the Rhodian Shore: Nature and Culture in Western Thought from Ancient Times to the End of the Eighteenth Century* (Berkeley: University of California Press, 1967), 532.
26. Benhabib, *Rights of Others*; T. Brennan, *At Home in the World: Cosmopolitanism Now* (Cambridge, Mass.: Harvard University Press, 1997).
27. Foucault, "What Is Enlightenment?" 70.
28. M. Foucault, "Questions on Geography," in *Power/Knowledge*, ed. C. Gordon (London: Harvester, 1980), 77.
29. The questions and replies, along with commentaries, some of them quite at odds with my own interpretation, can be found in *Space, Knowledge and Power: Foucault and Geography*, ed. J. Crampton and S. Elden (Aldershot, Hants.: Ashgate Publishing, 2007)
30. The peculiar way in which Kant compromised between Newton and Leibniz makes my assertions as to the absolute outcome of Kant's arguments controversial. The important point is his strict separation of history from geography in his theory of knowledge, and the only view of space and time consistent with this is absolute. That Kant in effect sealed in the absolute view is supported, among others, by E. Casey, "How to Get from Space to Place in a Fairly Short Stretch of Time," in *Senses of Place*, ed. S. Feld and K. Basso (Phoenix, Ariz.: School of American Research Advanced Seminar Series, 1996), 14.
31. May, *Kant's Concept of Geography*.

32. R. Hartshorne, *The Nature of Geography: A Critical Survey of Current Thought in the Light of the Past* (Lancaster, Pa.: Association of American Geographers, 1939); K. Sauer, *Land and Life* (Berkeley: University of California Press, 1965).
33. For an appreciative view of Foucault's arguments on local knowledges, see C. Philo, "'Bellicose History' and 'Local Discursivities': An Archaeological Reading of Michel Foucault's *Society Must Be Defended*," in *Space, Knowledge and Power,* ed. Crampton and Elden, 342–67.
34. H. Arendt, *Lectures on Kant's Political Philosophy* (Chicago: University of Chicago Press, 1989), 76.
35. Nussbaum, "Kant and Stoic Cosmopolitanism," citing the Stoics, 10.

2. The Postcolonial Critique of Liberal Cosmopolitanism

1. U. Mehta, *Liberalism and Empire: A Study in Nineteenth-century British Liberal Thought* (Chicago: University of Chicago Press, 1999), 51; E. Stokes, *English Utilitarians in India* (Oxford: Clarendon Press, 1959); D. Chakrabarty, *Provincializing Europe: Postcolonial Thought and Historical Difference* (Princeton: Princeton University Press, 2000).
2. Mehta, *Liberalism and Empire,* 129.
3. Ibid., 50, 92–93.
4. D. Clayton, *Islands of Truth: The Imperial Fashioning of Vancouver Island* (Vancouver: University of British Columbia Press, 1999).
5. Mehta, *Liberalism and Empire,* 32.
6. Cited in A. Badiou, *Metapolitics* (London: Verso, 2005), 131.
7. Chakrabarty, *Provincializing Europe,* 8.
8. Mehta, *Liberalism and Empire,* 84.
9. Ibid., 108–11.
10. Ibid., 119–20.
11. Ibid., 121–22.
12. Ibid., 21.
13. Ibid., 148.
14. Ibid., 41–42.
15. Ibid., 133.
16. H. Arendt, *Imperialism* (New York: Harcourt, Brace and Jovanovich, 1968), 56.
17. Mehta, *Liberalism and Empire,* 215.
18. Chakrabarty, *Provincializing Europe,* 254.
19. M. Katzenstein, U. Singh, and U.Thakar, "The Rebirth of Shiv-Sena: The Symbiosis of Discursive and Organizational Power," *Journal of Asian Studies* 56, no. 2 (1997): 371–90.
20. Mehta, *Liberalism and Empire,* 132.
21. C. Sauer, *Land and Life* (Berkeley: University of California Press, 1965), 147.
22. A. Pagden, "Introduction," in C. Sauer, *The Early Spanish Main* (Berkeley: University of California Press, 1992); W. Mignolo, *Local Histories/Global Designs*

(Princeton: Princeton University Press, 2000); Mignolo, *The Darker Side of the Renaissance: Literacy, Territoriality and Colonization* (Ann Arbor: University of Michigan Press, 2003).

23. A. Escobar, "Place, Economy, and Culture in a Post-Development Era," in *Places and Politics in an Age of Globalization,* ed. R. Prazniak and A. Dirlik (New York: Rowman and Littlefield, 2001).
24. M. Edney, *Mapping an Empire: The Geographical Construction of British India, 1765–1843* (Chicago: University of Chicago Press, 1990), 340.
25. Ibid., 333.
26. P. Chatterjee, *The Nation and Its Fragments: Colonial and Postcolonial Histories* (Princeton: Princeton University Press, 1993).
27. C. Mohanty, *Feminism without Borders: Decolonizing Theory, Practising Solidarity* (Durham, N.C.: Duke University Press, 2006).

3. The Flat World of Neoliberal Utopianism

1. T. Friedman, *The World Is Flat: A Brief History of the Twenty-first Century* (New York: Farrar, Strauss and Giroux, 2005), 3–5, 45–49.
2. Ibid., 314–15.
3. G. W. Bush, "Securing Freedom's Triumph," *New York Times,* 11 September 2002, A33.
4. D. Harvey, *A Brief History of Neoliberalism* (Oxford: Oxford University Press, 2005).
5. H. De Soto, *The Other Path: The Invisible Revolution in the Third World* (New York: Harper, 1989); De Soto, *The Mystery of Capital: Why Capitalism Triumphs in the West and Fails Everywhere Else* (New York: Basic Books, 2000).
6. T. Mitchell, "The Work of Economics: How a Discipline Makes Its World," *Archives européennes de sociologie* 46 (2005): 297–320.
7. J. Elyachar, *Markets of Dispossession: NGOs, Economic Development and the State in Cairo* (Durham, N.C.: Duke University Press, 2005); D. Gross, "Fighting Poverty with $2-a-Day Jobs," *New York Times,* 6 July 2006, Weekend in Review, 4 (quote); C. Brick, "Millions for Millions," *New Yorker,* 30 October 2006, 62–73; C. Prahalad, *The Fortune at the Bottom of the Pyramid: Eradicating Poverty through Profits* (Philadelphia: Wharton School Publishing, 2006).
8. M. Davis, *Planet of Slums* (London: Verso, 2006).
9. This account is drawn from Harvey, *Brief History of Neoliberalism;* see also N. Klein, *The Shock Doctrine: The Rise of Disaster Capitalism* (New York: Metropolitan Books, 2007).
10. Harvey, *Brief History of Neoliberalism,* chap. 6.
11. A. Appadurai, *Modernity at Large: Cultural Dimensions of Globalization* (Minneapolis: University of Minnesota Press, 1996); R. Appelbaum and W. Robinson, eds., *Critical Globalization Studies* (New York: Routledge, 2005), particularly 91–100.

12. Friedman, *World Is Flat*, 50.
13. See United Nations Development Program, *Human Development Report 1996* and *Human Development Report 1999* (New York: United Nations, 1999); E. Dash, "Off to the Races Again, Leaving Many Behind," *New York Times*, 9 April 2006, Business Section, 1, 5; P. Krugman, "Graduates versus Oligarchs," *New York Times*, 27 February 2006, A19; N. Munk, "Don't Blink. You'll Miss the 258th Richest American," *New York Times*, 25 September 2005,Weekend in Review, 3; J. Anderson, "Fund Managers Raising the Ante in Philanthropy," *New York Times*, 3 August 2005, Business Section, 1, 3.
14. Harvey, *Brief History of Neoliberalism*; E. Arvedlund, "Russia's Billionaires Club Now Totals 27 Members," *New York Times*, 7 May 2005, C1; E. Porter, "Mexico's Plutocracy Survives on Robber-Baron Concessions," *New York Times*, 27 August 2007, Editorial Observer.
15. Friedman, *World Is Flat*,382–83.
16. J. Stiglitz, *Globalization and Its Discontents* (New York: Norton, 2002), 129–30; J. Sachs, *The End of Poverty: Economic Possibilities for Our Time* (New York: Penguin, 2005), chap. 4.
17. A. Amsden, *Escape from Empire: The Developing World's Journey through Heaven and Hell* (Cambridge, Mass.: MIT Press, 2007).
18. S. Amin, *Beyond U.S. Hegemony? Assessing the Prospects for a Multipolar World* (London: Zed Books, 2006); S. George, *Another World is Possible IF . . .* (London: Verso, 2003); W. Bello, *Deglobalization: Ideas for a New World Economy* (London: Zed Books, 2002); A. Roy, *Power Politics* (Cambridge, Mass.: South End Press, 2001); B. Gills, ed., *Globalization and the Politics of Resistance* (New York: Palgrave, 2001); T. Mertes, ed., *A Movement of Movements* (London: Verso, 2004); P. Hawken, *Blessed Unrest: How the Largest Movement in the World Came into Being and Why No One Saw It Coming* (New York: Viking, 2007).
19. J. Gray, *False Dawn: The Illusions of Global Capitalism* (London: Granta Press, 1998), 207.
20. Critically cited in D. Robotham, *Culture, Society and Economy: Globalization and its Alternatives* (New York: Sage, 2005), chap. 7.
21. P. Krugman, *Development, Geography and Economic Theory* (Cambridge, Mass.: MIT Press, 1995).
22. D. Harvey, "The Art of Rent: Globalization, Monopoly and the Commodification of Culture," *Socialist Register* (2002): 93–110.
23. Harvey, *Brief History of Neoliberalism*, chap. 6.
24. D. Harvey, *The New Imperialism* (Oxford: Oxford University Press, 2003), chap. 4.
25. R. Wade and F. Veneroso, "The Asian Crisis: The High-Debt Model versus the Wall Street-Treasury-IMF Complex," *New Left Review* 228 (1998): 3–23.
26. B. De Sousa Santos and C. Rodriguez-Garavito, eds., *Law and Globalization from Below: Towards a Cosmopolitan Legality* (Cambridge: Cambridge University Press, 2005); A. Ong, *Neoliberalism as Exception: Mutations in Citizenship and Sovereignty* (Durham, N.C.: Duke University Press, 2006).

27. J. Brash, "Re-scaling Patriotism: Competition and Urban Identity in Michael Bloomberg's New York," *Urban Anthropology and Studies of Cultural Systems and World Economic Development* 35 (2006): 387–432.
28. D. Chandler, *From Kosovo to Kabul: Human Rights and International Intervention* (London: Pluto Press, 2002); T. Wallace, "NGO Dilemmas: Trojan Horses for Global Neoliberalism," *Socialist Register* (2003): 202–19.
29. Chandler, *From Kosovo to Kabul,* 230.
30. M. Edwards, and D. Hulme, eds., *Non-Governmental Organizations: Performance and Accountability* (London: Earthscan, 1995); Wallace, "NGO Dilemmas."
31. De Sousa Santos in De Sousa Santos and Rodriguez-Garavito, eds., *Law and Globalization from Below.*
32. A. Bartholomew and J. Breakspear, "Human Rights and Swords of Empire," *Socialist Register* XX (2003): 124–45.
33. Chandler, *From Kosovo to Kabul.*
34. Ibid., 235.
35. K. Marx, *Capital,* vol. 1 (New York: International Publishers, 1967): 225.
36. For my views on rights struggles more generally see Harvey, A *Brief History of Neoliberalism,* 175–82.
37. Sachs, *End of Poverty,* 81.
38. Ong, *Neoliberalism as Exception*; Gray, *False Dawn,* 207.

4. The New Cosmopolitans

1. P. Cheah, "Introduction Part II: The Cosmopolitical Today," in *Cosmopolitics: Thinking and Feeling Beyond the Nation,* ed. P. Cheah and B. Robbins (Minneapolis: University of Minnesota Press, 1998), 23.
2. For an account of Herder's position see J. Zammito, *Kant, Herder and the Birth of Anthropology* (Chicago: University of Chicago Press, 2002).
3. M. Nussbaum et al., *For Love of Country: Debating the Limits of Patriotism* (Boston: Beacon Press, 1996).
4. K. Marx and F. Engels, *Manifesto of the Communist Party* (Moscow: Progress Publishers, 1952).
5. Gramsci's views are summarized in A. Anderson, "Cosmopolitanism, Universalism and the Divided Legacies of Modernity," in *Cosmopolitics,* ed. Cheah and Robbins, 270–71; C. Calhoun, "The Class Consciousness of Frequent Travellers: Towards a Critique of Actually Existing Cosmopolitanism," in *Conceiving Cosmopolitanism: Theory, Context and Practice,* ed. S. Vertovec and R. Cohen (Oxford: Oxford University Press, 2002), 86–109; S. Sassen, *Territory, Authority, Rights: From Medieval to Global Assemblages* (Princeton: Princeton University Press, 2006), 299; R. Wilson, "A New Cosmopolitanism Is in the Air," in *Cosmopolitics,* ed. Cheah and Robbins, 352.
6. Cheah and Robbins, eds., *Cosmopolitics,* 9.
7. U. Beck, "The Cosmopolitan Perspective: Sociology in the Second Age of Modernity," in *Conceiving Cosmopolitanism,* ed. S. Vertovec and R. Cohen, 61.

8. U. Beck, *Cosmopolitan Vision* (Cambridge: Polity Press, 2006), 72–73.
9. U. Beck, "Living in the World Risk Society," Hobhouse Memorial Lecture, London School of Economics, 15 February, 2006
10. Beck's endorsement of military humanism is reported in R. Cohen, "A Generation of German Pacifists at Odds over the War," *New York Times*, 6 May 1999, A10.
11. Kant, cited in D. Held, *Democracy and the Global Order: From the Modern State to Cosmopolitan Governance* (Stanford: Stanford University Press, 1995), 229.
12. R. Fine and W. Smith, "Jürgen Habermas's Theory of Cosmopolitanism," *Constellations* 10, no. 4 (2003): 469–87.
13. Beck, *Cosmopolitan Vision*, 95.
14. De Sousa Santos, B., "Beyond Neoliberal Governance: The World Social Forum as Subaltern Cosmopolitan Politics," in *Law and Globalization from Below*, ed. De Sousa Santos and C. Rodriguez-Garavito (Cambridge: Cambridge University Press, 2005), 29–63.
15. A. Badiou, *Metapolitics*, trans. J. Barker (London: Verso, 2005), 138.
16. Ibid., 118; see also D. Harvey, *A Brief History of Neoliberalism* (Oxford: Oxford University Press, 2005), chap. 5.
17. D. Held, "Principles of Cosmopolitan Order," in *The Political Philosophy of Cosmopolitanism*, ed. G. Brock and H. Brighouse (Cambridge: Cambridge University Press, 2005), 10–27; Held, "Law of States, Law of Peoples," *Legal Theory* 8, no. 2 (2002): 1–44.
18. Held, "Principles of Cosmopolitan Order," 18.
19. Ibid., 20; the recent shifts toward "governance" are remarked upon by De Sousa Santos, "Beyond Neoliberal Governance"; for a more concrete example, see D. Harvey, *Spaces of Capital: Towards a Critical Geography* (Edinburgh: Edinburgh University Press, 2001), chap. 16.
20. Beck, *Cosmopolitan Vision*, 76.
21. Sassen, *Territory, Authority, Rights*, 338; C. Wright Mills, *The Sociological Imagination* (New York: Oxford University Press, 1959).
22. S. Benhabib, *The Rights of Others: Aliens, Residents and Citizens* (Cambridge: Cambridge University Press, 2004), 112; A. Ong, *Neoliberalism as Exception: Mutations in Citizenship and Sovereignty* (Durham, N.C.: Duke University Press, 2006).
23. Benhabib, *Rights of Others*, 122–27; M. Walzer, *Spheres of Justice* (Oxford: Basil Blackwell, 1983).
24. I. Young, *Justice and the Politics of Difference* (Princeton: Princeton University Press, 1990).
25. M. Nussbaum, *Frontiers of Justice: Disability, Nationality, Species Membership* (Cambridge, Mass.: Belknap Press, 2006), particularly 76–78.
26. J. Rawls. *The Law of the Peoples with The Idea of Public Reason Revisited* (Cambridge, Mass.: Harvard University Press, 1999); Nussbaum, *Frontiers of Justice*, 236.

27. Benhabib, *Rights of Others*, 77.
28. Nussbaum, *Frontiers of Justice*, 284–85.
29. Ibid., 306.
30. Ibid., 257.
31. Ibid., 317.
32. Young, *Justice and the Politics of Difference.*
33. De Sousa Santos and Rodriguez-Garavito, eds., *Law and Globalization from Below*, 14.
34. D. Harvey, *The New Imperialism* (Oxford: Oxford University Press, 2003).
35. De Sousa Santos, "Beyond Neoliberal Governance."
36. Sassen, *Territory, Authority, Rights*, 20.
37. Ibid., 311.
38. Cheah and Robbins, eds., *Cosmopolitics*, 2–3.

5. The Banality of Geographical Evils

1. K. Marx, *Capital*, vol. 1 (New York: International Publishers, 1967), 169–70.
2. G.W. Bush, The President's State of the Union Address, 29 January 2002; available online: http:www.whitehouse.gov/news/releases/2002/01/print20020129–11.html
3. First International Resources, Inc., *Economic Sanctions Survey* (Fort Lee, N.J.: First International Resources Inc., 2000).
4. M. Scheuer, *Imperial Hubris: Why the West Is Losing the War on Terror* (Dulles, Va.: Potomac Books, 2004).
5. R. Cooper, *The Breaking of Nations: Order and Chaos in the Twenty-first Century* (New York: Atlantic Monthly Press, 2003).
6. A. Nilsen, "The Valley and the Nation: The River and the Rage," Ph.D. diss., Department of Sociology, University of Bergen, 2006.
7. M. Hajer, *The Politics of Environmental Discourse: Ecological Modernisation and the Policy Process* (Oxford: Clarendon Press, 1995).
8. J. Sachs, *The End of Poverty: Economic Possibilities for Our Time* (New York: Penguin, 2005), 80–81.
9. T. Koopmans, and A. Beckman, "Assignment Problems and the Location of Economic Activities," *Econometrica* 25 (1957): 53–76; M. Fujita, P. Krugman, and A. Venables, *The Spatial Economy: Cities, Regions and International Trade* (Cambridge, Mass.: MIT Press, 2001).
10. W. Connolly, *The Ethos of Pluralization* (Minneapolis: University of Minnesota Press, 1995); Connolly, "Speed, Concentric Cultures and Cosmopolitanism," *Political Theory* 28 (2000): 596–618.
11. M. Shapiro, "The Events of Discourse and the Ethics of Global Hospitality," *Millennium* 27 (1998): 695–713.
12. S. Deshpande, "Hegemonic Spatial Strategies: The Nation-Space and Hindu Communalism in Twentieth Century India," *Public Culture* 10, no. 2 (1998): 249–83.

13. Ibid.
14. M. Walzer, *Spheres of Justice* (Oxford: Blackwell, 1983); J. Elster, *Local Justice: How Institutions Allocate Scarce Goods and Necessary Burdens* (New York: Russell Sage Foundation, 1992).
15. J. Clifford, "Mixed Feelings," in *Cosmopolitics*, ed. P. Cheah and B. Robbins (Minneapolis: University of Minnesota Press, 1998), 362–70.
16. E. Burke, cited in A. Appiah, *The Ethics of Identity* (Princeton: Princeton University Press, 2005), 241.
17. A. Appiah, "Cosmopolitan Patriots," in Nussbaum et al., *For Love of Country: Debating the Limits of Patriotism* (Boston: Beacon Press, 1996), 21–29; Appiah, *Cosmopolitanism: Ethics in a World of Strangers* (New York: Norton, 2006).
18. R. Falk, "Revisioning Cosmopolitanism," in Nussbaum et al., *For Love of Country*, 60.
19. Appiah, *Ethics of Identity*, chap. 6.
20. Appiah, *Cosmopolitanism*, 99.
21. W. Michaels, *The Trouble with Diversity: How We Learned to Love Diversity and Ignore Identity* (New York: Metropolitan Books, 2006).
22. M. Heidegger, *Poetry, Language, Thought* (New York: Harper and Row, 1971).
23. H. Arendt, *Eichmann in Jerusalem: A Report on the Banality of Evil* (Harmondsworth, Middlesex, England: Penguin, 1997).
24. J. Ree, "Cosmopolitanism and the Experience of Nationality," in *Cosmopolitics*, ed. Cheah and Robbins, 77–90.
25. I. Berlin, *The Sense of Reality: Studies in Ideas and Their History* (London: Chatto and Windus, 1997).
26. T. Brennan, *At Home in the World: Cosmopolitanism Now* (Cambridge, Mass.: Harvard University Press, 1997).
27. M. Nussbaum, *Frontiers of Justice: Disability, Nationality, Species Membership* (Cambridge, Mass.: Belknap Press, 2006), 257; Nussbaum, "Kant and Stoic Cosmopolitanism," *Journal of Political Philosophy* 5 (1997): 1–25.
28. The most sophisticated discussions of how geography has approached these questions are to be found in D. Livingston, *The Geographical Tradition: Episodes in the History of a Contested Enterprise* (Oxford: Blackwell, 1993), which is systematic but ends up reducing the "contestation" to a matter of conversations between different traditions; and D. Gregory, *Geographical Imaginations* (Oxford: Blackwell, 1994), which brilliantly connects critical geographical thinking with the social and literary theory tradition but unfortunately neglects the problems that arise from the strong traditions of physical and mathematical inquiry in the discipline's history.

6. Geographical Reason

1. W. Pattison, "The Four Traditions of Geography, *Journal of Geography* 63 (1964): 211–16.
2. J. Harley, P. Laxton, and J. Andrews, eds., *The New Nature of Maps: Essays in the*

History of Cartography (Baltimore: Johns Hopkins University Press, 2001); and the various volumes published by the history ot cartography project, edited initially by J. B. Harley and David Woodward, published by University of Chicago Press.

3. W. L. Thomas, ed., *Man's Role in Changing the Face of the Earth*, 2 vols. (Chicago: University of Chicago Press, 1956); C. Glacken, *Traces on the Rhodian Shore: Nature and Culture in Western Thought from Ancient Times to the End of the Eighteenth Century* (Berkeley: University of California Press, 1967).
4. I have examined this elsewhere; see D. Harvey, "The Sociological and Geographical Imaginations," *International Journal of Politics, Culture and Society* 18, nos. 3–4 (2005): 211–56.
5. A. Godlewska and N. Smith, eds., *Geography and Empire* (Oxford: Blackwell, 1997); D. Gregory, *The Colonial Present: Afghanistan, Palestine and Iraq* (Oxford: Blackwell, 2004).
6. R. Hartshorne, "'Exceptionalism in Geography' Re-examined," *Annals, Association of American Geographers* 45 (1955): 205–44; F. Schaeffer, "Exceptionalism in Geography: A Methodological Examination, *Annals, Association of American Geographers* 43 (1953): 57–84.

7. Spacetime and the World

1. A. Whitehead, *The Concept of Nature* (Cambridge: Cambridge University Press, 1920), 33.
2. This is a summary and an extension of my essay "Space as a Key Word," in D. Harvey, *Spaces of Global Capitalism: Toward a Theory of Uneven Geographical Development* (London: Verso, 2006), 119–48. For other geographical works, see N. Smith, *Uneven Development* (Oxford: Blackwell, 1984); D. Massey, *For Space* (London: Sage, 2005); Soja, E., *Postmodern Geographies: The Reassertion of Space in Critical Social Theory* (London: Verso, 1989); Yi-Fu Tuan, *Space and Place: The Perspective of Experience* (Minneapolis: University of Minnesota Press, 1977); R. Sack, *Conceptions of Space in Social Thought: A Geographic Perspective* (Minneapolis: University of Minnesota Press, 1980); Sack, *Human Territoriality: Its Theory and Its History* (Cambridge: Cambridge University Press, 1986). The themes of spatio-temporality have been the subject of extensive inquiry in other disciplines, of course, and among my favorite texts are the following: from history, A. Gurevich, *Categories of Medieval Culture* (London: Routledge, 1985); from anthropology, N. Munn, *The Fame of Gawa* (Cambridge: Cambridge University Press, 1986); from cultural studies, S. Kern, *The Culture of Time and Space, 1880–1918* (London: Weidenfeld and Nicolson, 1983). I examined many of these other works in D. Harvey, *Justice, Nature and the Geography of Difference* (Oxford: Blackwell, 1996), chaps. 9 and 10.
3. R. Osserman, *The Poetry of the Universe* (New York: Doubleday, 1995).
4. Ibid., 125–33.

5. The technical exposition of relative space in geography became most strongly evident in P. Haggett, *Locational Analysis in Geography* (London: Edward Arnold, 1965).
6. N. Rescher, *Leibniz's Metaphysics of Nature* (Dordrecht: Reidel, 1981).
7. B. Ollman, *Dialectical Investigations* (New York: Routledge, 1992); A. Whitehead, "La théorie relationiste de l'espace," *Revue de métaphysique et de morale* 23 (1916) : 423–54.
8. E. Grosz, "Bodies—Cities," in *Sexuality and Space*, ed. B. Colomina (Princeton: Princeton University Press, 1992), 241–54.
9. E. Casey, "How to Get From Space to Place in a Fairly Short Stretch of Time," in *Senses of Place*, ed. S. Feld and K. Basso (Phoenix, Ariz.: School of American Research Advanced Seminar Series, 1996), 13–51.
10. C. Garnett, *The Kantian Philosophy of Space* (Port Washington, N.Y.: Kennikat Press, 1965).
11. Whitehead, "La théorie relationiste de l'espace." *Revue de métaphysique et de morale* 23 (1916): 423–54.
12. D. Bohm, *Wholeness and the Implicate Order* (London: Ark Paperbacks, 1983); G. Deleuze, *The Fold: Leibniz and the Baroque* (Minneapolis: University of Minnesota Press, 1993); Deleuze and F. Guattari, *A Thousand Plateaus: Capitalism and Schizophrenia* (Minneapolis: University of Minnesota Press, 1987).
13. A. Naess, *Ecology, Community and Lifestyle* (Cambridge: Cambridge University Press, 1989); M. Hardt and T. Negri, *Empire* (Cambridge, Mass.: Harvard University Press, 2001); T. Negri, *Subversive Spinoza: (UN)contemporary Variations* (Manchester: Manchester University Press, 2004).
14. A. Badiou, *Being and Event* (London: Continuum, 2005).
15. W. Benjamin, *The Arcades Project* (Cambridge, Mass.: Belknap Press, 1999); for Sacré Coeur see D. Harvey, *Paris, Capital of Modernity* (New York: Routledge, 2003), chap. 18.
16. D. Harvey, *Social Justice and the City* (London: Edward Arnold, 1973), 13.
17. H. Lefebvre, *The Production of Space* (Oxford: Blackwell, 1991); E. Cassirer, *An Essay on Man* (New Haven: Yale University Press, 1944).
18. Yi-Fu Tuan, *Topophilia: A Study of Environment Perceptions, Attitudes and Values* (New York: Columbia University Press, 1990).
19. M. Foucault, *The Order of Things: An Archaeology of the Human Sciences* (New York: Random House, 1970); T. J. Clark, *Image of the People: Gustave Courbet and the 1848 Revolution* (London: Thames and Hudson, 1973).
20. J. Barry, "Voice Off," in *Third Berlin Biennal for Contemporary Art, Catalogue* (Berlin: Biennale, 2004), 48–49.
21. K. Marx, *The Eighteenth Brumaire of Louis Bonaparte* (New York: International Publishers, 1963); the letter to Cabet is cited in L. Marin, *Utopics: Spatial Play* (Atlantic Heights, N.J.: Humanities Press, 1984), 73–79.
22. K. Marx, cited in I. Mesjaros, *Beyond Capital* (New York: Monthly Review Press, 2000), 485.

23. E. Thompson, "Time, Work Discipline, and Industrial Capitalism," *Past and Present* 38 (1967): 56–97; R. Williams, *Resources of Hope* (London: Verso, 1989).
24. R. Williams, *People of the Black Mountains: The Eggs of the Eagle,* vol. 1 (London: Chatto and Windus, 1989), 10–12.
25. J. Clark, and C. Martin, eds., *Anarchy, Geography, Modernity: The Radical Social Thought of Elisée Reclus* (Lanham, Md.: Lexington Books, 2004).
26. K. Marx, *Capital,* vol. 1 (New York: International Publishers, 1967).
27. Ibid., 167.
28. Ibid., 275.
29. K. Cox, ed., *Spaces of Globalization: Reasserting the Power of the Local* (New York: Guilford, 1997).
30. M. Burawoy, *Manufacturing Consent: The Labor Process under Monopoly Capitalism* (Chicago: University of Chicago Press, 1982).
31. J. Rancière, *The Nights of Labor: The Workers' Dream in Nineteenth-century France* (Philadelphia: Temple University Press, 1989).
32. I reviewed some the anthropological and historical evidence in Harvey, *Justice, Nature and the Geography of Difference,*chap. 9.
33. D. Moore, *Suffering for Territory: Race, Place and Power in Zimbabwe* (Durham, N.C.: Duke University Press, 2005), 4.
34. J. Le Goff, *Time, Work, and Culture in the Middle Ages* (Chicago: University of Chicago Press, 1980); Kern, *Culture of Time and Space.* I reviewed much of this transition literature in D. Harvey, *The Condition of Postmodernity* (Oxford: Blackwell, 1989), Part III.
35. M. Kohn, *Radical Space: Building the House of the People* (Ithaca: Cornell University Press, 2003), 3–8.
36. Ibid.
37. Ibid., chap. 6.
38. Foucault, *Order of Things;* M. Foucault, "Heterotopias," *Diacritics* 16, no.1 (Spring 1986): 22–28.
39. M. Foucault, "Questions on Geography," in *Power/Knowledge,* ed. C. Gordon (London: Harvester, 1980); Foucault, *Security, Territory, Population: Lectures at the Collège de France, 1977–78* (Basingstoke: Palgrave Macmillan, 2007); *The Foucault Reader,* ed. P. Rabinow (Harmondsworth, Middlesex, England: Penguin, 1984); J. Crampton and S. Elden, eds., *Space, Knowledge and Power: Foucault and Geography* (Aldershot, Hants.: Ashgate Publishing, 2007).
40. H. Lefebvre, *The Urban Revolution* (Minneapolis: University of Minnesota Press, 2005).
41. J. Elyachar, *Markets of Dispossession: NGOs, Economic Development and the State in Cairo* (Durham, N.C.: Duke University Press, 2005); D. Graeber, *Towards an Anthropological Theory of Value: The False Coin of Our Own Dreams* (New York: Palgrave Macmillan, 2001).

8. Places, Regions, Territories

1. E. Casey, *The Fate of Place: A Philosophical History* (Berkeley: University of California Press, 1997); Casey, "How to Get From Space to Place in a Fairly Short Stretch of Time," in *Senses of Place*, ed. S. Feld and K. Basso (Phoenix, Ariz.: School of American Research Advanced Seminar Series, 1996),16-17.
2. M. Kohn, *Radical Space: Building the House of the People* (Ithaca, N.Y.: Cornell University Press, 2003).
3. G. Himmelfarb, "The Illusions of Cosmopolitanism," in M. Nussbaum et al., *For Love of Country: Debating the Limits of Patriotism* (Boston: Beacon Press, 1996), 72–77; A. Escobar, "Place, Economy and Culture in a Post-Development Era," in *Places and Politics in an Age of Globalization*, ed. R. Prazniak and A. Dirlik (Lanham, Md.: Rowman and Littlefield, 2002), 193–217; E. Burke, cited in A. Appiah, *The Ethics of Identity* (Princeton: Princeton University Press, 2005), 241.
4. Appiah, *Ethics of Identity*; A. Appiah, *Cosmopolitanism: Ethics in a World of Strangers* (New York: Norton, 2006).
5. Nussbaum et al., *For Love of Country*, 13; U. Hannerz, *Transnational Connections: Culture, People, Places* (New York: Routledge, 1996).
6. R. Williams, *Keywords: A Vocabulary of Culture and Society* (New York: Oxford University Press, 1985), 264–66. For some of the history of the regional concept in geography, see, e.g., R. Hudson, *Producing Places* (New York: Guilford, 2001); T. Cresswell, *Place: A Short Introduction* (Oxford: Blackwell, 2004); J. Agnew, *Place and Politics: The Geographical Mediation of State and Society* (London: Macmillan, 1987); Agnew and J. Duncan, eds., *The Power of Place: Bringing Together Geographical and Sociological Imaginations* (Boston: Unwin Hyman, 1989); N. Entriken, *The Betweenness of Place: Towards a Geography of Modernity* (London: Macmillan, 1991); G. Kimble, "The Inadequacy of the Regional Concept," in *London Essays in Geography*, ed. L. Stamp and S. Wooldridge (London: Longmans Green, 1957), 151–74; D. Massey, "In What Sense a Regional Problem?" *Regional Studies* 13 (1979): 233–43; M. Pudup, "Arguments within Regional Geography," *Progress in Human Geography* 12 (1988): 369–90.
7. K. Archer, "Regions as Social Organisms: The Lamarckian Characteristics of Vidal de la Blache's Regional Geography," *Annals, Association of American Geographers* 83 (1993): 498–514; A. Buttimer, *Society and Milieu in the French Geographical Tradition* (Washington, D.C.,:Association of American Geographers, 1971); A. Rossi, *The Architecture of the City* (Cambridge, Mass.: MIT Press, 1984).
8. On classificatory approaches to regions, see D. Grigg, "Regions, Models and Classes," in *Models in Geography*, ed. R. Chorley and P. Haggett (London: Methuen, 1967), 479–501. On regions and places more generally, see K. Anderson and F. Gale, eds., *Inventing Places: Studies in Cultural Geography* (Melbourne: Longman Cheshire, 1992); Hudson, *Producing Places*; Cresswell, *Place*; Yi-Fu Tuan, *Space and Place: The Perspective of Experience* (Minneapolis: University of Minnesota Press, 1977); A. Paasi, "Place and Region: Regional Worlds and Words," *Progress in Human Geography* 26 (2002): 802–11; T. Oakes, "Place and the Paradox

of Modernity," *Annals, Association of American Geographers* 87 (1997): 509–31; B. Anderson, *Imagined Communities: Reflections on the Origins and Spread of Nationalism* (London: Verso, 1983); A. Paasi, *Territories, Boundaries and Consciousness: The Changing Geographies of the Finnish-Russian Border* (New York: Wiley, 1997).

9. R. Ardrey, *The Territorial Imperative* (New York: Athenaeum, 1966); R. Sack, *Human Territoriality: Its Theory and Its History* (Cambridge: Cambridge University Press, 1986).
10. D. Delaney, *Territory: A Short Introduction* (Oxford: Blackwell, 2005), 9–11; for a particularly interesting ethnographic study of some of these issues, see S. Narotzky and G. Smith, *Immediate Struggles: People, Power, and Place in Rural Spain* (Berkeley: University of California Press, 2006).
11. P. Taylor, "The State as Container: Internationality, Interstatenesss, Interterritoriality, *Progress in Human Geography* 19 (1995): 1–15.
12. For a series of essays written on this topic in the 1970s, see D. Harvey, *Spaces of Capital: Towards a Critical Geography* (Edinburgh: Edinburgh University Press, 2001), Part 2; N. Smith, *Uneven Development* (Oxford: Blackwell, 1984); M. Storper, and R. Walker, *The Capitalist Imperative: Territory, Technology and Industrial Growth* (Oxford: Blackwell, 1989).
13. G. Deleuze and F. Guattari, *A Thousand Plateaus: Capitalism and Schizophrenia* (Minneapolis: University of Minnesota Press, 1987).
14. K. Basso, "Stalking with Stories: Names, Places and Moral Narratives among the Western Apache," in *1983 Proceedings of the American Ethnological Society* (Washington, D.C.: AES, 1984); Basso, "Wisdom Sits In Places: Notes on a Western Apache Landscape," in *Sense of Place*, ed. Feld and Basso, 52–87.
15. K. Basso, *Wisdom Sits in Places* (Albuquerque: University of New Mexico Press, 1995); D. Moore, *Suffering for Territory: Race, Place and Power in Zimbabwe* (Durham, N.C.: Duke University Press, 2005), 19.
16. Moore, *Suffering for Territory*, 21; D. DeLillo, *The Names* (New York: Vintage, 1989), 329–31.
17. M. de Certeau, *The Writing of History* (New York: Columbia University Press, 1988), 69; G. Bachelard, *The Poetics of Space* (Boston: Beacon Press, 1964), 6–7.
18. D. Morley and K. Robbins, "No Place Like Heimat: Images of Home(land)," in *Space and Place: Theories of Identity and Location*, ed. E. Carter, J. Donald, and J. Squires (London: Routledge, 1993), 3–31.
19. M. Gordon, "My Mother is Speaking from the Desert," *New York Times Magazine*, 19 March 1995, 47–70.
20. R. Williams, *Resources of Hope* (London: Verso, 1989); see also the essay "Militant Particularism and Global Ambition," in D. Harvey, *Justice, Nature and the Geography of Difference* (Oxford: Blackwell, 1996), chap. 1.
21. W. Benjamin, *Illuminations* (New York: Schocken Books, 1969).
22. C. Boyer, *The City of Collective Memory* (Cambridge, Mass.: MIT Press, 1996), 135.
23. Kohn, *Radical Space*, 149.
24. C. Norberg-Shulz, *Genius Loci: Towards a Phenomenology of Architecture* (New York: Rizzoli, 1980).

25. Rossi, *Architecture of the City.*; A. Loukaki, "Whose Genius Loci: Competing Interpretations of the Sacred Rock of the Acropolis," *Annals, Association of American Geographers* 87 (1997): 306–29; Loukaki, *Living Ruins: Value Conflicts* (Farnham, U.K.: Ashgate, 2008).
26. M. Heidegger, *Poetry, Language, Thought* (New York: Harper and Row, 1971), 165.
27. Ibid., 114–15.
28. Ibid., 160.
29. Ibid., 156; M. Heidegger, *Discourse on Thinking* (New York: Harper, 1966), 47–48; U. Mehta, *Liberalism and Empire: A Study in Nineteenth-century British Liberal Thought* (Chicago: University of Chicago Press, 1999), 215.
30. T. Relph, *Place and Placelessness* (London: Pion, 1976), 26–29.
31. Heidegger, *Poetry, Language, Thought,* 154; Casey, "How to Get from Space to Place," 37.
32. H. Lefebvre, *The Urban Revolution* (Minneapolis: University of Minnesota Press, 2005); A. Merrifield, "Place and Space: A Lefebvrian Reconciliation," *Transactions of the Institute of British Geographers* 16 (1991): 516–31.
33. B. Foltz, *Inhabiting the Earth: Heidegger, Environmental Ethics, and the Metaphysics of Nature* (Atlantic Park, N.J.: Humanities Press, 1995).
34. Tuan, *Space and Place.*
35. On Heidegger's supposed interest in the critique of West German reconstruction, see S. Elden, *Mapping the Present: Heidegger, Foucault and the Project of a Spatial History* (London: Continuum, 2001), 87; Bate, J., *Romantic Ecology: Wordsworth and the Environmental Tradition* (London: Routledge, 1991); Wiley, M., *Romantic Geography: Wordsworth and Anglo-European Spaces* (London: Macmillan, 1998).
36. On deep ecology, see A. Naess, *Ecology, Community and Lifestyle* (Cambridge: Cambridge University Press, 1989). For Heidegger and environmentalism, see Foltz, *Inhabiting the Earth;* and E. Reclus, *L'Homme et la Terre,* ed. B. Ghiblin, 2 vols., abridged (Paris: La Découverte, 1982).
37. Relph, *Place and Placelessness*; K. Sale, "What Columbus Discovered," *The Nation,* 22 October 1990, 444–46; R. Kunstler, *The Geography of Nowhere: The Rise and Decline of America's Man-Made Landscape* (New York: Free Press, 1994).
38. Escobar, "Place, Economy, and Culture."
39. Casey, *Fate of Place,* 30, 35.
40. D. Massey, *Space, Place and Gender* (Minneapolis: University of Minnesota Press, 1994), 5.
41. A. Dirlik, "Place-Based Imagination: Globalism and the Politics of Place," in *Places and Politics in an Age of Globalization,* ed. R. Prazniak and A. Dirlik (New York: Rowman and Littlefield, 2001), 15–51.
42. Casey, *Fate of Place,* 43.
43. I summarize Whitehead's views in *Justice, Nature and the Geography of Difference,* 261–64.
44. Moore, *Suffering for Territory,* 21; C. Katz, "On the Grounds of Globalization: A Topography for Feminist Political Engagement," *Signs* 26, no. 4 (2001): 1213–34.

45. A lot of work has been done in recent years on the significance of interurban competition in the dynamics of neoliberal capitalism. See N. Brenner, and N. Theodore, *Spaces of Neoliberalism: Urban Restructuring in North America and Western Europe* (Oxford: Blackwell, 2002); H. Leitner, J. Peck, and E. Sheppard, *Contesting Neoliberalism: Urban Frontiers* (New York: Guilford, 2006).
46. G. Deleuze, and M. Taormina, *Desert Islands and Other Texts (1953–74)* (London: Semiotexte, 2003).
47. Kohn, *Radical Space.*
48. Massey, *Space, Place and Gender,* depicts my views this way, and Dirlik, "Place-Based Imagination," takes her word for it. J. K. Gibson-Graham, "Beyond Global vs. Local: Economic Politics Outside the Binary Frame," in *Geographies of Power: Placing Scale,* ed. A. Herod and M. Wright Wiley-Blackwell, 2002),25–60.
49. D. Harvey, *Spaces of Hope* (Edinburgh: Edinburgh University Press, 2000).
50. Nussbaum et al., *For Love of Country,* 9.
51. K. Marx and F. Engels, *The Communist Manifesto* (London, Pluto Press, 2008).
52. Harvey, *Justice, Nature and the Geography of Difference,* chap. 1; Harvey, *Spaces of Hope,* chap. 10.
53. A. Etzioni, *The New Golden Rule: Community and Morality in a Democratic Society* (New York: Basic Books, 1998).
54. D. Harvey, *Spaces of Global Capitalism: Towards a Theory of Uneven Geographical Development* (London: Verso, 2006), chap. 2.
55. J. Conway, *Identity, Place, Knowledge* (Halifax: Fernwood Publishing, 2004); Katz, "On the Grounds of Globalization"; M. Keith, and S. Pile, eds., *Place and the Politics of Identity* (New York: Routledge, 1993); D. Hayden, *The Power of Place: Urban Landscapes as Public History* (Cambridge, Mass.: MIT Press, 1995).
56. M. Bookchin, *Remaking Society: Pathways to a Green Future* (Boston: South End Press, 1990), 182–85.
57. I. Young, *Justice and the Politics of Difference* (Princeton: Princeton University Press, 1990).

9. The Nature of Environment

1. J. Diamond, *Guns, Germs, and Steel: The Fates of Human Societies* (New York: Norton, 1997; rpt. 2003), 25, 408.
2. Ibid., 408.
3. Ibid., 417. For the West African rice culture, see J. Carney, *Black Rice: The African Origins of Rice Cultivation in the Americas* (Cambridge, Mass.: Harvard University Press, 2001); and for the problem of soil erosion, see G. Jacks and R. Whyte, *Vanishing Lands* (New York: Doubleday, 1949).
4. Diamond, *Guns, Germs, and Steel,* 453.
5. Ibid., 455.
6. Ibid., 414.
7. Ibid., 462.

8. J. Sachs, *The End of Poverty: Economic Possibilities for Our Time* (New York: Penguin, 2005), 163.
9. J. Sachs (with J. Gallup and A. Mellinger), "Is Geography Destiny," in *World Bank Conference on Development Economics,* ed. B. Pleskovic and J. Stiglitz (Washington, D.C.: World Bank, 1999),127–78; Sachs, *End of Poverty*, 165.
10. Sachs, *End of Poverty*, 166–67.
11. Sachs, *End of Poverty*, 167.
12. R. Haussmann, "A Case of Bad Latitude: Why Geography Causes Poverty," *Foreign Policy* (January–February 2001): 45–53. See D. Harvey, "Population, Resources and the Ideology of Science," in *Spaces of Capital: Towards a Critical Geography* (Edinburgh: Edinburgh University Press, 2001), chap. 3.
13. K. Wittfogel, *Oriental Despotism* (New Haven: Yale University Press, 1953).
14. D. Acemoglu, S. Johnson, and J. Robinson, "Reversal of Fortune: Geography and Institutions in the Making of the Modern World Income Distribution," *Quarterly Journal of Economics* 117 (2002): 1233.
15. D. Harvey, *Justice, Nature and the Geography of Difference* (Oxford: Blackwell, 1996), chap. 11.
16. A. Przeworski, "Geography vs. Institutions Revisited: Were Fortunes Reversed?" Department of Politics Working Paper, New York University, 2004.
17. C. Glacken, *Traces on the Rhodian Shore: Nature and Culture in Western Thought from Ancient Times to the End of the Eighteenth Century* (Berkeley: University of California Press, 1967).
18. E. C. Semple, *Influences of Geographical Environment on the Basis of Ratzel's System of Anthropogeographie* (New York: Henry Holt, 1911).
19. E. Huntington, *Civilization and Climate* (New Haven: Yale University Press, 1945); Huntington, *Mainsprings of Civilization* (New York: Mentor Books, 1965); D. Worster, *Dustbowl: The Southern Plains in the Great Depression* (New York: Oxford University Press, 1979).
20. P. O'Keefe, N. Smith, and B. Wisner, "Taking the Naturalness Out of Natural Disasters," *Nature* 260 (1976): 566–67; N. Smith, "Disastrous Accumulation," *South Atlantic Quarterly* 106, no. 4 (2007): 769–87.
21. On Griffith Taylor see J. Powell, *An Historical Geography of Modern Australia* (Cambridge: Cambridge University Press, 1988,) 129–49.
22. O. Spate, "Toynbee and Huntington: A Study in Determinism," *Geographical Journal* 118 (1952): 406–28.
23. G. Tatham, "Environmentalism and Possibilism," in *Geography in the Twentieth Century*, ed. G. Taylor (London: Methuen, 1951), 128–64.
24. P. Vidal de la Blache, *Principles of Human Geography* (London: Constable, 1926); K. Archer, "Regions as Social Organisms: The Lamarckian Characteristics of Vidal de la Blache's Regional Geography," *Annals, Association of American Geographers* 83 (1993): 498–514.
25. G. Marsh, *Man and Nature: Or, Physical Geography as Modified by Human Action* (Cambridge, Mass.: Harvard University Press, 1965).
26. Engels, cited in Harvey, *Justice, Nature and the Geography of Difference*, 184.

27. W. Leiss, *The Domination of Nature* (Boston: Beacon Press, 1974).
28. R. Williams, *Keywords: A Vocabulary of Culture and Society* (New York: Oxford University Press, 1985). I here follow the general argument laid out in Harvey, *Justice, Nature and the Geography of Difference.*
29. A. Lovejoy, *The Great Chain of Being* (Cambridge, Mass.: Harvard University Press, 1964), 7–14.
30. K. Soper, *What Is Nature?* (Oxford: Blackwell, 1995); N. Castree and B. Braun, eds., *Social Nature: Theory, Practice and Politics* (Oxford: Blackwell, 2001).
31. This is Neil Smith's fundamental argument in *Uneven Development.*
32. K. Marx, *Capital,* vol. 1 (New York: International Publishers, 1967), 493.
33. Emil Altvater has criticized my formulations because I am not sufficiently respectful of the limits set by the second law of thermodynamics. See E. Altvater, "Review of *Justice, Nature and the Geography of Difference,*" *Historical Materialism* 2 (1998): 225–35; The extreme version of this thesis can be found in K. Lee, *Social Philosophy and Ecological Scarcity* (London: Routledge, 1989).
34. I. Prigogine, and I., Stengers, *Order Out of Chaos* (Boston: Shambhala, 1984); R. Levins and R. Lewontin, *The Dialectical Biologist* (Cambridge, Mass.: Harvard University Press, 1985); T. Kuhn, *The Structure of Scientific Revolutions* (Chicago: University of Chicago Press, 1962). For an excellent overview of contemporary thinking in geography, see Castree, and Braun, *Social Nature.*
35. E. Wilson, *Consilience: The Unity of Knowledge* (New York: Knopf, 1998), 266.
36. Ibid., 266–67.
37. Ibid., 270.
38. Marx, *Capital,* vol. 1, 493–94.
39. Wilson, *Consilience,* 83.
40. Ibid., 128.
41. Ibid., 166.
42. Ibid., 168.
43. This is the sense that derives from the otherwise excellent work of A. Tsing, *Friction: An Ethnography of Global Connection* (Princeton: Princeton University Press, 2004).
44. A. Escobar, "Place, Economy, and Culture in a Post-Development Era," in *Places and Politics in an Age of Globalization,* ed. R. Prazniak and A. Dirlik (New York: Rowman and Littlefield, 2001), 193-217; J. Gibson-Graham, *The End of Capitalism (As We Knew It): A Feminist Critique of Political Economy* (Minneapolis: University of Minnesota Press, 2006).
45. D. Harvey, *Spaces of Hope* (Edinburgh: Edinburgh University Press, 2000); N. Smith, "Geography, Difference and the Politics of Scale," in *Postmodernism and the Social Sciences,* ed. J. Docherty, M. Graham, and M. Malek (London: Routledge, 1992); E. Swyngedouw, 1997: "Neither Global nor Local: "Glocalization" and the Politics of Scale," in *Spaces of Globalization: Reasserting the Power of the Local,* ed. K. Cox (New York: Routledge, 1997), 137–66.
46. R. Bhaskar, *Dialectic: The Pulse of Freedom* (London: Verso, 1993).
47. Leiss, *Domination of Nature*; M. Jay, *The Dialectical Imagination: A History of the*

Frankfurt School and the Institute of Social Research 1923–50 (Boston: Little Brown, 1973).

48. C. Caudwell, *Studies and Further Studies in a Dying Culture* (New York: Monthly Review Press, 1971).
49. Smith, *Uneven Development.*
50. N. Smith, "Nature as Accumulation Strategy," *Socialist Register* (2007): 16–36.
51. B. Braun, "Toward a New Earth and a New Humanity: Nature, Ontology, Politics," in *David Harvey: A Critical Reader,* ed. N. Castree and D. Gregory (Oxford: Blackwell, 2006), 191–222.
52. Cited in Harvey, *Justice, Nature and the Geography of Difference,* 48–57; Levins and Lewontin, *Dialectical Biologist.*
53. W. Cronon, *Changes in the Land: Indians, Colonists and the Ecology of New England* (New York: Hill and Wang, 1983), 13–14.
54. D. Bohm, *Wholeness and the Implicate Order* (London: Ark Paperbacks, 1983); M. Wilkins, "Complementarity and the Unity of Opposites," in *Quantum Implications,* ed. B. Hiley and F. Peat (London: Routledge, 1987), 338–60; A. Naess, *Ecology, Community and Lifestyle* (Cambridge: Cambridge University Press, 1989); M. Hardt and A. Negri, *Empire* (Cambridge, Mass.: Harvard University Press, 2001).
55. W. Thomas, ed., *Man's Role in Changing the Face of the Earth* (Chicago: University of Chicago Press, 1956).
56. Ibid., 68.
57. Marx., *Capital,* vol. 1, 133.
58. Harvey, *Justice, Nature and the Geography of Difference,* chap. 8.
59. Marx, *Capital,* vol. 1, 494.
60. D. Harvey, "The Fetish of Technology: Causes and Consequences," in "Prometheus's Bequest: Technology and Change," *Macalester International* 13 (2003): 3–30.
61. Marx, *Capital,* vol. 1., 133.
62. H. Lefebvre, *Critique of Everyday Life,* vol. 1 (London: Verso, 1991); N. Hartsock, *Money, Sex and Power* (London: Macmillan, 1973); M. Mies, *Patriarchy and Accumulation on a World Scale* (London: Zed Books, 1986); C. Katz, "Whose Nature, Whose Culture? Private Productions of Space and the Preservation of Nature," in *Remaking Nature: Nature at the End of the Millennium,* ed. N. Castree and B. Braun (London: Routledge, 1998), 46–63; F. Braudel, *Capitalism and Material Life, 1400–1800* (London: Weidenfeld and Nicolson, 1973); J. Habermas, *The Theory of Communicative Action,* Vol. 2: *Lifeworld and System: A Critique of Functionalist Reason* (Boston: Beacon Press, 1985).
63. See Mies, *Patriarchy and Accumulation on a World Scale,* in particular.
64. G. Cohen, *Karl Marx's Theory of History: A Defense* (Princeton: Princeton University Press, 1978).
65. K. Marx, *The Grundrisse* (Harmondworth, Middlesex, England: Penguin, 1973), 414–15.
66. Ibid., 704–5.

67. D. Haraway, "A Manifesto for Cyborgs: Science, Technology and Socialist Feminism in the 1980s," in *Feminism/Postmodernism*, ed. L. Nicholson (London: Routledge, 1990); Haraway, *Simians, Cyborgs and Women: The Reinvention of Nature* (London: Routledge, 1991); Diamond, *Guns, Germs and Steel.*
68. P. Hawken, *Blessed Unrest: How the Largest Movement in History Is Restoring Grace, Justice and Beauty to the World* (New York: Penguin, 2007).
69. Diamond, *Guns, Germs and Steel,* 111; D. Haraway, *Primate Visions: Gender, Race and Nature in the World of Modern Science* (London: Routledge, 1989); see also E. Martin, *Flexible Bodies: Tracking Immunity in American Culture: From the Days of Polio to the Age of AIDS* (Boston: Beacon Press, 1994).
70. Cited in M. Delanda, *A New Philosophy of Society: Assemblage Theory and Social Complexity* (London: Continuum Books, 2006), 121.
71. Ibid.
72. K. Marx, *A Contribution to the Critique of Political Economy* (New York: International Publishers, 1970).
73. Ibid.
74. For further elaboration on these lines, see D. Harvey, "On the Significance of a Certain Footnote in Marx's Capital," *Human Geography* 1, no. 2 (2008): forthcoming.

Epilogue

1. See D. Harvey, "The Sociological and Geographical Imaginations," *International Journal of Politics, Culture and Society* 18, nos. 3–4 (2005): 211–56.
2. T. Lemke, "'The Birth of Biopolitics': Michel Foucault's Lecture at the Collège de France on Neo-liberal Governmentality," *Economy and Society* 30 (2000): 190–207.
3. W. Benjamin, *Illuminations* (New York: Schocken Books, 1969), 255; A. Badiou, *Metapolitics,* trans. J. Barker (London: Verso, 2005).
4. B. Anderson, *Imagined Communities: Reflections on the Origins and Spread of Nationalism* (London: Verso, 1983).
5. E. Grosz, "Bodies-Cities," in *Sexuality and Space,* ed. B. Colomina (Princeton: Princeton University Press, 1992), 241–54; N. De Genova, *Working the Boundaries: Race, Space, and "Illegality" in Mexican Chicago* (Durham, N.C.: Duke University Press, 2005); P. Bourdieu, *Outline of a Theory of Practice* (Cambridge: Cambridge University Press, 1977).
6. R. Nozick, *Anarchy, State, and Utopia* (New York: Basic Books, 1974).
7. K. Marx and F. Engels, *Collected Works,* vol. 3 (Moscow: Progress Publishers, 1975), 154; Lemke, "'Birth of Biopolitics.'"
8. M. de Certeau, *The Practice of Everyday Life* (Berkeley: University of California Press, 1984).
9. R. Williams, *Loyalties* (London: Chatto and Windus, 1985).
10. J. Clark, and C. Martin, *Anarchy, Geography, Modernity: The Radical Social Thought of Elisée Reclus* (Lanham, Md.: Lexington Books, 2004).

11. See the trenchant critique in D. Robotham, *Culture, Society, Economy: Globalization and Its Alternatives* (New York: Sage, 2005).
12. P. Abrams, "Notes on the Difficulty of Studying the State," in *The Anthropology of the State*, ed. A. Sharma and A. Gupta (Oxford: Blackwell, 2006), 112–30.
13. T. Mitchell, "Society, Economy, and the State Effect," in *Anthropology of the State*, ed. Sharma and Gupta, 169–86.
14. Ibid., 174–82.
15. Cited in S. Kern, *The Culture of Time and Space, 1880–1918* (London: Weidenfeld and Nicolson, 1983).
16. Mitchell, "Society, Economy, and the State Effect," 183.
17. M. Biggs, "Putting the State on the Map: Cartography, Territory, and European State Formation," *Comparative Studies in Society and History* 41 (1999): 374–405.
18. D. Harvey, Spaces of Global Capitalism: Toward a Theory of Uneven Geographical Development (London: Verso, 2006).
19. T. Winichakul, *Siam Mapped: A History of the Geo-Body of a Nation* (Honolulu: University of Hawaii Press, 1994).
20. De Genova, *Working the Boundaries*, chap. 3.
21. Smith, *Endgame of Globalization*, 47.
22. J. Scott, *Seeing like a State: How Certain Schemes to Improve the Human Condition Have Failed* (New Haven: Yale University Press, 1999); Benhabib, *Rights of Others*.
23. M. Sparke, *In the Space of Theory: Postfoundational Geographies of the Nation-State* (Minneapolis: University of Minnesota Press, 2005), xxxiv, 116–17.
24. R. Trouillot, "The Anthropology of the State in the Age of Globalization: Close Encounters of the Deceptive Kind," *Current Anthropology* 42, no. 1 (2001): 125–34.
25. For an example of conceptualizing capitalism into quasi-oblivion, see J. Gibson-Graham, *The End of Capitalism (As We Knew It); A Feminist Critique of Political Economy* (Minneapolis: University of Minnesota Press, 2006).
26. M. Bookchin, *Remaking Society: Pathways to a Green Future* (Boston: South End Press, 1990), 194–95.
27. Kern, *Culture of Time and Space, 1880–1919*.
28. H. Lefebvre, *The Production of Space* (Oxford: Blackwell, 1991); D. Harvey, *The Condition of Postmodernity* (Oxford: Blackwell, 1989); C. Schorske, *Fin-de-Siècle Vienna* (New York: Vintage, 1981), 226.
29. Smith, *Endgame of Globalization*.
30. S. Kaviraj, "On the Enchantment of the State: Indian Thought on the Role of the State in the Narrative of Modernity," *European Journal of Sociology* 46 (2005): 263–96; P. Chatterjee, *The Nation and Its Fragments: Colonial and Postcolonial Histories* (Princeton: Princeton University Press, 1993).
31. Cited in D. Harvey, *Paris, Capital of Modernity* (New York: Routledge, 2003), 264.
32. M. Hardt and T. Negri, *Empire* (Cambridge, Mass.: Harvard University Press, 2001); J. Holloway, *Changing the World without Taking Power: The Meaning of Rev-*

olution Today (London: Pluto Press, 2002); Badiou, *Metapolitics;* J. Ranciere, *Disagreement: Politics and Philosophy* (Minneapolis: University of Minnesota Press, 1998); S. Žižek, *The Parallax View* (Cambridge, Mass.: MIT Press, 2003).

33. A. Badiou, "Communist Hypothesis," *New Left Review,* 2d ser., 49 (2008): 29–48.
34. Schorske, *Fin-de-Siècle Vienna,* 308.
35. D. Harvey, "Introduction," in K. Marx and F. Engels, *The Communist Manifesto* (London: Pluto Press, 2008).
36. Clark and Martin, *Anarchy, Geography, Modernity,* 249–50.

Bibliography

Abrams, P. "Notes on the Difficulty of Studying the State." In *The Anthropology of the State,* ed. A. Sharma and A. Gupta (Oxford: Blackwell, 2006), 112–30.

Acemoglu, D., S. Johnson, and J. Robinson. "Reversal of Fortune: Geography and Institutions in the Making of the Modern World Income Distribution." *Quarterly Journal of Economics* 117 (2002): 1231–94.

Agnew, J. *Place and Politics: The Geographical Mediation of State and Society.* London: Macmillan, 1987.

Agnew, J., and J. Duncan, eds. *The Power of Place: Bringing Together Geographical and Sociological Imaginations.* Boston: Unwin Hyman, 1989.

Alexander, D. "Bioregionalism: Science or Sensibility." *Environmental Ethics* 12 (1990): 161–73. Reprinted in McGinnis, M., ed. *Bioregionalism* (New York: Routledge, 1998), 161–73.

Allen, A. "Foucault and Enlightenment: A Critical Reappraisal." *Constellations* 10, no. 2 (2003): 180–98.

Altvater, E. "Review of *Justice, Nature and the Geography of Difference.*" *Historical Materialism* 2 (1998): 225–35.

Amin, S. *Beyond U.S. Hegemony? Assessing the Prospects for a Multipolar World.* London: Zed Books, 2006.

Amsden, A. *Escape from Empire: The Developing World's Journey through Heaven and Hell.* Cambridge, Mass.: MIT Press, 2007.

Anderson, A. "Cosmopolitanism, Universalism and the Divided Legacies of Modernity." In *Cosmopolitics,* ed. Cheah and Robins, 270–71.

Anderson, B. *Imagined Communities: Reflections on the Origins and Spread of Nationalism.* London: Verso,1983.

Anderson, J. "Fund Managers Raising the Ante in Philanthropy." *New York Times,* 3 August 2005, Business Section, 1, 3.

Anderson, K., and F. Gale, eds. *Inventing Places: Studies in Cultural Geography*. Melbourne: Longman Cheshire, 1992.

Anderson, P. *English Questions*. London: Verso, 1992.

Appadurai, A. *Modernity at Large: Cultural Dimensions of Globalization*. Minneapolis: University of Minnesota Press, 1996.

Appelbaum, R., and W. Robinson, eds. *Critical Globalization Studies*. New York: Routledge, 2005.

Appiah, A. *Cosmopolitanism: Ethics in a World of Strangers*. New York: Norton, 2006.

Appiah, A. "Cosmopolitan Patriots." In Nussbaum et al., *For Love of Country*, 21–29.

Appiah, A. *The Ethics of Identity*. Princeton: Princeton University Press, 2005.

Archer, K. "Regions as Social Organisms: The Lamarckian Characteristics of Vidal de la Blache's Regional Geography." *Annals, Association of American Geographers* 83 (1993): 498–514.

Ardrey, R. *The Territorial Imperative*. New York: Athenaeum, 1966.

Arendt, H. *Eichmann in Jerusalem: A Report on the Banality of Evil*. Harmondsworth, Middlesex, England: Penguin, 1997.

Arendt, H. *Imperialism*. New York: Harcourt, Brace and Jovanovich, 1968.

Arendt, H. *Lectures on Kant's Political Philosophy*. Chicago: University of Chicago Press, 1989.

Armstrong, P., A. Glyn, and J. Harrison. *Capitalism since World War II: The Making and Breaking Up of the Great Boom*. Oxford: Blackwell, 1991.

Arvedlund, E. "Russia's Billionaires Club Now Totals 27 Members." *New York Times*, 7 May 2005, C1.

Bachelard, G. *The Poetics of Space*. Boston: Beacon Press, 1964.

Badiou, A. *Being and Event*. London: Continuum, 2005.

Badiou, A. "Communist Hypothesis." *New Left Review*, 2d ser., 49 (2008): 29–48.

Badiou, A. *Metapolitics*. Trans. J. Barker. London: Verso, 2005.

Barry, J. "Voice Off." In *Third Berlin Biennal for Contemporary Art, Catalogue* (Berlin: Biennale, 2004), 48–49.

Bartholomew, A., and J. Breakspear. "Human Rights and Swords of Empire." *Socialist Register* (2003): 124–45.

Barzini, L. *The Italians*. New York: Athenaeum, 1967.

Basso, K. "Stalking with Stories: Names, Places and Moral Narratives among the Western Apache." In *1983 Proceedings of the American Ethnological Society* (Washington, D.C.: AES, 1984).

Basso, K. *Wisdom Sits in Places*. Albuquerque: University of New Mexico Press, 1995.

Basso, K. "Wisdom Sits in Places: Notes on a Western Apache Landscape." In *Sense of Place*, ed. Feld and Basso,52–91.

Bate, J. *Romantic Ecology: Wordsworth and the Environmental Tradition*. London: Routledge, 1991.

Beck, U. "The Cosmopolitan Perspective: Sociology in the Second Age of Modernity." In *Conceiving Cosmopolitanism*, ed. Vertovec and Cohen, 61–85.

Beck, U. *Cosmopolitan Vision*. Cambridge: Polity Press, 2006.

Beck, U. "Living in the World Risk Society." Hobhouse Memorial Lecture, London School of Economics, 15 February 2006.

Bello, W. *Deglobalization: Ideas for a New World Economy*. London: Zed Books, 2002.

Benhabib, S. *The Rights of Others: Aliens, Residents and Citizens*. Cambridge: Cambridge University Press, 2004.

Benjamin, W. *The Arcades Project*. Cambridge, Mass.: Belknap Press, 1999.

Benjamin, W. *Illuminations*. New York: Schocken Books, 1969.

Berlin, I. *The Sense of Reality: Studies in Ideas and Their History*. London: Chatto and Windus, 1997.

Bhaskar, R. *Dialectic: The Pulse of Freedom*. London: Verso, 1993.

Biggs, M. "Putting the State on the Map: Cartography, Territory, and European State Formation." *Comparative Studies in Society and History* 41 (1999): 374–405.

Blair, T. Speech to U.S. Congress, 18 July 2003, "History Will Forgive Us." Consulted online: http://politics.guardian.co.uk/speeches/story/0,1126,1008150,00.html

Bohm, D. *Wholeness and the Implicate Order*. London: Ark Paperbacks, 1983.

Bolin, R. "Immanuel Kant's *Physical Geography*." Trans. and annotated by R. L. Bolin. Master's thesis, Dept. of Geography, Indiana University, 1968.

Bookchin, M. *Remaking Society: Pathways to a Green Future*. Boston: South End Press, 1990.

Bourdieu, P. *Outline of a Theory of Practice*. Cambridge: Cambridge University Press, 1977.

Boyer, C. *The City of Collective Memory*. Cambridge, Mass.: MIT Press, 1996.

Brash, J. "Re-scaling Patriotism: Competition and Urban Identity in Michael Bloomberg's New York." *Urban Anthropology and Studies of Cultural Systems and World Economic Development* 35 (2006): 387–432.

Braudel, F. *Capitalism and Material Life, 1400–1800*. London: Weidenfeld and Nicolson, 1973.

Braun, B. "Toward a New Earth and a New Humanity: Nature, Ontology, Politics." In *David Harvey: A Critical Reader*, ed. Castree and Gregory, 191–222.

Bray, D. *Social Space and Governance in Urban China: The Danwei System from Origins to Reform*. Stanford: Stanford University Press, 2005.

Brennan, T. *At Home in the World: Cosmopolitanism Now*. Cambridge, Mass.: Harvard University Press, 1997.

Brenner, N., and N. Theodore. *Spaces of Neoliberalism: Urban Restructuring in North America and Western Europe*. Oxford: Blackwell, 2002.

Brick, C. "Millions for Millions." *New Yorker*, 30 October 2006, 62–73.

Brooks, D. "Ideals and Reality." *New York Times*, 22 January 2005, A15.

Burawoy, M. *Manufacturing Consent: The Labor Process under Monopoly Capitalism*. Chicago: University of Chicago Press, 1982.

Burdett, R., and D. Sudjic, eds. *The Endless City*. New York: Phaidon, 2008.

Bush, G. W. "Acceptance Speech to Convention Delegates in New York." *New York Times*, 3 September 2004, P4.

Bush, G. W. "Both Our Nations Serve the Cause of Freedom." *New York Times*, 20 November 2003, A14.

Bush, G. W. "The Inaugural Address: The Best Hope for Peace in Our World Is the Expansion of Freedom in All the World." *New York Times,* 21 January 2005, A12–13.

Bush, G. W. The President's State of the Union Address, 29 January 2002. Consulted online: http:www.whitehouse.gov/news/releases/2002/01/print20020129-11.html

Bush, G. W. "Securing Freedom's Triumph." *New York Times,* 11 September 2002, A33.

Buttimer, A. *Society and Milieu in the French Geographical Tradition.* Washington, D.C.: Association of American Geographers, 1971.

Calhoun, C. "The Class Consciousness of Frequent Travellers: Towards a Critique of Actually Existing Cosmopolitanism." In *Conceiving Cosmopolitanism,* ed. Vertovec and Cohen, 86–109.

Carney, J. *Black Rice: The African Origins of Rice Cultivation in the Americas.* Cambridge, Mass.: Harvard University Press, 2001.

Casey, E. *The Fate of Place: A Philosophical History.* Berkeley: University of California Press, 1997.

Casey, E. "How to Get from Space to Place in a Fairly Short Stretch of Time." In *Senses of Place,* ed. Feld and Basso, 13–51.

Cassirer, E. *An Essay on Man.* New Haven: Yale University Press, 1944.

Castree, N., and B. Braun, eds. *Social Nature: Theory, Practice and Politics.* Oxford: Blackwell, 2001.

Castree, N., and D. Gregory. *David Harvey: A Critical Reader.* Oxford: Blackwell, 2006.

Caudwell, C. *Studies and Further Studies in a Dying Culture.* New York: Monthly Review Press, 1971.

Chakrabarty, D. *Provincializing Europe: Postcolonial Thought and Historical Difference.* Princeton: Princeton University Press, 2000.

Chandler, D. *From Kosovo to Kabul: Human Rights and International Intervention.* London: Pluto Press, 2002.

Chatterjee, P. *The Nation and Its Fragments: Colonial and Postcolonial Histories.* Princeton: Princeton University Press, 1993.

Cheah, P. "Introduction Part II: The Cosmopolitical Today." In *Cosmopolitics,* ed. Cheah and Robbins, 20–44.

Cheah, P., and B. Robbins, eds. *Cosmopolitics: Thinking and Feeling beyond the Nation.* Minneapolis: University of Minnesota Press.

Chomsky, N. *The New Military Humanism: Lessons from Kosovo.* Monroe, Maine: Common Courage Press, 1999.

Chomsky, N. *On Power and Ideology.* Boston: South End Press, 1990.

Clark, J., and C. Martin, eds. *Anarchy, Geography, Modernity: The Radical Social Thought of Elisée Reclus.* Lanham, Md.: Lexington Books, 2004.

Clark, T. J. *Image of the People: Gustave Courbet and the 1848 Revolution.* London: Thames and Hudson, 1973.

Clayton, D. *Islands of Truth: The Imperial Fashioning of Vancouver Island.* Vancouver: University of British Columbia Press, 1999.

Clifford, J. "Mixed Feelings." In *Cosmopolitics*, ed. Cheah and Robins, 362–70.

Cohen, G. *Karl Marx's Theory of History: A Defense*. Princeton: Princeton University Press, 1978.

Cohen, R. "A Generation of German Pacifists at Odds over the War." *New York Times*, 6 May 1999, A10.

Connolly, W. *The Ethos of Pluralization*. Minneapolis: University of Minnesota Press, 1995.

Connolly, W. "Speed, Concentric Cultures and Cosmopolitanism." *Political Theory* 28 (2000): 596–618.

Conway, J. *Identity, Place, Knowledge*. Halifax: Fernwood Publishing, 2004.

Cooper, R. *The Breaking of Nations: Order and Chaos in the Twenty-first Century*. New York: Atlantic Monthly Press, 2003.

Cox, K., ed. *Spaces of Globalization: Reasserting the Power of the Local*. New York: Guilford, 1997.

Crampton, J., and S. Elden, eds. *Space, Knowledge and Power: Foucault and Geography*. Aldershot, Hants.: Ashgate Publishing, 2007.

Cresswell, T. *Place: A Short Introduction*. Oxford: Blackwell, 2004.

Cronon, W. *Changes in the Land: Indians, Colonists and the Ecology of New England*. New York: Hill and Wang, 1983.

Dash, E. "Off to the Races Again, Leaving Many Behind." *New York Times*, 9 April 2006, Business Section, 1, 5.

Davis, M. *Planet of Slums*. London: Verso, 2006.

De Certeau, M. *The Practice of Everyday Life*. Berkeley: University of California Press, 1984.

De Genova, N. *Working the Boundaries: Race, Space, and "Illegality" in Mexican Chicago*. Durham, N.C.: Duke University Press, 2005.

De Soto, H. *The Mystery of Capital: Why Capitalism Triumphs in the West and Fails Everywhere Else*. New York: Basic Books, 2000.

De Soto, H. *The Other Path: The Invisible Revolution in the Third World*. New York: Harper, 1989.

De Sousa Santos, B. "Beyond Neoliberal Governance: The World Social Forum as Subaltern Cosmopolitan Politics." In *Law and Globalization from Below*, ed. De Sousa Santos and Rodriguez-Garavito,29–63.

De Sousa Santos, B., and C. Rodriguez-Garavito, eds. *Law and Globalization from Below: Towards a Cosmopolitan Legality*. Cambridge: Cambridge University Press, 2005.

Delanda, M. *A New Philosophy of Society: Assemblage Theory and Social Complexity*. London: Continuum Books, 2006.

Delaney, D. *Territory: A Short Introduction*. Oxford: Blackwell, 2005.

Deleuze, G. *The Fold: Leibniz and the Baroque*. Minneapolis: University of Minnesota Press, 1993.

Deleuze, G., and F. Guattari. *A Thousand Plateaus: Capitalism and Schizophrenia*. Minneapolis: University of Minnesota Press, 1987.

Deleuze, G., and M. Taormina. *Desert Islands and Other Texts (1953–74)*. London: Semiotexte, 2003.

DeLillo, D. *The Names*. New York: Vintage, 1989.

Deshpande, S. "Hegemonic Spatial Strategies: The Nation-Space and Hindu Communalism in Twentieth Century India." *Public Culture* 10, no, 2 (1998): 249–83.

Diamond, J. *Guns, Germs, and Steel: The Fates of Human Societies*. New York: Norton, 1997; rpt. 2003.

Dirlik, A. "Place-Based Imagination: Globalism and the Politics of Place." In *Places and Politics in an Era of Globalization*, ed. Prazniak and Dirlik, 15–51.

Droit, R.-P. "Kant et les Fournis du Congo." *Le Monde*, 5 February 1999.

Edney, M. *Mapping an Empire: The Geographical Construction of British India, 1765–1843*. Chicago: University of Chicago Press, 1990.

Edwards, M., and D. Hulme, eds. *Non-Governmental Organizations: Performance and Accountability*. London: Earthscan, 1995.

Elden, S. *Mapping the Present: Heidegger, Foucault and the Project of a Spatial History*. London: Continuum, 2001.

Elster, J. *Local Justice: How Institutions Allocate Scarce Goods and Necessary Burdens*. New York: Russell Sage Foundation, 1992.

Elyachar, J. *Markets of Dispossession: NGOs, Economic Development and the State in Cairo*. Durham, N.C.: Duke University Press, 2005.

Entriken, N. *The Betweenness of Place: Towards a Geography of Modernity*. London: Macmillan, 1991.

Escobar, A. "Place, Economy, and Culture in a Post-Development Era." In *Places and Politics in an Age of Globalization*, ed. Prazniak and Dirlik,193–217.

Etzioni, A. *The New Golden Rule: Community and Morality in a Democratic Society*. New York: Basic Books, 1998.

Falk, R. "Revisioning Cosmopolitanism." In Nussbaum et al., *For Love of Country*, 53–60.

Feld, S., and K. Basso, eds. *Senses of Place*. Phoenix, Ariz.: School of American Research Advanced Seminar Series, 1996.

Fine, R., and W. Smith. "Jürgen Habermas's Theory of Cosmopolitanism." *Constellations* 10, no. 4 (2003): 469–87.

First International Resources, Inc. *Economic Sanctions Survey*. Fort Lee, N.J.: First International Resources, Inc., 2000.

Foltz, B. *Inhabiting the Earth: Heidegger, Environmental Ethics, and the Metaphysics of Nature*. Atlantic Park, N.J.: Humanities Press, 1995.

Foucault, M. "Commentary of Kant's Anthropology from a Pragmatic Point of View." Trans. Arianna Bove. Consulted online: http://www.generation-online.org/p/fpfoucault

Foucault, M. "Heterotopias." *Diacritics* 16, no. 1 (Spring 1986): 22–28.

Foucault, M. *Introduction to Kant's Anthropology*. Ed. R. Nigro. Los Angeles: Semiotext(e), 2008.

Foucault, M. *The Order of Things: An Archaeology of the Human Sciences*. New York: Random House, 1970.

Foucault, M. "Questions on Geography." In *Power/Knowledge*, ed. C. Gordon (London: Harvester, 1980),63–77.

Foucault, M. *Security, Territory, Population: Lectures at the College de France, 1977–78*. Basingstoke, U.K.: Palgrave Macmillan, 2007.

Foucault, M. "What Is Enlightenment?" In *The Foucault Reader*, ed. P. Rabinow (Harmondsworth, Middlesex, England: Penguin, 1984), 32–50.

Friedan, B. *The Feminine Mystique*. New York: Norton, 1963.

Friedman, T. *The World Is Flat: A Brief History of the Twenty-first Century*. New York: Farrar, Strauss and Giroux, 2005.

Fujita, M., P. Krugman, and A. Venables. *The Spatial Economy: Cities, Regions and International Trade*. Cambridge, Mass.: MIT Press, 2001.

Garnett, C. *The Kantian Philosophy of Space*. Port Washington, N.Y.: Kennikat Press, 1965.

George, S. *Another World Is Possible IF* ... London: Verso, 2003.

Gibson-Graham, J. K. "Beyond Global vs. Local: Economic Politics Outside the Binary Frame." In *Geographies of Power: Placing Scale*, ed. A. Herod and M. Wright: Wiley-Blackwell, 2002), 25–60.

Gibson-Graham, J. *The End of Capitalism (As We Knew It): A Feminist Critique of Political Economy*. Minneapolis: University of Minnesota Press, 2006.

Gills, B., ed. *Globalization and the Politics of Resistance*. New York: Palgrave, 2001.

Glacken, C. *Traces on the Rhodian Shore: Nature and Culture in Western Thought from Ancient Times to the End of the Eighteenth Century*. Berkeley: University of California Press, 1967.

Godlewska, A., and N. Smith, eds. *Geography and Empire*. Oxford: Blackwell, 1997.

Gordon, M. "My Mother Is Speaking from the Desert." *New York Times Magazine*, 19 March 1995, 47–70.

Graeber, D. *Towards an Anthropological Theory of Value: The False Coin of Our Own Dreams*. New York: Palgrave Macmillan, 2001.

Gray, J. *False Dawn: The Illusions of Global Capitalism*. London: Granta Press, 1998.

Gregory, D. *The Colonial Present: Afghanistan, Palestine and Iraq*. Oxford: Blackwell, 2004.

Gregory, D. *Geographical Imaginations*. Oxford: Blackwell, 1994.

Grigg, D. "Regions, Models and Classes." In *Models in Geography*, ed. R. Chorley and P. Haggett (London: Methuen, 1967), 479–501.

Gross, D. "Fighting Poverty with $2-a-Day Jobs." *New York Times*, 6 July 2006, Weekend in Review, 4.

Grosz, E. "Bodies-Cities." In *Sexuality and Space*, ed. B. Colomina (Princeton: Princeton University Press, 1992),241–54.

Gurevich, A. *Categories of Medieval Culture*. London: Routledge, 1985.

Habermas, J. *The Theory of Communicative Action*. Vol. 2: *Lifeworld and System: A Critique of Functionalist Reason*. Boston: Beacon Press, 1985.

Haggett, P. *Locational Analysis in Geography*. London: Edward Arnold, 1965.

Hajer, M. *The Politics of Environmental Discourse: Ecological Modernisation and the Policy Process*. Oxford: Clarendon Press, 1995.

Haraway, D. "A Manifesto for Cyborgs: Science, Technology and Socialist Feminism in the 1980s." In *Feminism/Postmodernism*, ed. L. Nicholson (London: Routledge, 1990),190–233.

Haraway, D. *Primate Visions: Gender, Race and Nature in the World of Modern Science.* London: Routledge, 1989.

Haraway, D. *Simians, Cyborgs and Women: The Reinvention of Nature.* London: Routledge, 1991.

Hardt, M., and A. Negri. *Empire.* Cambridge, Mass.: Harvard University Press, 2001.

Harley, J., P. Laxton, and J. Andrews, eds. *The New Nature of Maps: Essays in the History of Cartography.* Baltimore: Johns Hopkins University Press, 2001.

Hartshorne, R. "'Exceptionalism in Geography' Re-examined." *Annals, Association of American Geographers* 45 (1955): 205–44.

Hartshorne, R. *The Nature of Geography: A Critical Survey of Current Thought in the Light of the Past.* Lancaster, Pa.: Association of American Geographers, 1939.

Hartsock, N. "Globalization and Primitive Accumulation: The Contributions of David Harvey's Dialectical Marxism," in *David Harvey: A Critical Reader,* ed. Castree and Gregory, 167–90.

Hartsock, N. *Money, Sex and Power.* London: Macmillan, 1973.

Harvey, D. "The Art of Rent: Globalization, Monopoly and the Commodification of Culture," *Socialist Register* (2002): 93–110.

Harvey, D. *A Brief History of Neoliberalism.* Oxford: Oxford University Press, 2005.

Harvey, D. *The Condition of Postmodernity.* Oxford: Blackwell, 1989.

Harvey, D. "The Fetish of Technology: Causes and Consequences." In "Prometheus's Bequest: Technology and Change," *Macalester International* 13 (2003): 3–30.

Harvey, D. "Introduction." In K. Marx and F. Engels, *The Communist Manifesto.* London: Pluto Press, 2008.

Harvey, D. *Justice, Nature and the Geography of Difference.* Oxford: Blackwell, 1996.

Harvey, D. *The Limits to Capital.* London: Verso, 2007.

Harvey, D. "Marxism, Metaphors, and Ecological Politics." *Monthly Review* 49, no. 11 (April 1998): 1–38.

Harvey, D. *The New Imperialism.* Oxford: Oxford University Press, 2003.

Harvey, D. "On the Significance of a Certain Footnote in Marx's Capital." Forthcoming in *Human Geography* 2 (2008).

Harvey, D. *Paris, Capital of Modernity.* New York: Routledge, 2003.

Harvey, D. "Population, Resources and the Ideology of Science." In Harvey, *Spaces of Capital,* chap. 3.

Harvey, D. *Social Justice and the City.* London: Edward Arnold, 1973.

Harvey, D. "The Sociological and Geographical Imaginations." *International Journal of Politics, Culture and Society* 18, nos. 3–4 (2005): 211–56.

Harvey, D. *Spaces of Capital: Towards a Critical Geography.* Edinburgh: Edinburgh University Press, 2001.

Harvey, D. *Spaces of Global Capitalism: Toward a Theory of Uneven Geographical Development.* London: Verso, 2006.

Harvey, D. *Spaces of Hope*. Edinburgh: Edinburgh University Press, 2000.

Haussmann, R. "A Case of Bad Latitude: Why Geography Causes Poverty." *Foreign Policy* (January–February 2001): 45–53.

Hawken, P. *Blessed Unrest: How the Largest Movement in History Is Restoring Grace and Beauty to the World*. New York: Viking, 2007.

Hayden, D. *The Power of Place: Urban Landscapes as Public History*. Cambridge, Mass.: MIT Press, 1995.

Heidegger, M. *Discourse on Thinking*. New York: Harper, 1966.

Heidegger, M. *Poetry, Language, Thought*. New York: Harper and Row, 1971.

Held, D. *Democracy and the Global Order: From the Modern State to Cosmopolitan Governance*. Stanford: Stanford University Press, 1995.

Held, D. "Law of States, Law of Peoples." *Legal Theory* 8, no. 2 (2002): 1–44.

Held, D. "Principles of Cosmopolitan Order." In *The Political Philosophy of Cosmopolitanism*, ed. G. Brock and H. Brighouse (Cambridge: Cambridge University Press, 2005): 10–27.

Himmelfarb, G. "The Illusions of Cosmopolitanism." In M. Nussbaum et al., *For Love of Country*, 72–77.

Holloway, J. *Changing the World without Taking Power: The Meaning of Revolution Today*. London: Pluto Press, 2002.

Hudson, R. *Producing Places*. New York: Guilford, 2001.

Huntington, E. *Civilization and Climate*. New Haven: Yale University Press, 1945.

Huntington, E. *Mainsprings of Civilization*. New York: Mentor Books, 1965.

Jacks, G., and R. Whyte. *Vanishing Lands*. New York, 1949.

Jay, M. *The Dialectical Imagination: A History of the Frankfurt School and the Institute of Social Research 1923–50*. Boston: Little Brown, 1973.

Jayamaha, B., D. Smith, J. Roebuck, O. Mora, E. Sandmeir, Y. Gray, and J. Murphy. "The War as We Saw It." *New York Times*, 19 August, 2007, Week in Review, 6.

Kant, I. "An Answer to the Question: 'What Is Enlightenment,'" in Kant, *Political Writings*, 54–60.

Kant, I. *Anthropology from a Pragmatic Point of View*. The Hague: Martinus Nijhoff, 1974.

Kant, I. *Geographie (Physische Geographie)*. Paris: Bibliothèque Philosophique, 1999.

Kant, I. "Immanuel Kant's *Physical Geography*." Trans. O. Reinhardt and D. Oldroyd. Unpublished manuscript, 2007.

Kant, I. *Kant: Political Writings*. Cambridge: Cambridge University Press, 1991.

Katz, C. "On the Grounds of Globalization: A Topography for Feminist Political Engagement." *Signs* 26, no. 4 (2001): 1213–34.

Katz, C. "Whose Nature, Whose Culture? Private Productions of Space and the Preservation of Nature," In *Social Nature*, ed. Castree and Braun, 46–63.

Katzenstein, M., U. Singh, and U. Thakar. "The Rebirth of Shiv-Sena: The Symbiosis of Discursive and Organizational Power." *Journal of Asian Studies* 56, no. 2 (1997): 371–90.

Kaviraj, S. "On the Enchantment of the State: Indian Thought on the Role of the State in the Narrative of Modernity." *European Journal of Sociology* 46 (2005): 263–96.

Keith, M., and S. Pile, eds. *Place and the Politics of Identity*. New York: Routledge, 1993.

Kern, S. *The Culture of Time and Space, 1880–1918*. London: Weidenfeld and Nicolson, 1983.

Kerner Commission. *Report of the National Advisory Commission on Civil Disorders*. Washington, D.C.: Government Printing Office, 1968.

Kimble, G. "The Inadequacy of the Regional Concept." In *London Essays in Geography*, ed. L. Stamp and S. Wooldridge (London: Longmans Green, 1957), 151–74.

Klein, N. *The Shock Doctrine: The Rise of Disaster Capitalism*. New York: Metropolitan Books, 2007.

Kohn, M. *Radical Space: Building the House of the People*. Ithaca, N.Y.: Cornell University Press, 2003.

Koopmans, T., and A. Beckman. "Assignment Problems and the Location of Economic Activities." *Econometrica* 25 (1957): 53–76.

Krugman, P. *Development, Geography and Economic Theory*. Cambridge, Mass.: MIT Press, 1995.

Krugman, P. "Graduates versus Oligarchs." *New York Times*, 27 February 2006, A19.

Kuhn, T. *The Structure of Scientific Revolutions*. Chicago: University of Chicago Press, 1962.

Kunstler, R. *The Geography of Nowhere: The Rise and Decline of America's Man-Made Landscape*. New York: Free Press, 1994.

Lee, K. *Social Philosophy and Ecological Scarcity*. London: Routledge, 1989.

Lefebvre, H. *Critique of Everyday Life*. Vol. 1. London: Verso, 1991.

Lefebvre, H. *The Production of Space*. Oxford: Blackwell, 1991.

Lefebvre, H. *The Urban Revolution*. Minneapolis: University of Minnesota Press, 2005.

Le Goff, J. *Time, Work, and Culture in the Middle Ages*. Chicago: University of Chicago Press, 1980.

Leiss, W. *The Domination of Nature*. Boston: Beacon Press, 1974.

Leitner, H., J. Peck, and E. Sheppard. *Contesting Neoliberalism: Urban Frontiers*. New York: Guilford, 2006.

Lemke, T. "'The Birth of Biopolitics': Michel Foucault's Lecture at the Collège de France on Neo-liberal Governmentality." *Economy and Society* 30 (2000): 190–207.

Levins, R., and R. Lewontin. *The Dialectical Biologist*. Cambridge, Mass.: Harvard University Press, 1985.

Livingston, D. *The Geographical Tradition: Episodes in the History of a Contested Enterprise*. Oxford: Blackwell, 1993.

Loukaki, A. *Living Ruins: Value Conflicts*. Farnham, U.K.: Ashgate, 2008.

Loukaki, A. "Whose Genius Loci: Competing Interpretations of the Sacred Rock of the Acropolis." *Annals, Association of American Geographers* 87 (1997): 306–29.

Lovejoy, A. *The Great Chain of Being*. Cambridge, Mass.: Harvard University Press, 1964.

Marsh, G. *Man and Nature: Or, Physical Geography as Modified by Human Action.* Cambridge, Mass.: Harvard University Press, 1965.

Martin, E. *Flexible Bodies: Tracking Immunity in American Culture: From the Days of Polio to the Age of AIDS.* Boston: Beacon Press, 1994.

Marx, K. *Capital.* Vol. 1. New York: International Publishers, 1967.

Marx, K. *Capital.* Vol. 3. New York: Penguin, 1981.

Marx, K. *The Eighteenth Brumaire of Louis Bonaparte.* New York: International Publishers, 1963.

Marx, K. *The Grundrisse.* Harmondsworth, Middlesex, England: Penguin, 1973.

Marx, K., and F. Engels. *Collected Works.* Vol. 3. Moscow: Progress Publishers, 1975.

Marx, K., and F. Engels. *Manifesto of the Communist Party.* London: Pluto Press, 2008.

Massey, D. *For Space.* London: Sage, 2005.

Massey, D. "In What Sense a Regional Problem?" *Regional Studies* 13 (1979): 233–43.

Massey, D. *Space, Place and Gender.* Minneapolis: University of Minnesota Press, 1994.

May, J. *Kant's Concept of Geography and Its Relation to Recent Geographical Thought.* Toronto: University of Toronto Press, 1970.

Mehta, U. *Liberalism and Empire: A Study in Nineteenth-century British Liberal Thought.* Chicago: University of Chicago Press, 1999.

Merrifield, A. "Place and Space: A Lefebvrian Reconciliation." *Transactions of the Institute of British Geographers* 16 (1991): 516–31.

Mertes, T., ed. *A Movement of Movements.* London: Verso, 2004.

Mesjaros, I. *Beyond Capital.* New York: Monthly Review Press, 2000.

Michaels, W. *The Trouble with Diversity: How We Learned to Love Diversity and Ignore Identity.* New York: Metropolitan Books, 2006.

Mies, M. *Patriarchy and Accumulation on a World Scale.* London: Zed Books, 1986.

Mignolo, W. *The Darker Side of the Renaissance: Literacy, Territoriality and Colonization.* Ann Arbor: University of Michigan Press, 2003.

Mignolo, W. *Local Histories/Global Designs.* Princeton: Princeton University Press, 2000.

Mitchell, T. "Society, Economy, and the State Effect." In *Anthropology of the State,* ed. Sharma and Gupta, 169–86.

Mitchell, T. "The Work of Economics: How a Discipline Makes Its World." *Archives européennes de sociologie* 46 (2005): 297–320.

Mohanty, C. *Feminism without Borders: Decolonizing Theory, Practising Solidarity.* Durham, N.C.: Duke University Press, 2006.

Moore, A. "Rethinking Scale as a Geographical Category: From Analysis to Practice." *Progress in Human Geography* 32, no. 2 (2008): 203–25.

Moore, D. *Suffering for Territory: Race, Place and Power in Zimbabwe.* Durham, N.C.: Duke University Press, 2005.

Morley, D., and K. Robbins. "No Place Like Heimat: Images of Home(land)." In *Space and Place: Theories of Identity and Location,* ed. E. Carter, J. Donald, and J. Squires (London: Routledge, 1993), 3–31.

Moses, R. "What Happened to Haussmann?" *Architectural Forum* 77 (1942): 1–10.

Munk, N. "Don't Blink: You'll Miss the 258th Richest American." *New York Times*, 25 September 2005, Weekend in Review, 3.

Munn, N. *The Fame of Gawa*. Cambridge: Cambridge University Press, 1986.

Naess, A. *Ecology, Community and Lifestyle*. Cambridge: Cambridge University Press, 1989.

Narotzky, S., and G. Smith. *Immediate Struggles: People, Power, and Place in Rural Spain*. Berkeley: University of California Press, 2006.

Negri, T. *Subversive Spinoza: (UN)contemporary Variations*. Manchester: Manchester University Press, 2004.

Nilsen, A. "The Valley and the Nation: The River and the Rage." Ph.D. diss., Department of Sociology, University of Bergen, 2006.

Norberg-Shulz, C. *Genius Loci: Towards a Phenomenology of Architecture*. New York: Rizzoli, 1980.

Nozick, R. *Anarchy, State, and Utopia*. New York: Basic Books, 1974.

Nussbaum, M. *Frontiers of Justice: Disability, Nationality, Species Membership*. Cambridge, Mass.: Belknap Press, 2006.

Nussbaum, M. "Kant and Stoic Cosmopolitanism." *Journal of Political Philosophy* 5 (1997): 1–25.

Nussbaum, M., et al. *For Love of Country: Debating the Limits of Patriotism*. Boston: Beacon Press, 1996.

Oakes, T. "Place and the Paradox of Modernity." *Annals, Association of American Geographers* 87 (1997): 509–31.

O'Keefe, P., N. Smith, and B. Wisner. "Taking the Naturalness Out of Natural Disasters." *Nature* 260 (1976): 566–67.

Ollman, B. *Dialectical Investigations*. New York: Routledge, 1992.

Ong, A. *Neoliberalism as Exception: Mutations in Citizenship and Sovereignty*. Durham, N.C.: Duke University Press, 2006.

Osserman, R. *The Poetry of the Universe*. New York: Doubleday, 1995.

Paasi, A. "Place and Region: Regional Worlds and Words." *Progress in Human Geography* 26 (2002): 802–11.

Paasi, A. *Territories, Boundaries and Consciousness: The Changing Geographies of the Finnish-Russian Border*. New York: Wiley, 1997.

Pagden, A. "Introduction." In C. Sauer, *The Early Spanish Main* (Berkeley: University of California Press, 1992), xii–xvii.

Pagden, A. "Stoicism, Cosmopolitanism, and the Legacy of European Imperialism." *Constellations* 7, no. 1 (2000): 3–22.

Pattison, W. "The Four Traditions of Geography." *Journal of Geography* 63 (1964): 211–16.

Philo, C. "'Bellicose History' and 'Local Discursivities': An Archaeological Reading of Michel Foucault's *Society Must Be Defended*." In *Space, Knowledge, and Power*, ed. Crampton and Elden, 342–67.

Polanyi, K. *The Great Transformation: The Political and Economic Origins of Our Time*. Boston: Beacon Press, 1957.

Porter, E. "Mexico's Plutocracy Survives on Robber-Baron Concessions." *New York Times*, 27 August 2007, Editorial Observer.

Powell, J. *An Historical Geography of Modern Australia*. Cambridge: Cambridge University Press, 1988.

Prahalad, C. *The Fortune at the Bottom of the Pyramid: Eradicating Poverty through Profits*. Philadelphia: Wharton School Publishing, 2006.

Prazniak, R., and A. Dirlik, eds. *Places and Politics in an Age of Globalization*. New York: Rowman and Littlefield, 2001.

Prigogine, I., and I. Stengers. *Order Out of Chaos*. Boston: Shambhala, 1984.

Przeworski, A. "Geography vs. Institutions Revisited: Were Fortunes Reversed?" Department of Politics Working Paper, New York University, 2004.

Pudup, M. "Arguments within Regional Geography." *Progress in Human Geography* 12 (1988): 369–90.

Rancière, J. *Disagreement: Politics and Philosophy*. Minneapolis: University of Minnesota Press, 1998.

Rancière, J. *The Nights of Labor: The Workers' Dream in Nineteenth-century France*. Philadelphia: Temple University Press, 1989.

Rawls, J. *The Law of Peoples with The Idea of Public Reason Revisited*. Cambridge, Mass.: Harvard University Press, 1999.

Reclus, E. "The Feeling for Nature in Modern Society." In *Anarchy, Geography, Modernity*, ed. Clark and Martin,119–28.

Reclus, E. *L'Homme et la Terre*. Ed. B. Ghiblin. 2 vols., abridged. Paris: La Découverte, 1982.

Ree, J. "Cosmopolitanism and the Experience of Nationality." In *Cosmopolitics*, ed. Cheah and Robins, 77–90.

Relph, T. *Place and Placelessness*. London: Pion, 1976.

Rescher, N. *Leibniz's Metaphysics of Nature*. Dordrecht: Reidel, 1981.

Robotham, D. *Culture, Society, Economy: Globalization and Its Alternatives*. New York: Sage, 2005.

Roy, A. *Power Politics*. Cambridge, Mass.: South End Press, 2001.

Sachs, J. *The End of Poverty: Economic Possibilities for Our Time*. New York: Penguin, 2005.

Sachs, J. (with J. Gallup and A. Mellinger). "Is Geography Destiny." In *World Bank Conference on Development Economics*, ed. B. Pleskovic and J. Stiglitz (Washington, D.C.: World Bank, 1999), 127–78.

Sack, R. *Conceptions of Space in Social Thought: A Geographic Perspective*. Minneapolis: University of Minnesota Press, 1980.

Sack, R. *Human Territoriality: Its Theory and Its History*. Cambridge: Cambridge University Press, 1986.

Sale, K. "What Columbus Discovered." *The Nation*, 18. October 1990, 444–46.

Sassen, S. *Territory, Authority, Rights: From Medieval to Global Assemblages*. Princeton: Princeton University Press, 2006.

Sauer, K. *Land and Life*. Berkeley: University of California Press, 1965.

Sayre, N. "Ecological and Geographical Scale: Parallels and Potential for Integration." *Progress in Human Geography* 29, no. 3 (2005): 276–90.

Schaeffer, F. "Exceptionalism in Geography: A Methodological Examination." *Annals, Association of American Geographers* 43 (1953): 57–84.

Scheuer, M. *Imperial Hubris: Why the West Is Losing the War on Terror.* Dulles, Va.: Potomac Books, 2004.

Schorske, C. *Fin-de-Siècle Vienna.* New York: Vintage, 1981.

Schwab, K., and C. Smadja. "Globalization Needs a Human Face." *International Herald Tribune,* 28 January 1999, 8.

Scott, J. *Seeing like a State: How Certain Schemes to Improve the Human Condition Have Failed.* New Haven: Yale University Press, 1999.

Semple, E. C. *Influences of Geographical Environment on the Basis of Ratzel's System of Anthropogéographie.* New York: Henry Holt, 1911.

Shapiro, M. "The Events of Discourse and the Ethics of Global Hospitality." *Millennium* 27 (1998): 695–713.

Sharma, A., and A. Gupta, eds. *The Anthropology of the State.* Oxford: Blackwell, 2006.

Sheppard, E., and R. McMaster, eds. *Scale and Geographic Inquiry.* Oxford: Wiley-Blackwell, 2004.

Smith, N. *American Empire: Roosevelt's Geographer and the Prelude to Globalization.* Berkeley: University of California Press, 2003.

Smith, N. "Disastrous Accumulation." *South Atlantic Quarterly* 106, no. 4 (2007): 769–87.

Smith, N. *The Endgame of Globalization.* New York: Routledge, 2005.

Smith, N. "Geography, Difference and the Politics of Scale." In *Postmodernism and the Social Sciences,* ed. J. Docherty, M. Graham, and M. Malek (London: Routledge, 1992).

Smith, N. "Nature as Accumulation Strategy." *Socialist Register* (2007): 16–36.

Smith, N. *Uneven Development.* Oxford: Blackwell, 1984.

Soja, E. *Postmodern Geographies: The Reassertion of Space in Critical Social Theory.* London: Verso, 1989.

Soper, K. *What Is Nature?* Oxford: Blackwell, 1995.

Sparke, M. *In the Space of Theory: Postfoundational Geographies of the Nation-State* (Minneapolis: University of Minnesota Press, 2005).

Spate, O. "Toynbee and Huntington: A Study in Determinism." *Geographical Journal* 118 (1952): 406–28.

Stiglitz, J. *Globalization and Its Discontents.* New York: Norton, 2002.

Stokes, E. *English Utilitarians in India.* Oxford: Clarendon Press, 1959.

Storper, M., and R. Walker. *The Capitalist Imperative: Territory, Technology and Industrial Growth.* Oxford: Blackwell, 1989.

Swyngedouw, E. "Neither Global nor Local: 'Glocalization' and the Politics of Scale." In *Spaces of Globalization: Reasserting the Power of the Local* (New York: Routledge, 1997),.137–66.

Tatham, G. "Environmentalism and Possibilism." In *Geography in the Twentieth Century,* ed. G. Taylor (London: Methuen, 1951), 128–64.

Taylor, P. "The State as Container: Internationality, Interstateness, Interterritoriality." *Progress in Human Geography* 19 (1995): 1–15.

Thomas, W., ed. *Man's Role in Changing the Face of the Earth.* Chicago: University of Chicago Press, 1956.

Thompson, E. *The Making of the English Working Class.* Harmondsworth, Middlesex, England: Penguin, 1968.

Thompson, E. "Time, Work Discipline, and Industrial Capitalism." *Past and Present* 38 (1967): 56–97.

Trouillot, R. "The Anthropology of the State in the Age of Globalization: Close Encounters of the Deceptive Kind." *Current Anthropology* 42, no. 1 (2001): 125–34.

Tsing, A. *Friction: An Ethnography of Global Connection.* Princeton: Princeton University Press, 2004.

Tuan, Yi-Fu. *Space and Place: The Perspective of Experience.* Minneapolis: University of Minnesota Press, 1977.

Tuan, Yi-Fu. *Topophilia: A Study of Environment Perceptions, Attitudes and Values.* New York: Columbia University Press, 1990.

United Nations Development Program. *Human Development Report 1996* and *Human Development Report 1999.* New York: United Nations, 1999.

Van de Pitte, F. "Introduction." In I. Kant, *Anthropology from a Pragmatic Point of View* (The Hague: Martinus Nijhoff, 1974), xi–xxii.

Vertovec, S., and R. Cohen, eds. *Conceiving Cosmopolitanism: Theory, Context and Practice.* Oxford: Oxford University Press, 2002.

Vidal de la Blache, P. *Principles of Human Geography.* London: Constable, 1926.

Wade, R., and F. Veneroso. "The Asian Crisis: The High-Debt Model versus the Wall Street-Treasury-IMF Complex." *New Left Review* 228 (1998): 3–23.

Wallace, T. "NGO Dilemmas: Trojan Horses for Global Neoliberalism." *Socialist Register* (2003): 202–19.

Walzer, M. *Spheres of Justice.* Oxford: Blackwell, 1993.

Wheatley, P. *The Pivot of the Four Quarters.* Chicago: University of Chicago Press, 1971.

Whitehead, A. "La théorie relationiste de l'Espace." *Revue de métaphysique et de morale* 23 (1916): 423–54.

Wiley, M. *Romantic Geography: Wordsworth and Anglo-European Spaces.* London: Macmillan, 1998.

Wilkins, M. "Complementarity and the Unity of Opposites." In *Quantum Implications,* ed. B. Hiley and F. Peat (London: Routledge, 1987), 338–60.

Williams, R. *Keywords: A Vocabulary of Culture and Society.* New York: Oxford University Press, 1985.

Williams, R. *Loyalties.* London: Chatto and Windus, 1985.

Williams, R. *People of the Black Mountains: The Eggs of the Eagle.* Vol. 1. London: Chatto and Windus, 1989.

Williams, R. *Resources of Hope.* London: Verso, 1989.

Wilson, E. *Consilience: The Unity of Knowledge.* New York: Knopf, 1998.

Wilson, R. "A New Cosmopolitanism Is in the Air." In *Cosmopolitics,* ed. Cheah and Robins, 351–61.

Winichakul, T. *Siam Mapped: A History of the Geo-Body of a Nation.* Honolulu: University of Hawaii Press, 1994.

Wittfogel, K. *Oriental Despotism.* New Haven: Yale University Press, 1953.

Worster, D. *Dustbowl: The Southern Plains in the Great Depression.* New York: Oxford University Press, 1979.

Wright Mills, C. *The Sociological Imagination.* New York: Oxford University Press, 1959.

Young, I. *Justice and the Politics of Difference.* Princeton: Princeton University Press, 1990.

Zammito, J. *Kant, Herder, and the Birth of Anthropology.* Chicago: University of Chicago Press, 2002.

Zeldin, T. *The French.* New York: Vintage, 1984.

Zeldin, T. *An Intimate History of Humanity.* New York: Harper Collins, 1995.

Žižek, S. *The Parallax View.* Cambridge, Mass.: MIT Press, 2006.

Index